A MANUAL OF
AMERICAN LITERATURE

MJP
PUBLISHERS

A MANUAL OF
AMERICAN LITERATURE

Theodore Stanton, M.A.

MJP
PUBLISHERS

Chennai   Trichy   Tirunelveli   New Delhi

MJP
PUBLISHERS

ISBN 978-81-8094-368-3 **MJP Publishers**

All rights reserved No. 44, Nallathambi Street,
Printed and bound in India Triplicane, Chennai 600 005

MJP   328 © Publishers, 2019

Publisher : C. Janarthanan

Project Editor : C. Ambica

PUBLISHER'S NOTE

The legacy of a country is in its varied cultural heritage, historical literature, developments in the field of economy and science. The top nations in the world are competing in the field of science, economy and literature. This vast legacy has to be conserved and documented so that it can be bestowed to the future generation. The knowledge of this legacy is slowly getting perished in the present generation due to lack of documentation.

Keeping this in mind, the concern with retrospective acquiring of rare books has been accented recently by the burgeoning reprint industry. MJP Publishers is gratified to retrieve the rare collections with a view to bring back those books that were landmarks in their time.

In this effort, a series of rare books would be republished under the banner, "MJP Publishers". The books in the reprint series have been carefully selected for their contemporary usefulness as well as their historical importance within the intellectual. We reconstruct the book with slight enhancements made for better presentation, without affecting the contents of the original edition.

Most of the works selected for republishing covers a huge range of subjects, from history to anthropology. We believe this reprint edition will be a service to the numerous researchers and practitioners active in this fascinating field. We allow readers to experience the wonder of peering into a scholarly work of the highest order and seminal significance.

MJP Publishers

EDITOR'S PREFACE

This book has been prepared for publication as No. 4000, a "Memorial Volume," of the "Tauchnitz Edition." Perhaps it may be well to explain to American readers what the "Tauchnitz Edition" is and what a "Memorial Volume" is in this collection.

The "Collection of British Authors," or, as it is more popularly known on the European Continent, the "Tauchnitz Edition," was instituted in 1841, at Leipsic, by one of the most distinguished of German publishers, the late Baron Bernhard Tauchnitz, whose son is now at the head of the house. The father records that he was "incited to the undertaking by the high opinion and enthusiastic fondness which I have ever entertained for English literature: a literature springing from the selfsame root as the literature of Germany, and cultivated in the beginning by the same Saxon race.... As a German-Saxon it gave me particular pleasure to promote the literary interest of my Anglo-Saxon cousins, by rendering English literature as universally known as possible beyond the limits of the British Empire." In another place, Baron Tauchnitz describes "the mission" of his Collection to be the "spreading and strengthening the love for English literature outside of England and her Colonies."

Baron Tauchnitz early felt that the general title of the series, "Collection of *British* Authors," was a misnomer, which might even give offence to an important branch of the English-speaking race; for, though Bulwer and Dickens led off in the Collection, "Pelham" being the first volume issued and "The Pickwick Papers" the second, the fourth volume, added at the beginning of the second year of publication, in 1842, was Fenimore Cooper's "The Spy," followed in the same year by a second volume of the same author. Furthermore, the year 1843 opened with Washington Irving's "Sketch Book," immediately followed by a third novel by Cooper; and, though it was not till 1850 that another American work gained admittance into this charmed circle, not fewer than three of Irving's books succeeded one another in the single twelvemonth. In 1852, Hawthorne was welcomed with "The Scarlet Letter" and Mrs. Stowe with "Uncle Tom's Cabin"; from that time on, scarcely a year has passed without some new American book being included in the Collection, and under the present routine each year's issue, comprising some seventy-five volumes, includes several American works.

In fact, the representation of American authors in the "Tauchnitz Edition" is now so considerable that the list calls for a place by itself at the end of this volume, where it presents an interesting evidence of the growth of the popularity of American literature in Europe. The reader will notice that there are cases where some of the best works of an author are not included in the "Tauchnitz Edition." The cause of these omissions is sometimes other than taste or choice. But the catalogue is suggestive just as it stands.

The "Memorial Volumes" form a little series of special issues published at turning-points. This Manual has been made a Memorial Volume out of compliment to American literature and is dedicated, with his permission, to President Roosevelt. In this way, the present Baron Tauchnitz has striven to show his high appreciation of the group of American authors in the Edition, and to follow in the footsteps of his high-minded father.

In his Preface to the first Memorial Volume, No. 500, entitled "Five Centuries of the English Language and Literature," being a collection of characteristic specimens of British writers from Wycliffe to Thomas Gray, the first Baron Tauchnitz refers to the literature "on the other side of the Atlantic," and says in a footnote to this Preface: "A glance at my list of authors will show that America has contributed no small part to my Collection. Nevertheless I did not deem it necessary to alter the title under which my undertaking was started, as I thought that the term 'British Authors' might not improperly be applied to writers employing the language common to the two nations on either side of the Atlantic." No. 1000—Tischendorf's edition of The New Testament—is dedicated "to my English and American Authors," while in No. 2000—"Of English Literature in the Reign of Victoria, with a Glance at the Past"—the author, the late Professor Henry Morley, who long filled the chair of English Literature at the University of London, opens his Preface with these words: "When Baron Tauchnitz asked me to write this little book, he also wished me to include in it some record of the literature of America. But Baron Tauchnitz cordially agreed to a suggestion that the kindred literature of America, though we are proud in England to claim closest brotherhood with our fellow-countrymen of the United States, has a distinct interest of its own, large enough for the whole subject of another memorial volume, and that an American author would best tell the story of its rise and progress."

Another work in the "Tauchnitz Edition," but not a Memorial Volume, offered a good opportunity to present American literature to the attention of the European public. I refer to the two volumes of the late George L. Craik, sometime Professor of English Literature at Queen's College, Belfast, entitled "A Manual of English Literature, and of the History of the English Language, from the Norman Conquest; with Numerous Specimens." Here again no space is given to our authors, though they are mentioned once in a reference to "the leading poetical writers who have arisen in the American division of the English race, two or three of whom may be reckoned as of the second rank, though certainly not one as of the first."

Towards the end of 1893, as the time was approaching for the issuing of No. 3000, and again, in 1900, when No. 3500 was soon to be reached, I hinted to my Leipsic friends the peculiar fitness of singling out one of these possible Memorial Volumes and making it a sketch of our literary life, in accordance with the promise made in Professor Morley's Preface. I even suggested that Professor Moses Coit Tyler, who had then just completed his great work on our literature, be invited to perform the task. The last letter I ever received from this genial spirit, dated from the Isle of Wight, September 5, 1897, contains this passage: "I appreciate the honour you have done me in mentioning my name to Baron Tauchnitz, in connection with a proposed volume on American literature." Nothing, however, came of this; and when, some ten years later, I was invited to prepare the present volume, my first thought was to utilise the *magnum opus* of Professor Tyler, who had, in the meanwhile, passed away. So my chief care has been the first two chapters, drawn, with the kind permission of the publishers, Messrs. G. P. Putnam's Sons, and of the family of Professor Tyler, from his four authoritative volumes, "A History of American Literature during the Colonial Period," and "The Literary History of the American Revolution," to which Sir George Otto Trevelyan refers in his "American Revolution" as "a remarkable specimen of the historical faculty."

The chief labour in the preparation of this volume has fallen upon my friends and collaborators of the Department of English and the Sage School of Philosophy of my Alma Mater. Acknowledgment is, further, particularly due to Professors J. M. Hart and M. W. Sampson, also of Cornell University, for valuable suggestions and considerable help. The work of seeing the American edition through the press has been done by Professors Northup and Cooper.

Theodore Stanton.

PARIS, September, 1908.

CONTENTS

COLONIAL LITERATURE

I. FIRST PERIOD (1607–1676)

The Beginning.—The present race of Americans who are of English lineage—that is, the most numerous and decidedly the dominant portion of the American people of to-day—are the direct descendants of the crowds of Englishmen who came to America in the seventeenth century. Our first literary period, therefore, fills the larger part of that century in which American civilisation had its planting; even as its training into some maturity and power has been the business of the eighteenth and the nineteenth centuries. Of course, also, the most of the men who produced American literature during that period were immigrant authors of English birth and English culture; while the most of those who have produced American literature in the subsequent periods have been authors of American birth and of American culture. Notwithstanding their English birth, these first writers in America were Americans: we may not exclude them from our story of American literature. They founded that literature; they are its Fathers; they stamped their spiritual lineaments upon it; and we shall never deeply enter into the meaning of American literature in its later forms without tracing it back, affectionately, to its beginning with them. At the same time, our first literary epoch cannot fail to bear traces of the fact that nearly all the men who made it were Englishmen who had become Americans merely by removing to America. American life, indeed, at once reacted upon their minds, and began to give its tone and hue to their words; and for every reason, what they wrote here, we rightfully claim as a part of American literature; but England has a right to claim it likewise as a part of English literature. Indeed England and America are joint proprietors of this first tract of the great literary territory which we have undertaken to survey.

Since the earliest English colonists upon these shores began to make a literature as soon as they arrived here, it follows that we can fix the exact date of the birth of American literature. It is that year 1607, when Englishmen, by transplanting themselves to America, first began to be Americans. Thus may the history of our literature be traced back from the present hour, as it recedes along the track of our national life, through the early days of the republic, through five generations of colonial existence, until, in the first decade of the seventeenth century, it is merged in its splendid parentage—the written speech of England.

The First Writer.—Among those first Englishmen huddled together behind palisadoes in Jamestown in 1607, were some who laid the foundations of American literature, and there was one who still has a considerable name in the world. When he first set foot in Virginia, Captain John Smith was only twenty-seven years old; but even then he had made himself somewhat famous in England as a daring traveller in Southern Europe, in Turkey and the East. This extremely vivid and resolute man comes before us for study, not because he was the most conspicuous person in the first successful American colony, but because he was the writer of the first book in American literature. *A True Relation of Virginia* is of deep interest to us, not only on account of its graphic style and the strong light it throws upon the very beginning of our national history, but as being unquestionably the earliest book in American literature. It was written during the first thirteen months of the life of the first American colony, and gives a simple and picturesque account of the stirring events which took place there during that time, under his own eye. After all the abatements which a fair criticism must make from the praise of Captain John Smith either as a doer or as a narrator, his writings still make upon us the impression of a certain personal largeness in him, magnanimity, affluence, sense, and executive force. As a writer his merits are really great—clearness, force, vividness, picturesque and dramatic energy, a diction racy and crisp; and during the first two decades of the seventeenth century he did more than any other Englishman to make an American nation and an American literature possible.

William Strachey.—During the first decade of American literature a little book was written in Virginia, which, as is believed by some authors, soon rendered an illustrious service to English literature by suggesting to Shakespeare the idea of one of his noblest masterpieces, *The Tempest*. It was in May, 1610, that Sir Thomas Gates, with two small vessels and 150 companions, had at last found his way into the James River after a voyage of almost incredible difficulty and peril. Among those who had borne a part in this ghastly and almost miraculous expedition was William Strachey, of whom but little is known except what is revealed in his own writings. He was a man of decided literary aptitude. Soon after his arrival here he was made secretary of Virginia, and in July, 1610, he wrote at Jamestown and sent off to England *A True Reportory of the Wrack and Redemption of Sir Thomas Gates, Kt., upon and from the Islands of the Bermudas*. Whoever reads this little book will be quite ready to believe that it may have brought suggestion and inspiration even to the genius of William Shakespeare. It is a book of marvellous power. Its account of Virginia is well done; but its most striking merit is its delineation of his dreadful sea-voyage, and particularly of the tempest which, after the terror and anguish of a thousand deaths, drove them upon the rocks of the Bermudas. Here his style becomes magnificent; it has some sentences which for imaginative and pathetic beauty, for vivid implications of appalling danger and disaster, can hardly be surpassed in the whole range of English prose.

George Sandys.—The last one of this group of early writers, George Sandys, was perhaps the only one of all his fellow-craftsmen here who was a professed man of letters. He was well known as a traveller in Eastern lands, as a scholar, as an admirable prose-writer, but especially as a poet. His claim to the title of poet then rested chiefly on his fine metrical translation of the first five books of Ovid's *Metamorphoses*. This fragment was a specimen of literary workmanship in many ways creditable; and that he was able, during the next few years, robbing sleep of its rights, to complete his noble translation of the fifteen books, is worthy of being chronicled among the heroisms of authorship. In 1626, he brought out in London, in a folio volume, the first edition of his finished work. The writings which precede this book in our literary history were all produced for some immediate practical purpose, and not with any avowed literary intentions. This book may well have for us a sort of sacredness, as being the first monument of English poetry, of classical scholarship, and of deliberate literary art, reared on these shores. And when we open the book, and examine it with reference to its merits, first, as a faithful rendering of the Latin text, and, second, as a specimen of fluent, idiomatic, and musical English poetry, we find that in both particulars it is a work that we may be proud to claim as in some sense our own, and to honour as the morning-star at once of poetry and of scholarship in the New World.

The Burwell Papers.—In the year 1676 there occurred in Virginia an outburst of popular excitement which, for a hundred and fifty years afterward, was grotesquely misrepresented by the historians, and which only within recent years has begun to work itself clear of the traditional perversion. This excitement is still indicated by the sinister name that was at first applied to it, Bacon's Rebellion. With this remarkable event the literary history of Virginia now becomes curiously involved.

In the spring of 1676, at the very moment when the minds of men were torn by anxieties at the lawless interference of the King and Parliament with their most valuable rights, suddenly there swept toward them the terror of an aggressive Indian war. The people called upon the royal Governor, Sir William Berkeley, to take the necessary measures for repelling these assaults. For reasons of jealousy, indolence, selfishness, and especially avarice, this Governor gave to the people promises of help, and promises only. Then the people arose in their anger, and since their Governor would not lead them to the war, with unanimous voice they called upon one of their own number to be their leader, Nathaniel Bacon, a man only thirty years of age, of considerable landed wealth, of high social connections, a lawyer trained in the Inns of Court in London, an orator of commanding eloquence, a man who by his endowments of brain and eye and hand was a natural leader and king of men. He obeyed the call of the people and led them against the Indians, whom he drove back with tremendous punishment. But by the jealous and haughty despot in the governor's chair, he was at once proclaimed a rebel; a price was set upon his head; and the people who followed him were put under ban. Then followed a series of swift conflicts, military and political, between Bacon and the Governor; and at last, in that same year, Bacon himself died, suddenly and mysteriously, and twenty-five persons were hung or shot.

Shortly after our Revolutionary War, it was discovered that in an old and honourable family in the Northern Neck of Virginia, some manuscripts had been preserved, evidently belonging to the seventeenth century, evidently written by one or more of the adherents of Nathaniel Bacon. These manuscripts are sometimes called the Burwell Papers, from the name of a family in King William County by whom they were first given to the public. The author of the prose portion of these manuscripts reflects, on this side of the ocean, the literary foibles that were in fashion on the other side of the ocean. But apart from the disagreeable air of verbal affectation and of effort in these writings, they are undeniably spirited; they produce before us departed scenes with no little energy and life; and the flavour of mirth which seasons them is not unpleasant.

As the cause of Bacon's death was a mystery, so a mystery covered even the place of his burial; for his friends, desiring to save his lifeless body from violation at the hands of the victorious party, placed it secretly in the earth. And the love of Bacon's followers, which in his lifetime had shown itself in services of passionate devotion, and which, after his death, thus hovered as a protecting silence over his hidden grave, found expression also in some sorrowing verses that, upon the whole, are of astonishing poetic merit. Who may have been the author of these verses, it is perhaps now impossible to discover. They are prefaced by the quaint remark that after Bacon "was dead, he was bemoaned in lines drawn by the man that waited upon his person as it is said, and who attended his corpse to their burial-place." Of course this statement is but a blind; the author of such a eulogy of the dead rebel could not safely avow himself. But certainly no menial of Bacon's, no mere "man that waited upon his person," could have written this noble dirge, which has a stateliness, a compressed energy, and a mournful eloquence, reminding one of the commemorative verse of Ben Jonson.

Early Literature in Virginia and New England.—During the first epoch in the history of American literature, there were but two localities which produced in the English language anything that can be called literature,—Virginia and New England. As we have seen, there were in Virginia, during the first twenty years of its existence, authors who produced writings that live yet and deserve to live. But at the end of that period and for the remainder of the century, nearly all literary activity in Virginia ceased; the only exception to this statement being the brief anonymous literary memorials which have come down to us from the uprising of the people under Nathaniel Bacon. Even of those writers of the first two decades, all excepting one, Alexander Whitaker, "the Apostle of Virginia," flitted back to England after a brief residence in Virginia: so that besides Whitaker, the colony had during all that period no writer who gave his name to her as being willing to identify himself permanently with her fate, and to live and die in her immediate service. This, as we shall see, is in startling contrast to the contemporaneous record of New England, which, even in that early period, had a great throng of writers, nearly all of whom took root in her soil.

New England Traits in the Seventeenth Century.—Did the people of New England in their earliest age begin to produce a literature? Who can doubt it? With their incessant activity of brain, with so much both of common and of uncommon culture among them, with intellectual interests so lofty and strong, with so many outward occasions to stir their deepest passions into the same great currents, it would be hard to explain it had they indeed produced no literature. Moreover, contrary to what is commonly asserted of them, they were not without a literary class. In as large a proportion to the whole population as was then the case in the mother-country, there were in New England many men trained to the use of books, accustomed to express themselves fluently by voice and pen, and not so immersed in the physical tasks of life as to be deprived of the leisure for whatever writing they were prompted to undertake. It was a literary class made up of men of affairs, country-gentlemen, teachers, above all of clergymen; men of letters who did not depend upon letters for their bread, and who thus did their work under conditions of intellectual independence.

For the study of literature, they turned with eagerness to the ancient classics; read them freely; quoted them with apt facility. Though their new home was but a province, their minds were not provincial: they had so stalwart and chaste a faith in the ideas which brought them to America as to think that wherever those ideas were put into practice, there was the metropolis. In the public expression of thought they limited themselves by restraints which, though then prevalent in all parts of the civilised world, now seem shameful and intolerable: the printing-press in New England during the seventeenth century was in chains. The first was set up at Cambridge in 1639, under the auspices of Harvard College; and for the subsequent twenty-three years the president of that college was in effect responsible for the good behaviour of the terrible machine. His control of it did not prove sufficiently vigilant. The fears of the clergy were excited by the lenity that had permitted the escape into the world of certain books which tended "to open the door of heresy"; therefore, in 1662 two official licensers were appointed, without whose consent nothing was to be printed. Even this did not make the world seem safe; and two years afterward the law was made more stringent. Other licensers were appointed; excepting the one at Cambridge no printing-press was to be allowed in the colony; and if from the printing-press that was allowed, anything should be printed without the permission of the licensers, the peccant engine was to be forfeited to the government and the printer himself was to be forbidden the exercise of his profession. But even the new licensers were not severe enough. In the leading colony of New England legal restraints upon printing were not entirely removed until about twenty-one years before the Declaration of Independence.

The chief literary disadvantages of New England were, that her writers lived far from the great repositories of books, and far from the central currents of the world's best thinking; that the lines of their own literary activity were few; and that, though they nourished their minds upon the Hebrew Scriptures and upon the classics of the Roman and Greek literatures, they stood aloof, with a sort of horror, from the richest and most exhilarating types of classic writing in their own tongue. In many ways their literary development was stunted and stiffened by the narrowness of Puritanism. Nevertheless, what they lacked in symmetry of culture and in range of literary movement, was something which the very integrity of their natures was sure to compel them, either in themselves or in their posterity, to acquire.

William Bradford.—William Bradford, of the *Mayflower* and Plymouth Rock, deserves the pre-eminence of being called the father of American history. After he had been in America ten years and had seen proof of the permanent success of the heroic movement in which he was a leader, his mind seems to have been possessed by the historic significance of that movement; and thenceforward for twenty years he gave his leisure to the composition of a work in which the story of the settlement of New England should be told in a calm, just, and authentic manner. The result was his *History of Plymouth Plantation*. There is no other document upon New England history that can take precedence of this either in time or in authority. Governor Bradford wrote of events that had passed under his own eye, and that had been shaped by his own hand; and he had every qualification of a trustworthy narrator. His mind was placid, grave, well-poised; he was a student of many books and of many languages; and being thus developed both by letters and by experience, he was able to tell well the truth of history as it had unfolded itself during his own strenuous and benignant career. His history is an orderly, lucid, and most instructive work; it contains many tokens of its author's appreciation of the nature and requirements of historical writing; and though so recently—1855—published in a perfect form, it must henceforth take its true place at the head of American historical literature, and win for its author the patristic dignity that we have ascribed to him.

John Winthrop.—In the early spring of 1630, a fleet of four vessels sailed out into the sea from a beautiful harbour in the Isle of Wight, their prows pointed westward. On board that fleet were the greatest company of wealthy and cultivated persons that have ever emigrated in any one voyage from England to America. They were prosperous English Puritans. Foremost among them in intellectual power and in weight of character was John Winthrop, already chosen Governor of the Massachusetts Company, and qualified by every personal trait to be the conductor and the statesman of the new Puritan colony of Massachusetts Bay. Immediately upon going on board ship he began a piece of writing, which he continued to work at not only during the rest of the voyage but during the rest of his life, and which is a treasure beyond price among our early historic memorials,—*The History of New England*. His plan was to jot down significant experiences in the daily life of his company, not only while at sea but after their arrival in America. For almost twenty years the story went forward, from 1630 until a few weeks before the writer's death in 1649. It is quite evident that Winthrop wrote what he did with the full purpose of having it published as a history; but he wrote it amid the hurry and weariness of his unloitering life, with no anxiety about style, with no other purpose than to tell the truth in plain and honest fashion. There is one portion of this History that has acquired great celebrity: it is the one embodying Winthrop's speech, in 1645, in the general court, on his being acquitted of the charge of having exceeded his authority as deputy-governor. One passage of it, containing Winthrop's statement of the nature of liberty, is of pre-eminent merit, worthy of being placed by the side of the weightiest and most magnanimous sentences of John Locke or Algernon Sidney. A distinguished American publicist has declared that this is the best definition of liberty in the English language, and that in comparison with it what Blackstone says about liberty seems puerile.[1]

Descriptions of Nature.—A delightful group of writings belonging to our earliest age is made up of those which preserve for us, in the very words of the men themselves, the curiosity, the awe, the bewilderment, the fresh delight, with which the American Fathers came face to face for the first time with the various forms of nature and of life in the New World. Examples of this class of writings were produced by the early men of Virginia; and among the founders of New England there was no lack of the same sensitiveness to the vast, picturesque, and novel aspects of nature which they encountered upon the sea and the land, in their first journeys hither. The evidence of this fact is scattered thick through all their writings, in letters, sermons, histories, poems; while there remain several books, written by them immediately after their arrival here, describing in the first glow of elated feeling the vision that unfolded itself before them of the new realms of existence upon which they were entering.

---

1   "There is a twofold liberty, natural, and civil or federal. The first is common to man with beasts and other creatures. By this, man, as he stands in relation to man simply, hath liberty to do what he lists; it is a liberty to evil as well as to good. This liberty is incompatible and inconsistent with authority, and cannot endure the least restraint of the most just authority. The exercise and maintaining of this liberty makes men grow more evil, and in time to be worse than brute beasts. This is that great enemy of truth and peace, that wild beast, which all the ordinances of God are bent against, to restrain and subdue it. The other kind of liberty I call civil or federal; it may also be termed moral, in reference to the covenant between God and man, in the moral law, and the politic covenants and constitutions amongst men themselves. This liberty is the proper end and object of authority, and cannot subsist without it; and it is a liberty to that only which is good, just, and honest. This liberty you are to stand for, with the hazard not only of your goods but of your lives, if need be. Whatsoever crosseth this, is not authority, but a distemper thereof. This liberty is maintained and exercised in a way of subjection to authority.... So shall your liberties be preserved in upholding the honour and power of authority amongst you."—*History of New England*, ii., 279–282.

Theological Writers.—Without doubt, the sermons produced in New England during the colonial times, and especially during the seventeenth century, are the most authentic and characteristic revelations of the mind of New England for all that wonderful epoch. The theological and religious writings of early New England may not now be readable; but they are certainly not despicable. They represent an enormous amount of subtile, sustained, and sturdy brain-power. They are, of course, grave, dry, abstruse, dreadful; to our debilitated attentions they are hard to follow; in style they are often uncouth and ponderous; they are technical in the extreme; they are devoted to a theology that yet lingers in the memory of mankind only through certain shells of words long since emptied of their original meaning. Nevertheless, these writings are monuments of vast learning, and of a stupendous intellectual energy both in the men who produced them and in the men who listened to them. Of course they can never be recalled to any vital human interest. They have long since done their work in moving the minds of men. Few of them can be cited as literature. In the mass, they can only be labelled by the antiquarians and laid away upon shelves to be looked at occasionally as curiosities of verbal expression, and as relics of an intellectual condition gone for ever. They were conceived by noble minds; they are themselves noble. They are superior to our jests. We may deride them, if we will; but they are not derided.

Of all the great preachers who came to New England in our first age, there were three who, according to the universal opinion of their contemporaries, towered above all others,—Thomas Hooker, Thomas Shepard, John Cotton. These three could be compared with one another; but with them could be compared no one else. They stood apart, above rivalry, above envy. In personal traits they differed; they were alike in bold and energetic thinking, in massiveness of erudition, in a certain overpowering personal persuasiveness, in the gift of fascinating and resistless pulpit oratory.

"The Simple Cobbler of Agawam."—Soon after his arrival in Massachusetts, Nathaniel Ward became minister to a raw settlement of Puritans at Agawam, the beautiful Indian name of that district, afterward foolishly exchanged for Ipswich. Early in 1645, he commenced writing the remarkable book, *The Simple Cobbler of Agawam*, which will

keep for him a perpetual place in early American literature. It had the good fortune to fit the times and the passions of men; it was caught up into instant notice, and ran through four editions within the first year. *The Simple Cobbler of Agawam* may be described as a prose satire upon what seemed to the author to be the frightful license of new opinions in his time, both in New England and at home; upon the frivolity of women and the long hair of men; and finally upon the raging storm of English politics, in the strife then going forward between sects, parties, Parliament, and King. It is a tremendous partisan pamphlet. After all, the one great trait in this book which must be to us the most welcome, is its superiority to the hesitant, imitative, and creeping manner that is the sure sign of a provincial literature. The first accents of literary speech in the American forests seem not to have been provincial, but free, fearless, natural. Our earliest writers, at any rate, wrote the English language spontaneously, forcefully, like honest men. We shall have to search in some later period of our intellectual history to find, if at all, a race of literary snobs and imitators—writers who in their thin and timid ideas, their nerveless diction, and their slavish simulation of the supposed literary accent of the mother-country, make confession of the inborn weakness and beggarliness of literary provincials.

Roger Williams.—From his early manhood even down to his late old age, Roger Williams stands in New England a mighty and benignant form, always pleading for some magnanimous idea, some tender charity, the rectification of some wrong, the exercise of some sort of forbearance toward men's bodies or souls. He became an uncompromising Separatist. By the spectacle of the white men helping themselves freely to the lands of the red men, he became an assailant of the validity, in that particular, of the New England charters. Roger Williams also held that it was a shocking thing—one of the abominations of the age—for men who did not even pretend to have religion in their hearts, to be muttering publicly the words of religion with their mouths; and that such persons ought not to be called on to perform any acts of worship, even the taking of an oath. Finally, he held another doctrine, that the power of the civil magistrate "extends only to the bodies and goods and outward state of men," and not at all to their inward state, their consciences, their opinions. For these four crimes, particularly mentioned by Governor Haynes in pronouncing sentence upon him, Massachusetts deemed it unsafe to permit such a nefarious being as Roger Williams to abide anywhere within her borders.

The illustrious Westminster Assembly of Divines had been in session since July, 1643. Already the Presbyterians in it had come to hard blows with the Congregationalists in it, with respect to the form of church government to be erected in England upon the ruins of the Episcopacy. On that subject Roger Williams had a very distinct opinion. While some were for having the new national church of this pattern, and others were for having it of that, Roger Williams boldly stepped two or three centuries ahead of his age, and affirmed that there should be no national church at all. Putting his argument into the differential form of mere questions, he published, in 1644, what he called *Queries of Highest Consideration*. This, of course, was stark and dreadful heresy; but it was heresy for which Roger Williams had already suffered loss and pain, and was prepared to suffer more. Above all, his nature had become absolutely clear in its adjustment of certain grand ideas, of which the chief was liberty of soul. On behalf of that idea, having now an opportunity to free his mind, he resolved to do so, keeping nothing back; and accordingly, almost upon the heels of the little book that has just been mentioned, he sent out another—not a little one; a book of strong, limpid, and passionate argument, glorious for its intuitions of the world's coming wisdom, and in its very title flinging out defiantly a challenge to all comers. He called it *The Bloody Tenet of Persecution for Cause of Conscience*. His book reached in due time the library of John Cotton, and stirred him up to make a reply, which bore a title reverberating that given by Roger Williams to his book: *The Bloody Tenet washed and made white in the Blood of the Lamb*. Cotton's book quickly found Roger Williams, at his home in Rhode Island, and of course aroused him to write a rejoinder. Its title is a reiteration of that given to his former work, and is likewise a characteristic retort upon the modification made of it by his antagonist: *The Bloody Tenet yet more Bloody, by Mr. Cotton's Endeavour to wash it white in the Blood of the Lamb*. This book is the most powerful of the writings of Roger Williams. There are three principal matters argued in it,—the nature of persecution, the limits of the power of the civil sword, and the tolerance already granted by Parliament.

With Roger Williams, the mood for composition seems to have come in gusts. His writings are numerous; but they were produced spasmodically and in clusters, amid long spaces of silence. He is known to have written two or three works which were never printed at all, and which are now lost. In 1652, he published, in addition to his rejoinder to John Cotton, two small treatises. From that time, no book of his was given to the press until the year 1676, when he published at Boston a quarto volume of nearly 350 pages, embodying his own report of a series of stormy public debates, which he had held in Rhode Island, not long before, with certain robust advocates of Quakerism. This book bears a punning title, *George Fox Digged out of his Burrows*. Besides those of his writings that were intended for books, there are many in the form of letters, some addressed to the public, most of them to his personal friends. In these letters, which cover his whole life from youth to old age, we seem to get very near to the man himself.

Puritanism and Poetry.—A happy surprise awaits those who come to the study of the early literature of New England with the expectation of finding it altogether arid in sentiment, or void of the spirit and aroma of poetry. The New Englander of the seventeenth century was indeed a typical Puritan; and it will hardly be said that any typical Puritan of that century was a poetical personage. In proportion to his devotion to the ideas that won for him the derisive honour of his name, was he at war with nearly every form of the beautiful. He himself believed that there was an inappeasable feud between religion and art; and hence the duty of suppressing art was bound up in his soul with the master-purpose of promoting religion. Hence, very naturally, he turned away likewise from certain great and splendid types of literature,—from the drama, from the playful and sensuous verse of Chaucer and his innumerable sons, from the secular prose writings of his contemporaries, and from all forms of modern lyric verse except the Calvinistic hymn. Nevertheless, the Puritan did not succeed in eradicating poetry from his nature. Of course, poetry was planted there too deep even for his theological grub-hooks to root it out. Though denied expression in one way, the poetry that was in him forced itself into utterance in another. If his theology drove poetry out of many forms in which it had been used to reside, poetry itself practised a noble revenge by taking up its abode in his theology. Though he stamped his foot in horror and scorn upon many exquisite and delicious types of literary art, yet the idea that filled and thrilled his soul was one in every way sublime, immense, imaginative, poetic. How resplendent and superb was the poetry that lay at the heart of Puritanism, was seen by the sightless eyes of John Milton, whose great epic is indeed the epic of Puritanism.

Turning to Puritanism as it existed in New England, we may perhaps imagine it as solemnly declining the visits of the Muses of poetry, sending out to them the blunt but honest message—"Otherwise engaged." Nothing could be further from the truth. It is an extraordinary fact about these grave and substantial men of New England, especially during our earliest literary age, that they all had a lurking propensity to write what they sincerely believed to be poetry,—and this, in most cases, in unconscious defiance of the edicts of nature and of a predetermining Providence. It is impressive to note, as we inspect our first period, that neither advanced age, nor high office, nor mental unfitness, nor previous condition of respectability, was sufficient to protect any one from the poetic vice. Here and there, even a town-clerk, placing on record the deeply prosaic proceedings of the selectmen, would adorn them in the sacred costume of poetry. Remembering their unfriendly attitude towards art in general, this universal mania of theirs for some forms of the poetic art—this unrestrained proclivity toward the "lust of versification"—must seem to us an odd psychological freak. Or, shall we rather say that it was not a freak at all, but a normal effort of nature, which, being unduly repressed in one direction, is accustomed to burst over all barriers in another? As respects the poetry which was perpetrated by our ancestors, it must be mentioned that a benignant Providence has its own methods of protecting the human family from intolerable misfortune; and that the most of this poetry has perished.

Anne Bradstreet.—There was, however, belonging to this primal literary period, one poet who, in some worthy sense, found in poetry a vocation. The first professional poet of New England was a woman. In the year 1650 there was published, in London, a book of poems written by a gifted young woman of the New England wilderness, Anne Bradstreet by name. She was born in England, in 1612. She was the laborious wife of a New England farmer, the mother of eight children, and herself from childhood of a delicate constitution. The most of her poems were produced between 1630 and 1642, that is, before she was thirty years old; and during these years she had neither leisure, nor elegant surroundings, nor freedom from anxious thoughts, nor even abounding health. Somehow, during her busy lifetime, she contrived to put upon record compositions numerous enough to fill a royal octavo volume of 400 pages,—compositions which entice and reward our reading of them, two hundred years after she lived.

II. SECOND PERIOD (1676–1765)

The Two Periods.—I have taken the year 1676 as the year of partition between the two periods into which our colonial age seems to fall. Before 1676, the new civilisation in America was principally in the hands of Americans born in England; after 1676, it was principally in the hands of Americans born in America, and the subjects of such training as was to be had here. Our first colonial period, therefore, transmits to us a body of writings produced by immigrant Americans; preserving for us the ideas, the moods, the efforts, the very phrases of the men who founded the American nation; representing to us, also, the earliest literary results flowing from the reactions of life in the New World upon an intellectual culture formed in the Old World. Our second colonial period does more: it transmits to us a body of writings, produced in the main by the American children of those immigrants, and representing the earliest literary results flowing from the reactions of life in the New World upon an intellectual culture that was itself formed in the New World.

Our first colonial period, just seventy years long, we have now briefly examined. For my part, I have no apology to make for it: I think it needs none. It was a period principally engaged in other tasks than the tasks of the pen; it laid, quietly and well, the foundation of a new social structure that was to cover a hemisphere, was to give shelter and comfort to myriads of the human race, was to endure to centuries far beyond the gropings of our guesswork. Had it done that deed alone, and left no written word at all, not any man since then could have wondered; still less could any man have flung at it the reproach of intellectual lethargy or neglect. But if, besides what it did in the founding of a new commonwealth, we consider what it also did in the founding of a new literature—the muchness of that special work, the downright merit of it—we shall find it hard to withhold from that period the homage of our admiration.

From the year 1676, when our first colonial period ends, there stretches onward a space of just eighty-nine years, at the end of which the American colonies underwent a swift and portentous change,—losing, all at once, their colonial content, and passing suddenly into the earlier and the intellectual stage of their struggle for independence. This space of eighty-nine years forms, of course, our second colonial period.

New England Verse-Writers.—Urian Oakes, born in 1631, was reared in the woods of Concord. The splendid literary capacity of this early American—this product of our pioneer and autochthonous culture—is seen in this: as his sermons are among the noblest specimens of prose to be met with, in that class of writings, during the colonial time, so the one example that is left to us of his verse reaches the highest point touched by American poetry during the same era. The poem thus referred to is an elegy upon the death of a man to whom the poet seems to have been bound by the tenderest friendship,—a poem in fifty-two six-lined stanzas; not without some mechanical defects; blurred also by some patches of the prevailing theological jargon; yet, upon the whole, affluent, stately, pathetic; beautiful and strong with the beauty and strength of true imaginative vision.

In contemporaneous renown, far above all other verse-writers of the colonial time, was Michael Wigglesworth, the explicit and unshrinking rhymer of the Five Points of Calvinism; a poet who so perfectly uttered in verse the religious faith and emotion of Puritan New England that, for more than a hundred years, his writings had universal diffusion there, and a popular influence only inferior to that of the Bible and the Shorter Catechism. No one holding a different theology from that held by Michael Wigglesworth can do justice to him as a poet, without exercising the utmost intellectual catholicity. His verse is quite lacking in art; its ordinary form being a crude, swinging ballad-measure, with a sort of cheap melody, a shrill, reverberating clatter, that would instantly catch and please the popular ear, at that time deaf to daintier and more subtle effects in poetry. In the multitude of his verses, Michael Wigglesworth surpasses all other poets of the colonial time, excepting Anne Brad-street. Besides numerous minor poems, he is the author of three poetical works of considerable length. One of these, *God's Controversy with New England*, was "written in the time of the great drought," 1662. The argument of the poem is this: "New England planted, prospered, declining, threatened, punished." The poet holds the opinion, common enough in his day, that before the arrival of the English in America, this continent had been the choice and peculiar residence of the Devil and his angels. Another large poem of Wigglesworth's is *Meat out of the Eater; or, Meditations concerning the Necessity, End, and Usefulness of Afflictions unto God's Children, all tending to prepare them for and comfort them under the Cross*. Here we have simply the Christian doctrine of comfort in sorrow, translated into metrical jingles. It was first published, probably, in 1669; ten years afterward, it had passed through at least four editions; and during the entire colonial age, it was a much-read manual of solace in affliction. But the masterpiece of Michael Wigglesworth's genius, and his most delectable gift to an admiring public, was that blazing and sulphurous poem, *The Day of Doom; or, A poetical Description of the great and last Judgment*. This great poem, which, with entire unconscious-ness, attributes to the Divine Being a character the most execrable and loathsome to be met with, perhaps, in any literature, Christian or pagan, had for a hundred years a popularity far exceeding that of any other work, in prose or verse, produced in America before the Revolution. The eighteen hundred copies of the first edition were sold within a single year; which implies the purchase of a copy of *The Day of Doom* by at least every thirty-fifth person then in New England,—an example of the commercial success of a book never afterward equalled in this country. Since that time, the book has been repeatedly published; at least once in England, and at least eight times in America—the last time being in 1867.

The Dynasty of the Mathers.—At the time of his arrival in Boston—August, 1635—Richard Mather was thirty-nine years of age; a man of extensive and precise learning in the classics, in the Scriptures, and in divinity; already a famous preacher. This man, "the progenitor of all the Mathers in New England," and the first of a line of great preachers and great men of letters that continued to hold sway there through the entire colonial era, had in himself the chief traits that distinguished his family through so long a period;—great physical endurance, a voracious appetite for the reading of books, an alarming propensity to the writing of books, a love of political leadership in church and state, the faculty of personal conspicuousness, finally, the homiletic gift. His numerous writings were, of course, according to the demand of his time and neighbourhood;—sermons, a catechism, a treatise on justification, public letters upon church government, several controversial documents, the preface to the Old Bay Psalm Book, and many of the marvels of metrical expression to be viewed in the body of that work.

Of the six sons of Richard Mather, four became famous preachers, two of them in Ireland and in England, other two in New England; the greatest of them all being the youngest, born at Dorchester, June 21, 1639, and at his birth adorned with the name of Increase, in graceful recognition of "the increase of every sort, wherewith God favoured the country about the time of his nativity." Even in childhood he began to display the strong and eager traits that gave distinction and power to his whole life, and that bore him impetuously through the warfare of eighty-four mortal years. In 1657, on his eighteenth birthday, he preached in his father's pulpit his first sermon. From 1661 to 1664 he divided his services between his father's church at Dorchester and the North Church of Boston. At last, in 1664, he consented to be made minister of the latter church, which, thenceforward, to the end of his own life, and to the end of the life of his more famous son, continued to be the tower and the stronghold of the Mathers in America. Here, then, was a person, born in America, bred in America,—a clean specimen of what America could do for itself in the way of keeping up the brave stock of its first imported citizens. As to learning, he even exceeded all other New Englanders of the colonial time, except his own son, Cotton. His power as a pulpit-orator was very great. It was a common saying of his contemporaries, that Increase Mather was "a complete preacher." From a literary point of view, his writings certainly have considerable merit. The publications of Increase Mather defy mention, except in the form of a catalogue. From the year 1669, when he had reached the age of thirty, until the year 1723, when he died, hardly a twelvemonth was permitted to pass in which he did not solicit the public attention through the press. An authentic list of his works would include at least ninety-two titles. Of all the great host of Increase Mather's publications, perhaps only one can be said to have still any power of walking alive on the earth,—the book commonly known by a name not given to it by the author, *Remarkable Providences*. It cannot be denied that the conception of the book is thoroughly scientific; for it is to prove by induction the actual presence of supernatural forces in the world. Its chief defect, of course, is its lack of all cross-examination of the witnesses, and of all critical inspection of their testimony, together with a palpable eagerness on the author's part to welcome, from any quarter of the earth or sea or sky, any messenger whatever who may be seen hurrying toward Boston with his mouth full of marvels.

In the intellectual distinction of the Mather family, there seemed to be, for at least three generations, a certain cumulative felicity. The general acknowledgment of this fact is recorded in an old epitaph, composed for the founder of the illustrious tribe:

> Under this stone lies Richard Mather,
> Who had a son greater than his father,
> And eke a grandson greater than either.

This overtopping grandson was, of course, none other than Cotton Mather, the literary behemoth of New England in our colonial era; the man whose fame as a writer surpasses, in later times and especially in foreign countries, that of any other pre-Revolutionary American, excepting Jonathan Edwards and Benjamin Franklin. The most famous book produced by him—the most famous book, likewise, produced by any American during the colonial time—is *Magnalia Christi Americana; or, The Ecclesiastical History of New England, from its first Planting, in the Year 1620, unto the Year of our Lord 1698*. The Magnalia is, indeed, what the author called it, "a bulky thing,"—the two volumes of the latest edition having upwards of thirteen hundred pages. The *Magnalia* has great merits; it has, also, fatal defects. In its mighty chaos of fables and blunders and misrepresentations, are of course lodged many single facts of the utmost value, personal reminiscences, social gossip, snatches of conversations, touches of description, traits of character and life, that can be found nowhere else, and that help us to paint for ourselves some living picture of the great men and the great days of early New England; yet herein, also, history and fiction are so jumbled and shuffled together that it is never possible to tell, without other help than the author's, just where the fiction ends and the history begins. On no disputed question of fact is the unaided testimony of Cotton Mather of much weight. The true place of Cotton Mather in our literary history is indicated when we say that he was the last, the most vigorous, and, therefore, the most disagreeable representative of the Fantastic School in literature; and that he prolonged in New England the methods of that school even after his most cultivated contemporaries there had outgrown them, and had come to dislike them. The expulsion of the beautiful from thought, from sentiment, from language; a lawless and a merciless fury for the odd, the disorderly, the grotesque, the violent; strained analogies, unexpected images, pedantries, indelicacies, freaks of allusion, monstrosities of phrase;—these are the traits of Cotton Mather's writing, even as they are the traits common to that perverse and detestable literary mood that held sway in different countries of Christendom during the sixteenth and seventeenth centuries. Its birthplace was Italy; New England was its grave; Cotton Mather was its last great apostle.

Samuel Mather, the son of Cotton Mather, was born in 1706. In him, evidently, the ancestral fire had become almost extinct. He had abundant learning; was extremely industrious; published many things; but there was not in them, as there was not in him, the victorious energy of an original mind, or even the winning felicity of an imitative one. He was a sturdy and a worthy man. He left no successor to continue the once-splendid dynasty of his tribe. He was the last, and the least, of the Mathers.

The Laity in New England Literature.—In the history of literature in New England during the colonial time, one fact stands out above all others,—the intellectual leadership of the clergy, and that, too, among a laity neither ignorant nor weak. This leadership was in every sense honourable, both for the leaders and the led. It was not due alone to the high authority of the clerical office in New England; it was due still more to the personal greatness of the men who filled that office, and who themselves made the office great. They were intellectual leaders because they deserved to be; for, living among a well-educated and high-spirited people, they knew more, were wiser, were abler, than all other persons in the community. Of such a leadership, it was an honour even to be among the followers. And in the literary achievements of New England in the colonial time, the clergy filled by far the largest space, because, in all departments of writing, they did by far the largest amount of work. After the first half-century of New England life, another fact comes into notice,—the advance of the laity in literary activity. By that time, many strong and good men, who had been educated there in all the learning of the age, either not entering the clerical profession or not remaining in it, began to organise and to develop the other learned professions— the legal, medical, and tuitionary—and, appealing to the public through various forms of literature, to divide more and more with the clergy the leadership of men's minds. Moreover, in the last decade of the seventeenth century, an attempt was made to establish a newspaper in New England. The attempt failed. In the first decade of the eighteenth century, another attempt was made, and did not fail; and long before the end of our colonial epoch, a new profession had come into existence, having a power to act on the minds of men more mightily than any other,—the profession of journalism.

The Almanac.—No one who would penetrate to the core of early American literature, and would read in it the secret history of the people in whose minds it took root and from whose minds it grew, may by any means turn away, in lofty literary scorn, from the almanac. The earliest record of this species of literature in America carries us back to the very beginning of printed literature in America; for, next after a sheet containing *The Freeman's Oath*, the first production that came from the printing-press in this country was *An Almanac calculated for New England, by Mr. Pierce*, and printed at Cambridge, in 1639. Thenceforward for a long time, scarcely a year passed over that solitary printing-press at Cambridge without receiving a similar salute from it. In 1676, Boston itself grew wise enough to produce an almanac of its own. Ten years afterward, Philadelphia began to send forth almanacs—a trade in which, in the following century, it was to acquire special glory. In 1697, New York entered the same enticing field of enterprise. The first almanac produced in Rhode Island was in 1728; the first almanac produced in Virginia was in 1731. In 1733, Benjamin Franklin began to publish what he called *Poor Richard's Almanac*, to which his own personal reputation has given a celebrity surpassing that of all other almanacs published anywhere in the world. Thus, year by year, with the multiplication of people and of printing-presses in this country, was there a multiplication of almanacs, some of them being of remarkable intellectual and even literary merit. Throughout our colonial time, when larger books were costly and few, the almanac had everywhere a hearty welcome and frequent perusal.

History and Biography in New England.—The one form of secular literature for which, during the entire colonial age, the writers of New England had the most authentic vocation is history. Our second literary period produced four considerable historians,—William Hubbard, Cotton Mather, Thomas Prince, Thomas Hutchinson: the first two excelling in popularity all other historians of the colonial time; the last two excelling all others in specific training for the profession of history, and in the conscious accumulation of materials for historic work. Of that species of history which is devoted to the lives of individuals rather than of communities, there were many specimens produced in the colonial epoch. But it is a singular fact that, in literary quality, the biographies written in colonial New England are far inferior to its histories.

Pulpit Literature in New England.—In our progress over the various fields of literature in New England during the colonial time, we encounter not one form of writing in which we are permitted to lose sight of the clergy of New England,—their tireless and versatile activity, their learning, their force of brain, their force of character. The immigrant clergy of New England—the founders of this noble and brilliant order—were, in nearly all qualities of personal worth and greatness, among the greatest and the worthiest of their time, in the mother-country,—mighty scholars, orators, sages, saints. And by far the most wonderful thing about these men is, that they were able to convey across the Atlantic, into a naked wilderness, all the essential elements of that ancient civilisation out of which they came; and, at once, to raise up and educate, in the New World, a line of mighty successors in their sacred office, without the least break in the sequence, without the slightest diminution in scholarship, in eloquence, in intellectual energy, in moral power.

Jonathan Edwards.—Jonathan Edwards, the most original and acute thinker yet produced in America, was born in 1703; in 1758 he was installed as president of the College of New Jersey, and died a few weeks afterward. Both by his father and by his mother, he came of the gentlest and most intellectual stock in New England. In early childhood, he began to manifest those powerful, lofty, and beautiful endowments, of mind and of character, that afterward distinguished him,—spirituality, conscientiousness, meekness, simplicity, disinterestedness, and a marvellous capacity for the acquisition of knowledge and for the prosecution of independent thought. It is, perhaps, impossible to name any department of intellectual exertion, in which, with suitable outward facilities, he might not have achieved supreme distinction. Certainly, he did enough to show that had he given himself to mathematics, or to physical science, or to languages, or to literature—especially the literature of imagination and of wit—he would have become one of the world's masters. The traditions of his family, the circumstances of his life, the impulses derived from his education and from the models of personal greatness before his eyes, all led him to give himself to mental science and divinity; and in mental science and divinity, his achievements will be remembered to the end of time.

III. GENERAL LITERARY FORCES IN THE COLONIAL TIME

Colonial Isolation.—The study of American literature in the colonial time is the study of a literature produced, in isolated portions, at the several local seats of English civilisation in America. Before the year 1765, we find in this country, not one American people, but many American peoples. At the various centres of our colonial life—Georgia, the Carolinas, Virginia, Maryland, Pennsylvania, New York, Connecticut, Rhode Island, Massachusetts—there were, indeed, populations of the same English stock; but these populations differed widely in personal and social peculiarities—in spirit, in opinion, in custom. The germs of a future nation were here, only they were far apart, unsympathetic, at times even unfriendly. No cohesive principle prevailed, no centralising life; each little nation was working out its own destiny in its own fashion. In general, the characteristic note of American literature in the colonial time is, for New England, scholarly, logical, speculative, unworldly, rugged, sombre; and as one passes southward along the coast, across other spiritual zones, this literary note changes rapidly toward lightness and brightness, until it reaches the sensuous mirth, the satire, the persiflage, the gentlemanly grace, the amenity, the jocular coarseness, of literature in Maryland, Virginia, and the farther South.

Colonial Fellowship.—On the other hand, the fact must not be overlooked that, while the tendency toward colonial isolation had its way, throughout the entire colonial age, there was also an opposite tendency—a tendency toward colonial fellowship—that asserted itself even from the first, and yet at the first faintly, but afterward with steadily increasing power as time went on; until at last, in 1765, aided by a fortunate blunder in the statesmanship of England, this tendency became suddenly dominant, and led to that united and great national life, without which a united and great national literature here would have been for ever impossible. This august fact of fellowship between the several English populations in America—a fellowship maintained and even strengthened after the original occasion of it had ceased—has perhaps saved the English language in America from finally breaking up into a multitude of mutually repellent dialects; it has certainly saved American literature from the pettiness of permanent local distinctions, from fitfulness in its development, and from disheartening limitations in its audience. Besides these general causes leading toward colonial union,—kinship, religion, commerce, dependence on the same sovereign, peril from the same enemies,—there were three other causes that may be described as purely intellectual—the rise of journalism, the founding of colleges, and the study of physical science. They worked strongly for the development of that intercolonial fellowship without which no national literature would ever have been born here, and, also, were in themselves literary forces of extraordinary importance.

Early American Journalism.—The first newspaper ever published in America appeared in Boston in 1690, and was named *Public Occurrences.* For the crime of uttering "reflections of a very high nature," it was immediately extinguished by the authorities of Massachusetts,—not even attaining the dignity of a second number. Under this rough blow, the real birth of American journalism hesitated for fourteen years. On April 4, 1704, was published in Boston the first number of an American newspaper that lived. It was called *The Boston News-Letter.* For fifteen years, it continued to be the only newspaper in America. At last, on December 21, 1719, a rival newspaper was started, named *The Boston Gazette*; and on the twenty-second day of the same month, in the same year, there appeared in Philadelphia the first newspaper published in this country outside of Boston. This was called *The American Weekly Mercury*. From that time onward, the fashion of having newspapers spread rapidly. Nearly all of these newspapers were issued once each week; many of them were on diminutive sheets; and for a long time all of them clung to the prudent plan of publishing only news and advertisements, abstaining entirely from the audacity of an editorial opinion, or disguising that dangerous luxury under pretended letters from correspondents. News from Europe,—when it was to be had,— and especially news from England, occupied a prominent place in these little papers; but, necessarily, for each one, the affairs of its own colony, and next, the affairs of the other colonies, furnished the principal items of interest. Thus it was that early American journalism, even though feeble, sluggish, and timid, began to lift the people of each colony to a plane somewhat higher than its own boundaries, and to enable them, by looking abroad, this way and that, upon the proceedings of other people in this country, and upon other interests as precious as their own, to correct the pettiness and the selfishness of mere localism in thought. Colonial journalism was a necessary and a great factor in the slow process of colonial union. Besides this, our colonial journalism soon became, in itself, a really important literary force. It could not remain for ever a mere disseminator of public gossip, or a placard for the display of advertisements. The instinct of critical and brave debate was strong even among those puny editors, and it kept struggling for expression. Moreover, each editor was surrounded by a coterie of friends, with active brains and a propensity to utterance; and these constituted a sort of unpaid staff of editorial contributors, who, in various forms,— letters, essays, anecdotes, epigrams, poems, lampoons,—helped to give vivacity and even literary value to the paper.

Our early journalism, likewise, included publications of a more explicit literary intention than the newspapers; publications in which the original work was done with far greater care, and in which far more space was surrendered to literary news and literary criticism, and to the exercise of many sorts of literary talent. The generic name for these pub-lications is the magazine; and the first one issued in this country was by Benjamin Franklin, at Philadelphia, in 1741. By far the most admirable example of our literary periodicals in the colonial time was *The American*

Magazine, published at Philadelphia from October, 1757, to October, 1758, and conducted, according to its own announcement, "by a society of gentlemen."

Early American Colleges.—No other facts in American history are more creditable to the American people than those which relate to their early and steady esteem for higher education, and especially to their efforts and their sacrifices in the founding of colleges. Before the year 1765, seven colleges were established here: Harvard, in 1636; William and Mary, in 1693; Yale, in 1700; New Jersey, in 1746; King's—now Columbia—in 1754; Philadelphia—now the University of Pennsylvania—in 1755; Rhode Island—now Brown University—in 1764. Though all these little establishments bore the name of colleges, there were considerable differences among them with respect to the grade and extent of the instruction they furnished,—those founded latest being, in that particular, the most rudimental. Nevertheless, at them all one noble purpose prevailed,—the study of the ancient classics. This extraordinary training in the ancient languages led to forms of proficiency that have no parallel now in American colleges. So early as 1649, President Dunster wrote to Ravius, the famous Orientalist, that some of the students at Harvard could "with ease dexterously translate Hebrew and Chaldee into Greek." In 1678, there was in that college even an Indian student who wrote Latin and Greek poetry; and this accomplishment continued to be an ordinary one there as late as the Revolutionary War; while the facile use of Latin, whether for conversation or for oratory, was so common among the scholars of Harvard and of Yale as to excite no remark. Nearly all the superior men in public life, after the immigrant generation, were educated at these little colleges; and in all the studies that then engaged the attention of scholars in the Old World, these men, particularly if clergymen, had a scholarship that was, in compass and variety, fully abreast of the learning of the time. The existence here of these early colleges was in many ways a means of colonial fellowship. Each college was itself, in all portions of the country, a point of distinction for its own colony; at each college were gathered some students from other colonies; between all the colleges there grew a sense of fraternity in learning and letters, and this re-enforced the general sense of fraternity in civic destinies; finally, at these colleges was trained no little of that masterly statesmanship of our later colonial time, which, at a glance, interpreted the danger that hung upon the horizon in 1765, proclaimed the imminent need of colonial union, and quickly brought it about. The vast influence that our early colleges exerted upon literary culture can hardly be over-stated. Among all the people, they nourished those spiritual conditions out of which, alone, every wholesome and genuine literature must grow; and in their special devotion to classical studies, they imparted to a con-siderable body of men the finest training for literary work that the world is yet possessed of. It was of incalculable service to American literature that, even in these wild regions of the earth, the accents of Homer, of Thucydides, of Cicero, were made familiar to us from the beginning; that a consciousness of the æsthetic principle in verbal expression was kept alive here, and developed, by constant and ardent study of the supreme masters of literary form; and that the great, immemorial traditions of literature were borne hither across the Atlantic from their ancient seats, and were here housed in perpetual temples, for the rearing of which the people gladly went to great cost. The tribute of most eloquent homage, which, in 1775, in the House of Lords, the Earl of Chatham paid to the in-tellectual force, the literary symmetry, and the decorum of the state-pa-pers then recently transmitted from America, and then lying upon the table of that House, was virtually an announcement to Europe of the astonishing news,—that, by means of an intellectual cultivation formed in America, in its own little colleges, on the best models of ancient and modern learning, America had already become not only an integral part of the civilised world, but even a member of the republic of letters.

The Study of Physical Science in America.—The study of physical science in this country began with the very settlement of the country. The writings of the first Americans are strewn with sharp observations on the geography of America, on its minerals, soils, waters, plants, an-imals; on its climates, storms, earthquakes; on its savage inhabitants, its diseases, its medicines; and on the phenomena of the heavens as they appeared to this part of the earth. There were here, even in our earliest age, several men of special scientific inclination, such as William Wood, John Josselyn, John Sherman, John Winthrop of Massachusetts, and John Winthrop of Connecticut. Indeed, the latter was recognised as an eminent physicist even among the contemporaneous physicists of England; and in Connecticut, where he founded the city of New London, and where he was for many years Governor, he pursued with great zeal his scientific researches, carrying them even into the fatal chase for the philosopher's stone. He was on terms of endearing intimacy with Watkins, Robert Boyle, and other great leaders of science in England; and it is said that under the menace of public calamities there, and drawn, likewise, by their friendship for Winthrop, these men had proposed to leave England, and to establish in the American colony over which Winthrop presided "a society for promoting natural knowledge." They were, however, induced by Charles II. to remain in England; and accordingly, with the co-operation of Winthrop, who happened to be in London at the time, they founded there, instead of in New London, the association that soon became renowned throughout the world as the Royal Society. Perhaps there was no one of these early American students of nature whom it is now pleasanter to recall than the Quaker naturalist, John Bartram. Born in Pennsylvania, in 1701, he founded near Philadelphia the first botanic garden in America. He was appointed American botanist to George III., and won from Linnæus the praise of being "the greatest natural botanist in the world." As John Bartram represents high attainments in science reached under all outward disadvantages, so John Winthrop of Harvard College represents still higher attainments in science reached under all outward advantages. A descendant of the first Governor of Massachusetts, from 1738 until his death in 1779 he served his Alma Mater with great distinction as professor of mathematics and natural philosophy. For extent and depth of learning in his special departments, he was probably the foremost American of his day. All things considered, he was probably the most symmetrical example both of scientific and of literary culture produced in America during the colonial time; representing what was highest and broadest in it, what was most robust and most delicate; a thinker and a writer born and bred in a province, but neither in thought nor in speech provincial; an American student of nature and of human nature, who stayed at home, and bringing Europe and the universe to his own door, made himself cosmopolitan.

Thus, from the earliest moment of American civilisation, there were, here and there in this country, eager and keen students of nature,—their number greatly multiplying with the passing of the years. But it belongs to the essence of such studies that they who pursue them should seek the fellowship of their own brethren, either for help in solving difficulties or for delight in announcing discoveries; and it is, beyond question, true that the union of the American colonies was first laid in the friendly correspondence and intellectual sympathies of students of physical science, who from an early day were dispersed through these colonies. By the year 1740, the American students of nature had become a multitude; and from that year to the year 1765, the glory of physical research among us culminated in the brilliant achievements of Benjamin Franklin, whose good fortune it then was to enable his country to step at once to the van of scientific discovery, and for a few years to be the teacher of the world on the one topic of physical inquiry then uppermost in men's thoughts. In proposing the formation of the American Philosophical Society, this wonderful man had announced to his own countrymen that the time had come for them to make new and greater exertions for the enlargement of human knowledge. Inspired by the noble enthusiasm of Franklin, whose position brought him into large personal acquaintance in all the colonies, the activity and the range of scientific studies in America were then greatly increased,—a bond of scientific communion that helped to prepare the way for political communion, whenever the hour for that should come. The direct impulse given by all this eager study of physical science to the development of American literature is to be seen not only in scientific writings like those of Winthrop and of Franklin, which have high and peculiar literary merit, but in the general invigoration of American thought, in the development of a sturdy rational spirit, and in a broadening of the field of our intellectual vision.

But, in spite of all these influences working toward colonial fellowship, the prevailing fact in American life, down to the year 1765, was colonial isolation. With that year came the immense event that suddenly swept nearly all minds in the several colonies into the same great current of absorbing thought, and that held them there for nearly twenty years. From the date of that event, we cease to concern ourselves with an American literature in the East or the South, in this colony or in that. Henceforward American literature flows in one great, common stream, and not in petty rills of geographical discrimination,—the literature of one multitudinous people, variegated indeed, in personal traits, but single in its commanding ideas and in its national destinies.

THE REVOLUTIONARY PERIOD

I. A GENERAL VIEW

The Three Stages.—In the intellectual process of the American Revolution, are to be observed three well defined stages of development on the part of the men who began and carried through that notable enterprise. The first stage—extending from the spring of 1763 to the spring of 1775—represents the noble anxiety which brave men must feel when their political safety is imperilled, this anxiety, however, being deepened in their case by a sincere and even a passionate desire, while roughly resisting an offensive ministerial policy, to keep within the bounds of constitutional opposition, and neither to forsake nor to forfeit that connection with the mother-country which they then held to be among the most precious of their earthly possessions. The second stage—extending from the spring of 1775 to the early summer of 1776—represents a rapidly spreading doubt, and yet at first no more than a doubt, as to the possibility of their continuing to be free men without ceasing to be English colonists. This doubt, of course, had been felt by not a few of them long before the day of the Lexington and Concord fights; but under the appalling logic of that day of brutality, it became suddenly weaponed with a power which mere words never had,—the power to undo swiftly, in the hearts of a multitude of liegemen, the tie of race, the charm of an antique national tradition, the loyalty, the love, and the pride of centuries. The third stage—extending from the early summer of 1776 to the very close of the whole struggle—represents a final conviction, at least on the part of a working majority of the American people, that it would be impossible for them to preserve their political rights and at the same time to remain inside the British Empire,—this conviction being also accompanied by the resolve to preserve those rights whether or no, and at whatsoever cost of time, or effort, or pain.

Of course, the intellectual attitude of the Loyalists of the Revolution—always during that period an immense and a very conscientious minority—correlated to that of the Revolutionists in each one of these three stages of development: in the first stage, by a position of qualified dissent as to the gravity of the danger and as to the proper method of dealing with it; in the second and third stages, by a position of unqualified dissent, and of implacable hostility, as regards the object and motive and method of the opposition which was then conducted by their more masterful fellow-countrymen.

The Predominant Note.—The chief trait of American literature during the period now under view is this: its concern with the problems of American society, and of American society in a peculiar condition—aroused, inflammable, in a state of alarm for its own existence, but also in a state of resolute combat for it. The literature which we are thus to inspect is not, then, a literature of tranquillity, but chiefly a literature of strife, or, as the Greeks would have said, of agony; and, of course, it must take those forms in which intellectual and impassioned debate can be most effectually carried on. The literature of our Revolution has almost everywhere the combative note; its habitual method is argumentative, persuasive, appealing, rasping, retaliatory; the very brain of man seems to be in armour; his wit is in the gladiator's attitude of offence and defence. It is a literature indulging itself in grimaces, in mockery, in scowls: a literature accented by earnest gestures meant to convince people, or by fierce blows meant to smite them down. In this literature we must not expect to find art used for art's sake.

Our next discovery is the rather notable one that such a period actually had a literary product very considerable in amount. Even in those perturbed years between 1763 and 1783, there was a large mass of literature produced in America. More than with most other epochs of revolutionary strife, our epoch of revolutionary strife was a strife of ideas: a long warfare of political logic; a succession of annual campaigns in which the marshalling of arguments not only preceded the marshalling of armies, but often exceeded them in impression upon the final result. An epoch like this, therefore,—an epoch in which nearly all that is great and dear in man's life on earth has to be argued for, as well as to be fought for, and in which ideas have a work to do quite as pertinent and quite as effective as that of bullets,—can hardly fail to be an epoch teeming with literature, with literature, of course, in the particular forms suited to the purposes of political co-operation and conflict.

We shall be much helped by keeping in mind the distinction between two classes of writings then produced among us: first, those writings which were the result of certain general intellectual interests and activities apart from the Revolutionary movement, and, secondly, those writings which were the result of intellectual interests and activities directly awakened and sustained by that movement. The presence of the first class we discover chiefly in the earlier years of this period, before the Revolutionary idea had become fully developed and fully predominant; and, again, in the later years of the period, when, with the success of the Revolution assured, the Revolutionary idea had begun to recede, and men's minds were free to swing again toward the usual subjects of human concern, particularly toward those which were to occupy them after the attainment of independence and of peace.

Literary Centres.—We shall find, within the first decade of this period and before its culmination into the final violence of the Revolutionary controversy, the beginnings of a new and a truer life in America. Of this new literary life there were, in general, two chief centres, one in the New England, one in the Middle Colonies. The New England literary centre was at New Haven, and was dominated by the influence of Yale College, within which, especially between 1767 and 1773, was a group of brilliant young men passionately devoted to the Greek and Roman classics, and brought into contact with the spirit of modern letters through their sympathetic study of the later masters of English prose and verse. The foremost man in this group was John Trumbull.

The new literary life of the Middle Colonies had its seat in the neighbourhood of New York and Philadelphia, and was keenly stimulated by the influence of their two colleges, and also by that of the College of New Jersey under the strong man—Witherspoon—who came to its presidency in 1768. The foremost representative of this new literary tendency was Philip Freneau, a true man of genius, the one poet of unquestionable originality granted to America prior to the nineteenth century. Of him and of his brother poet in New England, it is to be said that both began to do their work while still in youth; both seemed to have a vocation for disinterested literature in prose as well as in verse; both were reluctantly driven from that vocation by the intolerable political storm that then burst over the land; both were swept into the Revolutionary movement, and, thenceforward, the chief literary work of both was as political satirists. From about the year 1774, little trace of an æsthetic purpose in American letters is to be discovered until after the close of the Revolution.

Classification of the Revolutionary Writings.—The characteristic life of the period we now have in view was political, and not political only, but polemic, and fiercely polemic, and at last revolutionary; and its true literary expression is to be recognised in those writings, whether in prose or in verse, which gave utterance to that life. Such writings seem naturally to fall into nine principal classes.

First, may here be named the correspondence of the time; especially, the letters touching on public affairs which passed between persons in different portions of America, and in which men of kindred opinions found one another out, informed one another, stimulated, guided, aided one another, in the common struggle. Indeed, the correspondence of our Revolution, both official and unofficial, constitutes a vast, a fascinating, and a significant branch of its literature. Undoubtedly, the best of all the letter-writers of the time was Franklin; and next to him, perhaps, were John Adams, and Abigail Adams, his wife. Indeed the letters of Mrs. Adams, mostly to her husband, and covering this entire period, are among the most delightful specimens of such work as done by any American. Not far behind these first three letter-writers, if indeed they were behind them, must be mentioned Jefferson and John Dickinson; and, for shrewdness of observation, for humour, for lightness of touch, for the gracious *negligée* of cultivated speech, not far behind any of them was a letter-writer now almost unknown, Richard Peters of Philadelphia. Of course, no one goes to the letters of Washington, in the expectation of finding there sprightliness of thought, flexibility, or ease of movement; yet, in point of diligence and productiveness, he was one of the great letter-writers of that age.

The second form of literature embodying the characteristic life of our Revolutionary era is made up of those writings which were put forth at nearly every critical stage of the long contest, either by the local legislatures, or by the General Congress, or by prominent men in public office, and which may now be described comprehensively as State Papers. It is probable that we have never yet sufficiently considered the extraordinary intellectual merits of this great group of writings, or the prodigious practical service which, by means of those merits, they rendered to the struggling cause of American self-government, particularly in procuring for the insurrectionary colonists, first, the respectful recognition, and then the moral confidence, of the civilised world.

The third class of writings directly expressive of the spirit and life of the Revolution consists of oral addresses, either secular or sacred,—that is, of speeches, formal orations, and political sermons. "In America, as in the Grand Rebellion in England," said a Loyalist writer—Boucher—of our Revolutionary time, "much execution was done by sermons." Had it been otherwise, there would now be cause for wonder. Indeed, the preachers were then in full possession of that immense leadership, intellectual and moral, which had belonged to their order, in America ever since its settlement, in England ever since the middle of the sixteenth century; and though this tradition of leadership was beginning to suffer under the rivalry of the printing-press and under the ever-thickening blows of rationalism, yet, when aroused and concentrated upon any object, they still wielded an enormous influence over the opinions and actions of men,—even as to the business of this world. Without the aid "of the black regiment," as he facetiously called them, James Otis declared his inability to carry his points. Late in the year 1774, the Loyalist, Daniel Leonard, in an essay accounting for the swift and alarming growth of the spirit of resistance and even of revolution in America, gave a prominent place to the part then played in the agitation by "our dissenting ministers." "What effect must it have had upon the audience," said he, "to hear the same sentiments and principles, which they had before read in a newspaper, delivered on Sundays from the sacred desk, with a religious awe, and the most solemn appeals to heaven, from lips which they had been taught from their cradles to believe could utter nothing but eternal truths!" The literary history of the pulpit of the American Revolution is virtually a history of the pulpit-champions of that movement; since those preachers who were not its champions could seldom find a printer bold enough to put their sermons to press, or even an opportunity to speak them from the pulpit. Nor was it necessary that ministers should seem to go out of their way in order to discourse upon those bitter secular themes: indeed, they would have been forced to go out of their way in order to avoid doing so. Fast days, thanksgiving days, election days, the anniversaries of battles and of important acts of Congress and of other momentous events in the progress of the struggle, brought such topics to the very doors of their studies, and even laid them upon the open Bibles in their pulpits. Moreover, if any clergyman held back from political preaching, he was not likely to escape some reminder, more or less gentle, as to what was expected of him in such a time of awful stress and peril. "Does Mr. Wibird preach against oppression and the other cardinal vices of the time?" wrote John Adams to his wife, from Philadelphia, shortly after the battle of Bunker Hill. "Tell him, the clergy here of every denomination, not excepting the Episcopalian, thunder and lighten every Sabbath. They pray for Boston and the Massachusetts. They thank God most explicitly and fervently for our remarkable successes. They pray for the American army."

More than in all other publications, it was in the fourth class of writings, namely, the political essays of the period, that the American people, on both sides of the great controversy, gave utterance to their real thoughts, their real purposes, their fears, their hopes, their hatreds, touching the bitter questions which then divided them. The political essay, whether in the shape of the newspaper article or in that of the pamphlet, gives us the most characteristic type of American literature for that portion of the eighteenth century.

Closely associated with the political essay as the most powerful form of prose in the literature of the American Revolution, should be mentioned the political satire, as being likewise the most powerful form of verse during the same period, and as constituting the fifth class of writings directly expressive of its thought and passion. The best examples of satire to be met with among us before the Revolutionary dispute had reached its culmination may be seen in the earlier and non-political verse of Freneau and John Trumbull. It is true that no great place was given to satire until about the year 1775—that is, until the debate had nearly passed beyond the stage of argument. From that time, however, and until very near the close of the Revolution, this form of literature rivalled, and at times almost set aside, the political essay as an instrument of impassioned political strife. On the Revolutionist side, the chief masters of political satire were Francis Hopkinson, John Trumbull, and Philip Freneau. On the side of the Loyalists, the satirical poet who in art and in power surpassed all his fellows, was Jonathan Odell.

For the sixth class of writings characteristic of the period, we may take the popular lyric poetry of the Revolution,—the numberless verses, commonly quite inelaborate and unadorned, that were written to be sung at the hearth-stone, by the camp-fire, on the march, on the battle-field, in all places of solemn worship.

Our seventh class gathers up the numerous literary memorials of the long struggle as a mere wit-combat, a vast miscellany of humorous productions in verse and prose. The newspapers of the Revolutionary period are strewn with such productions,—satirical poems, long and short, of nearly all degrees of merit and demerit, some of them gross and obscene, some of them simply clownish and stupid, some absolutely brutal in their partisan ferocity, some really clever—terse, polished, and edged with wit.

For the eighth class, partly in prose, chiefly in verse, are brought together the dramatic compositions of the period,—a class not inconsiderable in number, in variety, in vigour, and thoroughly representative both of the humour and of the tragic sentiment of the period. Tentative and crude as are nearly all of these writings, they are not unworthy of some slight attention, in the first place, as giving the genesis of a department of American literature now become considerable; but, chiefly, as reproducing the ideas, the passions, the motives, and the moods of that stormful time in our history, with a frankness, a liveliness, and an unshrinking realism not approached by any other species of Revolutionary literature.

Finally, to the ninth class belong those prose narratives that sprang out of the actual experiences of the Revolution, and that have embodied such experiences in the several forms of personal diaries, military journals, tales of adventure on land or sea, and especially records of suffering in the military prisons. Besides these, there are several elaborate contemporary histories of the Revolution.

Perhaps no aspect of the Revolutionary War has touched more powerfully the imagination and sympathy of the American people, than that relating to the sufferings borne by their own sailors and soldiers who chanced to fall as prisoners into the hands of the enemy; and for many years after the war, the bitterness which it brought into the hearts of men was kept alive and was hardened into a perdurable race-tradition through the tales which were told by the survivors of the British prison-pens and especially of the British prison-ships.

II. THE PRINCIPAL WRITERS

James Otis.—After his graduation at Harvard, at the age of eighteen, James Otis spent a year and a half at home in the study of literature and philosophy; then, devoting himself to the law, he had begun its practice at Plymouth in 1748; after two years of residence there, he had removed to Boston, and in spite of his youth, he had quickly risen to the highest rank in his profession. Throughout his whole career, he held to his early love of the Roman and Greek classics, particularly of Homer; while in English his literary taste was equally robust and wholesome. He was a powerful writer, and he wrote much; but in the structure and form of what he wrote, there are few traces of that enthusiasm for classical literature which we know him to have possessed. Perhaps his nature was too harsh, too passionate and ill-balanced, to yield to the culture even of a literary perfection which he could fully recognise and enjoy in others. He was, above all things, an orator; and his oratory was of the tempestuous kind—bold, vehement, irregular, overpowering.

In July, 1764, he published his gravest and most moderate pamphlet, *The Rights of the British Colonies Asserted and Proved*. Of all his political writing, this is the most sedate. It has even a tone of solemnity. Indeed, its moderation of tone, at the time, gave considerable offence to some of his own associates. The pamphlet was said to have satisfied nobody. Yet it gave food for thought to everybody; and it is the one work of Otis on which rests his reputation as a serious political thinker. The real object of Otis in this powerful pamphlet was not to bring about a revolution, but to avert one. But its actual effect was to furnish the starting-point for the entire movement of revolutionary reasoning, by which some two millions of people were to justify themselves in the years to come, as they advanced along their rugged and stormy path toward independence. It became for a time one of the legal text-books of the opponents of the ministry; it was a law-arsenal, from which other combatants, on that side, drew some of their best weapons. It expounded, with perfect clearness, even if with some shrinking, the constitutional philosophy of the whole subject; and it gave to the members of a conservative and a law-respecting race a conservative and a lawful pretext for resisting law, and for revolutionising the government.

John Adams.—Among the most striking of the literary responses to the news that, in disregard of all appeals from America, the Stamp Act had become a law, was one by a writer of extraordinary vigour in argument, of extraordinary affluence in invective, who chose to view the whole problem as having logical and historical relations far more extensive than had then been commonly supposed. This writer was John Adams, then but thirty years old, a rising member of the bar of Massachusetts, already known in that neighbourhood for his acuteness, fearlessness, and restless energy as a thinker and for a certain truculent and sarcastic splendour in his style of speech. To the very end of his long life, even his most offhand writings, such as diaries and domestic letters, reveal in him a trait of speculative activity and boldness. With the exception of Jefferson, he is the most readable of the statesmen of the Revolutionary period. A series of four essays by John Adams, which were first published, though without his name and without any descriptive title, in *The Boston Gazette*, in August, 1765, by their wide range of allusion, their novelty, audacity, eloquence, by the jocular savagery of their sarcasms on things sacred, easily and quickly produced a stir, and won for themselves considerable notoriety. In 1768, they were welded together into a single document, and as such were published in London under the somewhat misleading title of *A Dissertation on the Canon and the Federal Law*.

Francis Hopkinson.—On September 5, 1774, forty-four respectable gentlemen, representing twelve "colonies and provinces in North America," made their way into Carpenters' Hall, Philadelphia, and there began "to consult upon the present state of the colonies." Thus came into life the first Continental Congress, and with it the permanent political union of the American people. As they came out from that hall, some of them may have found, on stepping into Mr. John Dunlap's shop not far away, a lively-looking little book—*A Pretty Story*—just come from the printer's hands, in which book, under the veil of playful allegory, they could read in a few minutes a graphic and indeed a quite tremendous history of the very events that had brought them together in that place. Even a glance over this little book will show that here at last was a writer, enlisted in the colonial cause, who was able to defend that cause, and to assail its enemies, with a fine and a very rare weapon—that of humour. The personages included in *A Pretty Story* are few; its topics are simple and palpable, and even now in but little need of elucidation; the plot and incidents of the fiction travel in the actual footsteps of well-known history; while the aptness, the delicacy, and the humour of the allegory give to the reader the most delightful surprises, and are well sustained to the very end. Indeed, the wit of the author flashes light upon every legal question then at issue; and the stern and even technical debate between the colonies and the motherland is here translated into a piquant and a bewitching novelette. It soon became known that its author was Francis Hopkinson.

By this neat and telling bit of work, Hopkinson took his true place as one of the three leading satirists on the Whig side of the American Revolution,—the other two being John Trumbull and Philip Freneau. In the long and passionate controversy in which these three satirists bore so effective a part, each is distinguishable by his own peculiar note. The political satire of Freneau and of Trumbull is, in general, grim, bitter, vehement, unrelenting. Hopkinson's satire is as keen as theirs, but its characteristic note is one of playfulness. They stood forth the wrathful critics and assailants of the enemy, confronting him with a hot and an honest hatred, and ready to overwhelm him with an acerbity that was fell and pitiless. Hopkinson, on the other hand, was too gentle, too tender-hearted—his personal tone was too full of amenity—for that sort of warfare. As a satirist, he accomplished his effects without bitterness or violence. No one saw more vividly than he what was weak, or despicable, or cruel, in the position and conduct of the enemy; but in exhibiting it, his method was that of good-humoured ridicule. Never losing his temper, almost never extreme in emotion or in expression, with an urbanity which kept unfailingly upon his side the sympathies of his readers, he knew how to dash and discomfit the foe with a raillery that was all the more effective because it seemed to spring from the very absurdity of the case, and to be, as Ben Jonson required, "without malice or heat."

Francis Hopkinson was born in Philadelphia in 1737. Even in these days, he would have been regarded as a man of quite unusual cultivation, having in reality many solid as well as shining accomplishments. He was a distinguished practitioner of the law; he became an eminent judge; he was a statesman trained by much study and experience; he was a mathematician, a chemist, a physicist, a mechanician, an inventor, a musician and a composer of music, a man of literary knowledge and practice, a writer of airy and dainty songs, a clever artist with pencil and brush, and a humourist of unmistakable power. For us Americans, the name of Francis Hopkinson lives—if indeed it does live—chiefly on account of its presence in the august roll-call of the signers of the Declaration of Independence. He was a devotee to the law, who never took farewell of the Muses. And thus it came about that, from the autumn of 1774 on until the very close of the long struggle, the cause of the Revolution, at nearly every stage and emergency of it, was rescued from depression, was quickened, was cheered forward, was given strength, by the vivacity of this delightful writer.

For the development among the Americans in 1776 of the robust political courage invoked by their new doctrine of national separation, it was necessary that the amiable note of provincialism—the filial obtuseness of the colonial mind—should be broken up, and that the Englishmen who lived in America should begin to find food for mirth and even for derision in the peculiarities of the Englishmen who lived in England. Toward this important political result, Hopkinson made some contribution in his so-called *Letter written by a Foreigner on the Character of the English Nation.* Under an old device for securing disinterested judgments on national peculiarities, Hopkinson here represents a cultivated foreigner as spending some time in England in the latter part of 1776, and as giving to a friend in his own country a cool but very satirical analysis of the alleged vices, foibles, and absurdities of the English people, and of the weak and wrong things in their treatment of their late colonists in America. From these character-sketches by the supposed foreigner in London in the year 1776—themselves by no means despicable for neat workmanship and for humorous power—it is not difficult to make out just how Hopkinson's playful writings were adapted to the achievement of serious political results, as ridding colonial-minded Americans of the intellectual restraint imposed almost unconsciously by their old provincial awe of England, and helping them to subject the metropolitan race to caustic and even contemptuous handling, as a necessary condition of national free-mindedness and of bold dissent on questions of political authority and control.

The expedition of the year 1777, under the command of Sir William Howe, resulted in considerable temporary disaster to the American cause. Nevertheless, it was this very expedition, so full of prosperity for the British, which in its sequel gave to Hopkinson the occasion for his most successful stroke as a humorous writer. Sir William, having gained a brief succession of victories, finding Philadelphia an agreeable place of repose, concluded to settle himself down in that city. The surrounding inhabitants, who had at first regarded him and his army with no little terror, soon came to regard both with some derision, and to conceive the idea of practising upon both certain experiments which had in them an element of covert mirthfulness, as it were. By a very imaginative and a very rollicking expansion of the actual facts of this small affair, Hopkinson was enabled to compose his celebrated ballad, *The Battle of the Kegs*. The actual facts of the case are as follows, according to his own later testimony in prose: "Certain machines, in the form of kegs, charged with gunpowder, were sent down the river to annoy the British shipping at Philadelphia. The danger of these machines being discovered, the British manned the wharfs and shipping, and discharged their small arms and cannons at everything they saw floating in the river during the ebb tide." This jingling little story of *The Battle of the Kegs*—mere doggerel though it is—flew from colony to colony, and gave the weary and anxious people the luxury of genuine and hearty laughter in very scorn of the enemy. To the cause of the Revolution, it was perhaps worth as much, just then, by way of emotional tonic and of military inspiration, as the winning of a considerable battle would have been. From a literary point of view, *The Battle of the Kegs* is very far from being the best of Hopkinson's writings.

Nevertheless, for its matter and its manner and for the adaptation of both to the immediate enjoyment of the multitude of readers, it became in his own day the best known of all its author's productions, even as, since then, it is the only one that has retained any general remembrance in our literature.

Philip Freneau.—The work of Philip Freneau as poet and satirist in direct contact with the American Revolution was broken into two periods,—these periods being separated from each other by an interval of about two years. The first period embraces those months of the year 1775 wherein his own fierce passions, like the passions of his countrymen, were set aflame by the outbreak of hostilities. Thereafter occurred a mysterious lapse in his activity as a writer on themes connected with the great struggle to which he had professed his undying devotion;—he was absent from the country until some time in the year 1778. With the middle of the year 1778 began the second period of his work as Revolutionary poet and satirist, and it did not come to an end, except with the end of the Revolution itself.

After a considerate inspection of the writers and the writings of our Revolutionary era, it is likely that most readers will be inclined to name Philip Freneau as the one American poet of all that time who, though fallen on evil days and driven from his true course somewhat by stormy weather, yet had a high and questionless vocation for poetry. Of his own claim to recognition he was proudly conscious. Nor was he unconscious of all that was malign to his poetic destiny, both in the time and in the place on which his lot was cast. Even in the larger relations which an American poet in the eighteenth century might hold to the development of English poetry everywhere, Freneau did some work, both early and late, so fresh, so original, so unhackneyed, so defiant of the traditions that then hampered and deadened English verse, so delightful in its fearless appropriation of common things for the divine service of poetry, as to entitle him to be called a pioneer of the new poetic age that was then breaking upon the world, and therefore to be classed with Cowp-

er, Burns, Wordsworth, and their mighty comrades,—those poetic icon-
oclasts who, entering the temple of eighteenth-century English verse,
broke up its wooden idols, rejected its conventionalised diction, and si-
lenced for ever its pompous, monotonous, and insincere tune. Finally, of
Freneau, it remains to be said that, in a certain eminent sense, he was
the first American poet of Democracy; and that from the beginning to the
end of his career, and in spite of every form of temptation, he remained
true—fiercely, savagely true—to the conviction that his part and lot in
the world was to be a protagonist on behalf of mere human nature, as
against all its assailants whether in church or state. In the year 1795,
this combat-loving poet sent forth a second and an enlarged edition of
his poems, which had been first issued seven years before; and in some
verses which he therein inserted, entitled "To my Book," one may still
hear the proud voice with which he claimed for himself that, whether in
other ways successful or not, he was at least a poet militant—ever doing
battle on the people's side.

John Trumbull.—John Trumbull, with an inward vocation for a life
of letters, turned away to a calling far more likely to supply him with
bread—the profession of the law. It was in November, 1773, that he was
admitted to the bar of Connecticut. Being then but twenty-three years
of age, he wrote in verse an eternal farewell to verse-making. Notwithstanding all his vows of devotion to the new mistress whom he was to
serve, Trumbull could not forget his earlier love. Henceforward, all his
fine literary accomplishments, his subtlety, his wit, his gift for ridicule,
his training in satire, are to be at the service of the popular cause, and
are to produce in *M'Fingal* one of the world's masterpieces in political
badinage. The time of the poem is shortly after April, 1775. The scene is
laid in a certain unnamed New England town, apparently not far from
Boston. No literary production was ever a more genuine embodiment of
the spirit and life of a people, in the midst of a stirring and world-famous
conflict, than is *M'Fingal* an embodiment of the spirit and life of the
American people, in the midst of that stupendous conflict which formed
our great epoch of national deliverance. Here we find presented to us,
with the vividness of a contemporary experience, the very issues which
then divided friends and families and neighbourhood, as they did entire
colonies, and at last the empire itself; the very persons and passions of
the opposing parties; the very spirit and accent and method of political

controversy at that time; and at last, those riotous frolics and that hilarious lawlessness with which the Revolutionary patriots were fond of demonstrating their disapproval of the politics of their antagonists.

Satire is, of course, one of the less noble forms of literary expression; and in satire uttering itself through burlesque, there is special danger of the presence of qualities which are positively ignoble. Yet never was satire employed in a better cause, or for loftier objects, or in a more disinterested spirit. The author of *M'Fingal* wrote his satire under no personal or petty motive. His poem was a terrific assault on men who, in his opinion, were the public enemies of his country; and he did not delay that assault until they were unable to strike back. *M'Fingal* belongs, indeed, to a type of literature hard, bitter, vengeful, often undignified; but the hardness of *M'Fingal*, its bitterness, its vengeful force are directed against persons believed by its author to be the foes—the fashionable and the powerful foes—of human liberty; if at times it surrenders its own dignity, it does so on behalf of the greater dignity of human nature. That *M'Fingal* is, in its own sphere, a masterpiece, that it has within itself a sort of power never attaching to a mere imitation, is shown by the vast and prolonged impression it has made upon the American people. Immediately upon its first publication, it perfectly seized and held the attention of the public. It was everywhere read. Probably as many as forty editions of it have been issued in this country and in England. It was one of the forces which drove forward that enormous movement of human thought and passion which we describe as the American Revolution; and in each of the great agitations of American thought and passion which have occurred since that time, occasioned by the French Revolution, by the War of 1812, and by the war which extinguished American slavery, this scorching satire against social reaction, this jeering burlesque on political obstructiveness, has been sent forth again and again into the world, to renew its mirthful and scornful activity in the ever-renewing battle for human progress.

John Dickinson.—Among all the political writings which were the immediate offspring of the baleful Stamp Act dispute, there stand out, as of the highest significance, certain essays which began to make their appearance in a Philadelphia newspaper in the latter part of the year 1767. These essays very soon became celebrated, on both sides of the Atlantic, under the short title of the *Farmer's Letters*. Their full title was *Letters from a Farmer in Pennsylvania to the Inhabitants of the British Colonies*. Though published without the author's name, they were instantly recognised as the work of John Dickinson; and their appearance may perhaps fairly be described as constituting, upon the whole, the most brilliant event in the literary history of the Revolution. One distinction attaching to them is that they were written by a man who shared in the general excitement over the new attack upon colonial rights, but who desired to compose it rather than to increase it, and especially to persuade his countrymen so to bear their part in the new dispute as to save their rights as men, without losing their happiness as British subjects. Here was a man of powerful and cultivated intellect, with all his interests and all his tastes on the side of order, conservatism, and peace, if only with these could be had political safety and honour. No other serious political essays of the Revolutionary era quite equalled the *Farmer's Letters* in literary merit, including in that term the merit of substance as well as of form; and, excepting the political essays of Thomas Paine, which did not begin to appear until nine years later, none equalled the *Farmer's Letters* in immediate celebrity, and in direct power upon events. As they first came forth, from week to week, in the Philadelphia newspaper that originally published them, they were welcomed by the delighted interest and sympathy of multitudes of readers in that neighbourhood, and were instantly reproduced in all the twenty-five newspapers then published in America, with but four known exceptions. Within less than four weeks after the last letter had made its appearance, they were all collected and issued as a pamphlet, of which at least eight editions were published in different parts of America. On both sides of the Atlantic, the *Farmer's Letters* gained universal attention among the people interested in the rising American dispute. The name of John Dickinson became a name of literary renown surpassing that of any other American, excepting Benjamin Franklin. On the continent of Europe, these essays of the Pennsylvania Farmer became, for a time, the fashion: they were talked of in the salons of Paris; the Farmer himself was likened to Cicero; and almost the highest distinction then possible for any man was bestowed upon him through the notice and applause of Voltaire. Even in England, the success of these writings was remarkable, and was shown quite as much in the censures as in the praises which were lavished upon them. Among the English admirers of the *Farmer's*

Letters was Edmund Burke, who gave his sanction to their principle. In America, the admiration and the gratitude of the people were expressed in almost every conceivable form. Thanks were voted to the Farmer by political associations, by town-meetings, by grand juries. The College of New Jersey conferred on him the degree of Doctor of Laws. He became the favourite toast at public banquets. He was offered the membership of the choicest social clubs. On his entrance, one day, into a court-room, whither business called him, the proceedings were stopped in order to recognise his presence, and to make acknowledgment of the greatness and splendour of his services to the country. Songs were written in his praise.

The last of the *Farmer's Letters* was published in February, 1768. In the following May, the new commissioners of customs arrived at Boston; in June, these commissioners, attempting to execute their odious office on John Hancock's sloop, *Liberty*, were fiercely assaulted by the populace of Boston, and were driven for refuge to Castle William in Boston Harbour; whereupon Governor Bernard summoned thither General Gage with his troops from Halifax. Of these most ominous events in Boston, John Dickinson was an observer from his distant home on the Delaware; and even he, with all his deep loyalty and conscientious hesitation, was so stirred by them as then to utter what seems almost a ringing war-cry. Taking for his model Garrick's *Hearts of Oak*—the air of which was then so familiar to every one—he wrote the stanzas which he christened *A Song for American Freedom*,—a bit of versification obviously the work of a man neither born nor bred to that business; yet being quickly caught up into universal favour under the endearing name of the *Liberty Song*, its manly lines soon resounded over all the land; and thenceforward, for several years, it remained the most popular political song among us.

If we attempt to estimate the practical effects of John Dickinson's work as a political writer during the American Revolution, we shall find it not easy to disentangle and to separate them from the practical effects of his work as a politician. The two lines of power were closely interwoven; each, in the main, helped the other, as each was liable, in its turn, to be hindered by the other. At any rate, just as the politico-literary influence of James Otis was, upon the whole, predominant in America from 1764 until 1767, so, from the latter date until some months after the outbreak of hostilities in 1775, was the politico-literary influence of John Dickinson predominant here. Moreover, as he succeeded to James Otis in the development of Revolutionary thought, so was he, at last, succeeded by Thomas Paine, who held sway among us, as the chief writer of political essays, from the early part of 1776 until the close of the Revolution itself. The prodigious decline in the influence of John Dickinson, at the approach of the issue of independence, is a thing not hard to explain; it was due in part to his personal characteristics, in part to the nature of his opinions. From the beginning of the troubles until some months after the first shedding of blood, in 1775, public opinion in America had set strongly in favour of making demand—even armed demand—for our political rights, but without any rupture of the colonial tie. It was, therefore, a period calling for clear and resolute statements of our claims, but with loyalty, urbanity, and tact. To be the chief literary exponent of such a period, John Dickinson was in every way fitted by talent, by temperament, by training. A man of wealth, cultivation, and elegant surroundings, practically versed in the law and in politics, considerate, cautious, disinclined to violent measures and to stormy scenes, actuated by a passion for the unity and the greatness of the English race and for peace among all men, it was his sincere desire that the dispute with the mother country should be so conducted as to end, at last, in the perfect establishment of American constitutional rights within the empire, but without any hurt or dishonour to England, and without any permanent failure in respect and kindness between her and ourselves. Nevertheless, in 1775, events occurred which gave a different aspect to the whole dispute, and swept an apparent majority of the American people quite beyond the sphere of such ideas and methods. John Dickinson's concession to Parliament of a legislative authority over us, even to a limited extent, was roughly discarded; instead of which was enthroned among us the unhistoric and makeshift doctrine that American allegiance was due not at all to Parliament, but to the Crown only. Moreover, the moderation of tone, the urbane speech, the civility in conduct, exemplified by Dickinson in all this dispute with England, then became an anachronism and an offence. We were plunged at last into civil war—we had actually reached the stage of revolution; and the robust men who then ruled the scene were disposed, with no little contempt, to brush aside the moderate, conservative, and courteous Dickinson, who, either for advice or for conduct, seemed to them to have no further function to perform in the American world. His *Farmer's Letters* were declared by Jefferson to have been "really an 'ignis fatuus,' misleading us from true principles." Even Edward Rutledge, who, in June, 1776, agreed with Dickinson in his opposition to the plan for independence, nevertheless expressed some impatience with his intellectual fastidiousness and nicety,—declaring that the "vice of all his productions, to a considerable degree," was "the vice of refining too much."

Alexander Hamilton.—Within two or three weeks from the day on which the Congress announced its grand scheme for an agreement among the American colonists not to import or to consume the chief materials of the English carrying-trade, nor to export the chief products of their own farms, there came from the press of New York a pamphlet— *Free Thoughts on the Proceedings of the Continental Congress*—ostensibly written by a farmer, and addressed to farmers, and from the level of their particular interests subjecting the proposal of Congress to a sort of criticism that was well fitted to arouse against it the bitterest and most unrelenting opposition of the great agricultural class. The writer of this pamphlet—Samuel Seabury, a Loyalist clergyman—professed to be a "Westchester Farmer,"—a signature which at once became the target for vast applause and for vast execration. The first pamphlet was dated November 16, 1774. Twelve days from that date came his second one— as keen, as fiery, as powerful as the first. In less than four weeks from the day of his second pamphlet, the undaunted farmer was ready with a third one. No sooner was this pamphlet off his hands, than the "Westchester Farmer" seems to have set to work upon his fourth pamphlet.

Among the throng of replies which burst forth from the press in opposition to the tremendous pamphlets of the "Westchester Farmer," were two which immediately towered into chief prominence: *A Full Vindication of the Measures of the Congress*, and *The Farmer Refuted*. The extraordinary ability of these two pamphlets—their fulness in constitutional learning, their acumen, their affluence in statement, their cleverness in controversial repartee, their apparent wealth in the fruits of an actual acquaintance with public business—led both the "Westchester Farmer" and the public in general to attribute them to some American writer of mature years and of ripe experience—to some member of the late Congress, for example—particularly to John Jay or to William Livingston. It is not easy to overstate the astonishment and the incredulity with which the public soon heard the rumour that these elaborate and shattering literary assaults on the argumentative position of the Loyalists were, in reality, the work of a writer who was then both a stripling in years and a stranger in the country—one Alexander Hamilton, a West Indian by birth, a Franco-Scotsman by parentage, an undergraduate of King's College by occupation, a resident within the Thirteen Colonies but little more than two years, and at the time of the publication of his first pamphlet only seventeen years of age. In the exposition of his views touching the several vast fields of thought here brought under consideration,—constitutional law, municipal law, the long line of colonial charters, colonial laws and precedents, international polity as affecting the chief nations of Christendom, justice in the abstract and justice in the concrete, human rights both natural and conventional, the physical and metaphysical conditions underlying the great conflict then impending,—it must be confessed that this beardless philosopher, this statesman not yet out of school, this military strategist scarcely rid of his roundabout, exhibits a range and precision of knowledge, a ripeness of judgment, a serenity, a justice, a massiveness both of thought and of style, which would perhaps make incredible the theory of his authorship of these pamphlets, were not this theory confirmed by his undoubted exhibition in other ways, at about the same period of his life, of the same astonishing qualities.

Thomas Paine.—As the bitter events of 1775 rapidly unfolded themselves, not a few Americans became convinced that there was no true solution of the trouble except in that very independence which they had but a short time before dreaded and denounced. Of such Americans, Thomas Paine was one; and towards the end of the year, through incessant communication with the foremost minds in America, he had filled his own mind with the great decisive elements of the case, and was prepared to utter his thought thereon. Early in January, 1776, he did utter it, in the form of a pamphlet, published at Philadelphia, and entitled *Common Sense*,—the first open and unqualified argument in championship of the doctrine of American independence. During the first ten or twelve years of the Revolution, in just one sentiment all persons, Tories and Whigs, seemed perfectly to agree; namely, in abhorrence of the project of separation from the empire. Suddenly, however, and within a period of less than six months, the majority of the Whigs turned completely around, and openly declared for independence, which, before that time, they had so vehemently repudiated. Among the facts necessary to enable us to account for this almost unrivalled political somersault, is that of the appearance of *Common Sense*. This pamphlet was happily named: it undertook to apply common sense to a technical, complex, but most urgent and feverish, problem of constitutional law. In fact, on any other ground than that of common sense, the author of that pamphlet was incompetent to deal with the problem at all; since of law, of political science, and even of English and American history, he was ludicrously ignorant. But for the effective treatment of any question whatsoever that was capable of being dealt with under the light of the broad and rugged intellectual instincts of mankind,—man's natural sense of truth, of congruity, of fair-play,—perhaps no other man in America, excepting Franklin, was a match for this ill-taught, heady, and slashing English stranger. From the tribunal of technical law, therefore, he carried the case to the tribunal of common sense; and in his plea before that tribunal, he never for a moment missed his point, or forgot his method. The one thing just then to be done was to convince the average American colonist of the period that it would be ridiculous for him any longer to remain an American colonist; that the time had come for him to be an American citizen; that nothing stood in the way of his being so, but the trash of a few pedants respecting the authority of certain bedizened animals called kings; and that, whether he would or no, the alternative was at last thrust into his face upon the point of a bayonet,—either to declare for national independence, and a wide-spaced and resplendent national destiny, or to accept, along with subserviency to England, the bitterness and the infamy of national annihilation. With all its crudities of thought, its superficiality, and its rashness of assertion, *Common Sense* is a masterly pamphlet; for in the elements of its strength it was precisely fitted to the hour, to the spot, and to the passions of men. Even its smattering of historical lore, and its cheap display of statistics, and its clumsy attempts at some sort of political philosophy, did not diminish the homage with which it was read by the mass of the community, who were even less learned and less philosophical than Paine, and who, at any rate, cared much more just then for their imperilled rights, than they did either for philosophy or for learning. The immediate practical effects of this pamphlet in America, and the celebrity which it soon acquired in Europe as well as in America, are a significant part of its history as a potential literary document of the period. In every impassioned popular discussion there is likely to spring up a leader, who with pen or voice strikes in, at just the right moment, with just the right word, so skilfully, so powerfully, that thenceforward the intellectual battle seems to be raging and surging around him and around the fiery word which he has sent shrilling through the air. So far as the popular discussion of American independence is concerned, precisely this was the case, between January and July, 1776, with Thomas Paine and his pamphlet *Common Sense*. Within three months from the date of its first issue, at least 120,000 copies of it were sold in America alone. By that time, the pamphlet seemed to be in every one's hand and the theme of every one's talk.

Noble-minded and important as were the various services rendered by Paine to the American cause, on sea and land, in office and field, they could in no way be compared, as contributions to the success of the Revolution, with the work which he did during those same imperilled years merely as a writer, and especially as the writer of *The Crisis*. Between December, 1776, when the first pamphlet of that series was published, down to December, 1783, when the last one left the printer's hands, this indomitable man produced no less than sixteen pamphlets under the same general title, adapting his message in each case to the supreme need of the hour, and accomplishing all this literary labour in a condition of actual poverty.

Thomas Jefferson.—On June 21, 1775, Thomas Jefferson took his seat for the first time as a member of the Continental Congress. He had then but recently passed his thirty-second birthday, and was known to be the author of two or three public papers of considerable note. Early in June, 1776, Thomas Jefferson, receiving the largest number of votes, was placed at the head of the committee of illustrious men to whom was assigned the task of preparing a suitable Declaration of Independence, and thereby he became the draftsman of the one American state paper that has reached to supreme distinction in the world, and that seems likely to last as long as American civilisation lasts. Whatever authority the Declaration of Independence has acquired in the world has been due to no lack of criticism, either at the time of its first appearance or since then,—a fact which seems to tell in favour of its essential worth and strength. From the date of its original publication down to the present moment, it has been attacked again and again, either in anger or in contempt, by friends as well as by enemies of the American Revolution, by liberals in politics as well as by conservatives. It has been censured for its substance, it has been censured for its form; for its misstatements of fact, for its fallacies in reasoning, for its audacious novelties and paradoxes, for its total lack of all novelty, for its repetition of old and threadbare statements, even for its downright plagiarisms; finally, for its grandiose and vapouring style. Yet, probably no public paper ever more perfectly satisfied the immediate purposes for which it was sent forth. From one end of the country to the other, and as far as it could be spread among the people, it was greeted in public and in private with every demonstration of approval and delight. To a marvellous degree, it quickened the friends of the Revolution for their great task. Moreover, during the century and more since the close of the Revolution, the influence of this state paper on the political character and the political conduct of the American people has been great beyond all calculation.

No man can adequately explain the persistent fascination which it has had, and which it still has, for the American people, or for its undiminished power over them, without taking into account its extraordinary literary merits—its possession of the witchery of true substance wedded to perfect form:—its massiveness and incisiveness of thought, its art in the marshalling of the topics with which it deals, its symmetry, its energy, the definiteness and limpidity of its statements, its exquisite diction, at once terse, musical, and electric; and, as an essential part of this literary outfit, many of those spiritual notes which can attract and enthrall our hearts,—veneration for God, veneration for man, veneration for principle, respect for public opinion, moral earnestness, moral courage, optimism, a stately and noble pathos, finally, self-sacrificing devotion to a cause so great as to be herein identified with the happiness, not of one people only, or of one race only, but of human nature itself. We may be altogether sure that no genuine development of literary taste among the American people in any period of our future history can result in serious misfortune to this particular specimen of American literature.

Samuel Adams.—Samuel Adams was a man of letters, but he was so only because he was above all things a man of affairs. Of literary art, in certain forms, he was no mean master; of literary art for art's sake, he was entirely regardless. He was perhaps the most voluminous political writer of his time in America, and the most influential political writer of his time in New England; but everything that he wrote was meant for a definite practical purpose, and nothing that he wrote seemed to have had any interest for him aside from that purpose. Deep as is the obscurity which has fallen upon his literary services in the cause of the Revolution, the fame of those services was, at the time of them, almost unrivalled by that of any other writer, at least in the colonies east of the Hudson River. Born in Boston in 1722, graduated at Harvard in 1740, he early showed an invincible passion and aptitude for politics. One principal instrument by means of which Samuel Adams so greatly moulded public opinion, and shaped political and even military procedure, was the pen. Of modern politicians, he was among the first to recognise the power of public opinion in directing public events, and likewise the power of the newspaper in directing public opinion. It was, therefore, an essential part of his method as a politician to acquire and to exercise the art of literary statement in a form suited to that particular end. He had the instinct of a great journalist, and of a great journalist willing to screen his individuality behind his journal. In this service, it was not Samuel Adams that Samuel Adams cared to put and to keep before the public,—it was the ideas of Samuel Adams. Accordingly, of all American writers for the newspapers between the years 1754 and 1776, he was perhaps the most vigilant, the most industrious, the most effective, and also the least identified. Ever ready to efface himself in what he did, he realised that the innumerable productions of his pen would make their way to a far wider range of readers, and would be all the more influential, if they seemed to be the work, not of one writer, but of many. Therefore, he almost never published anything under his own name; but, under a multitude of titular disguises which no man has yet been able to number, this sleepless, crafty, protean politician, for nearly a third of a century, kept flooding the community with his ideas, chiefly in the form of essays in the newspapers,—thereby constantly baffling the enemies of the Revolutionary movement, and conducting his followers victoriously through those battles of argument which preceded and then for a time accompanied the battles of arms. In the long line of his state papers—

the official utterances of the several public bodies with which he was connected and which so long trusted him as their most deft and unerring penman—one may now trace, almost without a break, the development of the ideas and the measures which formed the Revolution. If we take into account the strain of thought and of emotional energy involved in all these years of fierce political controversy and of most perilous political leadership, we shall hardly fear to overestimate the resources of Samuel Adams in his true career of agitator and iconoclast;—especially the elasticity, the toughness, the persistence of a nature which could, in addition to all this, undertake and carry through, during the same long period, all the work he did in literary polemics,—work which alone might seem enough to employ and tire the strength even of a strong man who had nothing else to do.

The traits of Samuel Adams the writer are easily defined—for they are likewise the traits of Samuel Adams the politician, and of Samuel Adams the man. His fundamental rule for literary warfare was this— "Keep your enemy in the wrong." His style, then, was the expression of his intellectual wariness,—a wariness like that of the scout or the bushwhacker, who knows that behind any tree may lurk his deadly foe, that a false step may be his ruin, that a badly-aimed shot may make it impossible for him ever to shoot again. Whether in oral or in written speech his characteristics were the same,—simplicity, acuteness, logical power, and strict adaptation of means to the practical end in view. Nothing was for effect—everything was for effectiveness. He wrote pure English, and in a style severe, felicitous, pointed, epigrammatic. Careful as to facts, disdainful of rhetorical excesses, especially conscious of the strategic folly involved in mere overstatement, an adept at implication and at the insinuating light stroke, he had never anything to take back or to apologise for. In the wearisome fondness of his country for Greek and Roman analogies, he shared to the full; and, in a less degree, in its passion for the tags and gewgaws of classical quotation. Of course, his style bears the noble impress of his ceaseless and reverent reading of the English Bible. To a mere poet, he seldom alludes. Among secular writers of modern times, his days and nights were given, as occasion served, to Hooker, Coke, Grotius, Locke, Sidney, Vattel, Montesquieu, Blackstone, and Hume.

John Witherspoon.—Although John Witherspoon did not come to America until the year 1768,—after he had himself passed the middle line of human life,—yet so quickly did he then enter into the spirit of American society, so perfectly did he identify himself with its nobler moods of discontent and aspiration, so powerfully did he contribute by speech and act to the right development of this new nation out of the old cluster of dispersed and dependent communities, that it would be altogether futile to attempt to frame a just account of the great intellectual movements of our Revolution without some note of the part played in it by this eloquent, wise, and efficient Scotsman—at once teacher, preacher, politician, law-maker, and philosopher, upon the whole not undeserving of the praise which has been bestowed upon him as "one of the great men of the age and of the world." Born in 1722, at the age of forty-six he accepted an invitation to the presidency of the College of New Jersey. At the time of his removal to America, he had achieved distinction as a preacher and an ecclesiastical leader. Even as an author, also, he had become well known. His advent to the college over which he was to preside was like that of a prince coming to his throne. The powerful influence which, through his published writings, Witherspoon exerted upon the course of Revolutionary thought, may be traced in the very few sermons of his which touch upon the political problems of that time, in various Congressional papers, and especially in the numerous essays, long or short, serious or mirthful, which he gave to the press between the years 1775 and 1783, and commonly without his name. As a writer of political and miscellaneous essays, it is probable that Witherspoon's activity was far greater than can now be ascertained; but his hand can be traced with certainty in a large group of keen and sprightly productions of that sort. Of all these writings, the chief note is that of a virile mind, well-balanced, well-trained, and holding itself steadily to its own independent conclusions,—in short, of enlightened and imperturbable common sense, speaking out in a form always temperate and lucid, often terse and epigrammatic.

John Woolman.—It is no slight distinction attaching to American literature for the period of the Revolution, that in a time so often characterised as barren of important literary achievement, were produced two of the most perfect examples of autobiography to be met with in any literature. One of these, of course, is Franklin's *Autobiography*, the first, the largest, and the best part of which was written in 1771,—a work that has long since taken its place among the most celebrated and most widely read of modern books. Almost at the very time at which that fascinating story was begun, the other great example of autobiography in our Revolutionary literature was finished—*The Journal of John Woolman*, a book which William Ellery Channing long afterward described as "beyond comparison the sweetest and purest autobiography in the language." It is a notable fact, however, that while these two masterpieces in the same form of literature are products of the same period, they are, in respect of personal quality, very nearly antipodal to each other; for, as Franklin's account of himself delineates a career of shrewd and somewhat selfish geniality, of unperturbed carnal content, of kindly systematic and most successful worldliness, so the autobiography of Woolman sets forth a career which turns out to be one of utter unworldliness, of entire self-effacement, all in obedience to an Unseen Leadership, and in meek and most tender devotion to the happiness of others—especially slaves, poor toiling white people, and speechless creatures unable to defend themselves against the inhumanity of man.

John Woolman, who was of a spirit so unpresuming that he would have wondered and have been troubled to be told that any writing of his was ever to be dealt with as literature, was born in 1720 in Northampton, New Jersey, his father being a farmer, and of the Society of Friends. Until his twenty-first year, he lived at home with his parents, and, as he expressed it, "wrought on the plantation." Having reached his majority, he took employment in the neighbouring village of Mount Holly, in a shop for general merchandise. In this occupation he passed several years; after which he began to give himself almost wholly to the true work of his life—that of an apostle, with a need to go from land to land in fulfilment of his apostleship, and able, like one of the greatest of all apostles, to minister to his own necessities by the labours of a lowly trade. For, long before he set out upon these travels, even from his early childhood, he had entered, as he thought, into the possession of certain treasures of the spirit which he could not hoard up for himself alone,—which, if he could but share them with others, would make others rich and happy beyond desire or even imagination.

The autobiography of John Woolman was the gradual and secret growth of many years, beginning when he was of the age of thirty-six, and added to from time to time until, at the age of fifty-two, being in the city of York, in England, about the business of his Master, he was stricken down of the smallpox, whereof he died. Besides this story of his life, he left several ethical and religious essays. All these writings are, as Whittier has said, in the style "of a man unlettered, but with natural refinement and delicate sense of fitness, the purity of whose heart enters into his language." "The secret of Woolman's purity of style," said Channing, "is that his eye was single, and that conscience dictated the words." There is about John Woolman's writings that unconventionality of thought, that charity without pretence, that saintliness without sanctimony or sourness, that delicacy, that untaught beauty of phrase, by which we are helped to understand the ardour of Charles Lamb's love for him, as uttered in his impulsive exhortation to the readers of the *Essays of Elia*: "Get the writings of John Woolman by heart." "A perfect gem!" wrote Henry Crabb Robinson, in 1824, of Woolman's *Journal*, which Lamb had shortly before made known to him. "His is a 'schöne Seele.' An illiterate tailor, he writes in a style of the most exquisite purity and grace. His moral qualities are transferred to his writings." Perhaps, after all, the aroma that lingers about Woolman's words is best described by Woolman's true spiritual successor in American literature—Whittier—in the saying, that he who reads these writings becomes sensible "of a sweetness as of violets."

Benjamin Franklin.—For the period of the Revolution the writings of Franklin fall naturally into two principal divisions—first, those connected with the Revolutionary controversy, and, secondly, those almost entirely apart from it. Among the latter, of course, are to be reckoned his numerous papers on scientific discoveries and mechanical inventions; a considerable number of his personal letters—these being, perhaps, the wisest and wittiest of all his writings; many short sketches, usually playful in tone, often in the form of apologues or parables; finally, the first, and the best, part of his *Autobiography*, which, during the hundred years succeeding its first publication in 1791, has probably been the most widely read book of its class in any language. Here, then, as a product of Franklin's general literary activity during the Revolutionary period, is a considerable body of literature not concerned in the strifes of that bitter time, almost faultless in form, and so pervaded by sense, gaiety, and kindness, as to be among the most precious and most delightful of the intellectual treasures of mankind.

In Franklin's literary contributions to the Revolutionary controversy between 1763 and 1783, we find that his relation to that controversy had two strongly contrasted phases: first, his sincere and most strenuous desire that the dispute should not pass from the stage of words to that of blows, and thence to a struggle for American secession from the empire; and, secondly, after the stage of blows had been reached, his champion-ship of American secession through war as the only safe or honourable course then left to his countrymen. The line of division between these two phases of opinion and action falls across the spring and early sum-mer of 1775. Prior to that time, all his writings, serious or jocose, are pervaded by the one purpose of convincing the English people that the American policy of their government was an injustice and a blunder, and of convincing the American people that their demand for political rights would certainly be satisfied, if persisted in steadily and without fear, but also without disloyalty and without unseemly violence. Subsequent to that time, having accepted with real sorrow the alternative of war and of war for American secession, all his writings, serious and jocose, are pervaded by the one purpose of making that war a successful one,—a result to which, as a writer, he could best contribute by such appeals to public opinion in America as should nourish and quicken American confidence in their own cause, and by such appeals to public opinion in Europe as should win for that cause its moral and even its physical support. For reasons that must be obvious, his general literary activity was far greater during the first phase of this controversy than during the second.

Probably no writer ever understood better than he how to make dull subjects lively, and how, by consequence, to attract readers to the con-sideration of matters in themselves unattractive. As he well knew, the European public, whether upon the Continent or in Great Britain, were not likely to give their days and nights to the perusal of long and solemn dissertations on the rights and wrongs of his countrymen in the other hemisphere. Accordingly, such dissertations he never gave them, but, upon occasion, brief and pithy and apparently casual statements of the

American case; exposing, also, the weak points of the case against his own, by means of anecdotes, epigrams, *jeux-d'esprit*; especially contriving to throw the whole argument into some sort of dramatic form.

Franklin's favourite weapon in political controversy—a weapon which, perhaps, no other writer in English since Dean Swift has handled with so much cleverness and effect—was that of satire in the form of ludicrous analogue, thereby burlesquing the acts and pretensions of his adversary, and simply overwhelming him with ridicule. Moreover, with Franklin, as had been the case with Dean Swift before him, this species of satire took a form at once so realistic and so comically apt, as to result in several examples of brilliant literary hoaxing—a result which, in the controversy then going on, was likely to be beneficial to the solemn and self-satisfied British Philistine of the period, since it compelled him for once to do a little thinking, and also to stand off and view his own portrait as it then appeared to other people, and even in spite of himself to laugh at his own portentous and costly stupidity in the management of an empire that seemed already grown too big for him to take proper care of. As Franklin was by far the greatest man of letters on the American side of the Revolutionary controversy, so a most luminous and delightful history of the development of thought and emotion during the Revolution might be composed, by merely bringing together detached sayings of Franklin, humorous and serious, just as these fell from his tongue or pen in the successive stages of that long conflict: it would be a trail of light across a sea of storm and gloom. Nevertheless, not by illustrative fragments of what he wrote or said, any more than by modern descriptions, however vivid, can an adequate idea be conveyed of the mass, the force, the variety, the ease, the charm, of his total work as a writer during those twenty tremendous years. Undoubtedly, his vast experience in affairs and the sobriety produced by mere official responsibility had the effect of clarifying and solidifying his thought, and of giving to the lightest products of his genius a sanity and a sureness of movement which, had he been a man of letters only, they could hardly have had in so high a degree. It is only by a continuous reading of the entire body of Franklin's Revolutionary writings, from grave to gay, from lively to severe, that any one can know how brilliant was his wisdom, or how wise was his brilliancy, or how humane and gentle and helpful were both. No one who, by such a reading, procures for himself such a pleasure and such a benefit, will be likely to miss the point of Sydney Smith's playful menace to his daughter,—"I will disinherit you, if you do not admire everything written by Franklin."

Thomas Hutchinson.—Within the two decades of the American Revolution are to be found two distinct expressions of the historic spirit among this people. In the first place, from a consciousness of the meaning and worth of the unique social experiments then already made by each of the thirteen little republics, came the impulse which led to the writing of their local history. Afterward, from a similar consciousness of the meaning and worth of the immense events which began to unfold themselves in the collective political and military experience of these thirteen little republics, then rapidly melting together into a larger national life under the fires of a common danger, came the impulse which led to the writing of their general history.

Reaching the line which divides colonial themes from those of the Revolution, we confront a writer who, in his capacity as historian, not only towers above all his contemporaries, but deals with themes which are both colonial and Revolutionary. This writer is the man so famous and so hated in his day as a Loyalist statesman and magistrate, Thomas Hutchinson, the last civilian who served as governor of Massachusetts under appointment by the king. That he deserves to be ranked as, upon the whole, the ablest historical writer produced in America prior to the nineteenth century, there is now substantial agreement among scholars. In writing the early history of Massachusetts, Thomas Hutchinson was in effect writing the history of his own ancestors, some of whom had been eminent, some of whom had been notorious, in the colony almost from the year of its foundation. He was born in Boston in 1711. From the age of twenty-six when he was elected to his first office, until the age of sixty-three when he resigned his last one, he was kept constantly and conspicuously in the public service. Before the outbreak of the great controversy between the colonies and the British government, no other man in America had, to so high a degree as Hutchinson, the confidence both of the British government on the one hand, and of his own countrymen on the other. Had his advice been taken in that controversy by either of the two parties who had so greatly confided in him, the war of the Revolution would have been averted. While the writing of history was for Hutchinson but the recreation and by-play of a life immersed in outward business, the study of history seems to have been a passion with him almost from his childhood. It should be added that Hutchinson had the scientific idea of the importance of primary documents. Through his great eminence in the community, and through his ceaseless zeal in the collection of such documents, he was enabled in the course of many years to bring together a multitude of manuscript materials of priceless value touching the history of New England. With such materials at his command, and using with diligence those fragments of time which his unflagging energy enabled him to pluck from business and from sleep, he was ready, in July, 1764, amid the first mutterings of that political storm which was to play havoc with these peaceful studies and to shatter the hopes of his lifetime, to send to the printer, in Boston, the first volume of *The History of the Colony of Massachusetts Bay*. He published his second volume in the early summer of the year 1767,—not far from the very day on which Parliament, by the passage of the Townshend Act, perpetrated the ineffable folly of plunging the empire into such tumults as led to its disruption. Notwithstanding the lurid and bitter incidents amid which it was written, the second volume of Hutchinson's history of Massachusetts, like the first one, has the tone of moderation and of equanimity suggestive of a philosopher abstracted from outward cares, and devoted to the disinterested discovery and exposition of the truth.

From the time of the publication of the second instalment of his work, sixty-one years were to elapse before the public should receive ocular evidence that the author had had the fortitude, amid the calamities which overwhelmed his later years, to go on with his historical labours, and to complete a third and final volume, telling the story of Massachusetts from the year 1750 until the year 1774—the year in which he laid down his office as governor and departed for England. Borne down with sorrow, amazed and horror-stricken at the fury of the storm that was overturning his most prudent calculations, and was sweeping him and his party from all their moorings out into an unknown sea, he found some solace in resuming in England the historical task which he had left unfinished. In his diary for October 22, 1778, its completion is recorded in this modest note: "I finished the revisal of my History, to the end of my Administration, and laid it by." Laid by certainly it was, and not until the year 1828 was it permitted to come forth to the light of day, and then, largely, through the magnanimous intervention of a group of noble-minded American scholars in the very city which, in his later lifetime, would not have permitted his return to it.

A great historian Hutchinson certainly was not, and, under the most favourable outward conditions, could not have been. He had the fundamental virtues of a great historian—love of truth, love of justice, diligence, the ability to master details and to narrate them with accuracy. Even in the exercise of these fundamental virtues, however, no historian in Hutchinson's circumstances could fail to be hampered by the enormous preoccupation of official business, or to have his judgment warped and coloured by the prepossessions of his own political career. While Hutchinson was, indeed, a miracle of industry, it was only a small part of his industry that he was free to devote to historical research. However sincere may have been his purpose to tell the truth and to be fair to all, the literary product of such research was inevitably weakened, as can now be abundantly shown, by many serious oversights and by many glaring misrepresentations, apparently through his failure to make a thorough use of important sources of information then accessible to him, such as colonial pamphlets, colonial newspapers, the manuscripts of his own ancestors and of the Mathers, and especially the General Court records of the province in which he played so great a part. As to the rarer intellectual and spiritual endowments of a great historian,—breadth of vision, breadth of sympathy, the historic imagination, and the power of style,—these Hutchinson almost entirely lacked. That he had not the gift of historical divination, the vision and the faculty divine to see the inward meaning of men and events, and to express that meaning in gracious, noble, and fascinating speech—Hutchinson was himself partly conscious.

His first volume seems to have been written under a consciousness that his subject was provincial, and even of a local interest altogether circumscribed. In the second volume, one perceives a more cheery and confident tone, due, probably, to the prompt recognition which his labours had then received not only in Massachusetts but in England. In the third volume are to be observed signs of increasing ease in composition, a more flowing and copious style, not a few felicities of expression. That, in all these volumes, he intended to tell the truth, and to practise fairness, is also plain; to say that he did not entirely succeed, is to say that he was human. Of course, the supreme test of historical fairness was reached when he came to the writing of his third volume,—which was, in fact, the history not only of his contemporaries but of himself, and of himself in deep and angry disagreement with many of them. It is much to his praise to say that, throughout this third volume, the prevailing tone is calm, moderate, just, with only occasional efforts at pleading his own cause, with only occasional flickers of personal or political enmity. But no one should approach the reading of Hutchinson's *History of Massachusetts Bay* with the expectation of finding in it either brilliant writing or an entertaining story. From beginning to end, there are few passages that can be called even salient—but almost everywhere an even flow of statesmanlike narrative; severe in form; rather dull, probably, to all who have not the preparation of a previous interest in the matters discussed; but always pertinent, vigorous, and full of pith. Notwithstanding Hutchinson's modest opinion of his own ability in the drawing of historical portraits, it is probable that in such portraits of distinguished characters, both among his contemporaries and among his predecessors, the general reader will be likely to find himself the most interested.

Samuel Peters.—Somewhere in the debatable land between history, fiction, and burlesque, there wanders a notorious book, first published anonymously in London in 1781, and entitled *A General History of Connecticut*. Though the authorship of this book was never acknowledged by the man who wrote it, there is no doubt that it was the work of Samuel Peters, an Anglican clergyman and a Loyalist, a man of commanding personal presence, uncommon intellectual resources, powerful will, and ill-balanced character. He opposed with frank and bitter aggressiveness the Revolutionary politics then rampant. He sailed for England in October, 1774. There he abode until his return to America in 1805. During the five or six years immediately following his arrival in England, he seems to have had congenial employment in composing his *General History of Connecticut*, as a means apparently of wreaking an undying vengeance upon the sober little commonwealth in which he was born and from which he had been ignominiously cast out. The result of this long labour of hate was a production, calling itself historical, which was characterised by a contemporary English journal—*The Monthly Review*—as having "so many marks of party spleen and idle credulity" as to be "altogether unworthy of the public attention." In spite, however, of such censure both then and since then, this alleged *History* has had, now for more than a hundred years, not only a vast amount of public attention, but very considerable success in a form that seems to have been dear to its author's heart—that of spreading through the English-speaking world a multitude of ludicrous impressions to the dishonour of the people of whom it treats. It cannot be denied that for such a service it was most admirably framed; since its grotesque fabrications in disparagement of a community of Puritan dissenters seem to have proved a convenient quarry for ready-made calumnies upon that sort of people there and elsewhere.

Jonathan Carver.—In the year 1763, at the close of that famous war which resulted in the acquisition of Canada by the English, there was in New England an enterprising young American soldier, named Jonathan Carver, stranded as it were amid the threatened inanities of peace and civilisation, and confronting a prospect that was for him altogether insipid through its lack of adventure, and especially of barbaric restlessness and discomfort. "I began to consider," so he wrote a few years afterward, "having rendered my country some services during the war, how I might continue still serviceable, and contribute, as much as lay in my power, to make that vast acquisition of territory gained by Great Britain in North America, advantageous to it. To this purpose, I determined to explore the most unknown parts of them." The project thus clearly wrought out in 1763 by this obscure provincial captain in New England anticipated by forty years the American statesmanship which, under President Jefferson, sent Meriwether Lewis and William Clark to penetrate the passes of the Rocky Mountains and to pitch their tents by the mouth of the Columbia River; even as it anticipated by a hundred years the Canadian statesmanship which, under Sir John Macdonald, has in our time beaten out an iron way across the continent at its greatest breadth.

It seems to have taken Carver about three years to complete his preparations for the tremendous enterprise which then inspired him. Not until June, 1766,—in the political lull occasioned by the repeal of the Stamp Act—was he able to start. After passing Albany, he plunged at once into the wilderness which then stretched its rough dominion over the uncomputed spaces to the western sea. In June, 1768, he began his journey homeward. In the October following, he reached Boston, "having," as he says, "been absent from it on this expedition two years and five months, and during that time travelled near seven thousand miles. From thence, as soon as I had properly digested my journal and charts, I set out for England, to communicate the discoveries I had made, and to render them beneficial to the kingdom." In 1778, nine years after his arrival there, he succeeded in bringing out his noble and fascinating book of *Travels through the Interior Parts of North America*. It was in consequence of the publication, soon after his death, in the year 1780, of the tale of Carver's career as an explorer in America, and especially of the struggles and the miseries he encountered as an American man of letters in London, that, for the relief in future of deserving men of letters there, the foundation was laid for that munificent endowment, now so celebrated under the name of "The Royal Literary Fund." His best monument is his book. As a contribution to the history of inland discovery upon this continent, and especially to our materials for true and precise information concerning the "manners, customs, religion, and language of the Indians," Carver's book of *Travels* is of unsurpassed value. Besides its worth for instruction, is its worth for delight; we have no other "Indian book" more captivating than this. Here is the charm of a sincere, powerful, and gentle personality—the charm of novel and significant facts, of noble ideas, of humane sentiments, all uttered in English well-ordered and pure. In evidence, also, of the European celebrity acquired by his book, may be cited the fact that it seems to have had a strong fascination for Schiller, as, indeed, might have been expected; and Carver's report of a harangue by a Nadowessian chief over the dead body of one of their great warriors—being itself a piece of true poetry in prose—was turned into verse by the German poet, and became famous as his *Nadowessiers Totenlied*,—a dirge which pleased Goethe so much that he declared it to be among the best of Schiller's poems in that vein, and wished that his friend had written a dozen such.[2]

St. John Crèvecœur.—In 1782, there was published in London an American book written with a sweetness of tone and, likewise, with a literary grace and a power of fascination then quite unexpected from the

---

2   See "The Indian Death-Dirge," in *The Poems and Ballads of Schiller*, by Bulwer Lytton, Tauchnitz Edition, pp. 26–27.

western side of the Atlantic. It presented itself to the public behind this ample title-page:—"Letters from an American Farmer, describing certain provincial situations, manners, and customs, not generally known, and conveying some idea of the late and present interior circumstances of the British Colonies in North America: written for the information of a friend in England, by J. Hector St. John, a farmer in Pennsylvania." The name of the author as thus given upon his title-page, was not his name in full, but only the baptismal portion of it. By omitting from the book his surname, which was Crèvecœur, he had chosen to disguise to the English public the fact—which could hardly have added to his welcome among them—that though he was an American, he was not an English American, but a French one,—having been born in Normandy, and of a noble family there, in 1731. While really an American farmer, Crèvecœur was a man of education, of refinement, of varied experience in the world. When but a lad of sixteen, he had removed from France to England; when but twenty-three, he had emigrated to America.

As an account of the American colonies, this book makes no pretension either to system or to completeness; and yet it does attain to a sort of breadth of treatment by seizing upon certain representative traits of the three great groups of colonies,—the northern, the middle, and the southern. There are in this book two distinct notes—one of great peace, another of great pain. The earlier and larger portion of the book gives forth this note of peace: it is a prose pastoral of life in the New World, as that life must have revealed itself to a well-appointed American farmer of poetic and optimistic temper, in the final stage of our colonial era, and just before the influx of the riot and bitterness of the great disruption. This note of peace holds undisturbed through the first half of the book, and more. Not until, in the latter half of it, the author comes to describe slavery in the Far South, likewise the harsh relations between the colonists and the Indians, finally the outbreak of the tempest of civil war, does his book give out its second note—the note of pain. By its inclusion of these sombre and agonising aspects of life in America, the book gains, as is most obvious, both in authenticity and literary strength. It is not hard to understand why, at such a time, a book like this should soon have made its way into the languages of Europe, particularly those of France, Germany, and Holland; nor why it should have fascinated multitudes of readers in all parts of the Continent, even beguiling many of them—too many of them, perhaps—to try their fortunes in that blithe and hospitable portion of the planet where the struggle for existence seemed almost a thing unknown. In England, likewise, the book won for itself, as was natural, a wide and a gracious consideration; its praises lasted among English men of letters as long, at least, as until the time of Hazlitt and Charles Lamb; while its idealised treatment of rural life in America wrought quite traceable effects upon the imagination of Campbell, Byron, Southey, and Coleridge, and furnished not a few materials for such captivating and airy schemes of literary colonisation in America as that of "Pantisocracy."

THE NINETEENTH CENTURY

I. THE HISTORIANS

Early Dearth of Good Writers.—Among the consciously useful forms of literature there is none in which, by common consent, American men of letters have so uniformly distinguished themselves as in history. Bradford and Winthrop in the seventeenth century are as conspicuous among their countrymen and as respectable before the world as Prescott and Parkman in the nineteenth. Prince and Stith are as minutely conscientious—and almost as dull—as the most scientific of modern students; and Hutchinson, when judged by the prevailing standards of his own times, will be found not less diligent or judicious than Adams and Rhodes are thought to-day. Indeed, there is in our literature but one period destitute of historians of merit, and that period falls in the years immediately after the Revolution, precisely in the years when we should most expect historical writing to flourish; for those last years of the eighteenth century seem, as we look back upon them, to be full of encouragement for national pride. In 1781, Lord Cornwallis had surrendered at Yorktown. In 1783, King George acknowledged the independence of his rebellious subjects in America. Under a constitution since renowned, they soon instituted for themselves a federal government upon a continental scale. The prediction of Jefferson's Declaration seemed to be justified. The United States were ready "to assume among the powers of the earth that separate and equal station to which the laws of nature and of nature's God entitle them."

Popular revolutions such as this have often been followed by a period of great literary fruitfulness, particularly in history. So it proved in Holland, in France, in Italy. But in America nothing of the sort occurred. The twenty-five years after Yorktown, barren in literature of every kind, are exceptionally devoid of historical writers who deal with large subjects in a large way. There were, of course, narratives of the war by participants and panegyrists. Such were David Ramsay's "History of the American Revolution" (1789), Mrs. Mercy Warren's "Rise, Progress, and Termination of the American Revolution" (1805), and the "History of the American Revolution" which appeared in 1819 under the name of Paul Allen. But none of these works shows largeness of view, and none is distinguished by literary qualities. They serve a good purpose, however, in reflecting the feeling of the Revolution. This is particularly true of Mrs. Warren's book. She was a sister of James Otis, whose argument against the writs of assistance in 1761 marks the beginning of the Revolutionary agitation, and the wife of General Joseph Warren, who fell on Bunker Hill; and her intimacy with these and other New England patriots lends a certain representative value to her forgotten discursiveness. A similar value attaches also to the more readable, but not less bitter "Life of James Otis, containing Notices of Contemporary Characters and Events," written by William Tudor; likewise, though in a less degree, to several other early biographies of Revolutionary worthies, among which the most weighty is the "Life of George Washington," in five volumes (1804–1807), based upon his original papers and compiled by his fellow-Virginian John Marshall, afterwards famous as Chief Justice of the Supreme Court. For students of American history, this is a useful book, such as a man of Marshall's ability could not fail to produce when dealing with subjects with which he was thoroughly familiar and in which he was deeply interested. But it is hastily written, far too long, and, save for its partisanship, altogether colourless. Nevertheless, it occupies a relatively high rank among its coevals, for, taken all in all, American writers on national history in the years 1780–1820 are few and weak.

Causes of this Inferiority.—In explanation of this circumstance various conjectures have been advanced. Indubitably, the proscription of the Loyalists after the war deprived the thirteen States of wealth and intelligence which might otherwise have afforded to American literature an American support. But the effect upon letters of that social loss is easily exaggerated. The promptness with which serious English books were reprinted in America, even in the years when, as Goodrich discovered, it was "positively injurious to the commercial credit of a bookseller to undertake American works," proves sufficiently that a reading public still remained. Another reason why, in the earlier years of our national life, there were few historians, may be found in the exaggerated value which most Americans then set upon certain abstract and therefore absolute theories in politics. Among the leaders of the Anti-Federalist or Democratic party, especially, a sort of political orthodoxy grew up. Theirs became a party with a creed, but without a programme. In the Southern States, they developed, in defence of their principles, an extensive literature of political and economic theory, far surpassing in variety of argument, subtlety of reasoning, and clearness of exposition anything that the North could show. But throughout it all, they appealed for support to the unchanging text of written constitutions, or to the immemorial prescriptions of natural law; upon history they looked as a tedious tale of ignorance and error. The Federalists, on the other hand, like the Whigs and the Republicans who succeeded them, were a party rather of measures than of principles. For their practical aims, a knowledge of human experience was serviceable. They inclined, therefore, to historical studies, and it is in New England, where their hold had been strongest, that the most significant of American historians at length appear. But even the stoutest Federalist among the contemporaries of Jefferson could discern in the recent experience of the nation at large little to stimulate patriotic ardour. In the estimation of men as yet unaccustomed to "think continentally," the new government had brought few blessings: its burdens seemed innumerable. Taxes were high. Money was bad, and scarce as well. The Revolution had loosened the bonds of traditional authority, and internal disorder was rife. The mutual obligations assumed by England and by the United States at the Peace of 1783 were disregarded on both sides; and a new treaty, whose stipulations the vast majority of Americans deemed humiliating to themselves and dishonourable towards their French allies, served chiefly to prolong internal dissensions by introducing as an unwelcome issue in American politics the conflicting sympathies of the Federalists with England and of the Democrats with France. What wonder, then, that those who concerned themselves with the history of America at all turned from the Union to their several States, each of which, in their view, had been made separately sovereign by the events of the Revolution. Their temper is well expressed by the title of David Ramsay's "History of the Revolution of South Carolina from a British Province to an Independent State" (1785). Ramsay's "South Carolina" was soon followed by Belknap's "New Hampshire" (1784–92),

Proud's "Pennsylvania" (1797), Minot's "Continuation of the History [Hutchinson's] of Massachusetts" (1798), Burke's "Virginia" (1804), Williamson's "North Carolina" (1812), and Trumbull's "Connecticut" (1818). Among these books, Belknap's justly holds the highest rank. Its style is vigorous and flexible, and in the opinion of de Tocqueville, "the reader of Belknap will find more general ideas and more strength of thought than are to be met with in other American historians" of the same period.

Washington Irving.—The life of Washington Irving as a man of letters is followed elsewhere in this volume; but no account of American historical writers, however slight, can omit his name. In the more laborious paths of the historian's vocation he seldom walked. Research was foreign to his temperament, and in his histories references to authorities are few. He makes no pretence of disclosing new facts, or even of suggesting new theories concerning facts already known. But "the picturesque distances of earth's space and the romantic remoteness of history" kindled his imagination, and his travels, which were extended for an American of his day, produced enduring results in a series of books dealing with the countries, and in part with the history of the countries, which he visited. One reason for his assuming the duties, not over-serious, of an *attaché* of the American legation in Madrid was Minister Everett's suggestion that he make an English version of the matter relating to America in Navarrete's work on the voyages and discoveries of the Spanish at the end of the fifteenth century, which had then been recently published. This project presently expanded into Irving's "Life and Voyages of Christopher Columbus, to which are added Those of his Companions" (1828). It was followed in the next year by "The Conquest of Granada," and in 1832 by "Tales of the Alhambra." Returning to America, Irving travelled extensively west of the Mississippi, and presently published his "Astoria" (1836) and "The Adventures of Captain Bonneville" (1837). Of these books, which, with an unimportant "Life of Mahomet and his Successors" (1849) and a five-volume "Life of Washington" (1855–59), constitute Irving's historical writings, the "Columbus" is justly the most esteemed. It gained for its author the gold medal of the Royal Society of Literature and the Oxford degree of D.C.L. And not without reason, for it embodies, in a skilful narrative, not merely the substance of Navarrete's documents, which Irving rendered with fidelity into excellent English, but also the results of other studies which were, for him, exceptionally thorough. Modern criticism has been very busy with the life of Columbus since Irving wrote. The narratives of Ferdinand Columbus and of Las Casas, upon which he largely relied, have been somewhat discredited, and the character of the discoverer himself has not altogether escaped. Nor can it be denied that Irving's lively fancy led him to embellish his account of certain dramatic passages in the life of Columbus with details which, while not improbable in themselves, are unsupported by documentary or other direct evidence. But the attempt of some subsequent writers, and notably of Irving's countryman Winsor, to discredit him on that account has been carried beyond reason. Irving's narrative of facts in the "Columbus" is conscientiously based upon primary sources; and his judgments, though occasionally over-indulgent of his hero, are in general sound. Columbus may not have been in all respects such a man as Irving represents him, but it is, at least, ennobling for the reader to believe that he was such a man.

In writing his "Chronicle of the Conquest of Granada from the MSS. of Fray Antonio Agapida," Irving recurred to a device which he had already employed with success. Fray Antonio is no less mythical than the "small elderly gentleman, dressed in an old black coat and cocked hat, by the name of Knickerbocker," who was supposed to have left behind him, in his rooms at the Independent Columbian Hotel, that "very curious kind of a written book in his own handwriting" which, being presently printed "to pay off the bill for his board and lodging," brought to its real author his first popularity. Nor can the "Granada" lay much stronger claim to be considered authentic history than Irving's burlesque account of New York "from the beginning of the world to the end of the Dutch dynasty." It is not, of course, predominantly humorous; but it is, in reality, merely a historical romance, adorned with bits from old chroniclers. In it Irving gave his imagination loose rein; and for that reason it is the most readable of his Spanish books.

His writings upon American history are less sympathetic. The matter of "Captain Bonneville" was fine in its facts, but it contained too little of the last to stimulate Irving's romantic imagination, and it remained cold and almost crude under his shaping hand. In the founding of the settlement by which a butcher's boy from Waldorf hoped to seize the mighty river of the West, there was also the stuff "of Romance," and Irving's "Astoria, or Anecdotes of Enterprise beyond the Rocky Mountains," should transport the reader to

> the continuous woods
> Where rolls the Oregon, and hears no sound
> Save his own dashings.

In fact it continually brings his mind back to the ledgers of a too prosperous counting-house. Into the "Life of Washington" Irving was never able to put his heart. The book was the task-work of his declining years. It was undertaken at the suggestion of enterprising publishers, to whom he listened the more readily because the number of those dependent upon him had increased as the income from his earlier works declined. Its composition dragged from the outset. When at length the volumes appeared, they achieved a pronounced *succès d'estime*; but the work shows neither the firm grip of its subject nor the sustained vigour of treatment which might rank it among great biographies. It is rather a history of the United States during the latter half of the eighteenth century. There are entertaining anecdotes in it, vivid descriptions of battles, and sturdy American feeling. But of Washington himself there is only a pale shadow.

Irving's position in American historiography is a peculiar one. He was not primarily a historian. In a sense he stands outside the main currents of our historical writing. Nevertheless, he had a strong influence in determining their course. His "Knickerbocker History of New York," essentially a work of humour, was taken seriously by various of his fellow-townsmen, who were thus incited, much to Irving's amusement, to undertake extensive studies in local history for the purpose of clearing their Dutch progenitors from his ridicule. He was the earliest among American men of letters to choose historical subjects for the exercise of his craft, and thus became the founder of the "picturesque school" of American historians, in which Prescott, Motley, and Parkman are his followers. And he was the first to feel the fascination which the power of Spain, in the Old World and in the New, has not ceased to exercise upon American writers of history ever since.

The New England School.—When the events of 1814, which promised a prolonged peace to Europe, had put an end likewise to the second war between Great Britain and her former colonists, the people of the United States, freed at last from their long subserviency to the inherited animosities of Europe, turned with confident elation to face the future problems of America. For the next half-century, while the frontier was advancing from the Ohio to the Mississippi, to the Missouri, to the "Great Stony Mountains," and beyond them to the shores of the Pacific, the Western man was too much engrossed in the bustling business of making an empire to find time for writing its annals. It was, therefore, only in New England, in the section of the country farthest removed from the course of that breathless rush across the continent, that there existed the leisure as well as the wealth necessary for the study of historical books and documents. To wealth and leisure we must add, moreover,—as important conditions underlying the historical productiveness of New England—literary and political traditions, the possession of documents and other instruments of research, and, finally, the general intellectual tone of the extreme Eastern States—that part of the country most strongly affected by the civilisation of Europe. As Tyler points out, the earliest development of New England letters had taken place in those fields of half-literary effort which seek to provide the instruments or to record the acts of statesmen, in oratory and in history. And when, at the close of the Napoleonic wars, the intellectual influence of Europe upon America began to revive, and those forces which were to produce upon the Continent the Revolution of 1830 helped, on this side of the Atlantic, to excite the democratic turmoil of the Jacksonian era, it is not surprising that the new literary strivings, which manifested themselves somewhat widely in fiction and poetry, should take on in New England the form of historical narrative. The manner of this new historical movement was, in large measure, determined by the influence of German scholarship. It was from Göttingen that George Ticknor, afterward the historian of Spanish literature, wrote to his father in 1815, lamenting the "mortifying distance there is between an European and an American scholar. We do not know," said he, "what a Greek scholar is; we do not even know the process by which a man is to be made one." And it was in those bare halls of the old Georgia Augusta, at the feet of Heeren and Eichhorn and Dissen and Blumenbach, that other grateful New Englanders—among them George Bancroft and Edward Everett in Ticknor's time, and Longfellow and Motley at a later day—learned something of the spirit of Continental scholarship. In this spirit the New England School of historians attempted, on the whole, to work. They were somewhat swerved, no doubt, by the esteem in which their countrymen still held the elaborate formalism of such orators as Webster and Everett, and, also, more to their advantage, by their own admiration for the picturesqueness of Irving, whose example encouraged them to treat by preference of foreign subjects. Still they stood firmly upon their native soil. Born among a people whose temperament, though shot through with a strain of idealism and even dashed at times with a touch of imagination, was still fundamentally sober, they were predisposed to honest care in inquiry and, save when the temptations of rhetoric seduced them, to accuracy of statement.

Thus even those historians of the New England School who had not enjoyed the advantage of European study preserved most of the traits of those who had. If Jared Sparks, a home-bred scholar who successfully conducted *The North American Review* in its earlier days (1817–18, 1823–30) and lived to become professor of history (1839–49) and president (1849–53) of Harvard University, had better understood the standards of Ranke and the "Monumenta Germaniæ Historica," he might, indeed, have allowed himself less latitude than he actually took in editing the "Diplomatic Correspondence of the American Revolution" (1829–30, 12 volumes), the "Works of Benjamin Franklin" (1836–40, 10 volumes), and especially the "Life and Writings of George Washington" (1834–37, 12 volumes). But the extent of his fault was greatly exaggerated by certain of his critics, and not even the most rigorous training could have enhanced the diligence with which he preserved these and other less important sources of our Revolutionary history. Mention of Sparks naturally suggests the name of Peter Force (1790–1868), another diligent compiler of facts. Force's "American Archives ... a Documentary History" etc. (1837–53, 9 volumes, left incomplete) was published by Congress.

When we pass to the more illustrious writers of what has been called the classical period of historical writing in America, we discover two tolerably distinct tendencies. The one tendency appears in those men who were led to write by the spirit of the time and the place, and who wrote of America out of an ardent interest and a profound belief in the country and its political and social institutions. Foremost among these men stands George Bancroft. The other tendency appears in Prescott, Motley, and Parkman, who, though trained in the same atmosphere, were first men of letters and afterward Americans. They sought, not national and political, but picturesque and dramatic subjects, and these subjects lay, in large part, outside the history of their own country.

George Bancroft.—Bancroft spent the greater part of his long life (1800–91) upon his monumental history of the United States, a work that has occupied a high position among historical writings upon America. It was his ambition, as he announces in the Preface to his first volume (1834), to write "a history of the United States from the discovery of the American continent to the present time." Although he anticipated years of work in the completion of the task, he could not have foreseen either that it was to consume more than half a century of his industrious life, or that the history itself was to end near the real beginning of the Republic. Bancroft was a writer inspired by his theme and exalted by the conception of his undertaking. Witness the opening sentences:

> The United States of America constitute an essential portion of a great political system, embracing all the civilised nations of the earth. At a period when the force of moral opinion is rapidly increasing, they have the precedence in the practice and the defence of the equal rights of man. The sovereignty of the people is here a conceded axiom, and the laws, established upon that basis, are cherished with faithful patriotism. While the nations of Europe aspire after change, our constitution engages the fond admiration of the people, by which it has been established....

The rhetorical flavour of the passage is characteristic. Critics have been inclined to regard the style of the "History" as extravagant and perfervid. They have, perhaps, tended to overlook the influence of the sincere enthusiasm and robust patriotism of the early days of national organisation and growth. The book was undoubtedly suited to the spirit and the national ideals of the period. Note the tenor of contemporary opinion. Bancroft's friend, Edward Everett, devoured the first volume as it fell from the press and hastened to congratulate the author (October 5, 1834): "I think that you have written a work which will last while the memory of America lasts; and which will instantly take its place among the classics of our language.... I could almost envy you to have found so noble a theme, while yet so young." On the score of method, the "History" was generously applauded for its "exceedingly scrupulous care" by A. H. L. Heeren, the German historian and Bancroft's earlier teacher at Göttingen. It was inevitable, however, that the patriotic fervour and sanguine tone of the book should suggest to wise heads a danger and a source of weakness. "Let me entreat you," writes Gov. John Davis, the author's brother-in-law, "not to let the partisan creep into the work. Do not imbue it with any present feeling or sentiment of the moment which may give impulse to your mind.... The historian is the recorder of truth and not of his own abstract opinions." In still plainer speech did Thomas Carlyle complain that Bancroft was too didactic, going "too much into the origin of things generally known, into the praise of things only partially praisable, only slightly important." And at a later time (1852) Henry Hallam wrote: "I do not go along with all your strictures on English statesmen and on England, either in substance, or, still more, in tone.... Faults there were, but I do not think that all were on one side. At all events, a more moderate tone would carry more weight. An historian has the high office of holding the scales." In the midst of public affairs and political duties, the great labour of the "History" progressed. A second volume appeared in 1837, and a third in 1840. These volumes covered the colonial period down to 1748. Their conspicuous success contributed to Bancroft's appointment, in 1846, as Minister to England; and there, as subsequently in Germany, his official position, added to his established reputation, opened to him unusual stores of historical material. He writes from England to Prescott, his "brother antiquary": "I am getting superb materials, and had as lief a hundred should treat the same subject as not. If they do it with more heart than I, don't you see that as a good citizen of the Republic I must applaud and rejoice in being outdone?" Under the circumstances, the democratic humility of the man is perhaps slightly overdone; although the unusual riches laid under contribution might well have offered a temptation to pride, for both public and private collections of great value were placed absolutely at his disposal. An unrivalled collection of historical manuscripts (now in the Lenox Library, New York City) bears testimony to his thoroughness and his wisdom in the use of extraordinary advantages.

But Bancroft, once established in London, soon found his literary labours pushed into the background. He confesses in 1849: "Here in London, to write is impossible.... Mr. Macaulay says, one man can do but one thing well at a time.... I am of his opinion, now in my approaching old age." The eighteen years of private life at home that followed the ministry to England (1846–49) were much more productive. Between 1849 and 1867 six more volumes (iv. to ix.) of the "History" were brought out, a volume of "Literary and Historical Miscellanies" (1855), and the official eulogy pronounced upon Abraham Lincoln in the House of Representatives (1866). A passage from the "Miscellanies" on the conception of history displays Bancroft's style in his more oratorical vein:

> But history, as she reclines in the lap of eternity, sees the mind of humanity itself engaged in formative efforts, constructing sciences, promulgating laws, organising commonwealths, and displaying its energies in the visible movement of its intelligence. Of all pursuits that require analysis, history, therefore, stands first. It is equal to philosophy; for as certainly as the actual bodies forth the ideal, so certainly does history contain philosophy. It is grander than the natural sciences; for its study is man, the last work of creation, and the most perfect in its relations with the Infinite.

It was with gratification that Bancroft accepted in 1867 and held until 1874 the ministerial post at Berlin. The honour may have come as Bancroft's reward for writing President Johnson's first annual message (1865). At the close of the ministry appeared the tenth volume of the History: "The American Revolution. Epoch Fourth Continued. Peace between America and Great Britain, 1778–82" (1874). This at seventy-four years of age!

It was impossible, of course, that Bancroft should, at his advanced age, carry his work, as originally planned, through the nineteenth century. He determined, instead, to write the history of the organisation of the Federal Government. In 1882 came, accordingly, his "History of the Formation of the Constitution of the United States of America" (2 volumes). Thus, at eighty-two, he had set forth in twelve generous volumes what may be called an introduction to the history of the country. It is indeed more than that, for, as the author himself somewhere remarks, the history of the United States begins with the united resistance of the colonies to Great Britain.

As an historical writer, Bancroft belongs to the period of his first volumes and not to that of his last. His interpretation of men and events rests upon his political philosophy, and his political philosophy was a heritage of the times of Andrew Jackson. To this philosophy he was faithful. Ranke, the German historian, once said to him, "Your history is the best book ever written from the democratic point of view." Bancroft was aware of his democratic bias; but he would have denied with vehemence that this bias infused a subjective taint into his candour or laid a tinge of partiality upon his judgment. The "History" has been called an "epic of liberty." It is philosophical, at times rhapsodical—not scientific—history. It treats an heroic theme in an heroic manner. Recent criticism of his method and political theories tends to obscure the brilliancy of his services to American historiography. Over and above the serious spirit in which he set about his task, the exacting search among contemporary sources, the unceasing devotion to truth, and an unsparing and prodigious industry, the broad and national character of the whole achievement calls for grateful recognition. Bancroft raised the history of America above the plane of provincialism and local interests, and set forth both the total march of internal events incident to national development and the manifold relations of the United States to the history of Europe. This wide perspective of events and causes would hardly have been possible except for years of residence, both as student and diplomat, in the capitals of Germany and Great Britain. In the matter of method also, Bancroft's services to historical research must not be overlooked. He presented to Americans an object-lesson in the collection, criticism, and use of scattered materials. His distinction, then, as the founder of a new American school rests upon a double basis: his wide conception of a national history and his improved methodology in research. He reaped abundant success, both in the popular enthusiasm with which his books were hailed and in the extraordinary personal honours bestowed upon him until the time of his death. And it is no disparagement of his services to say that his great popularity rests rather upon a genius for catching up and reflecting the youthful spirit of genuine and uncritical Americanism than upon a capacity for setting down without passion and for interpreting without prejudice the human events of an inspiring epoch.

Contemporaries of Bancroft.—The writers of American history who came nearest to rivalling Bancroft in his own day were Richard Hildreth (1807–65), a vigorous New England leader writer and anti-slavery pamphleteer, and George Tucker (1775–1861), a Southern lawyer, who served for twenty years as professor of philosophy and political economy in the University of Virginia. Hildreth's "History of the United States" (1849–52, 6 volumes) comes down to 1821, Tucker's (1856–58, 4 volumes) to 1841. Both did careful work, though both have been criticised for their partisan leanings. Each gives a relatively large space to the Colonial and Revolutionary history of his own section. In the constitutional period, Hildreth commonly accepts the view of events most favourable to the Federalist party, whereas Tucker inclines to side even more strongly with the Democrats, of whose leader, Jefferson, he had published, in 1837, a sympathetic life. In connection with this branch of the New England School should be mentioned John Gorham Palfrey's illustrious "History of New England" (1858–75, 4 volumes; a supplemental volume, edited by F. W. Palfrey, 1890). Palfrey was a graduate of Harvard and for several years the editor of *The North American Review*. His work is commonly regarded as the best of the colonial histories of New England; it occupies besides a secure place in American literature.

William Hickling Prescott.—Eminent among the men of the "classical" period who wrote picturesque and romantic histories, stands Prescott (1796–1859), author of "The History of the Reign of Ferdinand and Isabella the Catholic" (1838), "The History of the Conquest of Mexico with a Preliminary View of the Ancient Mexican Civilization and the Life of the Conqueror Hernando Cortés" (1843), "The History of the Conquest of Peru, with a Preliminary View of the Civilization of the Incas" (1847), "The History of the Reign of Philip the Second, King of Spain" (1855–58), and other historical and literary works. "The Reign of Philip" was not finished, as Prescott suffered, during its preparation (1858), a shock of apoplexy, and died the following year. After working for ten years—so quietly that but few of his friends knew of the undertaking—upon his "Ferdinand and Isabella," Prescott, upon its publication, found himself suddenly famous. "Love of the author gave the first impulse," declared the author's friend, Gardiner; "the extraordinary merits of the work did all the rest." The American demand for the "History" was unparalleled, and all Europe sent liberal and judicious praise. Translations were called for in Russia, France, Spain, Italy, and Germany.

A bodily affliction, the partial loss of sight in early manhood, has lent a peculiar personal interest to Prescott's heroic performances. He has been called, with but little exaggeration, "the blind historian." During his junior year at Harvard, an accident destroyed the sight of one eye, and not long afterward the uninjured eye became permanently affected. A career in the practice of law had to be abandoned. Much of his subsequent life was spent in the dark. A great part of his historical labours had to be done with the aid of readers and secretaries. The task of mastering a language (he began Spanish at twenty-eight) and of collecting materials from libraries and archives would have seemed to be impossible. Nevertheless it was accomplished. The histories bear but little evidence of the writer's physical infirmities. They are renowned for their accuracy and thoroughness. Recent ethnological discovery and advancement in historical method have, it is true, necessitated revision in certain statements of fact (e. g., regarding the social and private life of the Aztecs); but that is an accident of time. His thoroughness is attested by Jared Sparks, who knew of no historian, "in any age or language, whose researches into the materials with which he was to work have been so extensive, thorough, and profound as those of Mr. Prescott." But the wide popularity of Prescott's historical writings rests first upon their literary merits. He wrote in a clear, graceful, and dignified style upon epochs and personages that were surrounded by charm and romance. His power for pictorial representation was great. The admirable qualities of his books strongly suggest the author himself. He was cheerful, amiable, spontaneous, warm-hearted, and much beloved. At forty-five, Sumner said of him that he possessed the "freedom and warmth and frolic of a boy." At the same time, Prescott's capacity for self-criticism and for rigorous discipline was unusual. Without these qualities, he would hardly have succeeded in the face of painful disabilities. For many years it was his custom to analyse his powers and weaknesses, and to formulate exacting rules for his own guidance. At twenty-eight he wrote in his journal: "To the end of my life I trust I shall be more avaricious of time and *never* put up with a smaller average than seven hours' intellectual occupation per diem." About this time he wrote down a list of "rules for composition." Among them are to be found these: "Rely upon myself for estimation and criticism of my composition;" "write what I think without affectation upon subjects I have examined;" "never introduce what is irrelevant or superfluous or unconnected for the sake of crowding in more facts." He was early attracted toward historical writing, although he devoted much time to biography and critical reviews. The interest in Spanish history seems to have come from Ticknor's lectures on Spanish literature, which Prescott heard at Harvard. The Ferdinand and Isabella theme first came to him in 1826. "The age of Ferdinand," he remarks at this time, "is most important as containing the germs of the modern system of European politics.... It is in every respect an interesting and momentous period of history; the materials ample, authentic,—I will chew upon this matter, and decide this week." The decision came, however, only after two years of further consideration. With Irving, Ticknor, and Motley, Prescott stands as one of the men who gave to the English-speaking world a clear and brilliant account of the history and literature of Spain. It is, however, a fact of still greater moment to American letters that Prescott should have embodied in permanent form a series of histories of great men and great events that is the common possession of the Old World and the New, and that marks the advancement of American historical writing beyond the limits of national feeling and national interest.

John Lothrop Motley.—Bancroft, Prescott, Motley (1814–77), and Parkman were all born and reared in the vicinity of Boston, and all were graduated from Harvard University. Motley and Bancroft continued their studies at Göttingen and Berlin. While in Germany, Motley enjoyed the friendship of Prince Bismarck, who was his fellow-student. "We lived," said Bismarck, "in the closest intimacy, sharing meals and outdoor exercise." In 1841 Motley was appointed secretary to the American Legation at St. Petersburg; but he soon relinquished the post and returned to America. Ten years later he took up his residence in Europe, where he remained for half a decade pursuing historical studies. At the end of this time (1856) appeared "The Rise of the Dutch Republic: A History." In 1860 came the first two volumes of "The History of the United Netherlands," and in 1868 the last two. The continuation of the Dutch history came out in biographical form (1874) as "The Life and Death of John of Barneveld, Advocate of Holland; with a View of the Primary Causes and Movements of the Thirty Years' War." Meanwhile, Motley had been appointed to the American Ministry to Austria (1861) and to England (1869). Both appointments ended unhappily. An interesting circumstance connects Motley's career with Prescott's and, indirectly, with Washington Irving's. With noble generosity, Irving had abandoned his well-formed plan of writing a Conquest of Mexico when he learned, through a common friend, of Prescott's intentions in the same field. This act involved real sacrifice. "I had," Irving afterward confesses, "no other subject at hand to supply its place. I was dismounted from my *cheval de bataille*, and have never been completely mounted since." Prescott was presently to realise the cost of Irving's surrender. For Motley, in turn, essayed to enter the field made illustrious by the author of "Ferdinand and Isabella." In ignorance of Prescott's plans for "The History of Philip," Motley began his study of related subjects. The news then came to him as a blow. "For I had not," Motley says, "first made up my mind to write a history, and then cast about to take up a subject. My subject had taken me up, drawn me on, and absorbed me into itself." Prescott listened to the younger man's proposal to retire, "with frank, ready, and liberal sympathy," and insisted that Motley should proceed. More than this, he made handsome allusion, in the Preface to his "Philip," to the forthcoming work on the revolt of the Netherlands. Motley wrote with zeal and enthusiasm. He loved liberty. The story of a people fighting for freedom fired his imagination. His ardour led him, naturally, toward the advocacy of favourite characters and parties; and the greater moderation of the Dutch historians themselves tends to support the charge of partiality. But Motley's partiality was not mere partisanship. It rested upon a nice discrimination of the good and the bad, of the noble and the mean. His Dutch history is classic. It is renowned for its scholarly qualities and for its vivid colouring. Froude, without previous knowledge of the writer or of his work, placed "The Rise of the Dutch Republic" among "the finest histories in this or in any language." While, by the more exacting standards of current schools, it is criticised for its lack of philosophical insight, it is still justly regarded as a faithful and striking picture of an heroic people.

Francis Parkman.—The New England School had told the story of the Spaniard in America and in the Netherlands. It was further to enrich its native literature by another brilliant history of the struggle for conquest of a great nation in foreign lands. Parkman (1823–93) is the historian of the rise and decline of France's power in North America. Like Motley, he was captivated by an impressive and dramatic cycle of events, and—again like Motley—he possessed breadth of vision and tenacity of purpose sufficient to his task. Parkman had a passion for the wilderness;—a passion which he fed in youth and early manhood by excursions, large and small, to the woods, the prairies, and the mountains. In his twenties, he appears, a picturesque figure in the great West, living and hunting with Indians, eating pemmican, and playing host at a feast of dog-meat and tea. In spite of outdoor life and travel, Parkman was seldom well. A serious affection of the eyes, and nervous troubles which may have emanated from it, kept him, from his undergraduate days, either incapacitated or on the border-line of invalidism. He was tortured till his death by pain, lameness, insomnia, and at times almost complete blindness. His suffering and infirmities recall Prescott. It is not easy to decide which of the two men struggled more heroically against overwhelming odds. As early as his sophomore year at Harvard, Parkman planned to write the history of the "Old French War" for the conquest of Canada; "for here, as it seems to me,"—so he writes—"the forest drama was more stirring and the forest stage more thronged with appropriate actors than in any other passage of our history." "The Oregon Trail"—an account of his adventures on the great plains and beyond—began to appear in *The Knickerbocker Magazine* in 1847, and "The Conspiracy of Pontiac" came out in 1851. Later, the plan widened to include the whole course of the conflict in America between France and England. The result was a series of books unexcelled in western historiography: "The Pioneers of France in the New World" (1865), "The Jesuits in North America" (1867), "La Salle and the Discovery of the Great West" (1869), "The Old Régime" (1874), "Count Frontenac and New France under Louis XIV" (1877), "Montcalm and Wolfe" (1884), and, finally, "A Half-Century of Conflict" (1892). The series received the general title, "France and England in North America." In his "Montcalm and Wolfe," Parkman reached the height of his fame. Wretched health turned the author's attention to horticultural diversions. In 1871 he was appointed professor of horticulture in Harvard University; in 1866 he published his famous

"Book of Roses." His intimate knowledge of the scenes and peoples of whom he wrote and an engaging and finished manner impart to his historical books an unusual vivacity and charm. His work, while it is, as he intended, "a history of the American forest," is also the history of two powerful and opposing systems of civilisation—"feudal, militant, and Catholic France in conflict with democratic, industrial, and Protestant England." Less impulsive than Motley and less serene than Prescott, Parkman possessed at once the ardour and the restraint necessary to the vivid and impartial rendering of a glowing theme vastly important in the history of the New World. Himself cast in an heroic mould and exhibiting a fine type of the Puritan spirit, he was at home among chivalrous men and bold and impressive deeds. Jameson, writing of him shortly before his work was finished (see "The History of Historical Writing in America," 1891), declares him to be, "next after one or two who survived from the preceding period, the most conspicuous figure in the American historiography of the last twenty-five years, the only historian who can fairly be called classical."

Recent Historical Writings.—Since the Civil War America has been prolific in historical records. General histories and local histories abound; histories of administrations, of periods, of popular movements, indefatigable and scholarly researches in politics, war, finance, and social and economic institutions. The literary value of these records is not, however, to be inconsiderately judged from their bulk. Times and standards in American historiography have changed. Among the multitude of authors one must not look for many names which may be written down with those of Prescott, Motley, and Parkman. Not that the modern period is wanting in good work or able writers. These are to be found in abundance. But most of the work belongs to science and not to letters; and besides, eminence is not fostered by the catholic distribution of talent and training. Jameson picks up Amiel's blunt opinion that "the era of mediocrity in all things is commencing" and applies it to American historians. At the same time, this wise critic inclines to the belief that the vast improvement in technical process and workmanship realised within the present generation is the natural means to the development of a more substantial and more profound school of historians than the West has thus far created. The term "mediocrity" does not, indeed, do full justice to the period and the authors in question, and we must seek other grounds of excuse for the brevity of our review of them. These grounds are found, first, in the indirect importance to literature of the great mass of recent work, and, secondly, in the impossibility of setting the achievements of contemporary workers in just perspective.

The writers, great and little, of the periods already surveyed were, in large measure, self-trained. Until the last two or three decades, colleges and universities offered little incentive to methodical work upon historical subjects. Even Harvard, from whose doors went one after another the men who were to make the New England School famous, taught history only incidentally. Now, an academic school has arisen. Young men and women are trained in undergraduate and graduate studies by teachers who are themselves historical writers and investigators. Students are taught the discriminating use of historical instruments, and sound methods of reconstruction and interpretation. The change has been wrought under the unequal pressure of external influence, emphasis laid upon scientific method, a quickened consciousness of the importance and dignity of American history, and, finally, the example of those graceful and inspiring writers who gave to Western historiography an honourable place in the world's literature. The academic school owes its existence to no single founder. It is, by its nature, a school of coöperative endeavour,—coöperation, first, between teacher and pupil, and coöperation, later, in the conjoint and organised labour of productive hands and brains. Among its early advocates and promoters were Charles Kendall Adams, university professor and president, teacher and historian, who adapted the German seminary method to the American university; Henry Adams, professor at Harvard University and author of a brilliant history in nine volumes (1889–91) of the country under Jefferson and Madison (1801–17); Justin Winsor, librarian, bibliographer, and editor of the useful and scholarly "Narrative and Critical History of America" (1884–89), and Herbert Baxter Adams, of Johns Hopkins, historian and instructor of historical students. The coöperative labours of the period have borne abundant fruit. Besides Winsor's volumes should be mentioned "The American Nation: a History from Original Sources by Associated Scholars," a gigantic work in twenty-seven volumes just finished (1904–8) under the editorship of Albert Bushnell Hart. The authorship is divided among a number of competent historical writers. The collection lays claim to being "the first comprehensive history of the United States, now completed, which covers the whole period" from the discovery of America to the present. Similar undertakings are, however, in progress, and a number of coöperative works of smaller scope are already in print. Other notable histories covering comparatively long periods of time are Edward Channing's "A History of the United States," to be completed in eight volumes; a series of nine volumes relating to preconstitutional times written by John Fiske, after the manner of Parkman, and including "The Critical Period of American History" (1888), "The Beginnings of New England" (1889), "The American Revolution" (1891), "The Discovery of America" (1892), etc.; James Schouler's "History of the United States under the Constitution" (1880–99); "A Popular History of the United States" (1876–81), by William Cullen Bryant and Sydney H. Gay; "A History of the People of the United States from the Revolution to the Civil War" (6 of the 7 volumes published, 1883–1906), by John B. McMaster; "The Constitutional and Political History of the United States," (1877–92), by Hermann E. von Holst, and "A History of the American People" (1902), by President Woodrow Wilson of Princeton University. Channing's attempt to cover, by the labours of a single competent scholar, the entire history of the country is comparable to that of George Bancroft. John Fiske wrote readable and popular narratives of historical events. He did much, both by books and lectures, to arouse general interest in matters of American life past and present. McMaster's substantial and illuminating history is social rather than political. He seeks to portray the whole life of the people. Von Holst's aim was, on the other hand, political. The author was a German-American. He held, among academic posts, professorships at Freiburg and the University of Chicago. His critical review, often disparaging to democratic institutions, may be taken as a counterblast to the ebullient patriotism of earlier, native writers. As the work of a foreign observer of American affairs, it suggests the reflections of de Tocqueville, of James Bryce, and of Goldwin Smith. President Wilson's five volumes contain a wise and judicial commentary, in the form of a long and attractive essay, on the main course of events since the days of discovery. For the multitude of American historical writers who have treated single epochs, space permits mention of only one or two names. James Ford Rhodes' "History of the United States from the Compromise of 1850" (7 volumes, 1902–6), the work of "nineteen years' almost exclusive devotion," is commonly regarded as the most thorough and best balanced study of the Civil War, its causes and its consequences. Henry Adams has, in his "History of the United States," etc., investigated with competence and penetration the administrations of Jefferson and Madison.

This meagre list of the more important productions of the academic school clearly reveals the attraction of the American theme for the present American historian. Capable and impressive studies of foreign subjects there have been, it is true;—David Jayne Hill's "History of Diplomacy in the International Development of Europe" and Henry C. Lea's work on the medieval church are conspicuous instances;—but the great mass of research and writing has been gathered at home. Governmental affairs and political events loom large. Less interest has been taken in the subtler phases of national character and individual motive; although Fiske and McMaster and Woodrow Wilson and certain of the best biographers (whose important service to literature deserves separate consideration) represent a current tendency toward reflective and philosophical writing of a literary quality, which augurs well for the future of American historiography.

II. THE NOVELISTS

The Beginnings.—American fiction was one of the latest types of native literature to appear. The hard conditions of life imposed on the colonists by the necessity of clearing the forests and keeping the Indians in check were evidently unfavourable to sustained efforts in imaginative writing. And there were other reasons for the late growth of the novel. Except as they had a religious turn or an evident moral, stories were likely to be looked upon by the Puritans as a species of useless frivolity, which could have no part in the saving of souls.[3] Again, in the struggle with the mother country the robust and scholarly intellects of America had other matters to think of besides the elements of pure literature. The rights of man, the basis of resistance to tyranny, the principles of statecraft, the elements of democracy, were among the interests that absorbed

---

3   In her valuable study of "The Early American Novel," New York, 1907 (published after these pages were in type), Miss Lillie Deming Loshe remarks: "It is a significant fact that nearly all the directly didactic novels are by known writers—writers of literary or educational importance in their day—while, on the other hand, the stories designed chiefly for amusement, but related to their didactic contemporaries by similarity of sentiment and manner, are almost invariably by unknown authors." Miss Loshe enumerates only thirty-five novels published before 1801.

the Washingtons, the Otises, and the Hamiltons of the latter part of the eighteenth century. But perhaps the most important reason for the tardy appearance of American fiction was the lack of tradition and legend. Of this Hawthorne complained as late as 1859, in the preface to "The Marble Faun":

> No author, without a trial, can conceive of the difficulty of writing a romance about a country where there is no shadow, no antiquity, no mystery, no picturesque and gloomy wrong, nor anything but a commonplace prosperity, in broad and simple daylight, as is happily the case with my dear native land. It will be very long, I trust, before romance-writers may find congenial and easily handled themes, either in the annals of our stalwart republic, or in any characteristic and probable events of our individual lives. Romance and poetry, ivy, lichens, and wall-flowers need ruin to make them grow.

Thus it was that for a long time Defoe and Fielding, Smollett and Sterne found no imitators in America. The American novel-reader, for the most part, was content with British provender, and satisfied his appetite for the marvellous with Walpole's "Castle of Otranto," Lewis' "Monk," and Mrs. Radcliffe's "Romance of the Forest" and "The Mysteries of Udolpho." Toward the end of the eighteenth century several writers essayed the novel, but not with lasting success. In "The Foresters" (published serially in *The Columbian Magazine*, and in book form in 1792), Jeremy Belknap (1774–98) produced an ingenious though trivial allegorical tale of the colonisation of America and the rebellion of the colonies. In this, Peter Bullfrog stood for New York, Ethan Greenwood for Vermont, Walter Pipeweed for Virginia, Charles Indigo for South Carolina, and so on. Ann Eliza Bleecker (1752–83) was the author of "The History of Maria Kittle," which in the form of a letter sets forth some harrowing experiences among the savages during the French and Indian War; and of "The Story of Henry and Anne," a tale, "founded on fact," of the misfortunes of some German peasants who finally settled in America; both of these were published posthumously in her "Works" in 1793. Mrs. Susanna Haswell Rowson's "Charlotte Temple" (1790), a story of love, betrayal, and desertion, despite its absurdly stilted phrases and its long-drawn melancholy, has ever been popular with a certain class of readers; the editor of the latest edition (1905), Mr. Francis W. Halsey, has examined 104 editions, and his list is incomplete. An avowed antidote to "Charlotte Temple," Mrs. Tabitha G. Tenney's satirical "Female Quixotism" (1808), suggests to Professor Trent "an expurgated Smollett"; it is now unknown. Mrs. Hannah W. Foster, the wife of a clergyman in Massachusetts, wrote "The Coquette, or The History of Eliza Wharton, a Novel Founded on Fact" (1797), a story of desertion, showing the marked influence of Richardson. In the same year, appeared "The Algerine Captive," by Royall Tyler, who was one of the first to turn to American life as a fruitful subject for fiction. His story is a broadly humorous picaresque tale, of the Smollett type, which introduces rather too many wearisome details of customs in Algiers; a fault for which his generally spirited style and his powerful description of the horrors of a slave-ship partially atone.

Hugh Henry Brackenridge (1748–1816), the classmate at Princeton of James Madison and Philip Freneau, wrote "Modern Chivalry, or The Adventures of Captain John Farrago and Teague O'Regan, His Servant" (Philadelphia and Pittsburgh, published in four parts, 1792–7), a modern "Don Quixote" narrating his experiences in the Whisky Insurrection of 1794. Though widely read in its day, especially by artisans and farmers, its literary worth was not sufficient to preserve it. "The Gamesters," published in 1805 by Mrs. Catharine Warren, was likewise popular in its day; it attempted "to blend instruction with amusement."

Charles Brockden Brown.—The history of the novel in America, therefore, properly begins with Charles Brockden Brown (1771–1810), who has been called "the first professional man of letters and important creative writer of the English-speaking portion of the New World." He was born in Philadelphia of a good Quaker family; just forty years earlier, his uncle, Charles Brockden, had drawn up the constitution of the old Philadelphia Library Company. From early childhood, books were familiar to the youthful Brown, who became an omnivorous reader, and at Robert Proud's school undermined his health by excessive devotion to reading and study, so that he was always an invalid. He took up the study of law, but soon abandoned it, despite the protest of his family, for the career of "book-making." After some writing of verse and of essays, he published in 1798 a successful novel, "Wieland, or The Transformation," and at once followed this with five others, "Ormond, or The Secret Witness," (1799), "Arthur Mervyn, or Memoirs of the Year 1793" (1799–1800), in which he gave an account of the ravages of the yellow fever in Philadelphia, "Edgar Huntly, or The Adventures of a Sleep-Walker," "Clara Howard" (1801), and "Jane Talbot" (published in England in 1804). From 1798 till 1801, Brown lived amid congenial surroundings in New York; in the former year he nearly died of yellow fever, to which his friend Dr. Elihu H. Smith succumbed. Returning to Philadelphia in 1801, he spent the remainder of his life there; marrying happily in 1804, editing *The Literary Magazine*, and writing political pamphlets and works on geography and Roman history, until consumption brought his busy and useful life to a premature end.

Brown's novels mostly belong with the "tales of terror" so popular in his day. A radical thinker and analyst, he rejects supernatural agencies in his explanation of events, and relies wholly on natural causes; but this does not diminish the number of marvels in his tales. The plots of one or two of his stories will give an idea of the character of all. The scene of "Wieland" is laid on the banks of the Schuylkill, in Pennsylvania. The Wielands are a cultivated German family. Wieland's father has died mysteriously by what is explained as self- or spontaneous combustion, and the son has inherited a melancholy and superstitious mind, which develops into fanaticism. The family hear strange voices giving commands or warnings or telling of events beyond the reach of human knowledge. A mysterious man, Carwin, appears, with such powers of pleasing that he becomes very intimate with the family. At length Wieland, at the command of what he takes to be a heavenly voice, sacrifices to God his wife and children. Confined in a maniac's dungeon, he bears his fate with a sense of moral exaltation. Having escaped, he attempts to offer up also his sister, the narrator of the story, when he learns that he has been deceived by the ventriloquism of Carwin, whom malice has thus led to trick the family. In a frenzy, Wieland kills himself; Carwin disappears; and the story ends with the marriage of the sister and Pleyel, a brother of Wieland's late wife and now a widower. Less powerful than "Wieland," but still superior to Brown's other works, is "Ormond." An artist, Stephen Dudley, engaging in pharmacy to support his family, is brought to beggary through the villainy of his partner. His daughter Constantia bears up bravely through severe trials. Just when life appears brighter,

Ormond comes upon the scene, a mysteriously powerful man, much like Falkland in Godwin's "Caleb Williams," of great wealth, strong mind, and base morals; he deserts Helena Cleves, who commits suicide, and pursues Constantia. Stephen Dudley is murdered by an unknown hand. Having a legacy from Helena, Constantia is about to sail for Europe with her friend (who narrates the story) when Ormond, finding her invincible, assaults her in a lonely house and meets death by her hand, after he has himself slain Craig, now revealed as the assassin of Dudley at Ormond's instigation. Constantia afterward lives quietly with her friend in Europe. Brown's plots are usually disfigured by irrelevant incidents and superfluous characters; he frequently changed his plans and even his heroines, and, writing with great rapidity, often with a greedy printer at his elbow, he utterly failed to weld together the elements of his stories and often to give them proper motivation. His characters are drawn in bold and clear outlines, but are frequently uninteresting—being too sentimental or inconsistent, or given to long and prosy soliloquies. It cannot be affirmed that Brown understood human nature well. Of style he had none; his pages are innocent of epigram or humorous turn; he employs very little dialogue and makes but scanty and awkward use of dialect. Yet in certain passages, in describing great crises, he exhibits considerable vividness and power. Brown's chief merit consists in the sense of reality with which he contrives to invest his scenes of gloom and terror.

> The power possessed by this rare genius, says Mr. James H. Morse,[4] of throwing gloomy characteristics into his theme, was equalled by no other American writer. In the matter of morbid analysis, Poe, in comparison with Brown, was superficial, Hawthorne was cheerful, and the modern school of French writers are feeble. With Poe, we can see that the gloom came by an effort of a spurred imagination; with Hawthorne, that it was the work of an artistic sense; but with Brown, it seems to have been constitutional—the gift at once of temperament and circumstances.

Brown was an admirer of William Godwin and obviously imitated not only his method of developing characters but also his style. It may be added that Brown in turn found many readers in England, where several of his novels were republished and where, as we have seen,

4   *The Century Magazine*, xxvi. 289.

"Jane Talbot" was first published. Professor Dowden quotes Peacock as saying that of all the works with which Shelley was familiar, those which took the deepest root in his mind were Brown's four novels, Schiller's "Robbers," and Goethe's "Faust." Brown's influence upon subsequent American writers, moreover, was not inconsiderable, and his place in our literature, if not high, is at least honourable.

John Davis, an Englishman about whom little is known, wrote several novels of American life, most of which were published here, and became somewhat popular. He lived in the United States from 1798 till 1802, and travelled over a large part of the country. His first novel, "The Original Letters of Ferdinand and Elizabeth" (1798), was a conventional story of seduction and suicide. It was followed by "The Farmer of New Jersey" (1800), "The First Settlers of Virginia" (1805), a pioneer historical novel, crude and ill managed, "Walter Kennedy, an American Tale" (London, 1805), and "The Post Captain" (1813). The most that can be said of these stories is that their author was shrewd and observant, and had some journalistic skill.

Mrs. Sally Keating Wood (1760–1855), wife of General Abiel Wood, of Maine, may be mentioned as the author of "Julia and the Illuminated Baron" (1800), which recalls the mysterious evil power and atheistic tendencies attributed to the Bavarian order of the Illuminati, established in 1775, which, though suppressed in 1780 by the Elector, was supposed to have secretly persisted and spread over Europe. Mrs. Wood wrote also "Dorval, or The Speculator" (1801), "Amelia, or The Influence of Virtue" (1802), "Ferdinand and Elmira, a Russian Story" (1804), and "Tales of the Night" (1827), besides several novels that were never published. Mrs. Wood placed many of her scenes in Europe.

Isaac Mitchell.—At Poughkeepsie, New York, in 1811, was published in two volumes "The Asylum, or Alonzo and Melissa, an American Tale, Founded on Fact." Of the author of this Gothic romance, Isaac Mitchell,[5] little is known save that he was successively the editor of *The Farmer's Journal*, *The Political Barometer*, and *The Republican Crisis*, all of Albany, New York, and that after losing his position through political changes, he moved to Poughkeepsie. The story was later abridged

---

5   See Mr. Edward B. Reed's note in *The Nation*, December 8, 1904, lxxix. 458.

and compressed into one volume by Daniel Jackson, Jr. (Mitchell's name disappearing from the title-page), and in this form was long popular throughout America; Mr. Reed thinks that for nearly a quarter of a century a new edition appeared practically every year. The narrative is full of elaborate descriptions of nature.

Washington Irving.—In general Irving will be discussed rather with the essayists than with the novelists; but his stories and tales must be considered here. They have contributed largely if not chiefly to his enduring reputation. His first book, "Knickerbocker's History of New York" (1809), in which he works out a grotesquely humorous drama of the Dutch fathers wrestling with the weighty problems of statecraft, is of course in the main fictitious. No doubt it is at times pretentious or overdone, and the humour is occasionally a little too broad for the decorum of to-day; but the irrepressible spirit of comedy, the delightfully burlesqued descriptions of stolid Dutch character, the vivid though leisurely narrative, give it a supreme place in our humorous literature. "Rip Van Winkle" and "The Legend of Sleepy Hollow" are doubtless the most read parts of "The Sketch Book" and have long since become classics; no more faithful narratives of quaint old Dutch life have ever been written. In them the boisterous exuberance of the "History" gives way to a more graceful, refined, and mature style, which invests the homely simplicity and contentment of colonial Dutch life with a kind of idyllic charm. Only a little less successful were Irving's other stories of early New Amsterdam life—notably "The Money-Diggers" in "Tales of a Traveller," and "Dolph Heyliger" in "Bracebridge Hall." Inferior because more conventional and less spontaneous are the first three parts of the "Tales"; yet even here, in dealing with the sentimental and the terrible, Irving compares favourably with other story-tellers of his day. In the stories scattered through "The Alhambra," Irving showed clearly that he had found another source of inspiration in the romantic legends of Spain and the Moors—legends full of Oriental mystery and of the splendid glories of old Spain, so charmingly and truthfully set forth that the Spaniards themselves spoke of him as "the poet Irving." And "poet" he is in the large sense that he has created imperishable scenes and characters in that realm of romance in which we delight to wander, far from the prosaic world and the madding crowd.

James Kirke Paulding.—A contrast with Irving in more than one respect is afforded by James K. Paulding (1778–1860), the friend and collaborator of Washington Irving and the brother-in-law of William Irving. The author of "The Sketch Book" gave his whole life to the profession of letters; for Paulding, on the other hand, literary composition was only an avocation. The genial humour of Irving, too, differs from the satirical and ironical vein too often indulged in by his friend. Born in Dutchess County, New York, Paulding went to New York City while a young man and became associated with the Irvings in writing *Salmagundi*, the success of which gave Paulding confidence in himself and led him to further literary efforts. "The Diverting History of John Bull and Brother Jonathan" (1812), a loosely constructed and amateurish satire in the style of Arbuthnot, became very popular both in America and in England. "Koningsmarke, the Long Finne" (1823), now remembered only for the familiar assertion that "Peter Piper picked a peck of pickled peppers," was a burlesque on Cooper's "Pioneers." Paulding's most successful work, which deserves to live, was "The Dutchman's Fireside" (1831), in which are charming descriptions of quaint Dutch customs and personages, of the picturesque scenery of the Hudson, and of the vast expanse of wilderness that stretched to the westward. In general, however, Paulding's work was characterised by a too harsh and obstreperous Americanism, an immoderate and amusing hostility to foreigners, and a carelessness of workmanship which prevented it from enduring long.

Samuel Woodworth.—As a curiosity must here be mentioned the long-forgotten "Champions of Freedom" (1816) of Samuel Woodworth (1785–1842). It was his one essay in fiction; a history of the War of 1812 in the style of a romance. It must be described as a chaotic miscellany, blending wild romance with commonplace realism, and conducting the reader from ballroom to battlefield and back again with the least possible suspicion of method or motive.

John Neal.—Born in Portland, Maine, and beginning life as a shop-boy in Boston, John Neal (1793–1876) became in turn a wholesale dry-goods merchant, a lawyer, and a voluminous critic, poet, and novelist. He boasted that in thirty-six years he had written enough altogether to fill a hundred octavo volumes; yet to-day he is little more than a name. His first novel, "Keep Cool," which he afterward spoke of with justice as a "paltry, contemptible affair," appeared in 1817. His best novels are "Seventy-Six" (1823), a lively story of the Revolution, "Rachel Dyer" (1828), a story of the Salem Witchcraft, and "The Down-Easters" (1833), an extravagant tale which deals with the ways of steamboat passengers, and into which he manages to introduce plenty of horrors. Neal has been well styled "the universal Yankee, whittling his way through creation, with a half-genius for everything, a robust genius for nothing." He is said to have been the originator of the woman's suffrage movement, the first person to establish a gymnasium in America, and the first to encourage Edgar A. Poe.[6]

James Fenimore Cooper.—The first American to win universal recognition as a powerful novelist was James Fenimore Cooper. Born at Burlington, New Jersey, on September 15, 1789, of English Quaker and Swedish parentage, he was taken, when a year old, to the Central New York wilderness, where his father, having become the owner of large tracts of land, had laid out the village of Cooperstown. Here, on the shores of the beautiful Otsego Lake, in a motley frontier settlement, the boy Cooper passed his earliest years. In due time entering the family of an Albany clergyman as a private pupil, Cooper proceeded in 1803 to Yale College, where he became a member of the class of 1806. An escapade in his third year led to his dismissal; after which he served a marine apprenticeship of a year and then entered the navy, serving as midshipman for nearly four years. In 1811, he married Susan A. De Lancey, a lady of Huguenot and Tory family, and a sister of Bishop De Lancey of Western New York; and at her request resigned his commission, to become an amateur farmer, successively at Mamaroneck, on Long Island Sound, at Cooperstown, and at Scarsdale, Westchester County, all in New York State. Thus he arrived at the age of thirty without having even dreamed of a career of authorship. One day, reading a novel descriptive of English society, he impatiently threw down the book and exclaimed that he could write a better story himself. Challenged by his wife to do so, he wrote and published "Precaution" (1820), a dull and conventional story of English social life, purporting to be the work of an Englishman. Although the novel was not very successful, his friends urged Cooper to try again, and this time to write of scenes of which he had some personal knowledge. The publication of "The Spy, a Tale of the

---

6   In a note in the Boston *Yankee* for September, 1829.

Neutral Ground," in December, 1821, marks the beginning of a long series of successes. "The Spy" met with a large sale both in America and in England. It was soon translated into most of the cultivated languages of Europe; and its popularity has never greatly waned. It is a story of the American Revolution, in which the patriotic hero, Harvey Birch, signally aids the American cause and exhibits a rare combination of the spy and the gentleman.

During the twenty-nine years remaining to Cooper, he produced thirty-two further volumes, chiefly romances. Of these, many are now rarely read, but the following have retained their popularity for successive generations:

"The Spy," already referred to.

"The Leatherstocking Tales," comprising (in the chronological order not of their production, but of the narrative):

"The Deerslayer, or The First War Path," 1841.

"The Last of the Mohicans, a Narrative of 1757," 1826.

"The Pathfinder, or The Inland Sea," 1840.

"The Pioneers," 1823, and "The Prairie," 1827; and ten volumes of the "Sea Tales":

"The Pilot," 1823.

"The Red Rover," 1828.

"The Two Admirals," 1842.

"Homeward Bound, or The Chase," 1838.

"The Water-Witch, or The Skimmer of the Seas," 1830.

"The Wing-and-Wing, or Le Feu-Follet," 1842.

"Afloat and Ashore," 1844.

"Miles Wallingford," 1844, published in England as "Lucy Harding." A sequel to "Afloat and Ashore."

"Jack Tier, or The Florida Reefs," 1848.

"The Sea Lions, or The Lost Sealers," 1849.

The popularity which Cooper achieved, and which reached its height with the publication of "The Last of the Mohicans," was most remarkable; no other American has ever enjoyed anything like it. Not only were his stories read in well-nigh every household, but they were promptly dramatised, and furnished subjects for numerous paintings and poetical effusions. In Europe, his fame fairly rivalled that of Scott. In 1833, Samuel F. B. Morse, the inventor of the electric telegraph, wrote: "In every city of Europe that I visited the works of Cooper were conspicuously placed in the windows of every bookshop. They are published, as soon as he produces them, in thirty-four different places in Europe. They have been seen by American travellers in the languages of Turkey and Persia, in Constantinople, in Egypt, at Jerusalem, at Ispahan."

In 1822 Cooper removed with his family to New York, in order to be near his publisher and to put his daughters into school. There he founded a club, commonly known as the Bread and Cheese, to which many of the noted men of the time belonged. The years 1826–33 he spent in Europe, being for a part of this time United States consul at Lyons. On his return, he lived a few winters in New York; he then took up his permanent residence at Otsego Hall, Cooperstown, where he died in September, 1851.

In his later years, Cooper presented the singular spectacle of a popular novelist who was the most cordially hated man of his time. The fact is significant and helps to account for the failure of many of Cooper's later stories. An ardent lover of his country and its republican institutions, he boldly rebuked the ignorance and supercilious condescension of European critics; he wrote "The Bravo" (1831), "The Heidenmauer" (1832), and "The Headsman" (1833), for the avowed purpose of assailing monarchical and praising democratic institutions, and kept this purpose in mind much too constantly to produce artistic work. On his return to America, contrasting the restless exertion and bustle, the material progress which obscured higher ideals than money-making, with the leisure and dignified culture of European lands, he did not hesitate to speak plainly of the defects in the American character. This naturally brought him much abuse from the press; and an unfortunate dispute with the citizens of Cooperstown over the ownership of Three-Mile Point on Otsego Lake, though the right was wholly on his side, only made him more intensely disliked.

In the early '40's, certain issues arose in New York State between the tenants of the old Patroons who held their large estates under original grants, and their landlords, the tenants attempting to secure under State legislation a title in fee to their rented lands. Cooper, whose family interests were themselves likely to be affected by these claims, threw himself with full force and bitterness into the contest. In addition to a number of magazine articles and speeches, he devoted three volumes to the presentation of the claims of the landlords, volumes which are now read but little, excepting by special students of the subject. They are entitled respectively:

> "Satanstoe, or The Littlepage Manuscripts," 1845;
>
> "The Chainbearer," 1846; and
>
> "The Redskins, or Indian and Injin," 1846.
>
> "The Ways of the Hour" (1850) was also a novel with a purpose, which overweighted its interest as a story; the purpose was the reform of court procedure in the State of New York.

In "Homeward Bound" and its sequel, "Home as Found" (1838), the latter being one of his worst stories, Cooper lashed the petty vices of his countrymen and sought to show them what ought to be. As he might have expected, he only confirmed the public in its hatred of him, while he materially impaired his reputation as a story- teller. Had he been more tactful, philosophical, and far-seeing, he would have saved himself years of stormy conflict.

In Lakewood Cemetery at Cooperstown, on the hill overlooking Otsego Lake, is a majestic monument to Fenimore Cooper, twenty-five feet in height, and surmounted by a statue of the hunter Leatherstocking and his dog. As enduring as bronze is this character in our American fiction; the hero that will live longest of Cooper's creations. In him

Lowell found "the protagonist of our New World epic, a figure as poetic as that of Achilles, as ideally representative as that of Don Quixote, as romantic in his relation to our homespun and plebeian myths as Arthur in his to the mailed and plumed cycle of chivalry." The series in which he appears, "The Deerslayer," "The Pathfinder," "The Last of the Mohicans," "The Pioneers," and "The Prairie," the group which Cooper himself preferred to his other stories, is now (excepting always "The Spy") more read than all Cooper's other works put together. Drawn at first from life, Natty Bumppo becomes an idealised character, the perfect type of the bold frontiersman and scout, who read nature as an open book, and who was most at home when farthest from the haunts of the civilised world. Worthy to stand by his side is the noble Indian Chingachgook, "grave, silent, acute, self-contained," as Mr. James H. Morse says of him; "sufficiently lofty-minded to take in the greatness of the Indian's past, and sufficiently farsighted to see the hopelessness of his future,—with nobility of soul enough to grasp the white man's virtues, and with inherited wildness enough to keep him true to the instincts of his own race." Famous among Cooper's sailor folk is Long Tom Coffin, of "The Pilot"—type of the rough but honest seaman, superstitious like all seamen but devoutly religious, faithful to the last and capable of the most heroic self-sacrifice. Other characters scarcely less well drawn, if less famous, move through Cooper's pages—rough, uncouth waifs and strays of border life, grizzled old sea-dogs, soldiers' and sailors' wives and sweethearts, such as the wife of Ishmael Bush, Hetty and Judith Hutter, and Dew-of-June.

That he exhibited marked imperfections in style and technique no one will deny. He wrote too rapidly to attain to anything like elegance of style, and he is not infrequently obscure. He continually repeats words and expressions, to the great annoyance of the reader. The same carelessness that characterises his style is occasionally seen in the construction of his stories. Scenes are repeated. Mistakes due to forgetfulness occur, as in "Mercedes of Castile," where the heroine presents her lover, on his outward voyage, with a cross of sapphire stones, emblems, she tells him, of fidelity, which later appear as turquoise stones. Peculiarities of habit or manner are referred to so continually that the reader becomes weary and disgusted. Numerous characters are, it must be admitted, conventional in the extreme. Cooper failed signally in his fine women. They are not creatures of flesh and blood; they are purely imaginary creatures in petticoats, mere simulacra, invariably paragons of sweetness, discretion, and artlessness, ever saying and doing the correct thing until the reader longs for a little less of the angel and a good deal more of Mother Eve. Finally, his introductions are exceedingly prolix and tedious, though in this respect he sinned in company with Scott and many another of the time.

But we must not let this catalogue of Cooper's defects obscure his virtues. In spite of occasional carelessness of construction, all his best stories are highly interesting; he spins a good yarn. Never straining after effects, never loading his sentences with ornaments, when once started he moves straight ahead to his goal; one stirring scene follows another; there is wonderful fertility of resource, set forth with the confidence that begets faith. His was a large genius, which, though unsuccessful at miniature work, could manage a large canvas marvellously well. It must not be forgotten that Cooper was a pioneer; that he was the creator of our American romance of forest and prairie and sea. His descriptions of nature are done with the hand of a master. "If Cooper," remarked Balzac, "had succeeded in the painting of character to the same extent that he did in the painting of the phenomena of nature, he would have uttered the last word of our art." Moreover, Cooper's stories are honest and wholesome like himself; they breathe the same genuineness, the same sincerity and hatred of shams and meanness; they uniformly hold up noble and worthy ideals; their tone is always as healthful and invigorating as a breath of ozone. As Professor Trent remarks, he "lifted the story of adventure into the realms of poetry"; and as the poet of the primeval American forest he has never been superseded.

Professor Lounsbury, whose Life of Cooper, in the "American Men of Letters" Series, remains the authoritative biography, sums up the man and his work as follows:

> America has had among her representatives of the irritable race of writers many who have shown far more ability to get on pleasantly with their fellows than Cooper. She has had several gifted with higher spiritual insight than he, with broader and juster views of life, with finer ideals

of literary art, and, above all, with far greater delicacy of taste. But she counts on the scanty roll of her men of letters the name of no one who acted from purer patriotism or loftier principle. She finds among them all no manlier nature, and no more heroic soul.

Mr. W. C. Brownell prepared for the Iroquois Edition of Cooper's Works a critical introduction which may safely be accepted as the most just, most delicate, and most comprehensive analysis of the man and of his work. Mr. Brownell writes:

> There is a quality in Cooper's romance, however, that gives it as romance an almost unique distinction. I mean its solid and substantial alliance with reality. It is thoroughly romantic, and yet—very likely owing to his imaginative deficiency, if anything can be so owing—it produces, for romance, an almost unequalled illusion of life itself.... Cooper's ... work is in no sense a *jardin des plantes*; it is like the woods and sea that mainly form its subject and substance. Only critical myopia can be blind to the magnificent forest, with its pioneer clearings, its fringe of "settlements," its wood-embosomed lakes, its neighbouring prairie on the one side, and on the other the distant ocean with the cities of its farther shore—the splendid panorama of man, of nature, and of human life unrolled for us by this large intelligence and noble imagination, this manly and patriotic American representative in the literary parliament of the world.

The Elder Dana.—Richard Henry Dana (1787–1879), lawyer, politician, poet, critic, and novelist, was one of the group of Boston writers that laid the foundations of New England literature. His tales, "Tom Thornton" and "Paul Felton," are romantic stories of villainy and insanity, and give evidence of the influence of Brockden Brown. The narrative has at times an impetuous sweep that hurries the reader along in spite of himself; and the characterisation is wrought with powerful strokes. A collective edition of his "Poems and Prose Writings" appeared in 1833.

Miss Sedgwick and Mrs. Child.—Catherine Maria Sedgwick (1789–1867) was the daughter of Judge Theodore Sedgwick and was born at Stockbridge, Massachusetts, where she was principal of a young ladies' school for half a century. Her duties as a teacher did not prevent her from becoming a voluminous novelist. Her first story was "A New England Tale" (1822), which at once found favour. "Redwood" (1824) was translated into three or four Continental languages; on the title-page of the French translation, the novel was ascribed to Fenimore Cooper. Other novels which achieved great popularity for their faithful portraiture of early and contemporary New England life were "Hope Leslie, or Early Times in Massachusetts" (1827), "Clarence, a Tale of Our Own Times" (1830), "The Linwoods, or Sixty Years Since in America" (1835), and "Married or Single" (1857). While Miss Sedgwick never rises to the height of absorbing interest, she is rarely dull, and some of her women, if we allow for the difference in time, do not suffer in comparison with those of Mrs. Stowe and Mrs. Wilkins Freeman. Her descriptions of simple country life were superior to any that had hitherto appeared. Mrs. Child, born Lydia Maria Francis (1802–1880), who likewise spent her life in Massachusetts, began writing early, producing her first novel, "Hobomok," in 1824 and her second, "The Rebels," a year later. The former deals with Salem life in colonial times; the latter is a story of the Revolution, describing the sack of Governor Hutchinson's house and the Boston massacre. Although they give true pictures of early Puritan customs, they are not powerful as fiction. In 1836 she essayed a more ambitious flight in "Philothea," a romance of the days of Pericles, which, in spite of its stilted rhetoric, reveals some imaginative power and deserves mention as a pioneer attempt to interpret Greek life to America.

Timothy Flint.—A voluminous writer and in his day a well-known figure was Timothy Flint (1780–1840), a native of Reading, Massachusetts, and a graduate of Harvard in the class of 1800. Becoming a Congregational minister, in 1815, in search for health, he crossed the Alleghany Mountains with his family, and after travelling in Ohio, Indiana, and Illinois, became a missionary, first at St. Charles, Missouri, and then in Arkansas. The success of his "Recollections of the Last Ten Years" (1826) led him to publish a novel, "Francis Berrian, or The Mexican Patriot" (1826), dealing with adventures with the Comanche Indians, and with the Mexican struggle of 1821, which resulted in the fall of Iturbide.

The story was crude and improbable, but some of its descriptions found favour. "Arthur Clenning," his second novel, published in 1828, includes a shipwreck in the Southern Ocean, after which the hero and heroine arrive in New Holland and later settle in Illinois. He wrote some other novels, but none has survived. For a time (1833), Flint edited *The Knickerbocker*; and in 1835 he contributed some "Sketches of the Literature of the United States" to the London *Athenæum*.

William Austin (1788–1841) a lawyer of Charlestown, Massachusetts, deserves to be noticed for the remarkable story of "Peter Rugg, the Missing Man," which he wrote for *The New England Galaxy* (1827–8; reprinted in "The Boston Book," 1841, and in other books and papers). The theme is the same as that of "The Wandering Jew." While "originating in the inventive genius of its author," as Joseph Buckingham says of it, it doubtless owed something also to German romance.

Nathaniel Hawthorne.—The greatest genius among American writers of romance, by many held to be the supreme literary artist of America, was Nathaniel Hawthorne. He was peculiarly a product of New England and frankly admitted that New England was quite as large a lump of earth as his heart could take in. His ancestor, William Hathorne, came to the New World in 1630, in the ship with John Winthrop and Thomas Dudley, and became a leader in the colony. Hathorne's son John was one of the judges in the witchcraft trials at Salem in 1691. The grandfather and father of Nathaniel Hawthorne were both sea-captains. The novelist was born at Salem on July 4, 1804. Four years later, his father, never apparently a robust man, died at Surinam, and the widowed mother began to live in a deep seclusion which could not fail to have its effect upon the quick sensibilities of her son. In 1818, the family removed to Raymond, on the shore of Sebago Lake, in Maine, where his grandfather Manning owned large tracts of land. Hawthorne's boyhood environment, therefore, was not widely different from that of Fenimore Cooper. But he was more of a reader than Cooper. As a boy, he became familiar with Shakespeare, Milton, Bunyan, Clarendon, Froissart, Rousseau, and Godwin. Entering Bowdoin College, he was graduated in 1825 in the class with Longfellow. While he did not distinguish himself in his studies, he became a respectable Latin and English scholar; and he devoted much time to reading in the little library of the Athenæan Society. At graduation, he ranked eighteenth in a class of thirty-eight. Meanwhile his family had returned to Salem, and thither Hawthorne now went, to begin a period of literary apprenticeship. It was seemingly a bold undertaking to attempt to live by his pen; however, he seems to have drifted into the attempt through aversion to a more active life. In 1828, he published anonymously a novel called "Fanshawe," dealing with some of his college experiences and recalling vaguely the methods of Scott. Some characters, it must be said, are vigorously conceived, and here and there the volume gave promise of the author's future skill; but there is about the whole a suggestion of unreality, not to say crudeness. The book found, as it deserved, an indifferent public, and Hawthorne subsequently recalled as many copies as he could procure and burned them. For several years, he continued to live in seclusion, contributing stories and sketches to various annuals and periodicals. For the stories he got $35 each. In March, 1837, having been encouraged by his friend Horatio Bridge, he published the first volume to appear with his name, "Twice-Told Tales." They were eighteen in number, being only half of the stories he is known to have printed up to this time. The "Tales" gave Hawthorne a considerable reputation; Longfellow praised it in *The North American Review*, then influential in literary affairs. Again helped by his friends, in January, 1839, Hawthorne assumed the position of weigher and gauger in the Boston Custom-House. At first, the novelty of contact with the practical world interested him; but he soon found that his work, always monotonous, left him no time or strength for writing, and he was not sorry to lose his post when the Whigs came into power in 1841. For a few months, he tried life at Brook Farm, thinking that in this new community he should find a suitable way of combining manual and intellectual labour; but the work was too hard, and he had too little opportunity for writing. Accordingly in 1842 he left the Farm, married Miss Sophia A. Peabody, to whom he had been engaged for four years, and settled at the Old Manse, an idyllic retreat at Concord, Massachusetts. Meanwhile, he had published (1841) two volumes of historical tales for young people, "Grandfather's Chair" and "Famous Old People"; and to these he now added a third series, "The Liberty Tree," as well as a second series of "Twice-Told Tales" and a volume of "Biographical Stories for Children" (1842). Of these, none except the "Tales" rises much above the level of respectable writing to sell. In the next four years, Hawthorne wrote for periodicals some eighteen more tales, which, together with a number of earlier uncollected stories, he republished in 1846 as "Mosses from an Old Manse." Hawthorne now returned to his native Salem as surveyor of customs (1846–9), and proved an able administrator of the office. Another period of literary barrenness ensued, but in 1847 he resumed his writing and produced a few tales. The idea of a longer romance had come to him, and after his dismissal from office in 1849 he found the leisure necessary for writing "The Scarlet Letter." Once more, then, he exchanged the world of affairs for that realm of the imagination where he was so much more at home. Working resolutely amid sickness and poverty, he at length completed the splendid romance, the publication of which distinguishes the year 1850 in American letters as Tennyson's "In Memoriam" and Wordsworth's "Prelude" do in English poetry. Hawthorne had now entered upon a period of great productivity. In the next two years he published "The House of the Seven Gables" (1851), "A Wonder-Book for Girls and Boys" (1851), "The Snow Image and Other Tales" (1851), "Tanglewood Tales," (1852), "The Blithedale Romance" (1852), a tale based on his Brook Farm life, and a campaign "Life of Franklin Pierce," his college friend, now a candidate for the Presidency. Promptly after his election, President Pierce made Hawthorne consul at Liverpool, an office which he held from July, 1853, until September, 1857. Though rich in experience and in fruitful observation, his life in England was outwardly quiet and uneventful. The years 1857–9 the Hawthornes spent in Italy, where they mingled somewhat more with the world than had been their wont. The fruit of the Italian life was "The Marble Faun" (1860), written in Italy and at Redcar, on the shore of the North Sea, and published in England as "Transformation." Returning to America in 1860, Hawthorne passed the next four years at the Wayside, Concord. In 1863 he contributed "Our Old Home" to *The Atlantic Monthly* and began "The Dolliver Romance," which he was destined not to finish. He died suddenly on May 18, 1864, at Plymouth, N. H., while on a journey to the New Hampshire lakes in search of health.

His literary remains must be at least mentioned. In 1868 appeared "Passages from American Note-Books"; in 1870, "Passages from English Note-Books"; and in 1871, "Passages from French and Italian Note-Books." These volumes throw much light on Hawthorne's favourite haunts and wandering propensities, as well as his eagerness for minute observation. "Septimius Felton, or, The Elixir of Life" (1871) was to be a story, placed in Revolutionary times, of a man who sought earthly immortality. The theme was a powerful one; but Hawthorne's strength was evidently exhausted, and the story must be pronounced a failure. The last works to appear were "The Dolliver Romance" (1876) and "Doctor Grimshaw's Secret," which are fragmentary and ineffective studies of the same theme as "Septimius Felton." Their failure, in all probability, was due not only to the waning of Hawthorne's powers but also to the difficulties attending the theme itself.

Hawthorne was one of the shyest of men. Kenyon, in "The Marble Faun," says: "Between man and man there is always an insuperable gulf"; such a gulf at any rate separated Kenyon's creator from the rest of mankind. Always fond of solitude, he lived in a world of his own, apart from humankind; longing at times for more familiar converse with men, but never quite successful in establishing cordial relations (outside of his own family) with any but a few friends. Possessed of an exquisitely sensitive nature, he made no effort to conceal the pleasure which honest praise afforded him; and he was easily rebuffed by the coolness of his public. Perhaps the bane of his life was self-distrust. Each of his books when first written seemed to him well-nigh worthless. James T. Fields has told of the difficulty with which he extracted from Hawthorne the first manuscript of "The Scarlet Letter." "Thus it is with winged horses," says Hawthorne in "The Chimæra," "and with such wild and solitary creatures. If you can catch and overcome them, it is the surest way to win their love." Such was the devotion with which Hawthorne repaid those who had "captured" him that their confident encouragement greatly strengthened and inspired him. As might be supposed, however, with the world at large he was lacking in sympathy. His point of view was fixed; he could not see the world with the eyes of another. This helps to account for the effect of harshness and asperity which his chapter on "The Custom House" in "The Scarlet Letter" had upon the people of Salem whom he there described; and for the similar effect of the descriptions of English life in "Our Old Home" upon the English people in general. As Professor Woodberry remarks, too, he had "the critical spirit which is a New England trait, and with this went its natural attendant, the habit of speaking his mind." He had, moreover, deeply rooted prejudices and a natural hatred of shams. He disliked literary friendships. While in England, for example, he remained a stranger to the brilliant literary set in London where he might have been warmly welcomed. He saw Tennyson once in Manchester, but made no effort to meet the poet. Another of his aversions concerned the manifestations of spiritualism—rappings, tipping of tables, spirit writing, and the like; he was a good hater of shams in general.

To his family, Hawthorne was always deeply devoted. When his mother died, although there had always been "a sort of coldness of intercourse" between them, he spoke of the time as the darkest hour he had ever lived through. His wife worshipped him, and the attitude of his children is sufficiently indicated by the words of his son Julian: "In my thought of him he has a quality not to be described; that is associated with the early impressions which make the name of home beautiful; with a child's delight in the glory of nature; with a boy's aspirations towards a pure and generous career; with intimate conceptions of truth, bravery, and simplicity."

So much for the man; what now, shall be said of the artist? In the first place, as he was the peculiar product of New England Puritanism, so his genius was in a sense confined to setting forth New England and the problems of New England Calvinism. Even when he lays the scene of his tale in Rome, there is the same interest in the working out of the consequences of sin, and part of the characters are Americans living in the Eternal City. Hawthorne still stands alone in having given supreme literary expression to that earnest and virile if narrow and at times misguided life of early New England; its pathos, its tragedy, its legacy to modern times. Then it must be observed that in doing this he places himself in the ranks of the great masters in deducing from the individual the general experience; from the particular the universal moral life. In his earlier years he delighted in allegory, of which the "Tales" and the "Mosses" are full; and he was always fond of symbolism. Lady Eleanore's mantle, for example, is a symbol of pride; the scarlet letter is a symbol of sin; no less is Donatello a symbol, a type of universal innocence tasting of the knowledge of good and evil—the missing link, as it were, in the evolution of moral instincts. Hawthorne constantly describes the unseen in terms of the seen, the spiritual world by means of the every day, material world.

The "Tales" have been most elaborately characterised by Professor Woodberry in his admirable biography.[7] Many of them are intrinsically slight—descriptions of the common events of daily life, always somewhat moralised, and to an increasing extent as the author grew older. In some the fancy has free rein, as in "The Seven Vagabonds" and "The Great Stone Face." In "Tales of the Province House" and many others Hawthorne skilfully wove threads of colonial history with the rich woof of his imagination to produce a splendid romantic pageant. Sometimes he treats of individuals, as in "David Swan" and "Rappaccini's Daughter"; often he studies the group, or the crowd, as in the "The Celestial Railroad," "The Christmas Banquet," "The Procession of Life." In all, he studies the moral life and tries to understand the significance of some phase of universal human experience.

"The Scarlet Letter" has been called by Mr. James "the most distinctive piece of prose fiction that was to spring from American soil." It is a grim tragedy, in which the consequences of sin are depicted with a simplicity, a steady movement, and a relentlessness characteristic of the tragedies of Euripides. Hester Prynne and Arthur Dimmesdale living agonised lives which moved steadily towards the day of expiatory shame; Roger Chilingworth, outwardly the wise, benevolent physician, inwardly the ghastly demon gloating over his victim—these figures indeed move us to pity and fear, and give us a new sense of the depth and mystery of our human life, which no man liveth to himself alone, but which must be interpreted as the expression and result of racial upstriving through myriads of years. "The Scarlet Letter" is indeed, as Mr. W. C. Brownell says,[8] the Puritan "Faust"; and many will doubtless agree with him in calling it "our one prose masterpiece."

In "The House of the Seven Gables," Hawthorne returns to the present and studies the workings of heredity. Less gloomy than the earlier story, this one is still sombre and in part removed from the world of objective reality. Real enough, to be sure, are the commonplace features of daily life at the Seven Gables, the pinched features and heroic heart of Hepzibah, and the homely philosophising of Uncle Venner; but Jaffrey and Clifford Pyncheon are at best shadowy and unreal. Holgrave, too,

---

7   "Nathaniel Hawthorne," Boston, 1902 ("American Men of Letters"), pp. 124–58.
8   *Scribner's Magazine*, January, 1908, xliii. 84.

belongs to a type which, common enough in the days of Brook Farm Fourierism, has now well-nigh passed away. Phœbe Pyncheon is one of the most delicate and exquisite of all Hawthorne's portraits; as Dr. Holmes wrote to the author, "the flavour of the sweet-fern and the bayberry are not truer to the soil than the native sweetness of our little Phœbe." It is interesting to note that when the book appeared Hawthorne wrote to his friend Horatio Bridge:

> "The House of the Seven Gables," in my opinion, is better than "The Scarlet Letter"; but I should not wonder if I had refined upon the principal character a little too much for popular appreciation, nor if the romance of the book should be somewhat at odds with the humble and familiar scenery in which I invest it. But I feel that portions of it are as good as anything I can hope to write.

More able critics than one have pronounced "The Blithedale Romance" the most perfect of Hawthorne's stories. Although he wrote to George William Curtis that the story had essentially nothing to do with Brook Farm, it is certain that the community formed more than a background for the story, and furnished some of its incidents and the traits of some of the characters. Thus the romance may be said to approach more closely to real life than any other of the greater works. The characters are drawn with great distinctness of outline: Hollingsworth the reformer, earnest, stern, engrossed in his reform undertaking to the point of selfishness; Miles Coverdale, the dreamer, who bears the ear-marks of his artist creator, always a spectator of, rather than a participant in, the life at Blithedale; Priscilla, the timid maid who seemed to have dropped down from the clouds and sought protection in this retreat; Zenobia with her splendid beauty, her refinement, her ardour, her despair when disillusionment comes—all these are highly individualised. It has been complained, and with justice, that neither Zenobia nor Priscilla is a typical New England girl; but something may perhaps be conceded to the romantic atmosphere of the tale; the author did not promise a transcript from prosaic real life. The plot halts now and then, and does not move steadily and convincingly to its climax. The inserted story of "The Veiled Lady" does not materially further the plot. Yet as a whole the romance is a searching and remarkable presentment of Hawthorne's views of reform. He was never a reformer; he distrusted the excess of zeal, the narrowness of vision too often characteristic of the more ardent reformers of his day; and with great skill he has here set forth the illusory hopes, the discouragement, the sense of impotence and defeat that must attend the outcome of radical schemes for human improvement which are not grounded on sound and wide knowledge of man's nature.

Probably the most popular, as it was the most ambitious, of all the romances, has been "The Marble Faun." With consummate skill the author maintains the mystery necessary for the romantic atmosphere and at the same time draws in clear outlines the four characters in the little drama—this miniature world-tragedy, this "story of the fall of man repeated," as Miriam says. As Mr. Lathrop has pointed out, moreover, with the main theme, itself of abiding interest, is joined a study of the psychology of Beatrice Cenci's story; but, without stopping where Shelley stopped, Hawthorne went on to show how Miriam and Donatello might "work out their purification." Thus while the romance may, as one critic avers, "begin in mystery and end in mist," the end is nevertheless full of hope.

Hawthorne has never been, and doubtless never will be, a popular novelist. His stories are for the few, the thoughtful readers who are willing to read old favourites over and over again. But there will always be such persons, haply in increasing numbers; and for them Hawthorne will continue to be a unique personality, the "high untrammelled thinker," the interpreter of spiritual mysteries.

Charles Sealsfield.—Although not mentioned by most historians of American literature, the Austrian novelist Carl Postl ("Charles Sealsfield," 1793–1864) deserves to be recalled here from the fact that his works deal chiefly with American life and in their English form enjoyed considerable popularity in America. Born in Poppitz, Moravia, he became at first a priest of the order of the Kreuzherren von Pöltenberg; but, having broken with Catholic dogma, he fled from the cloister and arrived in New York in 1823 as Charles Sealsfield. He remained in America until 1832, travelling extensively and making close studies of life and character. His first novel, "Tokeah, or The White Rose; an Indian Tale" (Philadelphia, 1828), was republished at Zurich in 1833 as "Der Legitime und die Republikaner"; while never a popular story in America, it seems, as Professor Faust has discovered,[9] to have furnished Mrs. Jackson with some hints for her "Ramona" and Charles F. Hoffman with a *motif* for his "Vigil of Faith." After his return to Europe Sealsfield published, among other things, "Transatlantische Reiseskizzen" (1833), translated as "Life in the New World, or Sketches of American Society" (1844), which originally appeared in *The New York Mirror* in 1827–8 and which furnished Simms with some scenes for "Guy Rivers"; "Nathan der Squatter Regulator" (1837), translated as "Life in Texas" (1845); "Der Virey und die Aristokraten, oder Mexiko im Jahre 1812" (1834); "Morton, oder Die grosse Tour" (1835); "Das Cajütenbuch, oder Nationale Charakteristiken" (1841), translated as "The Cabin Book" (1844), which furnished Mayne Reid with the last ten chapters of his "Wild Life" without change; and "Süden und Norden" (1842–3), translated as "North and South, or Scenes and Adventures in Mexico" (1844). In his vigorous delineations of the crude American life of the twenties and thirties, Sealsfield exhibited great enthusiasm, a wide range of observation which overlooked nothing and which measured impartially, and a comprehension of the true inwardness of our young institutions such as no native American of his day possessed. If his exaggerating brush failed of the touch of an artist, he created some characters, such as Morton and Nathan Strong, who deserve immortality as typical Americans, and described with inimitable fidelity "the dauntless squatter and sturdy pioneer, the Southern planter and patriarchal slave-holder, the grasping millionaire and his emissaries, the New York dandy and the society belle, the taciturn Yankee sea-captain and the hot-blooded Kentuckian, the utilitarian alcalde and the reformed desperado."

William Leggett (1802–39), after spending some time at Georgetown College, accompanied his family in 1819 to make a settlement on the prairies of Illinois. He spent the years 1822–26 as a midshipman in the navy. His experiences of pioneer and sea life were graphically portrayed in "The Rifle," published in 1828 in *The Atlantic Souvenir*, and in "Tales by a Country Schoolmaster" (1835). For the remainder of his life he was engaged in journalism, from 1829 till 1836 as one of the editors of *The Evening Post*.

---

9   "Charles Sealsfield (Carl Postl), Materials for a Biography; a Study of his Style; his Influence upon American Literature," Baltimore, 1892.

Southern Novelists.—Thus far we have considered no native Southern writer of fiction. The novel ripened late in the South; indeed, only one writer of fiction of the first rank was produced by the South before the Civil War. Yet in the varied and picturesque life of the aristocratic planters, the frontiersmen, the "poor whites," and the negroes there were rich materials for the artist and the story-teller, who in due time began to avail themselves of their opportunity. "The Valley of the Shenandoah" (1824) by George Tucker (1775–1861), though reprinted in England and translated into German, possesses slight worth, and little more can be said of his "Voyage to the Moon" (1827), a satirical romance; yet these works gave promise of better things from the South. William A. Carruthers (1806–72), a voluminous contributor to magazines, wrote two novels, "The Cavaliers of Virginia" (1832) and "The Knights of the Horseshoe" (1845), which, in spite of serious defects, deal with colonial days in Virginia in a genial, vigorous, and unhackneyed manner.

"Davy" Crockett (1786–1836), crude, unlettered hunter, backwoodsman, and Congressman, published, in his "Autobiography" (1834), a collection of thrilling narratives of adventure remarkable for directness, vividness, and virility. The "Georgia Scenes, Characters, and Incidents" (1835) of Augustus B. Longstreet (1790–1870), who was for many years a college president, revealed the curious traits of the poor whites or "Crackers" of Georgia. "The Partisan Leader" (1836) by Nathaniel Beverley Tucker (1784–1851) dealt with the encroachments of the Federal Government upon the rights of the States, and prophesied with startling and accurate logic the terrible disruption which occurred a quarter of a century later. If artistically imperfect, it is a stirring tale, intense in its action, and of heroic strain. But it can scarcely be said that any of these works now survive. They are mainly important as illustrating the evolution of Southern fiction. With Kennedy and Simms, however, the South takes a high place in the fiction of America.

John Pendleton Kennedy.—For John Pendleton Kennedy (1795–1870), literature was never more than a pastime, a fact much to be regretted. Kennedy belonged to a prominent and wealthy family. He was born in Baltimore, was graduated from Baltimore College in 1812, and studied law. Entering political life, he employed his pen effectively in the defence of his political principles, but occasionally amused himself with ventures in lighter forms of literature. His first work of importance, "Swallow Barn" (1832), was distinctly declared not to be a novel; and indeed the action is of slight importance. His main purpose in writing it was to give, in connection with a slender plot, a picture of manners and customs in Virginia toward the end of the eighteenth century. Here is no subtle characterisation; the persons of the narrative are drawn broadly and naturally and the story moves easily, if a little slowly, to its end. The local scenery and institutions are delineated with the utmost fidelity. Frank Meriwether, the prosperous country gentleman and magistrate, has been called a Virginia Sir Roger de Coverley; and there is throughout observed the same quiet good humour, the same cheerful atmosphere, the same genial optimism that one finds in the pages of Addison. "Horse-Shoe Robinson, a Tale of the Tory Ascendency" (1835), was a story of early Tory days in South Carolina, and is now generally considered the best novel written in the South before the Civil War. The action centres about the battle of King's Mountain (1780), which is vividly and accurately described. The intrepid valour of the backwoods patriot, the bitterness and horror of civil war, the relieving and characteristic humour of primitive frontier life, are well portrayed. The blacksmith Galbraith Robinson is a typical American, worthy to rank with Cooper's Leatherstocking, and possibly truer to nature than Cooper's more famous creation. In 1838 appeared Kennedy's third novel, "Rob of the Bowl: a Legend of St. Inigoes," a story of Colonial Maryland and the struggles of the Catholic settlers, with which are interwoven traditions of the piratical "Brethren of the Coast." Nor must we fail to mention the humorous chronicle entitled "Quodlibet: Containing some Annals thereof, by Solomon Secondthought, Schoolmaster" (1840), in which are described the vagaries and absurdities of an early Presidential election. Had Kennedy made literature the serious business of life he would have won more lasting fame. As it is, he deserves to be more widely read than he is.[10]

William Gilmore Simms.—One of the most prolific of American novelists was William Gilmore Simms. Born in Charleston, South Carolina, April 17, 1806, he was early left, by the death of his mother and the removal of his father to Tennessee, to the care of his grandmother, from

---

10 It has been alleged that by invitation Kennedy wrote the fourth chapter of the second volume of Thackeray's "Virginians" (1857–9; Tauchnitz Edition, vols. 425, 441). Mrs. Ritchie, Thackeray's daughter, however, believes that Kennedy only gave her father many hints and facts.

whom he learned many a weird tale of peril and adventure. From the poor schools of his time he gained little, though he became an omnivorous reader. Apprenticed to a druggist, at eighteen he turned to the study of law. A long visit to his father in the South-west gave him a good opportunity to study the primitive life of the backwoodsmen, a life which he afterward described inimitably. At twenty he married and in another year he was admitted to the bar. Successful from the first, he resolutely turned, however, from the practice of law to a literary life. He had become well known as a poet when his first prose tale, "Martin Faber, the Story of a Criminal," appeared in 1833, revealing the influence of William Godwin and Brockden Brown, but also independent skill in the construction of an interesting narrative. In "Guy Rivers" (1834), a description of Georgia in the turbulent days of the gold fever, Simms began a series of border romances which, though marred by a slipshod style and by roughness of construction, are nevertheless in the main readable on account of the rapidity and energy of the narrative. In "The Yemassee" (1835), a story of the strife between South Carolina and the Indians in 1715, Simms is perhaps at his best, and his stirring narrative strongly reminds one of, though it does not rival, the work of Cooper. Then came a trilogy, "The Partisan" (1835), "Mellichampe: a Legend of the Santee" (1836), and "Katharine Walton, or The Rebel of Dorchester" (1851), in which he portrays every phase of social life in Charleston during the Revolutionary War, and delineates the military careers of Marion, Pickens, Moultrie, Sumter, and Hayne. Between 1836 and 1859 he published some twenty-five other novels and stories, generally in two volumes each, the best of which are "The Kinsmen" (1841), afterwards known as "The Scout," (1854), "The Sword and the Distaff," now known as "Woodcraft" (1852), "The Forayers, or The Raid of the Dog-Days" (1855), its sequel, "Eutaw" (1856), and "The Cassique of Kiawah" (1859). He also wrote numerous short stories for various periodicals; one of these, "Grayling, or Murder Will Out," published in *The Gift* for 1842, was pronounced by Poe the best ghost story he had ever read. A collection of thirteen of Simms' best stories was published in 1845–46 under the title of "The Wigwam and the Cabin." Notwithstanding his immense popularity before the Civil War, Simms is now well-nigh forgotten. Although a conscientious workman, he wrote much too rapidly to produce permanent literature, and his faulty style and his excessive fondness for portraying in detail scenes of carnage and crime strongly repel the reader of to-day. After the Civil War, which Simms did much to bring on and from which he suffered severe losses, his popularity rapidly waned, and he tried in vain to make good his losses. He died in his native city on June 11, 1870, having composed this epitaph for himself: "Here lies one who, after a reasonably long life, distinguished chiefly by unceasing labours, has left all his better works undone."

His remarkable achievement in the pioneer days of American letters, on the whole, entitles him to be remembered with gratitude; and the verdict of Poe, who ranked Simms, as a novelist, just below Cooper and Brockden Brown, has not been impugned.[11]

Edgar Allan Poe.—No American writer is more difficult to judge than Edgar Allan Poe (1809–49), whether as a man or as a writer; and perhaps no other writer has received more attention from critics, not only in America but also in Europe. Poe was born in Boston of Southern parents, in the year which saw the birth of Tennyson, Darwin, Gladstone, and Holmes. His mother, Elizabeth Arnold Poe, was an actress, who died in 1811 of consumption; his father, David Poe, Jr., for a time a strolling player, was a man of little force; tradition represents him as dying young, a victim of consumption and alcoholism. Adopted after his mother's death by John Allan of Richmond, Virginia, the boy Edgar Poe was wondered at and spoiled by his foster-parents, who were people of means and position. When they went abroad in 1815, Poe was entered at the Manor House School, Stoke Newington, near London; here he remained five years, imbibing the influences of a half-rural scene whose ancient buildings and historical associations have since been swallowed up by the metropolis. From 1820 to 1825 he was at school in Richmond. As a child, Poe was beautiful and clever; as a youth he was superior rather than abnormal. He learned quickly though not accurately; for the inaccuracy his teachers were in part to blame. He was lithe, swift of foot, an excellent swimmer, and, though proud and self-centred, could play the leader among his fellows. By the time he was ready for college, he showed the effects of indulgence on the part of the Allans, being imperious and wilful, unduly sensitive as to his state of orphanage, and squandering his too abundant pocket-money. During his brief residence at the University of Virginia (1826), Poe maintained high scholarship in Latin and French,

---

11   See Professor Trent's biography, "American Men of Letters" Series, 1892.

but lived the life of his companions, drinking (though apparently not to excess) and incurring gambling debts which his guardian repudiated. Set to work in the counting-room of Mr. Allan, the young man rebelled and ran away to Boston, probably under an assumed name, and without capital save a sheaf of immature poems. He soon enlisted as a private in the army, made his peace with his guardian, and was sent to West Point. Here again he proved a clever student; but, purposely neglecting the routine, in 1831 he was discharged.

Obliged henceforth to depend on his own resources, Poe now approached almost to the point of starvation, when by his "Manuscript Found in a Bottle" (1833) he gained a prize of one hundred dollars offered by the Baltimore *Saturday Visiter*, and through John P. Kennedy, whom Poe called "the first true friend I ever had," obtained temporary relief for his wants and help in getting literary work. He now became a contributor to, and soon the literary editor of, *The Southern Literary Messenger*. His numerous stories and criticisms did much to make the magazine successful and famous. In 1836 Poe married his beautiful cousin Virginia Clemm, who lacked three months of being fourteen years of age; but family ties could not prevent his morally weak nature from occasional indulgence in drugs and intoxicants, and his irregularities in January, 1837, brought about his dismissal from the editorial chair of the *Messenger*, for which, however, he continued to write. For a time the Poes now lived in New York, practically supported by Mrs. Clemm, who conducted a boarding-house. Here he completed and published his longest story, "The Narrative of Arthur Gordon Pym" (1838), a tale of an Antarctic cruise as far south as the 84th parallel, based on Benjamin Morell's "Narrative of Four Voyages to the South Seas and Pacific" (1832) with frequent dashes of Coleridge's "Ancient Mariner," but full of such situations of blood-curdling horror and such highly imaginative landscape-painting as only the genius of Poe could produce. The years 1838–44 Poe spent in Philadelphia. In 1839 he collected and published his "Tales of the Grotesque and the Arabesque." He wrote constantly for *Graham's Magazine*, of which he was editor from 1840 till 1843; critiques, essays, and tales flowed from his pen. In imaginative story-telling, this was the period of his best work. His occasional lapses into intoxication are partly explained by the fits of insanity brought on by anxiety over the precarious condition of his wife, who in 1841 ruptured a blood-vessel while singing and who hovered between life and death for six years. The year 1844 found him back in New York, associated first with N. P. Willis on *The Evening Mirror* and later with Charles F. Briggs on *The Broadway Journal*. The publication of "The Raven" in the *Mirror* (January 29, 1845) and of his "Tales" (1845) greatly increased his reputation; but with curious and fatal perversity he proceeded to make enemies by trying to palm off upon the Boston Lyceum (October 16, 1845) a juvenile poem, "Al Aaraaf," as a new work and by sharply castigating his literary contemporaries in "The Literati of New York." The next year he removed his family to Fordham, a suburb of New York. Here his young wife died in 1847, of consumption; and he never really recovered from the shock. He conceived various literary enterprises; but he had become virtually a physical and moral wreck, unable to work except at long intervals. Toward the end of 1848 he proposed marriage to Mrs. Sarah Helen Whitman, a Providence poet, and was accepted; but the match was broken off in consequence of Poe's drinking to excess. He now determined to go South to lecture and procure funds with which to publish a magazine to be called *The Stylus*. At Philadelphia he had an attack of delirium tremens. Recovering, he went on to Richmond, where he spent the summer of 1849. He proposed marriage to an old flame, Mrs. Sarah Elmira Shelton, then a widow, who gave him some encouragement. About this time he signed a pledge to abstain from all intoxicating drinks, and made a new start in life. A lecture at the Exchange Hotel brought him some $1500; and with this in his pocket he started for New York to close up some business and take Mrs. Clemm back with him; but stopping in Baltimore *en route* he was induced to drink some wine, went on a debauch, and a few days later (October 7th) died in a hospital of brain fever. There is ground for believing that he had been drugged by political toughs on election day (October 3d) and carried to various polls to vote for the Whig candidates.

Such was the pathetic and tragic career of one of the most brilliant of American literary men. Few lives have been the subjects of so much controversy. In estimating his character, justice must be tempered with mercy; and this is the easier now that it is seen that, during at least the latter part of his life, his mental condition was abnormal if not pathological.[12] He inherited tendencies which he was unable to control, and

---

12 See Émile Lauvrière, "Edgar Poe, sa vie et son œuvre, étude de psychologie pathologique," Paris, 1904.

with which his environment wholly unfitted him to cope. When sober and sane, he was a quiet, well-bred, and refined gentleman, who could talk fascinatingly and in whom women found "a peculiar and irresistible charm"; he was capable, moreover, of working hard and efficiently. When under the influence of opium or intoxicating liquors, he was a wholly different man, with whom, fortunately, we are not here concerned. With the two exceptions of his wife and mother-in-law, he formed no close and lasting attachments. He was always deeply self-centred and found it impossible to enter sympathetically into the lives, sorrows, and aspirations of others. Thus his sensitive temperament more and more withdrew into itself and found its kindred in the phantasms of his powerful imagination.

Poe's genius is probably best expressed in his tales. They are not bulky in extent; in the Putnam edition they fill five octavo volumes. Many of them are marred by journalistic looseness and mannerisms—too much use of the parenthesis, the too constant recurrence of favourite words and phrases. Occasionally he misses good opportunities for telling dramatic effects and contrasts; and in general it may be admitted that the element of human passion, "save in its minor chords of sorrow and despair," is notably absent from his works. A passionate lover himself, his artistic genius was not concerned with the ordinary love-story. His lack of a sense of humour, too, has been remarked. His attempts to be humorous cannot be pronounced successful. Finally, some of his tales, "Arthur Gordon Pym" for example, contain matter so repulsive that the wonder is that any person could endure reading them, much less writing them.

Yet the fact remains that on a large number of these tales is the unmistakable stamp of genius. It may be well to recall the classification of them adopted by Messrs. Stedman and Woodberry. We have first the "Romances of Death," of which the most famous are "The Fall of the House of Usher," "Ligeia," and "Eleonora"; then come the "Old World Romances," of which "The Masque of the Red Death," "The Cask of Amontillado," and "The Pit and the Pendulum" are probably most read. In the second volume we find three groups, "Tales of Conscience, Natural Beauty, and Pseudo-Science," the last including his "MS. Found in a Bottle" and "Hans Pfaall." In the third are "Tales of Ratiocination," including the famous "Gold-Bug," the harrowing "Murders in the Rue

Morgue," and the perfect detective story "The Purloined Letter"; and "Tales of Illusion," including the horrible "Oblong Box." Then come the "Extravaganzas and Caprices" and lastly the two "Tales of Adventure and Exploration," namely, "Arthur Gordon Pym" and "Julius Rodman." It will be evident that Poe achieved success in two markedly distinct classes of tales: those in which a purely intellectual puzzle is worked out, and those in which a definite emotional effect is produced. The "Tales of Ratiocination" were the forerunners of a long line of "detective stories"—by Gaboriau, De Boisgobey, Wilkie Collins, Conan Doyle, and others,—in none of which does one find a keener analytical mind than that of Monsieur Dupin. "The Gold-Bug" undoubtedly suggested to Stevenson some features of "Treasure Island." Likewise in such stories as "Hans Pfaall," Poe was the pioneer in compounding flights of imagination with bits of popular science, being followed by Jules Verne and others of his class. Of the tales charged with emotion, the best are probably the three "Romances of Death" mentioned above. In these, it has been said, we see the highest reach of the romantic element in Poe's genius. The lady Ligeia is pure spirit, without human qualities, the maiden of a dream. The framework of the tale is slight; it is merely a prose-rhapsody on the theme expressed in the words of old Glanvill, "Man doth not yield himself to the angels, nor unto death utterly, save only through the weakness of his own feeble will." This theme, the supremacy of mind over matter, was one over which Poe busied himself much; but to scientific thought on the subject he contributed little of value. It has been pointed out, however, that Poe was the first to write this sort of tale, the "psychical story," in which Stevenson and others later outdid him. He was a subtle psychologist of certain moods and qualities, and understood the fiercer passions of terror and remorse as have few other men; of this, "William Wilson" furnishes abundant proof. But his range is limited, and most readers, tired, like the Lady of Shalott, of shadows, soon long to change his world of mystery and madness and death for the real world of sane and kindly, if commonplace, men and women.

According to the old maxim, however, we must take the artist for what he is. Poe chose his material and his setting as his artistic genius guided him; that he made skilful use of this material there can be little doubt. Within his narrow range, he is absolute master. His intensity, his eloquence, his skill in the choice and repetition of words force the reader to yield to the spell and believe for the moment even in the impossible. His limitations have been well set forth by Professor Woodberry:

> Being gifted with the dreaming instinct, the myth-making faculty, the allegorising power, and with no other poetic element of high genius, he exercised his art in a region of vague feeling, symbolic ideas, and fantastic imagery, and wrought his spell largely through sensuous effects of colour, sound, and gloom, heightened by lurking but un-shaped suggestions of mysterious meanings.

Symbolism is indeed evident throughout his imaginative works; in "The Black Cat," for example, remorse is indicated by the cat's flaming eye; in "William Wilson," a guilty conscience is the man's double. Of or-namentation there is plenty; Poe revelled in a wealth of beautiful images of Oriental and Gothic splendour.

In some of his tales, Poe reveals a certain kinship with Hawthorne. Both are fond of dwelling in a remote world. Both depict states of the soul; brief experiences; evanescent dreams. But Hawthorne's is always a moral world; Poe's, while never immoral, is prevailingly unmoral. In Hawthorne's tales we are never long forgetful of the Puritan heritage of conscience; Poe's indifference to moral issues is a not surprising result of his cavalier temperament. Both writers undoubtedly owe something to the weird imagination of Ernst Hoffmann (1776–1822); Poe also contin-ues the literary tradition of Mrs. Radcliffe, "Monk" Lewis, and the "Tales of Terror." Comparison with these writers suggests two other facts: first, that Poe was not a novelist, but a writer of short stories; he knew little about ordinary life, and nothing of human character, save through study of his own; he preferred a small canvas whereon his picture should be painted with Pre-Raphaelite fidelity and elaborate pains, and was un-able or unwilling to undertake a work on the scale of what we now call novels; secondly, that he was always a romancer, with a bias for medi-evalism as pronounced as if his characters wore armour and his pages were full of tournaments and chivalry.

If Poe has often been without honour in his own country and in En-gland, he has been enthusiastically received on the Continent. In France he early became known through the magnificent translation of Charles

Baudelaire, and his influence has never waned.[13] In Spain, Italy, and Germany he continues to be widely read and is generally regarded as the foremost man of letters hitherto produced by America. Time, that relentless and perverse critic, has given him a place of honour among the makers of world-literature, and his fame is secure.

Some Minor Writers.—At the novel-writing contemporaries of Kennedy, Simms, and Poe we can take but a passing glance. James Lawson (1799–1880), a Scotchman who, graduating from the University of Glasgow, came to America in 1815 and engaged in the mercantile and insurance business, is remembered for his "Tales and Sketches by a Cosmopolite" (1830), mainly relating to Scottish domestic life and romance. He was a friend of Edwin Forrest and Gilmore Simms. Richard Penn Smith (1799–1854) was the author of "The Forsaken" (1831), a novel of the American Revolution still worth reading. Henry William Herbert (1807–58), eldest son of the Rev. William Herbert, dean of Manchester, was graduated from the University of Cambridge with distinction in 1829 and in 1830 came to America, engaging in teaching Greek and writing for magazines. In 1834 he published a historical novel, "The Brothers, a Tale of the Fronde," which he had begun in *The American Monthly Magazine*; following it up with "Cromwell" (1837), "Marmaduke Wyvil" (1843), and "The Roman Traitor" (1848), a romance founded on the conspiracy of Catiline. He also wrote many tales and sketches of romantic incidents in European history. As a writer on sports, under the name of "Frank Forester," he became a popular authority, and may be said to have been the first writer who introduced field sports into American fiction.

Robert Montgomery Bird (1805–54), a native of Delaware, began his literary career by writing tragedies; one of these, "The Gladiator," was frequently played by Edwin Forrest. His first two novels, "Calavar" (1834) and "The Infidel" (1835), were descriptions of life in Mexico during the Spanish conquest; while "Nick of the Woods, or The Jibbenainosay" (1837), powerfully portrayed the thirst for vengeance aroused in American backwoodsmen, and thus sharply contrasted the real Indians

---

13   See Louis P. Betz, "Edgar Poe in der französischen Literatur," in his "Studien zur vergleichenden Literaturgeschichte der neueren Zeit," Frankfurt a. M., 1902; "Edgar Poe in Deutschland," *Die Zeit*, xxxv. 8–9, 21–23, Vienna, 1903.

with the somewhat idealised types in Cooper's stories. He also wrote "Sheppard Lee" (1836), "The Hawks of Hawk Hollow" (1835), and "The Adventures of Robin Day" (1839), a romantic novel of adventure. Although conscientious, he was not a skillful writer, and his extravagant and exciting tales are no longer read. Theodore Sedgwick Fay (1807–98), a New York lawyer and journalist, was the author of "Norman Leslie" (1835), a somewhat tame and highly moralised picture of life in New York City at the beginning of the century; its poverty of artistic merit excited the wrath of Poe, who helped to consign it to a merciful oblivion. Fay also wrote two novels directed against the practice of duelling: "The Countess Ida" (1840), the scene of which is laid in Europe, and "Hoboken, a Romance of New York" (1843), the action of which takes place in a locality notorious for the duels fought there. In 1835 appeared "Grace Seymour" by Hannah F. Lee (1780–1865), a story for the young, and, like the stories of Fay, with a moral purpose. In "Clinton Bradshaw" (1835), Frederick William Thomas (1811–66) painted with moderate success the social life of New York in the early years of the century. Like Fay, however, Thomas was too easily led from the path of artistic virtue by his desire to improve the minds of his readers. Thomas also wrote "East and West" (1836), in which he ably described a Mississippi steamboat race, and "Howard Pinckney" (1840), a novel of contemporary life in which both plot and character are handled not without skill.

Daniel Pierce Thompson.—The moral and educational improvement of the reader is likewise an evident purpose in the work of Daniel Pierce Thompson (1793–1868), a Vermont jurist, whose "May Martin, or The Money-Digger" appeared in 1835. His most famous work, which is still widely read, was "The Green Mountain Boys, a Romance of the Revolution" (1840), in which are described the early methods of fighting the Indians. Other stories of New England life from his pen were "Locke Amsden, or The Schoolmaster" (1845), in which he evidently drew upon his own experience, "Lucy Hosmer" (1848), "The Rangers, or The Tory's Daughter" (1851), a story dealing with the Revolutionary campaigns of 1777 in Vermont, "Tales of the Green Mountains" (1852), "Gaut Gurley, or The Trappers of Lake Umbagog" (1857), and "The Doomed Chief" (1860).

Hall, Hildreth, Hoffman.—While Thompson was delineating Vermont life, James Hall (1793–1868) wrote of the then far West. Born in

Philadelphia, Hall saw service in the War of 1812, and in 1820 went to Illinois and engaged in law and newspaper work. His "Sketches of History, Life, and Manners in the West" (1835) and several later volumes of tales are characterised by a natural and easy style, much skill in narrative, and general fidelity to detail. The distinction of writing the first of the army of anti-slavery novels belongs to the historian Richard Hildreth (1807–65). "Archy Moore" (1837) was republished in England, being reviewed by *The Spectator* and other papers. A rather extravagant narrative, it purports to be the autobiography of a Virginia slave during the War of 1812. A second edition with a continuation was published in 1852 as "The White Slave." Charles Fenno Hoffman (1806–84), after studying at Columbia College and preparing for the bar, practised law for three years in New York, then abandoned it for journalism and literature. He was the founder of *The Knickerbocker Magazine*, associated later, for many years, with the name of its editor, Lewis Gaylord Clark, and was connected with various other periodicals. His two novels, "Greyslaer" (1840), founded on the celebrated Beauchamp murder case in Kentucky,—a novel of intense interest which reminds some readers of Cooper,—and "Vanderlyn" (published serially in *The American Monthly Magazine* in 1837), like his other writings, reflect a generous and refined character. His promising career was cut short in 1849 by insanity.

William Ware.—In March, 1836, there appeared in *The Knickerbocker Magazine* the first of a series of "Letters from Palmyra," which aroused much interest. They purported to be written by a young Roman noble who visited Palmyra in the reign of Zenobia. They vividly presented the everyday life of the Roman Empire and at once gave their author high rank as a classical scholar. William Ware (1797–1852) graduated from Harvard College in 1816 and became a Unitarian clergyman; for some years he edited *The Christian Examiner*. The "Letters from Palmyra" were published in book form in 1837; the book is now called "Zenobia," from the title of the English reprint. It was followed in 1838 by a sequel, "Probus," in which the last persecution of Roman Christians is ably and energetically described. The title of this book was afterward changed to "Aurelian." His third novel, "Julian, or Scenes in Judea" (1841), narrated many episodes in the life of Jesus of Nazareth, the crucifixion forming a powerful climax to the story.

Mathews and Briggs.—A highly imaginative and somewhat absurd romance entitled "Behemoth, a Legend of the Mound-Builders" (1839) was the work of Cornelius Mathews (1817–89), a New York dramatist and magazine writer. His "Career of Puffer Hopkins" (1841) set forth some phases of contemporary political life; it first appeared serially in *Arcturus*, which Mathews edited in 1840–42. Another novel of his was "Moneypenny, or The Heart of the World" (1850), a story of city and country life. All of Mathews' stories, however, have a journalistic flavour. In the same year with Mathews, Charles Frederick Briggs (1840–77), a New York journalist, entered the ranks of the novelists with his "Adventures of Harry Franco, a Tale of the Great Panic" (1839), following it with "The Haunted Merchant" (1843) and "The Trippings of Tom Pepper" (1847). All of his novels have a certain value as humorous pictures of New York City life; through them runs a vein of amusing satire. Briggs was later the first editor of *Putnam's Monthly*.

Henry W. Longfellow.—It was in 1839 also that Longfellow published his once popular "Hyperion, a Romance," in which, in connection with a pathetic love story, he mainly sought, in the style of Richter, to convey his romantic impressions of the life and traditions of the Old World. The volume is charged, if not surcharged, with sentiment. Paul Flemming's enthusiasm for the quaint and picturesque in European lore and scenery takes us back to the days when Continental Europe was for Americans a land of romance, and when visits to the Old World were still not accomplished without difficulty and had not lost their novelty. Of a wholly different texture is the only other prose tale written by Longfellow, "Kavanagh, a Tale," which appeared in 1849 and which probably suffered by coming so near the romantic and fascinating "Evangeline." It is a bookish and uneventful story of New England life; Hawthorne said of it, "Nobody but yourself would dare to write so quiet a book." Yet it is written in a characteristically graceful style, and shows that the scholar-poet was a good observer of the life around him, though he could not give that life an air of reality in his portraiture.

John Lothrop Motley.—The fame of Motley's historical work has obscured the reputation of his fiction. "Morton's Hope, or The Memoirs of a Provincial" (1839), like "Hyperion," recalls the interest in German university life which was becoming general in America—a life which Motley vividly describes. From Germany the hero returns to participate in the American Revolution, in which he distinguishes himself. In "Merry Mount, a Romance of the Massachusetts Colony" (1849), Motley utilised the story of Thomas Morton, the jolly Royalist who with his followers settled near Boston in 1626 and whose revelry shocked his staid Puritan neighbours. As a historical picture, it has high value. Both of these novels, abounding in carefully wrought descriptions and gleams of genuine humour, deserved greater success than they had.

Caroline M. Kirkland.—A similar service was done for life in Michigan by Caroline M. Kirkland (1801–64), whose humorous and lively descriptions of frontier life, "A New Home; Who'll Follow?" (1839), "Forest Life" (1842), and "Western Clearings" (1846), were in their day successful and popular. Mrs. Kirkland's early works were published over the pen-name of "Mrs. Mary Clavers." Her literary career extended over a quarter of a century, and she was long a popular contributor to magazines and annuals.

The Forties.—The decade of 1840–50 saw the advent of no writers of enduring reputation. "Charles Elwood, or The Infidel Converted" (1840), a kind of philosophical autobiography by Orestes A. Brownson (1803–76), is really an essay in the guise of a novel, and can here only be mentioned. Brownson was successively a Presbyterian, a Universalist, a Unitarian, and a Roman Catholic; as a thinker, he might be called a Christian Socialist. Epes Sargent (1813–80), a student at Harvard College, who became a journalist and a popular dramatist, was the author of several juveniles, two of which, "Wealth and Worth" (1840) and "What's to be Done?" (1841), had a large sale; and of two now forgotten novels, "Fleetwood, or The Stain of Birth" (1845) and "Peculiar, a Tale of the Great Transition" (1864), a story of changes in the South in the Civil War. Washington Allston's "Monaldi" (1841), an Italian romance with an Othello-like *motif*, really belongs to an earlier generation, having been written as early as 1821, and intended apparently for publication in Dana's *Idle Man*. It is a powerful but harrowing story in which the progress of jealousy is traced throughout its course. Maria J. McIntosh (1803–78), losing her fortune in the panic of 1837, adopted authorship as a means of support and wrote a number of juveniles, the first of which was "Blind Alice" (1841), and all of which were intended to illustrate the moral sentiments. Some of her stories were reprinted in London; and she continued to write for more than twenty years. Maria Brooks (1795–1845), a once highly praised but now forgotten poet, in 1843 privately printed a prose romance, "Idomen, or The Vale of Yumuri," which was really an autobiography, including much poetical description and reflection.

Sylvester Judd.—The most successful picture of old New England life ever written, down to the time of its publication (1845), was "Margaret, a Tale of the Real and Ideal." It was this book which Lowell, in his "Fable for Critics," spoke of as the first Yankee book With the *soul* of Down East in 't, and things farther East, As far as the threshold of morning, at least, Where awaits the fair dawn of the simple and true, Of the day that comes slowly to make all things new.

The author, Sylvester Judd (1813–53), was a native of Massachusetts and a graduate of Yale College, who had become a Unitarian clergyman and settled in Augusta, Maine; and his purpose in writing was "to promote the cause of liberal Christianity." Had he kept this purpose more in the background, his place among the greater novelists would have been sure; for he had observed closely every phase of Puritan life and possessed rare gifts of realistic and dramatic story-telling. Not only does he correctly describe the externals of New England places and people, down to the niceties of dialect; but he also interprets with rare and poetic insight the moral and spiritual conflicts into which his characters are drawn. Another novel similar to "Margaret," "Richard Edney and the Governor's Family," appeared in 1850; it deals with the career of a New England country youth. Like Margaret, the hero has altogether too many "experiences"—introduced in order to point the moral. Yet on the whole the realism of these novels is wholesome and fresh and true.

Herman Melville.—A follower of Cooper—though at some distance in point of quality—in writing stories of the sea, was Herman Melville (1819–91). A native of New York, he spent the greater part of the years 1837–44 in voyages to the Pacific. Of his observations and exciting experiences he made good use in a long series of tales, the first of which, "Typee" (1846), narrated his adventures in the Marquesas. The general perception of the growing importance of the Pacific doubtless aided in securing for Melville's stories the most favourable reception, both in America and in England. "Omoo, a Narrative of Adventures in the South Seas" (1847) continued the earlier story, with no less vivid pictures of sailor life, fights with savages, and thrilling escapes. His next story, "Mardi, and a Voyage Thither" (1849), was an attempt at a philosophical romance contrasting European civilisation and Polynesian savagery, and, though it contained some able descriptions, its vagaries and lack of sobriety doomed it to failure. "Redburn, His First Voyage" (1849) tells of a journey to England, and includes some realistic horrors; it could hardly be popular. "The White Jacket, or The World in a Man-of-War" (1850) is a photographic narrative of experiences on board a United States frigate. Melville's masterpiece was "Moby Dick, or The Whale" (1851); though an uneven work of excessive length, written partly in a strained, Carlylesque style, it nevertheless fills the reader with the fascination of the sea. The fierce contest of Captain Ahab with the great whale, which "becomes a representative of moral evil in the world," is not unworthy of the pen of a greater writer. Melville never afterward came up to the standard of this work, though he wrote several other stories and novels, among them "Pierre, or The Ambiguities" (1852), "Israel Potter" (1855), narrating the adventures of a Revolutionary soldier, and praised by Hawthorne for its portraits of Paul Jones and Benjamin Franklin, "The Piazza Tales" (1856), and "The Confidence Man" (1857).

Mrs. Judson and Others.—Mrs. Emily Chubbuck Judson (1817–54), third wife of the celebrated Baptist missionary Dr. Adoniram Judson, and best known by her pen name of "Fanny Forester," in her "Alderbrook" (1846), a collection of village sketches, described girl life in New England, winning a reputation which lasted for many years. Peter Hamilton Myers (1812–78), a Brooklyn lawyer, was for a brief time remembered for his historical romances, "The First of the Knickerbockers, a Tale of 1673" (1848), "The Young Patroon, or Christmas in 1690" (1849), "The King of the Hurons" (1849), and "The Prisoner of the Border, a Tale of 1838" (1857). Charles Wilkins Webber (1819–56), the son of a Kentucky physician, inherited from his mother a fondness for out-of-door life, and spent some years in Texas. Then he tried in succession medicine, theology, and authorship. His stories and descriptions of South-western life and adventure include "Old Hicks the Guide" (1848), "The Hunter Naturalist" (1851–53), illustrated by his wife, "Tales of the Southern Border" (1852), and "Shot in the Eye" (1853), his best story. He died in the battle of Rivas, in Central America.

Mayo, Kimball, and Wise.—William Starbuck Mayo (1812–95), a New York physician, travelled in the Barbary States, and on returning home wrote two popular novels, "Kaloolah, or Journeyings in the Djebel Kumri" (1849) and "The Berber, or The Mountaineer of the Atlas" (1850). The former purports to be the autobiography of Jonathan Romer, who, after numerous exciting adventures in the American woods, goes to Africa, has various hair's-breadth escapes, fights with slave-traders and natives, and marries a beautiful dusky princess. In its satirical remarks on civilised usages it imitates "Gulliver." "The Berber," a story of more regular construction, is still enjoyable. It recounts events supposed to take place in Africa at the close of the seventeenth century, and like its predecessor contains minutely accurate descriptions of tropical scenery and animal life. Richard B. Kimball's "St. Leger, or The Threads of Life" (1849), reprinted from *The Knickerbocker*, was a serious attempt to depict a mind in pursuit of truth in a story in which romantic adventure plays some part; but the characters are not strongly marked. Henry Augustus Wise (1819–69), son of a naval officer and himself a lieutenant in the Navy, saw the humorous and comic side of the seaman's life, and chronicled his impressions in "Los Gringos, or An Inside View of Mexico and California" (1849), and still more successfully in his sprightly and sentimental "Tales for the Marines" (1855), in which all sorts of marvellous and amusing things happen.

The Decade of 1850–60.—It can hardly be said that the next decade, 1850–60, saw any great improvement in the quality of our fiction; but there is evident an increasing preference for realistic studies of home life, and a growing indifference to the highly wrought and more or less melodramatic romances which had delighted the readers of an earlier day. For many reasons, Americans desired to see themselves in fiction, doing their daily work, struggling with everyday temptations, yielding or conquering according to their native strength or weakness. There was a growing sense of the artistic—and moral or didactic—value of common life. The reaction against romance was inevitable, and was no doubt accelerated by the coming of railroads, telegraphs, Atlantic cables, and the controversy over slavery.

Ik Marvel.—Significant, then, was the popularity, which has scarcely waned, of "Ik Marvel's" two books, "Reveries of a Bachelor" (1850) and "Dream Life" (1851). The author, Donald G. Mitchell (born in 1822), was a product of Connecticut and a graduate of Yale, whose experience had been enriched by European travel. The pernicious influence of Carlyle upon Mitchell's style is too evident; but the sentiment, or sentimentality, the enthusiasm, the tender pathos of these slight stories have appealed to thousands. In his "Dr. Johns" (1866), Mitchell brought the stern Calvinistic theology of New England into relief by contrasting it with French frivolity.

Edward Everett Hale.—Edward Everett Hale's literary activity has extended over something like sixty years. Born in Boston in 1822, and graduated from Harvard at seventeen, he became a journalist, story-teller, minister, historian, and antiquarian. His "Margaret Percival in America," a religious novel, appeared in 1850, and he has since written others, "If, Yes, and Perhaps" (1868), "Ten Times One Is Ten" (1870), "In His Name" (1874), a truthful and glowing narrative of the Waldenses, "Philip Nolan's Friends" (1876), the gallant hero of which, the Kentuckian Philip Nolan, was "the protomartyr to Mexican treachery," "The Fortunes of Rachel" (1884), a slight but clever tale, and "East and West" (1892). But Dr. Hale is best known in literature by his short stories. "My Double and How He Undid Me," published in *The Atlantic* for September, 1859, was a clever and amusing piece which made a great hit and immortalised some of the bores of his parish. "The Man Without a Country" (*The Atlantic*, December, 1863) brought its author national reputation and has become a classic. It has been justly pronounced "the best sermon on patriotism ever written." Speaking of sermons recalls the criticism often applied to Dr. Hale's stories, that the moral is too obvious; in general, however, the moral cannot be called obtrusive and hardly interferes with the general effect of the story.

Alice Cary.—Alice Cary (1822–71), better known as a poet, wrote pleasantly appreciative sketches of her Ohio home under the title of "Clovernook, or Recollections of our Neighbourhood in the West" (1852);

a second series of similar sketches was published in 1853. Her three novels, "Hagar" (1852), "Married, not Mated" (1856), and "The Bishop's Son" (1857), were characterised by power of observation and by careful literary workmanship.

The Warners.—Susan Warner (1819–1885), whose earlier work was done under the pen name of "Elizabeth Wetherell," became well known through the publication (1850) of her first book "The Wide, Wide World." This was a story of domestic life on the upper Hudson, which showed an exceptional power of description and of character study, and which secured very promptly wide acceptance on both sides of the Atlantic. With the single exception of "Uncle Tom's Cabin," it proved to be the most popular novel written up to that date in America, and it had the compliment of reproduction in a long series of unauthorised editions in Europe. "The Wide, Wide World" was followed by a series of stories, of which the most important were "Queechy" (1852), "The Hills of the Shatemuc" (1858), "Diana" (1859), "Wych Hazel" (1860), and "The Gold of Chickaree" (1861). She collaborated with her sister, Anna Bartlett Warner (born in 1820), in the production of "Dollars and Cents," which was issued in 1853, and in some successful books for the young, "Mr. Rutherford's Children," etc.

Harriet Beecher Stowe.—A diligent and painstaking writer of fiction for thirty years, Harriet Beecher Stowe (1811–96) is to-day remembered only as the author of a single book, and that one almost her first. The daughter of Dr. Lyman Beecher of Connecticut, she was born into a remarkably gifted family and inherited the best that New England Puritan culture could give. At twenty-one she was married to Professor Calvin E. Stowe, then a teacher in the divinity school in Cincinnati. Here she had an opportunity of studying the workings of slavery, and as a result entered heart and soul into the anti-slavery movement. In the year in which Hawthorne published his "House of the Seven Gables," Longfellow "The Golden Legend," and Melville "Moby Dick," she began in *The National Era* a serial which aroused wide and bitter discussion. The next year (1852), "Uncle Tom's Cabin" appeared in book form. Over three hundred thousand copies, according to the author, were sold within a year. The part played by the book in hastening the "irrepressible conflict" of the Civil War cannot be estimated. It is not hard to see blemishes in the story: tame description, careless and loose construction, the tone of the preacher; but these are rendered insignificant by the great merits of the book, its frequent touches of humour, its range and variety of characters, who are not merely types but are graphically individualised, its broad humanity, its fierce earnestness, its kindling emotion. These may not suffice to put the story among the great and enduring works of literature; but it will be long before America outgrows her fondness and admiration for it. Mrs. Stowe followed this book in 1856 with "Dred" (republished in 1866 as "Nina Gordon"), in which she continued to depict effectively the position of slavery with reference to the church and the law, and the defeat by mob violence of a high-minded slave-owner who sought to purify the unholy system. A more deliberate and carefully planned work than "Uncle Tom's Cabin," it has generally been considered as inferior in power, though Harriet Martineau thought it superior. Old Tiff is one of the great creations of negro character. As a picture, in the main true, of old-fashioned Southern life, it has a lasting charm. In "The Minister's Wooing" (1859), Mrs. Stowe turned to New England life at the beginning of the century, and dealt with the influence of the older Calvinism upon devout and sensitive minds. In artistic construction and effect it has been pronounced superior to all her other works; some of the characters, for example, Mary Scudder and Dr. Hopkins, are notably strong and impressive. Yet, like all her later works, it has been overshadowed by that one which was struck out in a white heat of passionate appeal. "The Pearl of Orr's Island" (1861) is a quiet story of Puritan life on the Maine coast, insufficiently relieved by a few thrilling episodes. In "Agnes of Sorrento" (1862), the result of a visit to Europe, Mrs. Stowe turned to Italy in the days of Savonarola, but achieved even less success than George Eliot did in the next year with "Romola." In 1863, the Stowes settled permanently at Hartford, Connecticut; and after the war they acquired a winter residence in Florida. The best of Mrs. Stowe's numerous later books is probably "Oldtown Folks" (1869), dealing with life in Norfolk County, Massachusetts, about the year 1800, and portraying some very realistic characters. Such stories as "Pink and White Tyranny" (1871), "My Wife and I" (1871), and "We and Our Neighbours" (1875), in which she aimed to reform fashionable society, though successful in respect to sales, were from an artistic point of view decided failures. In "Sam Lawson's Fireside Stories" (1871) and "Poganuc People" (1878), she returned to New England Yankees and the life she most successfully drew. On the whole it must be said that her reputation, while it lasts, will rest chiefly upon "Uncle Tom" and the New England stories.

John T. Trowbridge.—One of the most popular of writers for boys is John Townsend Trowbridge (born in 1827). Educated in the common schools, he learned Latin, Greek, and French by himself, taught school, worked a year on an Illinois farm, and then settled down to writing in New York City. Some of his books are "Father Brighthopes" (1853), "Burrcliff" (1853), "Martin Merrivale" (1854), "Neighbour Jackwood" (1857), a famous anti-slavery novel, perhaps a good second to "Uncle Tom's Cabin" in influence and popularity, "Cudjo's Cave" (1864), and "Coupon Bonds, and Other Stories" (1871). He has been a prolific writer of healthful and finished stories for boys. John Burroughs has well said of him: "He knows the heart of a boy and the heart of a man, and has laid them both open in his books."

John Esten Cooke.—A romancer of the old school was John Esten Cooke (1830–86), a younger brother of Philip Pendleton Cooke. A native of Virginia, he found inspiration in the romantic history of that State, drawing many of his characters from life. His first important publication was "Leather Stocking and Silk, or Hunter John Myers and His Times" (1854); his best story proved to be "The Virginia Comedians, or Old Days in the Old Dominion" (1854), which deals with the period just preceding the Revolution, and which, with its youthful enthusiasm and interesting descriptions of colonial manners, has been called by some critics the best novel written in the South down to the Civil War. After serving in the Confederate army, Cooke sought to utilise his military experiences in several dramatic stories; but his reputation had been made, and his day had gone by.

Maria S. Cummins.—In "The Lamplighter" (1854), Maria S. Cummins (1827–66) achieved a success comparable to that of "Uncle Tom's Cabin" and "Ben Hur." In "Mabel Vaughan" (1857) she produced probably a better book. Both of her stories, however, while in the main true delineations of girl and home life, are too evidently written with a didactic aim, and are at times laboured and diffuse. Her other stories, "El Fureidis" (1860), a story of Palestine, and "Haunted Hearts" (1864), are now entirely forgotten.

Mrs. Ann Sophia Stephens.—Mrs. Ann Sophia Stephens (1813–86) was in the fifties and sixties an immensely popular novelist. She was the daughter of John Winterbotham, an English woollen manufacturer who had come to America, and was born at Humphreysville, Connecticut. In 1831, she married Edward Stephens, a publisher, and began in 1835 to edit *The Portland Magazine*, founded by her husband. Later, she edited *The Ladies' Companion* and became an associate editor of *Graham's* and *Peterson's*, to which she contributed over twenty serials. Her first elaborate novel, "Fashion and Famine" (1854), had a very large circulation and was three times translated into French. A novel of affected intensity, it contained some excellent delineation of character. Among her other works were "Zana, or The Heiress of Clare Hall" (1854), republished as "The Heiress of Greenhurst," "The Old Homestead" (1855), "Sibyl Chase" (1862), "The Rejected Wife" (1863), "Married in Haste" (1870), "The Reigning Belle" (1872), and "Norton's Rest" (1877). She was attentive to details and wrote in a condensed and forcible style.

Marion Harland.—Marion Harland is the pseudonym under which Mrs. Mary Virginia Terhune (born in 1831), a Virginian of New England ancestry, became known for a number of short stories, novels, and miscellaneous matter. Her fiction is of the romantic type, full of incident, and dealing with brave personages. Some of her stories are "Alone, a Tale of Southern Life and Manners" (1854), "The Hidden Path" (1855), "Moss-Side" (1857), "Miriam" (1860), "Nemesis" (1860), "Husks" (1863), "Sunnybank" (1866), "At Last" (1870), "Judith" (1883), and "A Gallant Fight" (1888). She has been editorially connected with a number of juvenile magazines.

Curtis, Willis, Holland.—George William Curtis belongs in the main, of course, with the essayists, where his life will be narrated. He was the author of "Prue and I" (1856), a series of papers written originally for *Putnam's*, and together forming a slight story of charming domestic life, in which sentiment, fancy, and a broad optimistic philosophy are pervasive features; and of an unsuccessful novel, "Trumps" (1861), which he began in 1859 as a serial in *Harper's Weekly*. In view of the broad experience of its author, his fondness for good novels, his discriminating taste, his facility in expression, this failure of "Trumps" was remarkable. The truth is that Curtis had not rightly estimated his powers.

He could not manage an elaborate plot with skill, and he also made the same mistake that marred the work of many writers already noticed—he was too much concerned to point the moral. The general effect, as Mr. Cary points out,[14] is that "Trumps" becomes "a Sunday-school story, written by a man of rare gifts, some of which betray the elusive charm of genius, but still essentially of that class, producing, and apparently intended to produce, the impression that in the end virtue triumphs and vice comes to a miserable end." In the long run, this is eternally true; but the great artists do not talk about it very much. A similar failure, though for different reasons, was the one novel written by the prolific Nathaniel P. Willis, "Paul Fane, or Parts of a Life Else Untold" (1857), an early and dull experiment in the field of international novels. It was a story whose general distortion of things amounted almost to caricature, since it was based on superficial rather than deep and careful observation of character. In the same year Josiah Gilbert Holland (1819–81) made his *début* in the field of fiction with "The Bay Path," a story of the settlement of the Connecticut Valley, filled largely with historical characters, and generally faithful to the manners and thought of the age portrayed. A more ambitious story, "Miss Gilbert's Career" (1860), is a realistic modern novel in which a characteristic Yankee community is described with great fidelity. His later novels, "Arthur Bonnicastle" (1873), "The Story of Sevenoaks" (1875), and "Nicholas Minturn" (1877), cannot on the whole be said to possess high literary merit; the author was avowedly a moralist, and the best that can be said of them is that they did no harm.

Major John William de Forest.—Major John William de Forest (born in 1826) began writing fiction with a very romantic and very poor novel called "Witching Times," published serially in *Putnam's*, 1856–57, and followed it with a number of works which made him one of the most popular novelists of the seventies—"Seacliff" (1859), "Miss Ravenel's Conversion" (1867), a book out of his own experience, and his first in realistic vein, "Overland" (1871), "Kate Beaumont" (1872), "Honest John Vane" (1875), "Playing the Mischief" (1875), and many others. Of "Miss Ravenel's Conversion" Mr. Howells has said: "It was one of the best American novels that I had known, and was of an advanced realism before realism was known by that name."

---

14   In his "George William Curtis" ("American Men of Letters"), Boston, 1894, p. 124.

Robert Lowell.—In 1858 appeared "The New Priest of Conception Bay," in which the Rev. Robert Traill Spence Lowell (1816–91), an elder brother of James Russell Lowell, and an Episcopal clergyman, painted in bright and cheerful colours the rural life of Newfoundland with which he became familiar during his sojourn at Bay Roberts in 1843–47. No truer picture of the simple fisher folk of Newfoundland was ever produced— even to a delicate discrimination of dialects. Mr. Lowell's reputation was not ill sustained by his later though less known books, "Antony Brade" (1874) and "A Story or Two from an Old Dutch Town" (1878), which dealt with the quaint life in the Dutch villages of eastern New York.

Mrs. Harriet Prescott Spofford.—Mrs. Harriet Prescott Spofford (born in 1835), a native of Maine who has passed most of her life in Massachusetts, made her reputation with a short story of Parisian life, "In a Cellar," in *The Atlantic* in 1859. In "Sir Rohan's Ghost" (1859), "The Amber Gods" (in *The Atlantic*, 1860), which gave her a considerable reputation, "Azarian," (1864), and "A Thief in the Night" (1872), she produced sombre works vividly imaginative and intense in feeling. She was among the first to work the mine of ghostly romance. Her stories have never been very popular; her fondness for the sensuous and the splendid repels many readers. Yet for sheer and overwhelming intensity and for complete success in producing the effect sought, "A Thief in the Night" must be given a high place as a work of art.

Mrs. Miriam Coles Harris.—Mrs. Miriam Coles Harris (born in 1834), who has spent most of her life in and near New York City, wrote a number of stories popular in their day, some of them being still read. "Rutledge" (1860) and "The Sutherlands" (1862) were widely circulated. Her later stories include "A Perfect Adonis" (1875), "Phœbe" (1884), "Missy" (1885), and "An Utter Failure" (1890).

Theodore Winthrop.—Theodore Winthrop (1828–61) deserves more than passing mention, not so much for what he actually accomplished as for what his brief life gave promise of doing. Born in New Haven, Connecticut, a descendant of Governor John Winthrop of Connecticut and at twenty a graduate of Yale, he travelled much abroad, went to Panama in the employment of the Pacific Mail Steamship Company, and afterward sojourned in California and Oregon, visiting also the island of Vancouver and some of the Hudson's Bay Company's stations. He was admitted to the bar in 1855, but became more fond of politics and literature than of law. For several years, he worked on his novels; but though one was accepted for publication, none appeared in his lifetime. At the opening of the war he went to the front with the Seventh New York Regiment, and fell, bravely fighting, at Great Bethel. His descriptions of his march to Washington, in *The Atlantic Monthly*, had attracted much attention, and after his death his novels appeared in rapid succession, "Cecil Dreeme" in 1861 and "John Brent" and "Edwin Brothertoft" in 1862. The first is a gruesome tale of life in New York, full of broad sweep and passion, immature but not devoid of power. "John Brent," the best of his stories, is an imaginative tale into which he wove a record of his Western experiences; it "had the merit, in its day especially, of delineating Western scenes and characters with sympathy and skill, at a time when the West was almost virgin soil to literature." "Edwin Brothertoft" is a melodramatic story of the American Revolution, at times crude in expression, but strong in plot and in its play of light and shade. Had Winthrop lived, our literature beyond question would have been far richer. He comprehended as did few others the deep throbbing life of America, not only in its externals but in its less obvious features; and abating his youthful "breeziness," he would doubtless have reproduced some parts of that life on enduring canvas.

Fitz-James O'Brien.—Another brilliant writer whose career was cut short by the war was Fitz-James O'Brien (1828–62), a native of County Limerick, Ireland. He was educated at the University of Dublin; and after spending his inheritance of £8,000 in London, he came to America in 1852 and from that time on devoted himself to literature. In New York he became a prominent figure among the Bohemian set and won distinguished social and literary success. Besides much clever verse, he wrote for the magazines some marvellously ingenious tales, for example "The Diamond Lens," "The Wondersmith," "The Golden Ingot," and "Mother of Pearl." The reader is occasionally reminded of Poe and Hawthorne, but is more often led to wonder why O'Brien has so long lain in neglect; for some of his stories are powerful in a high degree. Like Winthrop, O'Brien in 1861 became a soldier in the Seventh New York Regiment and went to the front. On February 26, 1862 he was severely wounded in a skirmish, and in April he died. Nearly twenty years later, his friend William Winter edited "The Poems and Stories of Fitz-James O'Brien" (1881).

The Civil War.—It is not surprising that the Civil War partially, at least, dried up the springs of literature and art in America. It was an epoch of concentration, of action; men had little time for reading novels or writing them; the newspaper any day might chronicle as sublimely heroic or as pathetic events as could be found in fiction. Comparatively few novels of distinction were written, therefore, during the war and the two or three years following it, the Reconstruction period. Some worthy novels which appeared in those years, for example Mrs. Stoddard's "Morgesons," failed of an appreciative audience.

The close of the war marked the beginning of a new era in American fiction. As Mr. Morse points out, people no longer cared for stories about the Indians and about the Revolution. The Indians had retreated into that world of romance with which the modern world, ignorant of "Nick of the Woods," associates them; the Revolution was ancient history by the side of the more terrible conflict just ended, and a quarter of a century must elapse before the earlier war would make a background for fiction. Romance, which, as we have seen, had already begun to lose favour, must now yield to realism; there must be pictures of life at home, in the market-place, in the fields, in the teeming cities; there must be greater skill in handling the narrative so as to make it a transcript from daily life. The lover of romance will doubtless deplore this tendency; but it was inevitable, and it has dictated the path of fiction almost to the present day.

Oliver Wendell Holmes.—The many-sided activity of Dr. Holmes extended to the writing of three novels—"medicated novels" they have been called, but the term does not apply to all equally well. Certainly they all belong to the large and increasing group of "problem novels." The first, "Elsie Venner: a Romance of Destiny" (1861), published when the author had passed the half- century mark, made its first appearance as "The Professor's Story" in *The Atlantic Monthly*. The mother of Elsie Venner, a short time before giving birth to her child, was fatally bitten by a *crotalus* or rattlesnake, and from birth the child is partially endowed with a serpent nature, which enables her to exercise a peculiar influence over those with whom she is brought into contact, especially the sensitive schoolmistress Helen Darley. "The real aim of the story," says Dr. Holmes himself, "was to test the doctrine of 'original sin' and human responsibility for the disordered volition coming under that technical denomination. Was Elsie Venner, poisoned by the venom of a *crotalus* before she was born, morally responsible for the 'volitional' aberrations which, translated into acts, become what is known as sin, and, it may be, what is punished as crime? If, on presentation of the evidence, she becomes by the verdict of the human conscience a proper object of divine pity and not of divine wrath, as a subject of moral poisoning, wherein lies the difference between her position at the bar of judgment, human or divine, and that of the unfortunate victim who received a moral poison from a remote ancestor before he drew his first breath?" It will thus be seen that what the author intended was nothing less than an onslaught upon one of the great fundamental dogmas of orthodox theology. Fifty years ago, this was a bold undertaking indeed. The intensely tragic motive of the novel is relieved by some chapters of pure comedy, in which figure the mean, calculating, money-making Silas Peckham, the vulgar splurging Sprowles, and a varied group of other minor characters. "The Guardian Angel" (1867) forms a natural sequel to "Elsie Venner"; it deals with some of the problems of heredity, attempting "to show the successive evolution of some inherited qualities in the character of Myrtle Hazard," the heroine. Less tragic than the earlier tale, "The Guardian Angel" is more pleasant to read, and a more artistic creation. An interesting plot is skilfully worked out and the characterisation is subtle and true. In his third novel, "A Mortal Antipathy" (1885), Dr. Holmes at seventy-six plainly showed that he had passed his creative period. He yielded, to a much greater degree than in the other stories, to the rambling propensity which, charming and natural enough in "The Autocrat of the Breakfast Table," seriously mars the continuity of a novel in which plot-interest is intended to figure. In this the author deals with the influence on a man's after-life of an antipathy (toward womankind) arising from a severe shock received in early childhood—an antipathy which is happily removed when the hero, helpless on a sick-bed in a burning house, is borne out by a brave and athletic girl. In spite of its "medicated" character, the story is full of delightful gossip, amusing descriptions and characterisation, and thoughtful speculation over miscellaneous matters connected with the healing art. If, as some contend, Dr. Holmes has in these books emphasised the moral issue at the expense of artistic perfection, they still have great value as records of personality. In Mr. Noble's words, the author "is a man whose temperament makes him intensely interested in human nature, and whose bent of mind gives him a special interest in any development of human nature which, by exhibiting exceptional possibilities or limitations, casts some strange side-light upon its more ordinary and normal conditions."

Mrs. Elizabeth Barstow Stoddard.—Mrs. Elizabeth Barstow Stoddard (1823–1902), wife of the poet Richard Henry Stoddard, wrote three novels remarkable in their day, "The Morgesons" (1862), "Two Men" (1865), and "Temple House" (1867), which found few readers in their time and are now almost forgotten, but which evinced careful observation of life and customs, and decided if not eccentric individuality. Republished in 1888 and again in 1901, "The Morgesons" was praised by such judicious critics as Mr. Stedman, Mr. Julian Hawthorne, and Professor Beers (who declared he had read it four times); but it again failed of popular favour; it had become old-fashioned.

Edmund Kirke.—Under this pen name, James Roberts Gilmore (1822–1903) was for many years a well known writer. In 1857 he retired from business with a competency, and thereafter devoted himself mainly (except 1873–83) to literature. His earlier novels, "Among the Pines" (1862), "My Southern Friends" (1862), "Among the Guerillas" (1863), "Down in Tennessee" (1863), "Adrift in Dixie" (1863), and "On the Border" (1864), were concerned with the Southern life with which he became acquainted in war-time. In later life, he wrote "The Last of the Thorndikes" (1889) and "A Mountain-White Heroine" (1889). His earlier stories were popular and did much to acquaint readers with slavery.

Thomas Bailey Aldrich.—Thomas Bailey Aldrich (1836–1907) began his career as a novelist in 1862 with the publication in *The Atlantic Monthly* (June) of a little romance, "Père Antoine's Date Palm," which secured sympathetic recognition from Hawthorne. In the same year, he also published "Out of His Head, a Romance in Prose," a collection of six short stories; but these remained his sole efforts in fiction until 1869, when he published his largely autobiographical "Story of a Bad Boy." The hero of this little idyl of Portsmouth, New Hampshire, Tom Bailey, who is after all "not a very bad boy," has become a classic character in the fiction of boyhood. "Marjorie Daw, and Other Stories" (1873) are ingenious tales, in the first of which a surprising hoax is managed with consummate skill. "Prudence Palfrey" (1874) is an old-fashioned novel of incident in which a well-nigh impossible plot is made plausible. "The Queen of Sheba" (1877) is perhaps the most skilfully done of all his stories; the action takes place in New Hampshire and Switzerland, and the story is full of humour. "The Stillwater Tragedy" (1880) is a realistic portrayal of life in a New England manufacturing village, the *motif* being the detection of a murderer, and the sombreness of the situation being relieved by a love story. "Two Bites at a Cherry, and Other Tales," subtle, amusing, ingenious, appeared in 1893. Probably most of us will agree with Mr. Howells when he says that Aldrich was a worker in the novel with the instinct of a romancer, and was at his best in the romantic parts of his stories. Of his prose works his short stories will probably endure longest.

Mrs. Adeline D. T. Whitney.—Mrs. Adeline D. T. Whitney (born in 1824), a native of Boston and sister of the eccentric George Francis Train, wrote a number of stories for young people, beginning with "Boys at Chequasset" (1862) and "Faith Gartney's Girlhood" (1863) and including also "The Gayworthys" (1865), which ranks among the best of New England novels, "A Summer in Leslie Goldthwaite's Life" (1866), "Patience Strong's Outings" (1868), "Hitherto" (1869), "We Girls" (1870), "Bonnyborough" (1885), and "Ascutney Street" (1888). To some critics the didactic tone of her stories has seemed so prominent as to impair their artistic value; others, like Mrs. Stowe, defend her from the charge of being "preachy." A vein of mysticism runs through her stories. Her style is effective and her creations are real and lifelike.

Bayard Taylor.—The writing of novels did not play a great part in the life of Bayard Taylor, who felt himself to be first of all a poet; but his four novels are not without interest. Taylor had already tried his hand at writing stories for *The Atlantic Monthly* when he began in 1861 the writing of a novel. Before he left America for Russia he had written seven chapters. He finished the book in St. Petersburg and published it in 1863 under the title of "Hannah Thurston, a Story of American Life." Although the scene is nominally laid in central New York, the life is essentially that of Chester County, Pennsylvania. The plot is similar to that of Tennyson's "Princess." It is, however, of secondary importance; the author's main purpose apparently was to satirise the more or less superficial reforms of the time—abolition, total abstinence, spiritualism, vegetarianism, and the like. The homely and commonplace village life of his time Taylor described vividly and truthfully; but it cannot be said that his characters, amusing as many of them are, are distinctly individualised. Even so, the book was received with favour. It was promptly translated into German, Swedish, and Russian. Its success encouraged Taylor to further efforts. "John Godfrey's Fortunes, Related by Himself" appeared late in 1864. This is a story of life in Pennsylvania and in New York City. A good plot is worked out, and some of the characters are interesting, though for the most part they are too obviously good or bad. John Godfrey in a sense was Taylor himself, but the book can hardly be called an autobiography. In 1866 appeared "The Story of Kennett," in some respects the best of Taylor's novels. For it he drew largely upon his memories of Chester County, and most of the characters were drawn from life. The scene at the funeral of Abiah Barton, where the hero discovers his worthless and cowardly father, has been sharply censured; but Taylor contended that, because of the vein of superstition in Mary Potter, it was the most justifiable chapter in the book. "Joseph and His Friend: a Story of Pennsylvania," the last of Taylor's novels, appeared serially in *The Atlantic*, and was published in book form in 1870. It is a disagreeable story of duplicity, in Bismarck's view of which many have shared, that the villain gets off too easily. To the above should be added a volume of shorter stories issued under the title of "Beauty and the Beast." In general, Taylor's novels exhibit skilful workmanship and sympathetic and often vivid delineations of character.

Louisa May Alcott.—Louisa May Alcott (1832–88), daughter of Amos Bronson Alcott, became well known as a writer of wholesome fiction, especially for young readers. She began life as a teacher and during the Civil War was an army nurse. "Moods" (1864), her first novel, was widely read, and contains passages of strength. "Little Women" (1868–69), written as a girls' book, remains her best. A kind of sequel to it was "Little Men; Life at Plumfield with Jo's Boys" (1871), followed in its turn by "Jo's Boys and How They Turned Out" (1886). Other similar stories were "An Old-Fashioned Girl" (1870), "Work, a Story of Experience" (1873), partly autobiographical, "Eight Cousins" (1875) and its sequel, "Rose in Bloom" (1876), and "A Modern Mephistopheles" (1877), a disagreeable but vigorous and imaginative study of moral deterioration. Her stories continue to be popular with the young, though the newer juvenile fiction will in time supersede them.

Richard Malcolm Johnston.—Richard Malcolm Johnston (1822–98) was one of the most popular of the Southern writers of his time. The son of a Georgia planter and Baptist clergyman, he in time became a Roman Catholic. Graduating from Mercer University, Georgia, in 1841, he practised law for some years, in 1857 declining a judgeship to become professor of belles-lettres in the University of Georgia. From 1861 till 1882, he was engaged in conducting a boys' boarding-school, first at Sparta, Georgia, then near Baltimore. In 1864 he published, as "Georgia Sketches," four stories of life in Georgia. To these, others were added in 1874 under the title of "Dukesborough Tales," his best book. He afterward wrote "Old Mark Langston" (1884), "Mr. Absalom Billingslea and Other Georgia Folk" (1888), "Ogeechee Cross-Firings" (1889), "The Primes and Their Neighbours" (1891), "Mr. Billy Downs and His Likes" (1892), "Mr. Fortner's Marital Claims, and Other Stories" (1892), "Widow Guthrie" (1893), "Little Ike Templin, and Other Stories" (1894), "Old Times in Middle Georgia" (1897), and "Pearce Amerson's Will" (1898). In all he published more than eighty stories. He was not a master of plot, and the structure of his tales is loose and faulty in sequence; but his characters have the magic touch of reality, and his descriptions of ante-bellum Georgia days cannot be neglected.

William Mumford Baker.—William Mumford Baker (1825–83), a Princeton graduate and Presbyterian clergyman, was once popular but is now little read. From 1850 till 1865 he was minister of a church in Austin, Texas, where he had many of the experiences utilised in his stories. His most important fiction was "Inside, a Chronicle of Secession," which was written secretly during the war, ran as a serial in *Harper's Weekly*, and appeared in book form in 1866; it gives a vivid picture of Southern life and feeling. Some of his later books were "Oak Mot" (1868), "The New Timothy" (1870), "Mose Evans" (1874), "Carter Quarterman" (1876), "A Year Worth Living" (1878), "Colonel Dunwoodie" (1878), "His Majesty Myself" (1879), and "Blessed Saint Certainty" (1881). While not striking their roots very deeply into life and character, his books are marked by sincerity and intense earnestness.

S. Weir Mitchell.—Dr. Silas Weir Mitchell (born in 1830) is a distinguished physician of many-sided fame. A native of Virginia, he studied at the University of Pennsylvania and the Jefferson Medical College, from which he was graduated in 1850. He began writing fiction during the Civil War, and in July, 1866, contributed to *The Atlantic* a remarkable story, "The Case of George Dedlow." But it was not until about 1880 that he began to devote himself more seriously to literature. He has written "Hephzibah Guinness" (1880), three stories of Quaker life in Philadelphia; "In War Time" (1885); "Roland Blake" (1886), the earlier part of which deals with the Civil War; "Far in the Forest" (1889), a story of character influence, the scene of which takes place in the forest of Pennsylvania before the Revolutionary War; "Hugh Wynne, Free Quaker" (1897), a story of Philadelphia during the War of Independence, which ranks among the few great American novels; "The Adventures of François" (1898), a romance of the French Revolution, the hero being a light-hearted little waif who has some strange adventures; "The Autobiography of a Quack" (1900), a study of the mind of a professional medical knave; "Constance Trescot" (1905), a study of an unusual character, skilfully handled, the scene being Paris in the sixties; and "A Diplomatic Adventure" (1906). Dr. Mitchell's interest in problems of abnormal psychology has led him to treat some themes which in the hands of any but a born story-teller would have resulted in merely sensational novels. His stories all show keen powers of analysis and character-drawing and a kindly and wholesome optimism.

Beecher and Higginson.—Henry Ward Beecher (1813–87), amid the many activities of a busy clerical and journalistic life, found time to write one novel, "Norwood, or Village Life in New England" (1867), in which occur descriptive and narrative passages rich in insight and humour. There is only a slight plot; the movement is leisurely; we are chiefly interested in the characters, who include the usual personages to be found in a village and some curious and amusing people as well. The book is partly autobiographical, with a vein of romance running through it. Thomas Wentworth Higginson (born in 1823) is chiefly known as an essayist, but wrote one capital story, "Malbone, an Oldport Romance"

(1869), which deserves wider reading as a subtle study of temperament; the scene is obviously Newport, Rhode Island. It "is largely a transcript from actual life, the chief character being drawn from the same friend of Higginson, William Hurlbert, who figures as Densdreth in Winthrop's 'Cecil Dreeme.'"[15] In "Madame Delia's Expectations" (*The Atlantic*, January, 1871, reprinted in "Oldport Days," 1873), Colonel Higginson showed that he could tell a short story well.

Mark Twain.—The literary productions of Mr. Clemens will be recorded elsewhere; here a few words may be said of his place as a writer of fiction. In technique, it cannot be maintained that he stands high; his narrative wanders whither it listeth, blameless of compact construction or climax; his style is not free from faults. Yet in spite of these defects his name has become "a household word in all places where the English language is spoken, and in many where it is not." He has created two characters—Tom Sawyer and Huckleberry Finn—who will live long as humorously conceived but true American boys. Pudd'nhead Wilson and the Connecticut Yankee may fade into oblivion, but it seems unlikely that the heroes of Mark Twain's most typical books will soon be allowed to withdraw from our group of favourites. Moreover, Mr. Clemens has enshrined the Mississippi River of his youth in a kind of homely, virile prose-poetry; he has recorded, in narrative which Mr. Thompson rightly calls "firm and vigorous," the impression which the great river made upon his youthful mind. Nowhere else shall we find such descriptions of Mississippi River life in the fifties. Artistically defective his work is indeed; but to it cannot be denied the qualities of eloquence, naturalness, and sincerity. The work, like the man, is genuine.

Bret Harte.—The stirring, primitive, lawless life of early California found its painter in Francis Bret Harte, who early dropped his first name from his literary signature. He was a native of Albany, New York (1839), his ancestors being English, German, and Hebrew. His father, a teacher of Greek, died when the son was but a child. Receiving only a common-school education, Harte went with his family in 1854 to California, which for five years had been the Mecca of the gold-hunter and the gambler. At first he tried teaching and mining, gaining from either business little more than experience, of which he was to make good use in later

---

15   See Higginson's "Cheerful Yesterdays," pp. 107–111.

years. In 1857 he became a compositor for the San Francisco *Golden Era*. Some of his unsigned sketches attracted the notice of the editor, who ordered him to exchange his composing-stick for a writer's desk in the office. He later joined the staff of *The Californian*, to which he contributed the clever parodies on contemporary writers of fiction later published (1867) as "Condensed Novels." From 1864 till 1870, he was secretary of the United States Branch Mint; during this time he wrote much of his best poetry. When *The Overland Monthly* was projected in 1868, no other name than Harte's was considered for the editorship. Mr. Noah Brooks has told how he and Harte agreed to write each a short story for the first number, and how Harte with his usual fastidiousness about words was unable to finish his in time. When it did appear, however, "The Luck of Roaring Camp" and the story which followed it, "The Outcasts of Poker Flat," made Harte famous; the latter story is generally considered the most perfect of his works. In 1870, Mr. Harte was appointed professor of recent literature in the University of California; but in the following year he resigned this post, settled in New York, and devoted himself to lecturing and to writing, especially for *The Atlantic Monthly*. In 1878, he was appointed United States consul at Crefeld, Germany; from 1880 till 1885 he held a similar post at Glasgow. From 1885 until his death, in 1902, Harte lived in London, busily engaged in literary work. His best-known works are "Mrs. Skagg's Husbands" (1872), "Tales of the Argonauts, and Other Stories" (1875), "Gabriel Conroy," his only long novel (1876), "Drift from Two Shores" (1878), "The Twins of Table Mountain" (1879), "Flip; and Found at Blazing Star" (1882), "In the Carquinez Woods" (1883), effectively expressing the wonder and mystery of the forest, "On the Frontier" (1884), "Maruja" (1885), a melodramatic novel, "Snow-Bound at Eagle's" (1886), "A Millionaire of Rough and Ready" (1887), "The Crusade of the Excelsior" (1887), "A Phyllis of the Sierras" (1888), "The Argonauts of North Liberty" (1888), "A Sappho of Green Springs" (1891), "Colonel Starbottle's Client and Some Other People" (1892), "Sally Dows" (1893), "A Protégée of Jack Hamlin's" (1894), "The Three Partners" (1897), "Under the Redwoods" (1901). Throughout his life, it will be seen, he continued to write of the old California days, of a régime which has long since passed away, but which he immortalised.

It was Harte's rare privilege to be the first to work in a mine which has yielded rich ores to many since his day; to write of an elemental, half-savage life in which convention was all but unknown, and the background of which was the rugged simplicity and majesty of the Sierras. "His actual discovery," says Mr. Logan, "was Nature in an aspect always grand, sometimes awful, at a moment when her primeval solitude was invaded by a host that had cast human relationships behind, and came surging towards an unknown land, all under the sway of a devouring passion—the thirst for gold." He had his own way (possibly influenced by Dickens) of presenting these rough scenes. He did not idealise this primitive life; he did not as a rule weave it into romance (even Mr. Boyesen cites only "Gabriel Conroy" as a romantic novel); he did not seek to interpret it or to make it symbolise religious or moral ideas. To him it was a very real world; and with true eye and sure touch he sought to portray it impartially, as it was; the reader might draw his own moral—if he happened to need one. It is this unerring instinct of the artist that places Harte in the ranks of the greater story-tellers.

His powers, however, had their limitations. He found himself unable to sustain interest in a long story. "Gabriel Conroy," though it contains interesting scenes and some of his best characters, is quite without unity—a bundle of impressions in which the same characters are presented hardly twice alike. He has been criticised, too, for endowing otherwise worthless characters with some marked virtue; but perhaps it is only fair to say, with Mr. Logan, that "the virtue is generally a primitive one, and is rarely either inconsistent or improbable."

In his later years, Harte did little to increase his reputation. The same characters, the same types, appear again and again; but there is no added source of interest, no maturer observation of men and manners. His reputation continues to rest on the score of early tales, terse and full of energy, with which he dazzled and delighted the reading public of the later sixties and the seventies.

Elizabeth Stuart Phelps Ward.—It is of course a far cry from Harte to Mrs. Phelps Ward, who came into notice in the East in the same year in which *The Overland* was started. Mrs. Ward was born at Andover, Massachusetts, and was the daughter of Professor Austin Phelps of Andover Theological Seminary. In 1888 she was married to the Rev. Herbert D. Ward. She is the author of a long list of kindly and readable stories, none of which quite attains to distinction in point of quality, but several of which have been popular and influential. Beginning with "The Gates Ajar" (1868), half novel, half threnody, she continued with "The Silent Partner" (1870), "The Story of Avis" (1877), a favourite with many, "An Old Maid's Paradise" (1879) and its sequel "Burglars in Paradise" (1886), "Friends, a Duet" (1881), "Doctor Zay" (1882), "Beyond the Gates" (1883), which elaborates the idea of her first story, "A Singular Life" (1894), her best book, and "The Man in the Case" (1906). Her plots, sometimes conventional, are never complicated and are skilfully managed; and her women characters are generally true to life. Of her men, for example Emanuel Bayard, so much cannot be said. She collaborated with her husband in writing two or three novels which were not very successful.

Constance Fenimore Woolson.—A grandniece of Fenimore Cooper, Miss Woolson (1848–94) has taken a place among women novelists scarcely less honourable than that held by her kinsman among American novelists in general. Born at Claremont, New Hampshire, she was educated in Cleveland, Ohio, and at a French school in New York City. After her father's death in 1869, she spent her summers at Cooperstown, New York, or on the Great Lakes, and her winters in the South. Her first literary effort, "The Happy Valley" (*Harper's*, July, 1870) met with immediate approval. From then till her death, she contributed regularly to *Harper's*. She published "The Old Stone House" (1873), "Castle Nowhere; Lake Country Sketches" (1875), "Rodman the Keeper; Southern Sketches" (1880), "Anne" (1882), "For the Major" (1883), "East Angels" (1886), her most elaborate and perhaps her best novel, dealing with ante-bellum Georgia coast life, "Jupiter Lights" (1889), and "Horace Chase" (1894), by many preferred to any of her other works. Possessing decided gifts as a novelist, she had a high standard of excellence. Some of her plots are intricate, but all are skilfully worked out. Charles Dudley Warner spoke of her as one of the first in America to bring the short story as a social study to its present degree of excellence. Her best work should have more than a merely ephemeral life.

Henry James, Jr.—A subject of contention among critics, having an ardent if not a large following, but standing for something like caviare to the general public, Henry James is to-day one of the most striking figures among American novelists. He was born in New York, April 15, 1843, the son of Henry James the theologian, and a younger brother of William James the psychologist. His family was Irish on the father's side and Scotch on the mother's. He has told us of his early years and of how, while the other boys were at their games, he used to sit on the hearth-rug studying *Punch* and learning about the life which John Leech's pictures suggested to him. At eleven he was sent abroad and spent six years in England, France, and Switzerland, deeply interested in European culture, art, and social tradition. On his return, his family made their home at Newport, Rhode Island. In 1862 he entered the Harvard Law School, but found more pleasure in the lectures of James Russell Lowell on literature than in the reading of law. Soon after leaving Cambridge, having succeeded with some early ventures in *The Galaxy* and other magazines, he began to devote himself wholly to literature. Since 1869 he has lived abroad, chiefly in Paris, London, and Italy. His life has been a quiet, uneventful study of men and women, of books, of places.

Mr. James has been a fairly prolific writer, of constantly increasing subtlety and attention to finish. His first stories, curiously enough, revealed a romantic, at times even sensational, bent, which he soon outgrew. His first novel, "Watch and Ward" (1871), was promising but not otherwise significant; "Roderick Hudson" (1875) was quite equal to the best of his later work, combining profound analysis of character with perhaps more sentiment than appears in his later works. It is a study of the artistic temperament in the person of a young American sculptor who is taken to Italy by a rich virtuoso. The story deals with two favourite studies of Mr. James: the contrast between Americans and the older races with which they come into contact in Europe, and the contrast between the artistic and the prosaic person. The first of these contrasts forms the subject of "A Passionate Pilgrim" (1875), including that exquisite story "The Madonna of the Future," of "The American" (1877), and of "Daisy Miller, a Comedy" (1878), in which a burlesque element is noticeable. From the year 1875, then, may be said to date the "international novel" of comparison or contrast, which has become so immensely popular. In "The Europeans" (1878), the scene changes to Boston and the author shows how the life of the Puritans appears to foreign visitors. Other international studies are found in "An International Episode" (1879), "The Portrait of a Lady" (1881), one of his most popular longer novels, and "The Siege of London, The Pension Beaurepas, and The Point of View" (1883). In 1880 (dated 1881) appeared "Washington Square," a quiet story laid in a formerly aristocratic quarter of New York; the tale has been called "a miracle in monotone." Then came "The Bostonians" (1886), which Professor Richardson speaks of as typically "long, dull, and inconsequential, but mildly pleasing the reader, or at times quite delighting him, by a deliberate style which is enjoyable for its own sake, by a calm portraiture which represents the characters with silhouette clearness, and by some very faithful and delicately humorous pictures of the life and scenery of Eastern Massachusetts." "The Princess Casamassima" (1886) continues the career of an American adventuress, Christina Light, who has figured in "Roderick Hudson," to which it thus forms a kind of sequel. Less read than some others, it is one of the most remarkable of Mr. James' stories. In 1888 appeared "The Aspern Papers, and Other Stories" and "The Reverberator," a comedy of manners recalling "The American," and dealing with the incompatibility between the cultivated and the vulgar relatives of two lovers and with the odious violation of private life by modern journalism. "The Tragic Muse" (1890), a study of a psychological problem of art and love, is complicated and difficult in the extreme; a friend expressed a sound view of it to Mr. James: "I will say it is your best novel if you promise never to do it again," probably meaning that the extreme limit of elaboration had been reached. Three collections of stories, "The Lesson of the Master, and Other Stories" (1892), "The Real Thing, and Other Tales" (1893), and "Terminations" (1895), include various comic sketches, with some preciosities, and a well-told ghost-story, "Sir Edmund Orme," the *motif* of which was later repeated in "The Turn of the Screw" (1898), a horrible, nerve-racking tale. "The Other House" (1896) is a highly dramatic, even sensational, story of passion, culminating, strange to say, in a murder; yet Rose Armiger is Mr. James' one supremely passionate woman. In 1897 were published "The Spoils of Poynton" and "What Maisie Knew," the latter a rather unpleasant story of domestic unhappiness and sordid intrigue; Maisie being a little girl whose life was spent alternately in the company of divorced parents, equally guilty, each of whom had remarried. "In the Cage" (1898) is a tissue of shrewd guess-work woven by a lively telegraph girl who becomes interested in the love affair of two others. "The Two Magics" (1898) includes "The Turn of the Screw" and "Covering End," a pleasant comedy about an English country house.

"The Awkward Age" (1899) is a unique example of subtle, often elusive, analysis of character—of character which some might say was not worth analysis, with unimportant incidents and little action. "The Soft Side" (1900) is a collection of studies of abnormal character and curious psychical phenomena, in which the rhythm of the prose is at times remarkable for its suggestiveness. "The Sacred Fount" (1901) is a fanciful sketch dealing with the idea of youth as a rejuvenator of age. "The Wings of the Dove" (1902) has been called the most remarkable book that Mr. James has written. It is a long story of the old warfare between the flesh and the spirit, in which the unseen forces from another world play an unlooked-for part. Mr. James' most recent stories are "The Better Sort" (1903), "The Ambassadors" (1904), and "The Golden Bowl" (1905).

It is difficult to sum up in a few words the leading traits of Mr. James. It is easy to speak of him as reeling off volumes of abstruseness in which the petty ambitions of worthless Americans are analysed with a minuteness like that in which the leisurely student of anatomy delights; but such innocuous "criticism" does not even touch Mr. James. Undoubtedly it has been increasingly hard of late years to follow him; his later stories, with their proneness to excessive psychological delving, have a certain analogy to Browning's later poems, which became harder to follow. But judged by his best works, such as "Roderick Hudson," "The Princess Casamassima," and "The Other House," he must be pronounced a great artist, a keen analyst of the small section of life and the few types of character which he has chosen to study (and if one does not care for the types, one may still recognise the art with which they are presented); and as always a loyal American. He is not a master of style; yet at his best he embodies certain qualities of supreme excellence in style—ease, intimacy, suggestiveness, lucidity, sincerity. He is never a preacher, nor is he ever the mere idler and *dilettante*. He is very much in earnest; and in consequence the moral effect of his exposition of life is wholesome. "Out of the corruption," says Miss Cary,[16] "of a society which Mr. James depicts with unsparing detail and without satire or didactic comment, rises the flame of purity. Some one among his characters is sure to stand for invincible goodness." If the language of his later books becomes unintelligible, it will of course be a pity; but it seems

16   *Scribner's Magazine*, October, 1904, xxxvi. 399.

quite unlikely that the great works of his middle period will soon cease to have a large body of appreciative and delighted readers.

Edward Eggleston.—The Hoosier life of southern Indiana has been described by Edward Eggleston (1837–1902). A native of Vevay, Indiana, he received only a brief school education, but taught himself several languages. He first became (1857) an itinerant Methodist minister in southern Indiana and then for nine years was a Bible Society agent in Minnesota. From 1866 till 1879, he was engaged partly in journalism and partly in a Brooklyn pastorate; then he retired to his country place on Lake George to devote himself entirely to literature.

His first book to win attention was "The Hoosier Schoolmaster" (1871), which first appeared as a serial in *Hearth and Home*. Having read Taine's "Art in the Netherlands," he says, he proceeded to apply Taine's maxim, that an artist ought to paint what he has seen. The result was so faithful a picture that in spite of its faults it has a permanent value as a record of one phase of early Western life. Dr. Eggleston also wrote "The End of the World" (1872), which deals with the Millerites, who in 1842–3 proved by the Book of Daniel that the end of the world was at hand; "The Mystery of Metropolisville" (1873); "The Circuit Rider, a Tale of the Heroic Age" (1874), in which he drew on his own early experiences; "Roxy" (1878), a story of picturesque incident and character development laid in the time of the Tippecanoe campaign of 1840; "The Graysons, a Story of Illinois" (1888), a realistic picture of pioneer life in which Abraham Lincoln figures as a character; "The Faith Doctor" (1891), which deals with Christian Science and kindred phenomena in New York, and which shows the influence of Mr. Howells; and "Duffels" (1893), a collection of stories.

Dr. Eggleston himself spoke of his attitude in literature as a constant struggle "between the lover of literary art and the religionist, the reformer, the philanthropist, the man with a mission." We are not of course surprised to find an editor of *The Sunday School Teacher* making his moral too prominent. But while this mars much of his work, his novels may still be said to be fresh and genuine transcripts of life.

Julian Hawthorne.—Julian Hawthorne (born in 1846) inherited literary ability from his father, the romancer. As an infant he was delicate; at seven his health was good, but having been kept out of school he could neither read nor write. Entering Harvard in 1863, he became known as an all-around athlete. After leaving Harvard without graduating, he lived in Dresden for some years, then returned to America and became a hydrographic engineer in New York. In 1871 he began to win attention to his short stories, and since 1872 has devoted himself to literature and journalism, living successively in Dresden, London, and New York. "Bressant," his first novel, published in *Appleton's Journal* in 1872, is somewhat crude and not without sensational elements, but holds the interest. Then came "Idolatry" (1874), which, though rewritten in whole or in part seven times, is now unknown, "Garth" (1877), a long story of New Hampshire, the chief part being a painter's love-story, "Sebastian Strome" (1880), a study of the chastening of a selfish character, strongly reminding us of "Adam Bede," "Dust" (1883), a story of extreme self-sacrifice, "Fortune's Fool" (1884), "Archibald Malmaison" (1884), a novelette, and "Beatrix Randolph" (1884). In general his stories are not pleasant reading. Impossible characters are not infrequent and there is a tendency toward the choice of morbid subjects. Many descriptive passages, however, are superbly done, and the general impression one gets is that of power, but of power unrestrained, a strong imagination capable of greater things than Mr. Hawthorne has done. Yet the qualities characteristic of his best books, like "Archibald Malmaison," are such as led the late Richard Henry Stoddard, a man by no means deficient in judgment, and familiar with the best in modern literature, to pronounce Mr. Hawthorne "clearly and easily the first of living romancers."

In recent years, Mr. Hawthorne has forsaken the paths of pure literature, with which he seems never to have been in love,[17] for those of journalism.

William Dean Howells.—The apostle of latter-day realism, and one of the most noted of our writers of fiction, is Mr. Howells. He has been prominent in literary circles for more than forty years. The son of a journalist and printer, Mr. Howells was born at Martin's Ferry, Belmont County, Ohio, in 1837. His father had adopted Swedenborgian tenets and the

---

17   *Cf.* "Confessions and Criticisms" (1886), pp. 15–16.

boy was reared in this faith. His boyhood life has been admirably described in "A Boy's Town." The family lived successively at several places in Ohio, and young Howells was in turn compositor, correspondent, and news editor. In 1859 he began contributing to *The Atlantic Monthly*, his first poem, "Andenken," appearing anonymously in January, 1860. Nearly every volume of *The Atlantic* down to 1900 contains some of his work. A campaign "Life of Abraham Lincoln" (1860) netted him $160, and enabled him to make his first trip East and to meet Emerson, Lowell, and other New England writers; it also won for him the post of Consul at Venice, which he held from 1861 till 1865. The first fruits of his Italian residence were "Venetian Life" (1866) and "Italian Journeys" (1867), two descriptive works which revealed a truly poetic temperament and a refined taste. On his return to America, Mr. Howells became an editorial writer for the New York *Times* and a contributor to *The Nation*. The next year (1866), removing to Boston, he became assistant editor of *The Atlantic*; in 1871 he became the editor and made the magazine a stronger force than ever in criticism. On resigning this post in 1880, he spent a year or two abroad; since 1888 he has lived in New York, engaged chiefly in literary work. From 1886 till 1891 he conducted the Editor's Study in *Harper's*.

While Mr. Howells has been prolific in criticism, description, narratives of travel, literary and personal reminiscences, and lighter essays, his most significant work has been done in his novels. His first appearance as a writer of fiction was in 1871, with "Their Wedding Journey," a slight but delicately humorous tale of a Boston couple, the Marches, who go to Canada to spend their honeymoon. "A Chance Acquaintance" (1873) is a subtle study of incompatibility of temperament. "A Foregone Conclusion" (1875) transports us to Venice, where we watch the unhappy love story, dramatically told, of an agnostic priest and an American girl. "The Lady of the Aroostook" (1879) is an amusing, healthy story of New England provincial manners. The theme of "The Undiscovered Country" (1880) is spiritualism and mesmerism. "A Fearful Responsibility" (1881) is the story of an American professor in Venice whose charge, a young girl, is loved by an Austrian officer. In "Dr. Breen's Practice" (1881) we have pictures of summer life in a small seaside village in Maine and a study of modern Puritanism. With "A Modern Instance" (1881) may be said to begin the extremely realistic stories in Mr. Howells' later manner; others are: "A Woman's Reason" (1883), "The Rise of Silas Lapham" (1885), "Indian Summer" (1886), "The Minister's Charge, or The Apprenticeship of Lemuel Barker" (1887), "April Hopes" (1887), "Annie Kilburn" (1888), "A Hazard of New Fortunes" (1890), in which the Marches have characteristic experiences in New York, "The Quality of Mercy" (1892), a painful but well told story, "The Coast of Bohemia" (1893), "An Open-Eyed Conspiracy" (1897), "Ragged Lady" (1899), "The Flight of Pony Baker" (1902), a captivating boys' story, belonging with "A Boy's Town," "The Kentons" (1903), and "The Son of Royal Langbrith" (1905). From these novels, after the manner of Tolstoi, the romantic and even the ideal are rigorously excluded; we are treated to exhaustive, minutely detailed accounts of the daily lives of ordinary, generally commonplace people. Plot and incident are of secondary importance, although some chapters fairly bristle with incident; Mr. Howells holds that any transcript of real life, even though made at random, if skilfully handled, is of sufficient interest to form a good story. Naturally this view of the novel has found many opponents, and Mr. Howells' books have been somewhat less popular of late years than they were in the eighties. After all, the hunger for the ideal cannot be wholly appeased by disagreeable actualities; and there are people whom we know all too well in the flesh to care to see them, in all their pettiness and meanness and duplicity, in the pages of fiction. Mr. Howells' followers, however,—and there are many of them—contend that nothing is so interesting as real, actual, present life; that no detail of our daily round is without its significance; that the slightest act or omission of an act may affect our destiny. After all, the realists and the romanticists we have always with us; the former are just now in the majority; but the reaction is just as inevitable as the return of the pendulum.

In some of his later stories, as "The Traveller from Altruria" (1894) and "Through the Eye of the Needle" (1907), Mr. Howells has shown an increasing interest in the more serious problems of society—poverty, strikes, the causes of crime, "the tyranny of individualism," and the conditions that hinder the spread of sympathy and human brotherhood. The effect of this increased ethical and human interest has probably not been to enhance the artistic value of his work; and some deplore his lapse from the high ideal of art for art's sake. Others see in Mr. Howells' recent works a greater attention to substance, a firmer tissue, a broader humanity. And always, be it said, in reading Mr. Howells, one is conscious of that fine and careful workmanship, that care for correct and proper form, that artistic conscience, without which, whatever his literary creed, Mr. Howells could never have become the foremost and representative American novelist of his time.

Frances Hodgson Burnett.—Frances H. Burnett was born in Manchester, England, in 1849, but came to America with her parents in 1865 and lived for eight years, until her marriage, in New Market and Knoxville, Tennessee. Since then she has lived in Washington and in Kent, England. She first gained notice with "Surly Tim's Trouble" (*Scribner's Monthly*, June, 1872), a story of Lancashire, as were also "That Lass o' Lowrie's" (1877), "Dolly" (1877, republished in 1883 as "Vagabondia"), and "Haworth's" (1879) said to be a favourite with its author. With "Louisiana" (1880) she turned to America for material, describing life in the mountains of North Carolina. "Through One Administration" (1883) is a pathetic and powerful story of social and political life in Washington. "Little Lord Fauntleroy" (1886), the Anglo-American story of a seven-year-old hero, has become a children's classic; similar but less known are the tales in "Sara Crewe, and Other Stories" (1888), and "The Captain's Youngest, Piccino, and Other Stories" (1894). In "The Pretty Sister of José" (1889), Mrs. Burnett deals with picturesque and striking Spanish characters and scenes. "A Lady of Quality" (1896) and its sequel, "His Grace of Osmonde" (1897), are melodramatic stories of English aristocrats in the seventeenth and eighteenth centuries. "In Connection with the De Willoughby Claim" (1899) deals with country life in Tennessee in the early sixties. Her latest stories are "The Dawn of a To-Morrow" (1906) and "The Shuttle" (1907), the latter a fascinating international novel. She has thoroughly demonstrated her power to delineate character as moulded by passion.

Philander Deming.—Philander Deming (born in Carlisle, New York, in 1829), a lawyer by profession, in 1873 began publishing in *The Atlantic Monthly* stories and sketches the scene of which is laid in the Adirondack region of northern New York. Devoid of sensationalism, these stories portray simply and effectively the rude but sound life of plain country folk. Mr. Deming has published in book form "Adirondack Stories" (1880), "Tompkins and Other Folks" (1885), and "The Story of a Pathfinder" (1907).

Lew Wallace.—General Lewis Wallace (1827–1905), an Indiana lawyer and soldier in the Mexican and Civil Wars, was the author of three novels, "The Fair God" (1873), "Ben Hur, a Tale of the Christ" (1880), and "The Prince of India" (1893), which deserve mention chiefly because of their popularity. The second, especially, in this respect, ranks close to "Uncle Tom's Cabin." Written in a spirit of deep reverence for the traditional view of Jesus of Nazareth, and making small demands upon the imagination, it could hardly fail to make a strong appeal to a large body of readers. As literature, however, Wallace's books are of only transient importance.

Charles Dudley Warner.—Charles Dudley Warner (1829–1900) belongs mainly with the essayists, but wrote a few novels that deserve to live. With Mark Twain he wrote "The Gilded Age" (1873). "Their Pilgrimage" (1887) has a slight plot, but gives minute and accurate descriptions of Southern watering-places. "A Little Journey in the World" (1889) and its sequel, "The Golden House" (1895), are vivid pictures of decadent New York society. "That Fortune" (1899) is a picture, drawn from expert knowledge, of the New York financial world.

Hjalmar Hjorth Boyesen.—Hjalmar Hjorth Boyesen (1848–95) realised the dream of many in successfully combining the careers of authorship and teaching. Born at Frederiksvärn, Norway, and educated at Christiania, he came to America in 1869. He first became editor of a Scandinavian journal in Chicago. Then he studied philology at Leipsic for two years (1872–74). From 1874 till 1880 he was professor of German at Cornell University, and from 1881 till his death he filled a similar chair at Columbia University. Besides some poetry and essays, he wrote "Gunnar, a Norse Romance" (1874), his one effort in romance, "Tales from Two Hemispheres" (1876), "Falconberg" (1879), "Ilka on the Hilltop" (1881), a collection of short stories, "Queen Titania" (1881), "A Daughter of the Philistines" (1883), "Social Strugglers" (1893), "The Mammon of Unrighteousness" (1891), and "The Golden Calf" (1892). His later stories were realistic novels concerned with vital problems, such as the conflict between wealth and essential culture. Their vogue was not great, but their workmanship was genuine.

Blanche Willis Howard.—Blanche Willis Howard (1847–98) was born in Bangor, Maine, was educated in New York, and in 1878 went to Stuttgart, Germany, to engage in teaching and writing. In 1890 she was married to Baron von Teuffel, a physician. She wrote a number of novels, of which "One Summer" (1875), "Aunt Serena" (1880), "Guenn" (1882), "Aulnay Tower" (1886), "The Open Door" (1889), "No Heroes" (1893), a boys' story, and "Seven on the Highway" (1897), a collection of short stories, may be mentioned. In collaboration with William Sharp she wrote "A Fellowe and His Wife" (1892), in which a comic atmosphere prevails. Perhaps "Guenn," the pathetic story of a Breton maiden's hopeless love, is the book by which she will be longest remembered.

Edgar Fawcett.—Edgar Fawcett (1847–1904) was in his day a prominent and popular poet, dramatist, and novelist. Born and reared in New York, and at twenty graduated from Columbia College, he early saw the rich possibilities of the life around him, and confined himself to the delineation of New York people. The best of his novels are "Rutherford" (written in 1876, but not published in book form till 1884), "A Hopeless Case" (1880), "A Gentleman of Leisure" (1881), "An Ambitious Woman" (1883), "The House at High Bridge" (1886), perhaps his best story, "Fair Fame" (1894), "Outrageous Fortune" (1894), and "The Ghost of Guy Thyrle" (1897). He was fond of attacking the petty conventions of social life and his satire was not ineffective. Partly because of this unpleasant realism his books have already ceased to be much read.

Edwin Lassetter Bynner.—Edwin L. Bynner (1842–93), a New England lawyer and journalist, for a time librarian of the Boston Law Library, achieved success in the field of the historical romance. Beginning with "Nimport" (1877), he produced a large number of novels and short stories, of which the best are "Penelope's Suitors" (*The Atlantic*, December, 1884), "Agnes Surriage" (1887), "The Begum's Daughter" (1889), a story of New Amsterdam in 1689, and "Zachary Phips" (1892), which introduces the mysterious Western expedition of Aaron Burr. Accurate on the historical side, his works are not distinguished artistic successes; yet they make the past live again.

Sarah Orne Jewett.—Sarah Orne Jewett (born in 1849) has written some interesting and even powerful stories of the coast of New England.

She was reared at South Berwick, near the Maine coast. While accompanying her father, a physician, on his rounds, she heard from him many local and family histories and traditions. Her first story was "Deephaven" (1877); and she has since written, among others, "Country By-Ways" (1881), eight sketches; "The Mate of the *Daylight*, and Friends Ashore" (1884), short stories and sketches; "A Country Doctor" (1884), "A Marsh Island" (1885), and "A White Heron" (1886), three stories of rural New England; "Strangers and Wayfarers" (1890); "A Native of Winby, and Other Tales" (1893); "The Country of the Pointed Firs" (1896), which contains her most successful character studies; "The Queen's Twin, and Other Stories" (1899); "The Tory Lover" (1901), a love-story of the Revolution, introducing John Paul Jones, which cannot be pronounced successful. Miss Jewett is at her best in her kindly humorous and sympathetic interpretations of humble but self-respecting New Englanders of the present day. Her humour is healthy and contagious and her style is for the most part simple, clear, and vigorous.

Mrs. Ellen Olney Kirk.—Ellen Olney Kirk ("Henry Hayes," born in Connecticut in 1842) has been popular as a novelist. She received her education at Stratford, Conn., and was married to John Foster Kirk, the historian, in 1879. Her stories include "Love in Idleness" (1877), "A Lesson in Love" (1883), a study in character, "A Midsummer Madness" (1885), "The Story of Margaret Kent" (1886), "Queen Money" (1888), "The Story of Lawrence Garth" (1894), her best book, in which the difficult character of an adventuress is well drawn, "The Revolt of a Daughter" (1898), "Dorothy Deane" (1899), "Our Lady Vanity" (1901), "The Apology of Ayliffe" (1904), and "Marcia" (1907). The moral in her stories is generally not obtrusive and the humour is genial.

Edward Bellamy.—Edward Bellamy (1850–98), a native of Massachusetts, studied at Union College and in Germany, and in 1871 was admitted to the bar, but devoted his life to journalism and literature. After a year in the Sandwich Islands, in 1878 he published his first novel, "A Nantucket Idyl," which was followed by "Dr. Heidenhoff's Process" (1880), in its own way a supremely effective romance, and "Miss Ludington's Sister, a Romance of Immortality" (1884), none of them very successful with the public. His best known work, "Looking Backward, or 2000–1887" (1888), a Utopian romance, was unexpectedly received as a gospel of socialism; it was widely read and translated into many languages. Much inferior artistically was its sequel, "Equality" (1897). In his best work Bellamy showed a rare gift of romantic portraiture of average types "in the village environment by which he interpreted the heart of the American nation."

Mrs. Burton N. Harrison.—Mrs. Burton Harrison (born Constance Cary, at Vaucluse, Virginia, in 1846) has written interesting and highly realistic novels of New York City life, full of local colour and effective in background; and some novels of Virginia life. Mr. Harrison, to whom she was married in 1867, had been private secretary to President Jefferson Davis of the Confederacy. The couple soon removed to New York, which has since been their permanent home. Mrs. Harrison's first venture in literature was "A Little Centennial Lady" (*Scribner's Monthly*, July, 1876), a sprightly historical sketch. Her novels dealing with Northern society are "Golden Rod" (1878), "Helen Troy" (1881), "The Anglomaniacs" (1890), "Sweet Bells out of Tune" (1893), "A Bachelor Maid" (1894), "An Errant Wooing" (1895), "Good Americans" (1897), "A Triple Entanglement" (1897), "The Carcelline Emerald" (1899), and "The Circle of a Century." Perhaps the chief excellence of these stories is the dialogue, in the management of which Mrs. Harrison shows great skill. Although the attitude of the author is that of a satirist, her laughter at the foibles of society is not unkindly. Of Virginia she has written "Crow's Nest and Bellhaven Tales" (1892) and "A Son of the Old Dominion" (1897), which deals with pre-Revolutionary times. "A Daughter of the South" (1892) is an exquisitely told story of New Orleans Creole life thrown into the environment of Paris under the Second Empire.

Charles Egbert Craddock.—Charles Egbert Craddock is the pen name of Mary Noailles Murfree (born in 1850), who contributed to *The Atlantic* for several years before it was suspected that her stories were written by a woman. She is the daughter of a once prominent lawyer of Murfreesboro, Tennessee, who in 1883 removed to St. Louis. Because of an accident, Miss Murfree was for several years unable to walk. She was a diligent student and somehow gained an intimate knowledge of the mountaineers of Eastern Tennessee, who figure in all of her stories. Her first story of any importance was "The Dancin' Party at Harrison's Cove" (*The Atlantic*, May, 1878). It was largely due to Mr. Aldrich's urgent representations that her first collection of stories, "In the Tennessee Mountains," found a publisher (1884). Of this a writer in *The Nation* said, with justice: "We have not only one mountain valley, but a whole country of hills—not a man and a woman here and there, but the people of a whole district—not merely a day of winter or of summer, but all the year—not lives, but life." This is substantially true of all her works, in which she described prosaic and pathetic mountaineer life, being always inspired, however, by the solitude and grandeur of the Great Smoky Mountains. The list of her works is a long one: "Where the Battle was Fought" (1884); "Down the Ravine" (1885); "The Prophet of the Great Smoky Mountains" (1885), which recounts the history of "a Bunyan worsted by his doubts"; "In the Clouds" (1887), a tragic story likewise dealing with religious experiences; "The Story of Keedon Bluffs" (1887); "The Despot of Broomsedge Cove" (1889), the plot of which hinges on a mysterious murder; "In the Stranger People's Country" (1891); "His Vanished Star" (1894); "The Mystery of Witch-Face Mountain, and Other Stories" (1895); "The Juggler" (1897); "The Young Mountaineers" (1897), short stories; "The Champion" (1902); "A Spectre of Power" (1903), which is laid in the year 1763 and is full of Indian love; "The Frontiersmen" (1904); and "The Storm Centre" (1905). Her later work suffers from repetition of certain mannerisms and from excessive attention to description; possibly also from too rapid production. On the whole, however, in her ability to present the pathos and tragedy of simple lives, Miss Murfree has a place of honour among present-day writers.

Anna Katharine Green.—Through the publication, in 1878, of "The Leavenworth Case," a clever detective story, this author, then a girl of nineteen, was brought into immediate notice on both sides of the Atlantic. "The Leavenworth Case" was followed in successive years by "A Strange Disappearance," "The Sword of Damocles," "Hand and Ring," "Behind Closed Doors," "Marked 'Personal,'" "That Affair Next Door," "Lost Man's Lane," "One of My Sons," and other volumes. Some critics have spoken of Miss Green (who is now Mrs. Charles Rohlfs) as the "Wilkie Collins of America." Nearly all of her books have appeared in transatlantic editions. Mrs. Rohlfs is also responsible for two volumes of poems, "The Defence of the Bride" (1882) and "Risifi's Daughter" (1886).

Frank R. Stockton.—The unique and kindly humour of Mr. Stockton's books attracted many readers. He was born in Philadelphia in 1834 and was the son of William S. Stockton, an ardent temperance reformer, abolitionist, and Methodist layman who helped to establish the Methodist Protestant Church. Educated in the schools of Philadelphia, young Stockton first tried the study of medicine, then worked as a wood-engraver for some years, devoting his leisure time to prose and verse writing. In 1872, he gave up wood-engraving to join the staff of the Philadelphia *Morning Post*, and for the next ten years was engaged in editorial and journalistic work on *Scribner's Monthly*, *St. Nicholas*, *Hearth and Home*, etc. From 1882 until his death in 1902, Mr. Stockton was independently engaged in literary work, producing a large number of delightfully humorous stories and novels. The tale which made him famous was "Rudder Grange" (1879), which recounts the experiences of a young married couple who begin housekeeping in a castaway barge with an absurd handmaid named Pomona. "The Lady or the Tiger? and Other Stories" appeared in 1884; the title story is the best known of Stockton's works. Other stories are "The Late Mrs. Null" (1886); "The Casting Away of Mrs. Lecks and Mrs. Aleshine" (1886), a Crusoe-like narrative, a sequel to which is "The Dusantes" (1888); "The Hundredth Man" (1887); "The Merry Chanter" (1890); "The Squirrel Inn" (1891); "Pomona's Travels" (1894), which narrates the wedding journey of the amusing Pomona through England and Scotland; "The Adventures of Captain Horn" (1895) and its sequel, "Mrs. Cliff's Yacht" (1896), which deal with adventures in quest of the treasure of the Incas of Peru; "A Bicycle of Cathay" (1900); and "Afield and Afloat" (1901), a collection of short stories. While his style is remarkably simple and free from mannerisms, "the art that conceals art, until it can pass for nature itself," his method of handling plot and character is distinctively his own. His reasoning is always logical, but he contrives that it shall bring about the most amusing absurdities conceivable. If, as one writer alleges, "his whimsicality played on the surface of men and things," one may reply that that is precisely where it should play. His stories are none the less wholesome, even though he rarely or never touches on the pathetic. He was equally at home with the novel and the short story; but probably it is by his short stories that he will be longest known.

George Washington Cable.—George W. Cable (born in 1844) has immortalised the picturesque Creole life of Louisiana in the nineteenth century. Born in New Orleans of Virginian and New England stock, he had little school training and early became a clerk. At nineteen he entered the Confederate Army, serving till the close of the war. Then he became in succession a civil engineer and an accountant, contributing meanwhile to the New Orleans *Picayune*. Seven of his stories were collected and published in 1879 as "Old Creole Days." "The Grandissimes" (1880), which remains his best work, is a graphic and faithful picture of New Orleans life of a century ago, embodying romance and realism. "Madame Delphine" (1881) is a touching story of a heroic old quadroon woman. In "Dr. Sevier" (1884), Cable has studied in romantic vein an exceptional type of character, though not with marked success. "Bonaventure, a Prose Pastoral of Arcadian Louisiana" (1888), a better book, is a chapter of ethical history. "Strange True Stories of Louisiana" appeared in 1889. Less interesting as fiction, but valuable as a social study, is "John March, Southerner" (1894), a story of Southern Reconstruction. "The Cavalier" (1901) goes back to the Civil War, but subordinates interest in the conflict to interest in character; while "Bylow Hill" (1902) is a tragic story of insane jealousy, the scene being New England. Since 1885, Mr. Cable has lived at Northampton, Massachusetts. His later work, like that of many another, has probably suffered from a natural tendency to subordinate the artistic to the ethical. But in the province which he has made his own, the pioneer remains supreme. "Few recent American novelists," Professor Richardson justly remarks, "have shown so uniform an average of attainment in thought and art, or have thrown upon the quaintly real such new tints of ideal light."

Albion Winegar Tourgee.—Albion W. Tourgee (1838–1905), an Ohioan, studied (1858–61) at the University of Rochester, saw service in the Union Army, and afterward became an editor and lawyer at Greensboro, North Carolina. Most of his novels deal with phases of the Reconstruction Period in the South. The best of these were: "A Fool's Errand, by One of the Fools" (1879), doubtless his best known work, "Bricks Without Straw" (1880), and "The Invisible Empire" (1883). "Figs and Thistles" (1879) is a realistic story of early Ohio, in which the career of President Garfield is introduced; "Pactolus Prime" (1890) is the story of a Washington bootblack who has views on the negro problem. A man of strong opinions, Judge Tourgee could not write a novel which did not provoke thought; and he was by no means devoid of the true story-teller's cunning.

The Eighties.—The decade of 1880–90 beheld the growth of realism to vigorous maturity. Romances not a few were written, to be sure, such as the "Ramona" (1884) of Mrs. Helen Fiske Jackson ("H. H.," 1831–85), in which a romantic narrative clothes a strong plea for more humane treatment of the Indians, and the two Italian romances of William Waldorf Astor (born in 1848), "Valentino" (1885) and "Sforza, a Story of Milan" (1889). But these can hardly be called representative stories in a decade which saw the best work of Howells, James, Craddock, Fawcett, Bunner, Cable, and many others who wrote of the life they had seen and were content to employ present-day settings.

A few writers may here be grouped together for convenience. To the decade in question belong the best stories of George Parsons Lathrop (1851–98), the son-in-law of Hawthorne: "In the Distance" (1882), "An Echo of Passion" (1882), and "Would You Kill Him?" (1889), which amounts to a plea against capital punishment; and most of the fiction of Professor Arlo Bates (born in 1850): "The Pagans" (1884) and its sequel "The Philistines" (1889), "A Lad's Love" (1887), though "The Puritans" dates from 1898. Fine pictures of Italian life have been drawn by Julia Constance Fletcher ("George Fleming," born in 1853) in "Vestigia" (1882) and "Andromeda" (1885), the latter a story of high ideals and noble self-sacrifice. Illinois life in the unattractive baldness of pioneer days is portrayed by Major Joseph Kirkland (1830–94) in "Zury, the Meanest Man in Spring County" (1887) and "The McVeys, an Episode" (1888), in which Lincoln again figures as in Eggleston's "Graysons."

Henry Adams and John Hay.—"Democracy" (1880), an anonymous novel the authorship of which has hitherto baffled the critics, and which the present writer can now announce definitely to have been the work of the historian Henry Adams, is a keen and incisive study of political society in Washington, vividly portraying the corruption which perhaps inevitably attends the growth of the people's power, but concerning which the author is all too pessimistic. The bribery case which aids Mrs. Lee in unmasking the real character of Silas P. Ratcliffe finds a parallel in our contemporary history; and several of the characters are thought to have been drawn from real life. Happily, whatever may have been the state of affairs in Washington in 1880, the story would be very far from a true picture of the Washington of to-day. John Hay (1838–1905), lawyer, journalist, diplomatist, and statesman, was the author of a single novel, and his connection with that has been, up to the appearance of the present volume, only a conjecture. Prudence, however, obviously, required that "The Bread-Winners" (1883) should appear anonymously. As a politician, and as acting editor of *The Tribune*, Mr. Hay did not then wish to avow himself the author of a "frivolous novel"; besides, in the story he had spoken rather plainly about strikes and labour troubles. The story itself is well written, natural, and for the most part true to life. Of the two love scenes, the proposal of Maud Matchin is more convincing than is Farnham's to Alice Belding. The plot is well worked out; our interest in the story for itself almost never flags.

Joel Chandler Harris.—Joel Chandler Harris (1848–1908) used to describe himself as a journalist who became a literary man by accident. Few accidents have been luckier. He was born at Eatonton, Putnam County, Georgia. At fourteen he began to set type in a country newspaper office, contributing surreptitiously to its columns, setting his articles from the case instead of committing them to paper. Then he studied law and practised for a time at Forsyth, Georgia, at the same time doing literary work. In 1876, he joined the staff of the Atlanta *Constitution*, of which he became editor in 1890. To this paper he contributed the beast stories collected in 1881 under the title of "Uncle Remus: His Songs and His Sayings," which have ever since been immensely popular. Uncle Remus, a shrewd and witty old negro, has an inexhaustible supply of stories of Brer Rabbit, Brer Fox, and the other creatures; these "the little boy" and the rest of us never tire of hearing. The stories themselves, brought from Africa by the negroes, are interesting variant forms of the great beast epic, the classic example of which is "Reynard the Fox."[18] They celebrate the victory of craft over strength, of brain over brawn. Two other series afterward appeared, "Nights with Uncle Remus" (1883) and "Uncle Remus and His Friends" (1892); and now there is an *Uncle Remus' Magazine*. Mr. Harris' other books have helped to complete an

---

18   See Professor T. Frederick Crane's study of them in *The Popular Science Monthly*, April, 1881, xviii. 824–833.

admirably faithful picture of Middle Georgia rural life before, during, and after the Civil War. They include "At Teague Poteet's" (published in 1883 in *The Century*), "Mingo, and Other Sketches in Black and White" (1884), "Free Joe" (1887), "Balaam and His Master, and Other Sketches and Stories" (1891), in which melancholy and pathos predominate, "Aaron in the Wildwoods" (1897), "Tales of the Home Folks in Peace and War" (1898), "The Chronicles of Aunt Minervy Ann" (1899), "On the Wing of Occasions" (1900). With the single exception of "Gabriel Tolliver" (1902), which was not successful, Mr. Harris' constant work in journalism prevented him from undertaking any long novel of plantation life; shorter flights were better suited to his ability.

Maurice Thompson.—Maurice Thompson (1844–1901), of Indiana, wrote several romances. The first three, dealing with Southern life, "A Tallahassee Girl" (1882), "His Second Campaign" (1883), and "At Love's Extremes" (1885), were not very successful. In "A Banker of Bankersville" (1886) he succeeded better, giving a true and fresh picture of life in Indiana. The novel by which he is best known is "Alice of Old Vincennes" (1901), a stirring tale of French Indiana and the War of Independence. "Sweetheart Manette" (1901) gives an agreeable sketch of life in a Creole town on the Gulf Coast.

Francis Marion Crawford.—"The most versatile and various of modern novelists," if Mr. Andrew Lang's opinion is to be accepted, is Mr. F. Marion Crawford. Not only has he been prolific in a high degree, having written over thirty novels, but his scenes and characters have a wide range both in time and in place. He was born at Bagni di Lucca, Italy, in 1854, the son of Thomas Crawford the sculptor (who was of Scotch-Irish parentage) and Louisa Ward Crawford, a sister of Mrs. Julia Ward Howe. Prepared for college at St. Paul's School, Concord, New Hampshire, he entered Harvard, but remained there only a short time. He spent the years 1870–74 mainly at Trinity College, Cambridge, 1874–76 at Karlsruhe and Heidelberg, and 1877–78 at the University of Rome, where he studied Sanskrit. In 1879 he went to India and for two years was connected with the Allahabad *Indian Herald*. Returning to America, he spent two years in New York and Boston, continuing his Sanskrit and Zend studies under Professor Lanman of Harvard. No other American novelist save Mr. James has had so cosmopolitan a training. Relating a story of a Persian jewel merchant's adventure in India to his uncle, Samuel Ward, he was advised to make a novel of it; the result was the fascinating "Mr. Isaacs" (1882). Soon afterward Mr. Crawford returned to Italy, where, near Sorrento, he has since lived.

Mr. Crawford has a gift of rapid composition, sometimes completing a novel in less than a month; but his work as a whole is markedly free from slovenliness or signs of undue haste. His stories can be only briefly described: "Dr. Claudius" (1883), a highly romantic old- fashioned love-story of a learned Heidelberg Ph.D.; "To Leeward" (1883), a clever story of a wife's infidelity and of Roman society; "A Roman Singer" (1884), the story of an Italian peasant boy who became a great tenor and married a German countess; "An American Politician" (1885), which deals, in the style of Henry James, and with indifferent success, with the corruption in American politics; "Zoroaster" (1885), a strong romance written also in French, and brilliantly treating of the court of King Darius and the prophet Daniel; "A Tale of a Lonely Parish" (1886), a quiet and charming story of English rural life; "Paul Patoff" (1887), "a tale and nothing else," the scene of which is laid in modern Constantinople; "Marzio's Crucifix" (1887, written also in French), which is exceptional among his works in that it portrays Italian lower- and middle-class life, and which is considered by many his best work; "Saracinesca" (1887), "Sant' Ilario" (1889), "Don Orsino" (1892), and "Corleone" (1898), four novels forming a sequence and presenting on a broad canvas a remarkable picture of Roman society in the last third of the nineteenth century; "Greifenstein" (1889), a tragedy of the Black Forest, "a true story," containing accurate descriptions of German student life; "A Cigarette-Maker's Romance" (1890), a perfectly constructed romantic and absorbing story of Russian and Polish people living in Munich; "Khaled, a Romance of Arabia" (1891), of which a genie is the hero; "The Witch of Prague" (1891), which deals with hypnotism, a theme difficult to handle in fiction; "The Three Fates" (1892), a realistic story of New York society life and the best of Mr. Crawford's American studies; "Marion Darche" (1893), another story of New York and of the devotion of a forger's wife; "The Children of the King" (1893), a melodramatic story of Calabrian peasant life; "Pietro Ghisleri" (1893), in which both romantic and realistic elements are found and which pictures the gay society of Rome; "Katharine Lauderdale" and its sequel "The Ralstons" (1894), chronicles of a New York family; "Casa Braccio" (1895), a melodrama of passion; "Taquisara" (1896), an unpleasant story of the last representative of a great Saracen family and a princess of Acireale; "Via Crucis" (1899), a historical romance of the Second Crusade; "In the Palace of the King" (1900), a tale of passion, the hero of which is Don John of Austria, and the scene of which is the court of Philip II. of Spain; "Marietta, a Maid of Venice" (1901), a fifteenth-century story; "The Heart of Rome" (1903), the *motif* of which is modern Rome's treatment of its artistic heritage; "Fair Margaret" (1905), published in London as "Soprano, a Portrait," recounting the fascinating career of Margaret Donne, who becomes a successful opera singer; "Whosoever Shall Offend" (1905), an effective story of crime; and "A Lady of Rome" (1906), a study of character mould-ed by strong religious belief.

Of this remarkable series, the most noteworthy, though probably not the most popular, are those dealing with Italian life. Mr. Crawford has been markedly successful in his portraiture of Italian middle-class life, and only a little less so in writing of the aristocracy. He excels in representing agreeable, well-bred men and women; under his touch they are natural, human, lifelike. He is fertile in invention and lavish of characters and plot-incident, using in quite a subordinate connection materials which other novelists would reserve for the main plots of fu-ture novels. In general, his plots are skilfully constructed; occasionally, as in "Taquisara" (which is almost two separate stories), he fails to weld his material insolubly together. He has a remarkably bold and vigorous imagination, and does not hesitate to introduce daring conceptions and incidents; a romantic cast of mind is necessary if one would fully en-joy him. A Roman Catholic himself, he has had the amplest opportunity for studying the Catholic temperament and point of view, which he in-terprets admirably; it is natural that he should be weakest in portray-ing the characters of unbelievers or heretics. He is always dispassion-ate, calm, never losing himself in any storm of passion. His fiction as a whole is remarkably even, and it cannot be affirmed that his latest work shows deterioration. For the skill with which he has utilised vast stores of learning, for the effective though restrained use of a virile and pictur-esque imagination, for "astonishing literary tact" and breadth of view, Mr. Crawford has not his equal among living American writers, and his place is among the writers who only just miss the first rank.

Frederic Jesup Stimson.—Frederic J. Stimson, a native of Dedham, Massachusetts (born in 1855), has led a busy life as lawyer, legal writer, Harvard professor, and novelist. His earlier novels were published over the pen name of "J. S. of Dale." He has written, among others, "Guerndale" (1882), "The Crime of Henry Vane" (1884), the plot of which is unconvincing, "First Harvests" (1888), "Mrs. Knollys and Other Stories" (1894), "Pirate Gold" (1896), "King Noanett" (1896), carefully worked out, an exciting story of mystery and adventure, "Jethro Bacon of Sandwich" (1902), and "In Cure of Her Soul" (1906). Mr. Stimson has not taken high rank as a novelist, but his stories are generally interesting and the later ones may be commended to those who are fond of good romances. "The Weaker Sex" (*The Atlantic*, April, 1901) is a powerful short story.

Henry Cuyler Bunner.—Henry C. Bunner (1855–96), for many years the editor of *Puck*, wrote many short stories and some good novels. He was a native of Oswego, New York, and received his literary training in the school of journalism, being connected first with *The Sun* and then with *The Arcadian*, a literary weekly. "A Woman of Honor" (1883) gave some promise in plot and incident. "Love in Old Cloathes" (*The Century*, September, 1883) brought him a reputation as a clever story-teller. His next novel, "The Midge," an ingenious story of the New York French quarter, appeared in 1886; it was followed by "The Story of a New York House" (1887), the somewhat melancholy history of a house, typifying the family which occupies it. "Natural Selection" appeared serially in *Scribner's* (1888). "Zadoc Pine, and Other Stories" (1891) are tales the skilful construction of which shows how carefully Bunner studied Boccaccio; while in "Short Sixes" (1891), his most popular stories, he avowed his discipleship to Maupassant. He was more successful in his short stories than in his novels.

Arthur Sherburne Hardy.—Arthur S. Hardy (born in 1847 at Andover, Mass.), in 1902–6 United States Minister Plenipotentiary at Madrid, has had a varied career. Graduating at West Point in 1869, he served for a year in the Third United States Artillery, then became in succession professor of civil engineering, first at Iowa College, later at Dartmouth, professor of mathematics at Dartmouth, editor of *The Cosmopolitan*, and United States Minister to Persia, to Greece, Roumania, and Servia, and to Switzerland. Well known for several mathematical publications, he is the author of three novels, two of which are distinguished for happy description, graceful diction, and profound reflection rather than for individuality of plot or able development of character. "But Yet a Woman" (1883) is a story, somewhat deficient in local colour, of the coming of love to a French maiden destined for the convent. "The Wind of Destiny" (1886) is a story of a weak woman and two men which, though it lacks dramatic interest, offers some compensation in "the peculiarly noble air which pervades it, the extreme beauty of many of its passages, the revelation of life flashed occasionally as from a diamond of light, and perhaps more than all for the very subtle charm which hangs over the whole movement of the story."[19]"Passe Rose" (1889) is a charming poetical romance of Provence in the stirring times of Charles the Great, and is decidedly Mr. Hardy's most successful novel. His latest story is "His Daughter First" (1903). With rare sympathy, which he makes no attempt to conceal, he has interpreted several diverse types, and his men and women are alive.

Mary Hallock Foote.—Born at Milton-on-the-Hudson, New York, in 1847, Mary Hallock early showed artistic talent and at sixteen began to study design in Cooper Institute, New York City. She was married in 1876 to Arthur D. Foote, a California mining engineer, and travelled extensively in the Southwest. Her varied experiences have been utilised with marked literary skill in a series of stories, the first of which was "The Led Horse Claim" (1883), in which the story of Romeo and Juliet was repeated in a California mining camp, though with a happy ending. "The Chosen Valley" (1892) is a study in contrasts, recounting an episode in the reclaiming by irrigation of the waste lands of the West. In 1894 appeared "Cœur d'Alene," a love-story with a background in the labour troubles. She has also written "John Bowdoin's Testimony" (1886), "The Last Assembly Ball" (1889), "In Exile" (1894), and "The Cup of Trembling" (1895). Her latest stories, "The Desert and the Sown" (1902), a study of ideal self-sacrifice, and "A Touch of Sun, and Other Stories" (1903), are hardly up to the level of her earlier work, which, in its vivid representation of wild Western life, entitles her to a place with Bret Harte.

---

19   *The Atlantic Monthly*, July, 1886, lviii. 133.

Wolcott Balestier.—The promise of the too short life of Charles Wolcott Balestier (1861–91) deserves record. He was born at Rochester, New York, studied at Cornell University and the University of Virginia, and became first the editor of *Tid-Bits* and then the junior partner of Heinemann & Balestier, publishers of *The English Library*, an attempt to popularise British and American books on the Continent. His interest in literature was intense, and that he would have produced stories worth remembering, doubtless in the vein of Mr. Howells, whom he greatly admired, is evidenced by his few published works: "A Patent Philtre" (1884), "A Fair Device" (1884), "A Victorious Defeat" (1886), "A Common Story" (1891), "The Average Woman" (1892), three stories, with a memorial note by Henry James, and "Benefits Forgot" (1891), first published serially in *The Century*. With Mr. Kipling, his brother-in-law, he collaborated in "The Naulahka" (1892).

Robert Grant.—Born in Boston (1852), Robert Grant graduated from Harvard in 1873 and became Ph.D. in 1876 and LL.B. in 1879. He has followed law and letters side by side. In 1893 he was appointed Judge of the Probate Court and the Court of Insolvency for Suffolk County, Massachusetts. He has written, among other things, "The Confessions of a Frivolous Girl" (1880), "An Average Man" (1884), "The Knave of Hearts" (1886), "The Reflections of a Married Man" (1892), "The Opinions of a Philosopher" (1893), "The Bachelor's Christmas, and Other Stories" (1895), and "Unleavened Bread" (1900), his best known and most powerful story. Mr. Grant is a trenchant satirist of the foibles of certain aspirants to social prominence. Selma, in "Unleavened Bread," is a veritable incarnation of ignoble social ambition.

Henry Harland.—Henry Harland (1861–1905) was born in St. Petersburg, Russia, and was educated at the College of the City of New York, Harvard, Paris, and Rome. In 1886 he removed to London, where he became well known as the editor of *The Yellow Book*. His earlier stories, including "As It Was Written" (1885), a musician's story, "Mrs. Peixada" (1886), "The Land of Love" (1887), "My Uncle Florimond" (1888), and others, were published as by "Sidney Luska"; they circulated widely but were later condemned by Harland himself as trashy. He later wrote "Mea Culpa" (1893), "Comedies and Errors" (1898), "The Cardinal's Snuff-Box" (1900), which scored a decided success, and "My Lady Paramount" (1902). His brilliance and geniality are reflected in his works, but his vein was not an extensive one.

Thomas Nelson Page.—One of the leading novelists of the South to-day is Thomas Nelson Page. Born in 1853 at Oakland, Virginia, he studied (1869–72) at Washington and Lee University and (1873–74) at the University of Virginia. After practising law for some years, he turned, like many other lawyers, to literature. "Marse Chan" (*The Century*, April, 1884) met with great favour, and was followed by other short stories, which were collected in 1887 under the title "In Ole Virginia." The life in Virginia before and during the war was further presented in "Two Little Confederates" (1888), "On New Found River" (1891), "Elsket, and Other Stories" (1891), "The Burial of the Guns, and Other Stories" (1894), "Red Rock, a Chronicle of Reconstruction" (1898), "The Old Gentleman of the Black Stock" (1900), and "Gordon Keith" (1903). Mr. Page has a strong affection for the Old South, and vividly and powerfully delineates the life of the aristocracy and the negroes. While sympathetic, his descriptions of the system of slavery are free from bitterness and are entitled to consideration as truthful and convincing. Probably he has never surpassed his earlier short stories, which exhibit most distinctively the charm of his style; but "Red Rock," at least, has demonstrated his ability to write successfully also on a larger scale.

Thomas Allibone Janvier.—Thomas A. Janvier (born in 1849), a native of Philadelphia, became a New York journalist and then a writer of stories. He has been especially successful in depicting the Bohemian life of the metropolis. His "Color Studies: Four Stories" (1885), reprinted from *The Century*, narrate the struggles of a painter in New York; though slight, they are realistic and agreeable. Having made an exhaustive study of Mexico, he put his knowledge to good use in "The Aztec Treasure House: a Romance of Contemporaneous Antiquity" (1890), a successful romantic novel dealing with a legend of buried treasure and a story of wholesome flavour and sustained interest. He has also written "Stories of Old New Spain" (1895) and several others.

Some New England Women.—Here may be grouped several gifted daughters of the Puritans, some of whom deserve more space than can be given them. Mrs. Jane Goodwin Austin (1831–94) wrote several read-

able historical romances of colonial New England. Among her works
are "A Nameless Nobleman" (1881), "Dr. Le Baron and His Daughters"
(1890), sequel to the first, "Standish of Standish" (1889), and "David Al-
den's Daughter and Other Stories" (1892).

Mrs. Rose Terry Cooke (1827–92), a native of Connecticut, was
known as a poet for many years before she began to write short stories.
She published the following collections: "Happy Dodd" (1879), "Some-
body's Neighbours" (1881), "Root-Bound" (1885), "The Sphinx's Children" (1886), and "Huckleberries Gathered from New England Hills"
(1891). "The Deacon's Week" (1884) may count as her best story. In all
her stories the humours of New England Yankee character are set forth
with vigour and relish. She wrote a single novel, "Steadfast, the Story
of a Saint and a Sinner" (1889), dealing with early New England church
life, and ranking much above the average novel.

Mrs. Annie Trumbull Slosson, likewise of Connecticut, has shown
skill in dialect stories, of which "Fishin' Jimmy" (1889), "Seven Dream-
ers" (1890), "The Heresy of Mehetabel Clark" (1892), and "Dumb Fox-
glove, and Other Stories" (1898) may be mentioned. The grotesque elements of New England life especially appeal to her.

Mrs. Clara Louise Burnham (born at Newton, Massachusetts, in
1854) has lived in Chicago since childhood, but is fond of locating her
scenes in New England. She has written many stories, among them "No
Gentleman" (1881), "A Sane Lunatic" (1882), "Dearly Bought" (1884),
"Next Door" (1886), "Young Maids and Old" (1888), "Miss Bagg's Secretary" (1892), "Dr. Latimer" (1893), "The Wise Woman" (1895), "A West
Point Wooing" (1899), and "The Right Princess" (1902).

Alice Brown (born in New Hampshire in 1857), after teaching school
for several years, devoted herself to literature, and is now a member of
the staff of *The Youth's Companion*. She has written "Fools of Nature"
(1887), "Meadow-Grass" (1895), short tales of New England village
life, "The Day of His Youth" (1897), a story of disillusionment, "Tiverton
Tales" (1899), "King's End" (1901), "Margaret Warrener" (1901), "The
Mannerings" (1903), and "High Noon" (1904). Her stories are skilfully
constructed, and she writes with commendable restraint and dignity.

Mary E. Wilkins Freeman.—The more sombre and less attractive aspects of New England village and country life have been presented with great success in the numerous stories of Mary E. Wilkins (since 1902 Mrs. Charles M. Freeman). Born at Randolph, Massachusetts, in 1862, she was educated at Mt. Holyoke Seminary, South Hadley, Mass. Her stories include "The Adventures of Ann" (1886), "A Humble Romance" (1887), "A New England Nun, and Other Stories" (1891), "Jane Field" (1892), her first novel, "Pembroke" (1894), generally considered her greatest work, and distinguished for beauty of style and truthful and delicate character-drawing, "Madelon" (1896), "Jerome, a Poor Man" (1897), by some ranked higher than "Pembroke" in that it has a stronger central interest, "Silence and Other Stories" (1898), which includes some of her best work, especially "Evelina's Garden," one of her most artistic tales, "The Love of Parson Lord" (1900), "The Heart's Highway" (1900), a historical romance of Virginia in 1682, "The Portion of Labour" (1901), "Understudies" (1901), "Six Trees" (1903), "The Wind in the Rose Bush" (1903), "The Givers," eight stories (1904), and several magazine stories. Her place is easily in the first rank of those who have delineated New England life.

Harold Frederic.—Harold Frederic (1856–98) wrote a number of realistic stories, chiefly of country life in New York. A native of Utica, in that State, he began his career as proof-reader; at twenty-six he was editor of the Albany *Evening Journal*, and in 1884 he took charge of the foreign bureau of the New York *Times*, with headquarters in London. "Seth's Brother's Wife" (1887), first published serially in *Scribner's,* minutely describes the prosaic round of farming life and country journalism and elections. "The Lawton Girl" (1890) gives us the turmoil of a small manufacturing town. "In the Valley" (1890) is a Mohawk Dutchman's story of the Revolutionary struggle. "The Copperhead, and Other Stories of the North" (1893) and "Marséna, and Other Stories" (1894) are collections of Civil War stories, vigorous and daring. His best stories are "The Damnation of Theron Ware" (1896, published in England as "Illumination"), an absorbing study of the intellectual career of an earnest but narrow young Methodist minister and of the struggle of two religious ideals in his life, and "The Market-Place" (1899), a thoroughgoing study of the London Stock Exchange. His untimely death cut short a career of notable achievement and great promise.

Archibald Clavering Gunter.—Archibald Clavering Gunter (1847–1907), a native of Liverpool who became a California mining and civil engineer, chemist, and stock-broker, at forty began to write novels which violated most of the literary canons, but which in plot and incident were of absorbing interest. It was his avowed rule to make something happen in every five hundred words. This explains why a million copies of his first novel, "Mr. Barnes of New York" (1887), have been sold. He wrote thirty-nine novels in all, the best of which, in addition to his first, are "Mr. Potter of Texas" (1888), "That Frenchman" (1889), "Jack Curzon" (1899), and "A Manufacturer's Daughter" (1901). He also became well known as a playwright.

Octave Thanet.—Octave Thanet is the well known pen name of Alice French (born at Andover, Massachusetts, in 1850), who has achieved enviable success in her short stories of life in Iowa and Arkansas, a field in which she has few rivals. These stories include "Knitters in the Sun" (1887), "Expiation" (1890), vigorous, truly coloured, and accurate in details, "Stories of a Western Town" (1893), Iowa sketches, "The Missionary Sheriff" (1897), and "The Heart of Toil" (1898), full of the pathos of an unequal struggle with economic forces. Miss French writes sympathetically, with her eyes on the men and women who furnish her with characters.

Margaret Deland.—One of the most popular of living novelists, and justly so, is Mrs. Margaret Deland. Born Margaretta Campbell, in 1857, in Manchester, now a part of Allegheny, Pennsylvania, then a village "of dignified houses, pleasant gardens, and meadows sloping to a picturesque river," she was left an orphan at three and was cared for by an aunt. At sixteen, like Mrs. Foote, she entered a class in drawing and design in Cooper Institute, New York; she graduated at the head of her class, and won an appointment as instructor in design in the Girls' Normal College, a post which she filled till 1880. Then she was married to Mr. Lorin F. Deland and went to Boston. Eight years later appeared her first novel, "John Ward, Preacher." It is the story of the conflict of rigid Calvinism and modern liberalism, and it has been compared with Mrs. Ward's "Robert Elsmere." Two love-stories, one of which recalls Mrs. Gaskell's "Cranford," relieve the tragic gloom of the narrative. Ashurst is an idealised Manchester. In "Sidney" (1890) the author studies the question of the value of mortal sexual love; the problems of faith and doubt also recur. "The Story of a Child" (1892) delineates an uncontrolled imagination. "Mr. Tommy Dove, and Other Stories" (1893) is a collection including typical humour and pathos. "Philip and His Wife" (1894) has to do with an unhappy marriage. Her recent stories are "The Wisdom of Fools" (1898), "Old Chester Tales" (1899), "Dr. Lavendar's People" (1904), and "The Awakening of Helena Richie" (1906). Big-hearted, shrewd Dr. Lavendar, who figures in her last two stories, is one of the most lovable characters in American fiction; and her latest books show a distinctly stronger grasp of life and greater narrative power.

Mrs. Mary Hartwell Catherwood.—Mary Hartwell Catherwood (1847–1902) made a name for herself with some very successful historical romances of the French and Indian Wars and French Canadian and early Illinois life. "The Romance of Dollard" (1889), "The Lady of Fort St. John" (1891), "The White Islander" (1893), and "The Chase of Saint Castin, and Other Stories" (1894) are spirited narratives of battle and siege, of intrigue and jealousy, in which bold and noble characters play their parts well, and which contain vivid descriptions of scenery—in sunshine and storm. Of the early Middle West she wrote "Old Kaskaskia" (1893), "The Spirit of an Illinois Town" (1897), "Little Renault" (1897), "Spanish Peggy" (1899), "The Queen of the Swamp, and Other Plain Americans" (1899), and "Lazarre" (1901).

Rowland E. Robinson.—The dialect and manners of Vermont are reproduced with remarkable fidelity by Rowland E. Robinson (1833–1900) in "Sam Lovel's Camps" (1889), "Danvis Folks" (1894), and "Uncle 'Lisha's Shop" (1897). These stories are among our most valuable transcripts of the life of Northern New England.

Francis Hopkinson Smith.—F. Hopkinson Smith (born in Baltimore, 1838) had a varied career before he essayed the novel, at fifty-three. He began life as a clerk in some iron works; then, becoming an engineer and contractor, he took to building sea-walls and lighthouses, and afterwards became well known as an artist. In "Colonel Carter of Cartersville" (1891) he drew an alluring picture of the old *régime* in the South. "A Gentleman Vagabond, and Some Others" (1895) are varied character stories. "Tom Grogan" (1896) and "Caleb West, Master Diver" (1898) draw upon Mr. Smith's engineering experiences. He has also written "The Other Fellow" (1899), "The Fortunes of Oliver Horn" (1902), "The Under Dog" (1903), "Colonel Carter's Christmas" (1904), "At Close Range" (1905), and "The Wood Fire in No. 3" (1905). If some of his persons are conventional and indistinct, others stand out as skilfully characterised and permanent figures in his literary gallery.

James Lane Allen.—James Lane Allen has done for Kentucky what Mr. Page has done for Old Virginia and Miss Murfree for the Tennessee mountaineers. A native of Kentucky (born in 1849), he graduated from Transylvania University, at Lexington, Kentucky, and taught in schools and colleges for some years. Since 1884, however, he has devoted himself to literary work. Besides writing much for magazines he has published "Flute and Violin, and Other Kentucky Tales and Romances" (1891), "The Blue Grass Region, and Other Sketches" (1892), "John Gray" (1893), rewritten and enlarged into "The Choir Invisible" (1897), "A Kentucky Cardinal" (1894) and its sequel "Aftermath" (1895), "Summer in Arcady" (1896), "The Reign of Law" (1900), published in England as "The Increasing Purpose," and "The Mettle of the Pasture" (1903). A tendency toward didacticism and a lack of spontaneity mar the latest works of Mr. Allen; he is at his best in his earlier works, in which he revels in the beauty of the Blue Grass region and writes in the spirit of a disciple of Thoreau and Audubon. The romanticist in him was gradually transformed into the objective realist. Yet in all his work there are elements of strength and poetic beauty. By a curious coincidence another Kentucky James Lane Allen (born in 1848) a graduate of Bethany College, in which the first Mr. Allen taught, and now a Chicago lawyer, has also written numerous magazine sketches and stories.

Hamlin Garland.—The grim, dull life of the hard-worked farmer in the Middle West has been effectively recorded by Hamlin Garland. A native of La Crosse, Wisconsin (born in 1860), Mr. Garland saw at close range the life he was to describe, in Iowa, Illinois, and Dakota. His first book was a collection of six realistic stories, "Main-Travelled Roads" (1891), which gave him a reputation, and he has continued to write in similar vein, publishing "Prairie Folks" (1892), "A Little Norsk, or Ol' Pap's Flaxen" (1892), "A Spoil of Office" (1892), "Rose of Dutcher's Coolly" (1895), his best novel, "The Eagle's Heart" (1900), "Her Mountain

Lover" (1901), and "Money Magic" (1907). Mr. Garland has for the most part wisely obeyed his own dictum, to write only of what one knows; and his later work shows a notable increase in vigour and grasp of the story-teller's art.

Henry Blake Fuller.—Henry B. Fuller (born in Chicago, 1857) was intended for a mercantile career, but preferred literature. "The Chevalier of Pensieri-Vani" (1890), first published anonymously, was praised by Lowell and Norton. In 1892 appeared "The Chatelaine of La Trinité." In "The Cliff-Dwellers" (1893), he turned from the romantic to a sure realism in a story of Chicago life. "With the Procession" followed in 1895, being in similar vein. These stories show skill in individualisation, intense earnestness, facility, and ability to make an old theme interesting. "His picture," says Mr. Whibley, "is never overcharged; his draughtsmanship is always sincere."

Stephen Crane and Frank Norris.—Stephen Crane (1870–1900), born in Newark, New Jersey, and educated at Lafayette College and Syracuse University, first entered journalism and won some distinction as a war correspondent of the New York *Journal*. His first story, dealing with slum life, was "Maggie, a Girl of the Streets" (1891), which, as Mr. Howells thinks, remains his best work. "The Red Badge of Courage" (1895), a thoroughly realistic study of the mind of a soldier in action at the battle of Chancellorsville, was altogether a remarkable achievement; it took the public by storm and brought the author a wide reputation, which was not sustained by his later work. He also wrote "George's Mother" (1896), another slum story, "The Little Regiment" (1896), "Active Service" (1899), "The Monster, and Other Stories" (1899); and two collections of stories, "Wounds in the Rain" and "Whilomville Stories" (1900), tales of child life, which were published posthumously. His impressionism, though at times too little restrained, was often effective, and his highly coloured stories have found many admiring readers.

In the death of Frank Norris (1870–1902), another promising career was cut short. Norris managed to see a good deal of life. Born in Chicago, he studied art in Paris (1887–89) and literature at the University of California and Harvard. Like Crane he became a journalist. At the time of the Jameson Raid in South Africa he was the South African correspondent for a San Francisco paper and in 1898 did similar work in Cuba. He began publishing fiction as early as 1891 ("Yberville"), but it was not till 1899 that he became well known for "McTeague." His later stories were thoroughly realistic. With "The Octopus" (1901) he began a trilogy which should form "an epic of the wheat." In the first novel is described the growth of the wheat and the oppressive railroad monopoly encountered in its transportation. "The Pit" (1903) deals with the battles of the wheat speculators. "The Wolf," unfinished, was to have dealt with the struggle for bread in a European famine-stricken community. "The story of the wheat was for him," as Mr. Howells puts it, "the allegory of the industrial and financial America which is the real America." The largeness of the scope of his undertaking and the robust courage and confidence with which he attacked it deserve our admiration. What he accomplished shows that he would have been equal to his task.

Mrs. Ruth McEnery Stuart.—Mrs. Stuart has written highly amusing stories of negro life in the South. Born in the parish of Avoyelles, Louisiana, she was married in 1879 to Alfred O. Stuart, a cotton planter. Since 1885 she has lived in New York. Her stories include "The Golden Wedding, and Other Tales" (1893), "Carlotta's Intended" (1894), "The Story of Babette" (1894), "Moriah's Mourning" (1898), "Sonny" (1896), "Holly and Pizen" (1899), "The Woman's Exchange" (1899), and "River's Children" (1905). Writing in a natural and witty style, she has brought out with great skill the humour and pathos of the old plantation. She is a favourite contributor to the magazines.

Paul Leicester Ford.—Paul Leicester Ford (1865–1902), whose most serious and permanently valuable work was done in the field of American history, was the author of some notable works of fiction. "The Honourable Peter Sterling and What People Thought of Him" (1894) introduces an ideally noble statesman whose integrity triumphs over the sordid corruption of politics. Some points in the book are said to have been suggested by the career of President Cleveland. "Janice Meredith" (1899) is a sentimental romance of the Revolutionary War, in which a fascinating love-story is projected on an accurate historical background. Of less importance, but still most readable, are "The Great K. & A. Train Robbery" (1897) and "The Story of an Untold Love" (1897).

Edward Noyes Westcott.—Edward N. Westcott (1847–98), a banker of Syracuse, New York, was the author of a single book, which he was unable to get published in his lifetime, but which gave him posthumous fame. The hero of "David Harum" (1898) is a shrewd Central New York Yankee, a son of the soil who with characteristic energy rose to be a banker and successful man of affairs, and who retained all his amusing traits, including a weakness for trading horses—"an optimist who has wrung from the harsh conditions of life all that it can yield." The other characters are rather wooden, but the delineation of David Harum is strong, vital, and hence lasting. The plot is weak, but the story is true to the phases of life it depicts.

The Younger Generation.—Space forbids more than a mention of some of the other living writers. Owen Wister (born in Philadelphia, 1860) has become well known through "The Dragon of Wantley: His Tail" (1892) and "The Virginian" (1902), in which latter we have an exciting story of a Wyoming cowboy. The much-travelled Richard Harding Davis (also a Philadelphian, born in 1864) has written racy and characteristically humorous stories of New York club and street life in "Gallegher, and Other Stories" (1891), "Van Bibber, and Others" (1892), and "Episodes in Van Bibber's Life" (1899). Of his other stories the best known are "The Princess Aline" (1895), "Soldiers of Fortune" (1897), in which a South American revolution figures prominently, "In the Fog" (1901), a clever London tale, "Ranson's Folly" (1902), and "The Bar Sinister" (1904). Robert W. Chambers (born in Brooklyn, 1865) is well known both as an artist and a romancer, a weaver of strange and exciting plots. Among his best books are "The Red Republic" (1894), "A King and a Few Dukes" (1894), "The Haunts of Men" (1898), stories of American or Canadian life, "The Cambric Mask" (1899), "A Gay Conspiracy" (1900), which shows the influence of Anthony Hope's "Prisoner of Zenda," "Cardigan" (1901), and "Iole" (1905). Newton Booth Tarkington (born in 1869 in Indianapolis, a graduate of Princeton) won fame in 1899 with "The Gentleman from Indiana" and has followed this with "Monsieur Beaucaire" (1900), a romance laid in Bath in the eighteenth century, "The Two Vanrevels" (1902), "Cherry" (1903), "In the Arena" (1905), "The Conquest of Canaan" (1905), and "The Beautiful Lady" (1905). His later work shows a gain in power. Winston Churchill (born in 1871), a graduate of the Naval Academy at Annapolis, and now a resident of New Hampshire, pub-

lished "The Celebrity" in 1898. "Richard Carvel" (1899) made him famous; it is a Revolutionary story of Maryland and London. He has since
written "The Crisis" (1901), a substantial story of the Civil War, "Mr.
Keegan's Elopement" (1903), "The Crossing" (1904), and "Coniston"
(1906), a New England story of love and politics. The mountaineer life
of Kentucky furnishes John Fox, Jr., with the materials for his well told
stories, "A Cumberland Vendetta, and Other Stories" (1896), "The Kentuckians" (1897), "The Little Shepherd of Kingdom Come" (1903), and "A
Knight of the Cumberland" (1906).

Mrs. Gertrude Franklin Atherton (born in San Francisco, 1857) has
made a wide reputation with her stories of early California life; some
critics declare, however, that they do not accurately represent the California of old days. The first of them was "The Doomswoman" (1892).
Other novels are "A Whirl Asunder" (1895), "Patience Sparhawk and Her
Times" (1897), "The Californians" (1898), "American Wives and English
Husbands" (1898), and "The Conqueror" (1902), which is based on the
life of Alexander Hamilton. Mrs. Kate Douglas Wiggin (born in Philadelphia in 1857 and married to Samuel B. Wiggin in 1880) has written
charming juvenile stories, "The Birds' Christmas Carol" (1888), "The
Story of Patsy" (1889), and "Timothy's Quest" (1890), besides some stories of travel, such as "A Cathedral Courtship" (1893) and "Penelope's
Progress" (1898). Her husband died in 1889, and in 1895 she was married to George C. Riggs.

Irving Bacheller (born in 1859), a New York journalist, attracted
attention by his stories, "The Master of Silence" (1890) and "The Still
House of O'Darrow" (1894). His "Eben Holden" (1900), a novel of northern New York, was very successful. He has since written "Darrel of the
Blessed Isles" (1903) and "Vergilius" (1904). Robert Herrick (born in
1868), a Harvard graduate and now a Chicago University professor, has
written searching studies of American society in "The Gospel of Freedom" (1898), "The Web of Life" (1900), "The Real World" (1901), and
"The Common Lot" (1904). He is something of a pessimist, but not unwholesome.

Edith Wharton (born in New York in 1862) began her literary career with short stories of the metropolitan society with which she had

been familiar from birth: "The Greater Inclination" (1899), eight stories, "A Gift from the Grave" (1900), and "Crucial Instances" (1901). In "The Valley of Decision" (1902), "Sanctuary" (1903), and "The House of Mirth" (1905), she deals with scenes and characters of deep human interest but not easily managed; and she acquits herself with credit. Lily Bart is distinctly individualised and is worthy to be compared with Becky Sharp and Gwendolen Harleth.

Upton Sinclair (born in Baltimore, 1878), after writing a number of novels, produced in "Manassas" (1904) a thrilling romantic novel of the years just preceding the Civil War. "The Jungle" (1906), though much better known, is artistically far inferior to it. The creed of socialism is professed by both Mr. Sinclair and Jack London (born in San Francisco in 1876). London left the University of California to go to the Klondike, afterward went to Japan, and has since tramped through America and Canada for sociological study. In his best works, "The Son of the Wolf" (1900), "The Call of the Wild" (1903), and "The Sea Wolf" (1904), he has chosen to depict the tragedies of the animal world and the elemental passions in man.

Three Virginia women novelists have won distinction in recent years.

Molly Elliot Seawell (born in Gloucester County, Virginia, in 1860), a resident of Washington, began writing fiction in 1886. Among her stories are "Throckmorton" (1890), "Little Jarvis" (1890), a *Youth's Companion* prize story, "Midshipman Paulding" (1891), "The Sprightly Romance of Marsac" (1896), a lively story that won a New York *Herald* prize of $3000, "The Lively Adventures of Gavin Hamilton" (1899), "The House of Egremont" (1901), "Children of Destiny" (1903), and "The Great Scoop" (1905). Her plots are sometimes slight and inconsequential, and her narrative lacks reserve; but she shows skill in the management of dialogue, and is a favourite writer.

Ellen Glasgow (born in Richmond in 1874) has found many readers with her "Descendant" (1897), "Phases of an Inferior Planet" (1898), "The Voice of the People" (1900), "The Battle-Ground" (1902), and "The Deliverance" (1904). She does not manage to escape from improbabilities, and some of her plots are desultory; yet on the whole her work maintains a high average.

Mary Johnston (born at Buchanan, Virginia, in 1870) has realised the possibilities of early Virginia history in her successful romances, "Prisoners of Hope" (1898), published in England as "The Old Dominion," "To Have and to Hold" (1900), in England called "By Order of the Company," "Audrey" (1902), and "Sir Mortimer" (1904). She has a sure touch, and her narrative moves rapidly.

But we have already exceeded the limits of our space. The work of Margaret Sherwood, William A. White, Brand Whitlock, Will Payne, Meredith Nicholson, George Barr McCutcheon, Jesse Lynch Williams, David Graham Phillips, Mary R. Shipman Andrews, James B. Connolly, Nelson Lloyd, George Cary Eggleston, William N. Harben, Justus Miles Forman, and many others, excellent as much of it is, can only be referred to summarily. The great number of promising writers of to-day is a matter of congratulation.

Retrospect and Conclusion.—We have thus traced the American novel from its first crude beginnings through a little more than a century of healthy and constant growth. It took the American novelist some three or four decades to learn to stand on his own feet; since he has learned to walk he has required very little assistance from abroad. More and more the possibilities of American life have attracted the writers of prose fiction. In the earlier decades of the last century, as was the case in Europe, the romance was the only fiction in demand; and the romance has ever been the favourite of many readers who maintain that the chief function of literature is to give reality through the alembic of the imagination. Perhaps the creed of romanticism has never been better put than by Mr. Julian Hawthorne:

> The value of fiction lies in the fact that it can give us what actual existence cannot; that it can resume in a chapter the conclusions of a lifetime; that it can omit the trivial, the vague, the redundant, and select the significant, the forcible, and the characteristic; that it can satisfy expectation, expose error, and vindicate human nature. Life, as we

experience it, is too vast, its relations are too complicated, its orbit too comprehensive, ever to give us the impression of individual completeness and justice; but the intuition of these things, though denied to sense, is granted to faith, and we are authorised to embody that interior conviction in romance.... And stories of imagination are truer than transcripts of fact, because they include or postulate these, and give a picture not only of the earth beneath our feet, but of the sky above us, of the hope and freshness of the morning, of the mystery and magic of the night. They draw the complete circle, instead of mistrustfully confining themselves to the lower arc.[20]

Notwithstanding the attractiveness of this artistic creed, the ranks of the out-and-out romancers have gradually thinned, as we have seen. Professor Boyesen believed that Bret Harte was the last of these. Slowly the realists, led by Howells and James, have gained ground, and for the last twenty years have almost steadily held the field. Of late, indeed, there have been some signs of a reaction; but it has as yet taken no very pronounced form.

A necessary concomitant of this tendency toward realism has been an increase in the number of "novels of the soil." Writers have drawn what they knew best: Miss Woolson, the Lake region; Cable, Creole New Orleans; Ella Higginson and Emma Wolf, the Pacific coast; Allen, Kentucky; Miss Murfree, Tennessee; Fawcett and Bunner, New York; Henry B. Fuller and Miss Wyatt, Chicago; Miss Jewett and Mrs. Wilkins Freeman, New England. One reason why the "great American novel" has not yet been written is the very bigness of the country. No great personality has yet risen who can combine all the elements of our vast modern life into one harmonious structure. Meanwhile we have had most of the various sections of our country described in fiction by skilful hands. Types of a life that is passing away have been caught and preserved in a fiction which, though assuredly not immortal, is destined, we believe, to a long life.

Our critics have justly complained, however, of the limited range of our novelists. They are timid. They are content to paint a small can-

---

20   Quoted by Professor C. F. Richardson, "American Literature," ii. 448–449.

vas. They do not rise to great conceptions. They do not probe life to its depths; neither do they rise to the height of all its grandeur. This is, of course, only another way of saying that we have no supremely great novelists. But doubtless the mediocrity of our fiction is partly due to the disastrous effect of commercialism and professionalism on the novelist's trade; though Mr. Whibley's account of this (*Blackwood's*, March, 1908) is exaggerated. Certainly our writers must be less eager for immediate and substantial rewards. *Poeta nascitur, non fit*; too many "made" writers are pouring out fiction to-day.

Our fiction possesses one characteristic which has often been commented upon—a general excellence of moral atmosphere. There is little American fiction that must be kept from the curious Young Person. Some critics allege that the obligation to write what anyone may be permitted to read has prevented American novelists from discussing those darker problems of sex-relations which confront us, and which should find expression in a literature adequately reflecting our intellectual and moral life; that missing any rigorous attack on these problems they find our fiction tame, insipid, wanting in vitality. But such an opinion carries with it its own condemnation. If our fiction lacks vitality, it is probably from other causes; at any rate Americans are generally content to leave matters of moral pathology to their moral surgeons, whose diagnoses and discussions are not expected to circulate promiscuously; and it is not likely that our novelists will consent to defile their pages for the sake of securing comprehensiveness in their pictures of life.

The short story has been brought by American writers to a high degree of perfection. Irving was its American father; and in the hands of Hawthorne, Poe, Fitz-James O'Brien, Edward Everett Hale, Miss Woolson, Brander Matthews, Miss Jewett, Stockton, Page, Mark Twain, Mrs. Freeman, and many others, it has become a highly flexible instrument, capable of subtle adaptations. The limitations of range and environment have made for great delicacy and precision in the minute portraits and the *genres* to be found in large numbers throughout our short stories.

Yet notwithstanding the increase in the number and the advance in quality of our short stories, the novel continues as popular as ever. The immense vogue of the novel in America has been commented upon many times. The "best sellers" are almost always novels; and so many novels of more than average excellence are produced every year that many really superior stories do not get the immediate hearing, at least, which they deserve. That this demand for novels will continue unabated for some time is altogether likely. That another form of literature will soon take its place is quite improbable.

Apparently we have no great living poets; for various reasons we have no dramatists of note; of novelists who are at least possibilities, we have several.

What will be the type of the American novel of the future? Probably it is rash to make any prediction; but one may venture to believe that the prevailing attitude of our future novelists will be that of a sane and optimistic realism. The morbid books like "The Jungle" do not wear well; and, while such books may have their use in promoting needed reforms, they do not constitute additions to literature and can, therefore, secure no permanent place. The pleasant paths of romance will always tempt bold and imaginative writers; but they will be more than ever restrained by the demand of enlightened readers that they shall not wander far from the probable, and shall present, clear and undistorted, the best there is in the actual present. That there are immense possibilities in the varied and complex life of to-day, few will doubt; that the great artists are to appear who will make the most of these opportunities we may assume with confidence.

III. THE POETS

English Influence on American Poetry.—If we accept the popular belief, and identify poets with makers of verse, it must be allowed that American poetry at its best—in the nineteenth century—is in a peculiar sense unoriginal and derivative. To be derivative, to have a traceable pedigree, may, indeed, be no disadvantage, either for a national or an individual genius. In their way, all modern literatures are derivative and unoriginal; not merely influenced by each other, but ultimately dependent for the sources of their inspiration upon the basal civilisations of Palestine and Greece. "We are all Greeks," said Shelley. Milton might have said, "We are all Hebrews." And our best American poets might have added, "*We* are all Englishmen." Particular scenes on this continent, and the vast and ever growing extent of our territory, have both left their impress on our poets during the last five generations; they have touched the poetry of ten or twelve decades here and there with the undeniable stamp of reality, and given it now and then a largeness of range and freedom of atmosphere very proper to a nation whose sense of geography has been so elastic. Yet one can hardly say that our natural scenery has ever been really incarnate in our literature as a whole, or that a pervasive national spirit, a spirit at once large and precise, has entered fundamentally into our verse. What has been most effectual in our literature has been closely imitative, has followed at a little distance, yet step for step, the development of the English literature from which it sprang. This continuous imitation, now more superficial, now more indirect and elusive, has been the mainspring of our poetry even more than our prose, during the century just gone by.

American poetry, it is true, has probably been more plastic and mobile in its outer form than American prose, has been less steadily patterned after those literary standards in England which were bequeathed by the eighteenth century. The prose style of Irving betrays its descent from the essays of Addison; the style of Franklin was developed through conscious and painstaking emulation of the same models. Even fairly late in the eighteen hundreds, when perhaps only a trained ear can detect the lingering echoes of Pope and his school in our verse, the "Autocrat" of Wendell Holmes still retains an accent and a flavour from eighteenth-century, Ciceronian eloquence. No doubt the age of Pope and Johnson survived by many vestiges much longer in English prose than in English verse, for its habits of thought were more or less suited to argument and exposition in every time. Yet in the history of American letters it is easier to find parallels to Wordsworth and Shelley than to duplicate the prose rhapsodies—characteristic in nineteenth-century Europe—of De Quincey and Ruskin. To the transition in English literature that was marked by the appearance of "Lyrical Ballads" in 1798 our poetry was, in the main, more quickly responsive than our prose. None the less our prose, more conservative though it has been, less changeful in its manner of expression, has struck its roots far more deeply into our national being; and our verse, like the other fine arts, is still an exotic.

For our lack of a national art, a national poetry, a superficial reason is often assigned: in the conditions of a new country, in the struggle for existence, in the development of agriculture and commerce, in the assimilation of foreign races, there has been very little time for the nourishment of letters, very little of that leisure which the Greeks called *scholé*, and which is indispensable for a productive scholarship and for the flourishing of imagination. Yet we have had, or have taken, sufficient leisure to write and publish an immense amount of verse, judged merely by its bulk. Scarcely an American author can be mentioned in the nineteenth century that did not try his hand at metrical composition. The truth is, rather, that we have seldom approached the art of poetry with enough seriousness; that, having rebelled against the Puritan's unkindly conception of life, we have nevertheless to some extent acquiesced in his belittling estimate of imaginative art; that we have failed to recognise in the poet a necessary servant of the commonwealth, a leader worthy of a high and severe training. Our versifiers have rushed into print before they were ripe, and they have praised each other's work too easily; while the standards set by the public taste have been readily met when the rhymers succeeded in being "patriotic." Real patriotism demands such an admission.

Not that our poets have been wholly without a philosophy of criticism; though it is significant that the most subtle and sympathetic understanding of the poetic temperament, of its function as well as its perils, is to be found, not in the writings of any maker of verses but in those of a novelist, Hawthorne—for example, in "The House of Seven Gables" and "The Great Stone Face." Yet Bryant read, meditated, and wrote upon the art of poetry; Poe thought somewhat, if not deeply, upon it; Lanier made a worthy contribution to the science of meter; Longfellow was conversant with the literature of criticism; and Emerson's stimulating essay on "The Poet," while it may not have been the sort of medicine that our men of letters most needed, has doubtless exerted a wholesome influence. In Poe's day, several magazines were discussing the principles of imaginative composition. However, an "Art of Poetry" like Timrod's (published in *The Atlantic Monthly* for September, 1905) could lie for forty years in manuscript, without exciting any strong suspicion of its value; and in the long run there has been an amazing disproportion between the slender thread of fundamental tradition and sound critical theory on the one hand, and the swollen and rapid stream of naïve, uncultivated verse, gathering from every quarter, on the other. Whatever English poets furnished the models, the imitation was largely on the surface. First Pope and his successors in England, then Wordsworth and Coleridge, then Shelley and Keats, and Scott and Bryon, and subsequently Tennyson,— all had in turn their American devotees. But there seems to have been relatively little understanding like that of Bryant and Timrod for the conscious theory underlying the "experiments" in "Lyrical Ballads," or for the ideal demands which Shelley laid upon poetry and poets; nor did cisatlantic readers of Lord Byron much concern themselves about that Longinus whom he studied "o'er a bottle," or for the structural frame upon which was reared Tennyson's "Palace of Art."

Characteristics of the Period.—Of course in the following pages we shall deal as briefly as possible with those American poets in the last century who are touched to any great extent by strictures like these; for a history of literature is bound to treat as far as may be of writers that have made a wise use of tradition, and whose native insight has enabled them to train their genius in accordance with universal canons of art, and with a due appreciation of masterly technique. Meanwhile we may attempt to summarise the characteristics of the poetical era under consideration, and, in particular, of the earlier rather than the latter half of that era. The nearer we advance toward our own day, the wiser it is to refrain from general characterisation.

1. The relation between English literature and American in the initial twenty or thirty years of the last century has already been suggested. Aside from that, or very often through that, the influence of Rousseau was paramount. The doctrine that upheld the innocence of "man in a state of nature," and maintained the equality of all individuals, and the feeling, half pantheistic, for an external nature opposed to civilisation, since they entered into the vital tissue of our national thought,—and though they are at bottom contrary to science and all demonstrable experience—are among the very conditions, so to speak, of much of our poetry. From these sources, for example, it came about that while in actual practice we despised and maltreated that "natural man" the cruel Indian, we idealised him in poetical effusions; just as Fenimore Cooper, treading in the footsteps of Chateaubriand, idealised him in prose.

2. Our earlier poets, that is, immediately after the Revolution, but again, and especially, after the War of 1812 had confirmed our sense of national solidarity, are much given to the utterance of their patriotism; albeit only a few out of many more or less pretentious or tasteful efforts have survived. Key's "Star-Spangled Banner" (1814), conceived at the close of the second war, antedates "The American Flag" (1819) of Drake by but five years; these two, with Hopkinson's "Hail Columbia" (1798), and "America" (1832), the well-known hymn by S. F. Smith, whatever their relative or absolute merits as literature, remain our most cherished national poems.

3. However frequent or insistent the note of patriotism, the general temper of American poets has not been strongly optimistic. As one glances over a long list of the subjects chosen for treatment, a leaning toward the more sombre and melancholy elements and aspects of life becomes more and more apparent. Nor is this leaning confined to the multitude. Exceptions like Walt Whitman to the contrary notwithstanding, it is characteristic, in the main, of the leaders, whenever they escape from common or inherited themes, and give rein to their own personalities. That joy which is the well-spring of Wordsworth's vitality is greatly diminished in even his nearest American counterpart, Bryant; assuredly it is not akin to the subdued sadness of Longfellow, though this be not strictly "akin to pain."

4. On the other hand, the noblest American poetry has not been tragic. Tragedy and serious epic have been attempted, but, as in the case of Dwight, Barlow, and so many others, largely as academic exercitations, savouring of the desk and the library. With our national life they have had no essential connection. A central motive in our history like the death of Lincoln still awaits the imagination of a master-dramatist.

5. Though few have devoted their entire lives to it, most of our poets have begun the profession betimes, conceiving very often in haste, and publishing in their immaturity. The painful advice of Horace has not been to our liking. With the examples of Milton, Wordsworth, and Tennyson continually before us, we have yet failed to profit by their insistence upon generous preparation, meticulous technique, and laborious delay in publication. We have realised the brevity of life more fully than the length of art.

6. Our respect for the "practical" and for "common sense" is allied to a fondness shown in our poetry for common, everyday subjects. Here, of course, we have succeeded better in the comic than in the serious vein. To treat of homely topics so as to invest their essential dignity with the light of imagination—in painting the world about us, to "add the gleam"—was the task set for himself by an English mystic. It is a dangerous trade for men whose talk is of oxen. Homely minds on homely matters are prone to slip into the trivial or the pathetic. Even Longfellow cannot be freed from the charge of too much attention to the obvious commonplace, and, as a versifier at least, of too much love for the merely sentimental. For adequate imaginative handling of themes that are serious, complete, and of sufficient magnitude to produce the loftier effects of great literary art, we are in general forced to go to our best prose fiction.

7. So long as Puritan ideals, however modified and softened, continued to dominate any considerable part of American education, that is, up to a point somewhere within the past twenty-five years, our poetry has tended to be obviously didactic. Not only clerical but secular poets have seemed to regard themselves as direct teachers of morality. In satirical writers,—Freneau, Halleck,—or in literature that by virtue of its kind is pietistic, such a tendency is altogether normal and effective. But in supposedly imaginative poems such as "The Vision of Sir Launfal," though the basic moral order of the universe doubtless ought to be inherent, it just as certainly ought to contrive its own effect, without the adventitious aid of sermonising. To the present writer, much of the best—not of course the very best—in American poetry loses in ethical as well as æsthetic value through the intrusion of argument and exhortation on the subject of conduct or belief. The finest work of Holmes, for instance, "The Chambered Nautilus," may be thought to lose in this way. The spirit of the United States is a prosaic spirit, hence our verse, when it is at all substantial, rarely lacks some element or other from the style of the forensic orator.

8. On the other hand, since we can make no pretence to the possession of a tragic drama, and none to a truly national epic, it may safely be affirmed that our poetry has risen to its greatest heights in meditative and religious lyric; in meditative verse on nature, that is, such "na-

ture-poetry" as assumes the Divine immanence throughout the world of objective reality—in Bryant's "Thanatopsis"; and in the religious lyric, that is, in a few of our hymns.

The Earlier Poets.—We commence this survey of American poetry at the date to which the sections adapted from Tyler have conducted the literature as a whole, namely, the year 1784. The chief poets of the Revolutionary period, Barlow, Dwight, Trumbull, and Freneau, all lived well on into the next century, Barlow, in fact, being the only one of these who did not survive the War of 1812.

In Barlow's day, heroics were the fashion. His *magnum opus*, a rhymed epic on the discovery of America, had already taken shape in manuscript as early as 1781; in 1787 it appeared as "The Vision of Columbus"; by 1807 it had grown into the ponderous "Columbiad." It is an uninspired, pseudo-classical narrative, schematically and metrically correct, but organically lifeless, full of the "printer's devil personification" so characteristic of its time. With gratuitous industry, as it supplies all the lineage of personified abstractions like "Discord," so it begins the history of America at Creation, fetches the story down through colonial times to the Revolution, and includes in its sweep a glance at events yet to come. Similarly in his mock-heroic, "The Hasty Pudding" (1793), which is touched with fancy and is in every way more attractive than his "Columbiad," Barlow commences with the growth and harvesting of the maize which is to furnish the flour.

Dwight, who was at first a tutor, but from 1795 until his death, in 1817, president, of Yale College, in 1785 brought forth a Biblical epic entitled "The Conquest of Canaan," in which the narrative of Exodus is diversified by allusions to heroes in the American War of Independence, and by a tale of romantic love superadded. Dwight was a diligent reader of Pope and Goldsmith, but he did not confine his interest to the eighteenth century; he knew the enchantment of the poets' poet, Spenser; and like Thomson he could at times, as in "Greenfield Hill," look with his own eyes at things about him. He was a friend of Trumbull, Humphreys, and Barlow; on occasion he penned a bitter invective. But as a writer he will be remembered for his noble hymn, whose second stanza commences,

I love Thy Church, O God,

which is the key-note of his life.

Trumbull, though he lived to a great age (1750–1831), had completed his remarkable mock-heroic, "M'Fingal," prior to 1784; hence at this point he interests us chiefly on account of his friendship with Dwight and Barlow, and his effect on later satirists.

With Freneau the case is different. Some of his choicest verse did not appear until 1786, when he published a collection containing "The House of Night"; and in 1795 he brought together in another collection what he apparently considered best in his output for twenty-five years or more preceding. This was very uneven, including much that might better have been left unprinted, and other work which stamps Freneau as the one American of true poetical genius before 1800. He was not unaware of his powers, and aimed to develop them by frequent perusal of good models in ancient and modern literature; but he was not sufficiently self-critical. He prolonged a career of travel and rapid composition, in both poetry and prose, beyond the normal span of life, making still another collection of his works in 1815. His latter years were darkened by the thought that he was being unwarrantably neglected for men of lesser talent. A man of great bodily vigour, he was meditating yet another, a final, edition of his writings, when he came to his unfortunate end. In 1832 he lost his way as he was returning home through a snowstorm, and died from exposure. His once maligned personality has of late been duly vindicated, and his work has received generous praise. It is claimed that Scott and Campbell were content to borrow lines from him. Furthermore, he has been deemed a co-worker with Coleridge and Wordsworth in bringing about in literature the so-called "return to nature." The parallel might easily be carried too far. Until literary scholarship has broadened and deepened its knowledge of the entire period in which Freneau was active, neither the worth of his poetry nor the possible extent of his influence can be judicially determined. There can be no question that such poems as "The Wild Honeysuckle," "The Hurricane," "The Dying Indian," and "Eutaw Springs" have more than a transitory value. However, it is by his satirical verse that Freneau might seem more likely to persist; for the nature of satire tolerates in some measure a free and easy style such as he developed.

Early Minor Poets.—Of the minor poetry prior to 1815 there is little to be said by way of praise. We see in it how the influence of Akenside and other English didactic writers of a previous age gives ground before the newer spirit of Wordsworth and Coleridge; although the satires of the Revolution had a lineage, in Paine and others, that did not quickly die away; and although several other literary fashions had their intervals of existence, as, for example, the imitation of "Ossian" and the cult of the Della Cruscans. The intellect of Akenside made itself felt in such work as "The Power of Solitude" (1804), by Joseph Story (1779–1845), and the anonymous "Pains of Memory," published four years later. "Of much higher merit," thinks Professor Bronson, "are the didactic poems of Robert Treat Paine (1773–1811), a man of versatile and brilliant parts, but dissipated character. His lyrics, orations, and dramatic criticisms all show ability. But his best work is 'The Ruling Passion,' a poem delivered before the Phi Beta Kappa at Harvard in 1797." This is "frankly on the model of Pope, but so witty, vigorous, and pointed that it does honour to its original." William Cliffton's "Poems" (1800), and Thomas G. Fessenden's "Original Poems" (1804), can only be mentioned.

A word may be added on the poetesses of the time, several of whom, for example Mrs. Mercy Warren (1728–1814), having made themselves heard during the American struggle for liberty, continued to find an audience in the early years of the Republic. Mrs. Warren's poems were collected in 1790, Mrs. Susanna H. Rowson's in 1804. The sentimental Mrs. Sarah W. Morton may also be noted; she flourished somewhat later than the others (1759–1846). She is no longer interesting as the "American Sappho," nor is it generally recalled that she considered Paine to be the American "Menander." She was an exponent of the inane "Della Cruscan" style, which had its vogue in England until it was attacked by William Gifford, and in the United States until Gifford's "Baviad" and "Mæviad" were republished at Philadelphia (1799), seconded by a poetical epistle to their author from the pen of the young Quaker Cliffton.

Not less pernicious than the Della Cruscans were the imitators of MacPherson's "Ossian," including Joseph B. Ladd (1764–1786), Jonathan M. Sewall (1746–1808), and John Blair Linn (1777–1804). Both schools gave place when the Wordsworthian reaction set in against "poetic diction" and the habit of writing verse about natural objects without having looked at them.

When party spirit runs high, satire is likely to be thriving. Political tension during the latter part of Washington's presidency and during the administrations of Adams and Jefferson gave birth to a brood of satiric poems, many of them unacknowledged by their authors. Anonymous or otherwise, in most of them the writer's pen was wielded as a bludgeon rather than a knife. Freneau himself was none too delicate in his censure of the government, although he ill deserved the reputation of a man lacking in love for his country; but Freneau was merely the most gifted among a number, more partisan than he, who, according as they were Federalists or Democrats, bitterly assailed the measures of the opposing faction. The "Democratiad" and the "Guillotina" were anonymous attacks in 1795 and 1796 upon the Democrats. William Cobbett, the Englishman, and Alexander Hamilton, whose private life offered an easy target, were pilloried as representatives of the Federalist party, in Carey's "Porcupiniad" (1799) and a collection entitled "Olio" (1801).

Nor was factional spleen unrelated to a variety of patriotic sentiment which displayed itself in verse for holidays and state occasions; but, like all the satires, most of the post-Revolutionary effusions of patriotism have long since ceased to excite emotion. As has been noted, Hopkinson's "Hail Columbia" (1798) is one of the exceptions. Colonel David Humphreys (1753–1818), a large part of whose verse amounted to eulogies on Washington, to the general public is hardly so much as a memory; and his intention "to make use of poetry for strengthening patriotism, promoting virtue, and extending happiness" has gone the way of many similar purposes of great excellence unaided by genius.

Washington Allston.—The first poet of distinction who evidently represents the tradition of Wordsworth was the artist Washington Allston (1779–1843), a friend of Coleridge, and declared by him to have a genius for literature and painting "unsurpassed by any man of his age." Southey too was an enthusiastic admirer; and Wordsworth, who was chary of praise for the age in which he lived, commended the American painter ungrudgingly. In Allston's "Sylphs of the Seasons" (1813) there is evidence of the exact eye of an artist, and there is much delicacy of sentiment and gentle play of fancy; but great constructive and imaginative vigour are not present, and a certain tameness in the rhymes and obviousness in the succession of thoughts serve to explain why the poem has not secured a more lasting recognition. His "America and Great Britain" was included by Coleridge in "Sibylline Leaves" (1817), "for its moral no less than its patriotic spirit." As an attempt to incorporate in language the conception of abstract, so to speak, intellectual, beauty, "The Angel and the Nightingale" reminds one of Shelley.

Before Allston, there had been ballad-writers who dealt with themes that are now familiar to readers of Wordsworth and Coleridge. In particular, the motive of the young and innocent girl who has been betrayed, and through her betrayal crazed, was a notable favourite. Lucius M. Sargent's "Hubert and Ellen" (1812) is described as a poor imitation of Wordsworth, taking its cue, like Joseph Hutton's ballad on Crazy Jane ("Leisure Hours," 1812) and Henry C. Knight's "Poor Margaret Dwy," from one study or another of mental derangement in "Lyrical Ballads" or the "Poems" (by Wordsworth) of 1807. Doubtless a large number of parallels could be found in American literature to Wordsworth's "Ruth," and to his sympathetic treatment of other lowly types of humanity. In like manner, just as the same English poet fraternises with the robin and the butterfly, and Coleridge hails a young ass as his "brother," and as Shelley in 1815 claims kindred with "bright bird, insect, or gentle beast," so Knight addresses "The Caterpillar" (1821) as "cousin reptile." The Puritans had averred, Most sins, and all sinners, are equal; Rousseau and the French Revolutionists went further, declaring, All men are equal; and now, responsive to the doctrine of Coleridge and his Pantisocrats, American poets were implying, All creatures are equal. Thus thrives the principle of democracy and fraternity. Themistocles is at length no better than the boorish islander, and the Apostles have lost their superiority to sparrows. "Cousin reptile," of course, is an extreme case.

On its saner side, the new impulse set in motion several writers of not a little promise. Such was John Neal (1793–1876), whose poem "The Battle of Niagara" (1818) reflects Wordsworthianism at second hand through Shelley and Keats, with a touch of Byronic grandiloquence and tameness, but with a touch, too, of aboriginal nature, however crude. The native powers of Neal were later dissipated in journalism, novel-writing, and the like.

Joseph Rodman Drake.—Of great promise likewise, but cut short by a premature demise, was the career of Joseph Rodman Drake (1795–1820). Drake was a precocious spirit, working swiftly, and valuing his easily produced and quickly moving verses perhaps a little below their true worth. A friend of Halleck, and like Halleck under the sway of the novelist Fenimore Cooper, he reveals also how familiar he was with the half-luminous, half-misty style of Coleridge. In Drake's happiest attempt, "The Culprit Fay" (1816), he aimed to find an utterance for the poetry of the great American rivers, hitherto neglected, as he and his friends decided, in the native literature. The outcome of a discussion between Drake, Freneau, and Cooper, this fanciful story is nevertheless replete with the cadences of Coleridge's "Christabel" (1816), however difficult it may be to explain the resemblance. Needless to say, "The Culprit Fay" could not make a general appeal like that of "The American Flag," by the same author—a rhetorical and manneristic piece that, up to a few years ago, was on the lips of every American school-boy:

> When Freedom from her mountain height
> Unfurled her standard to the air,
> She tore the azure robe of night,
> And set the stars of glory there.

Set them where? In spite of the fact that it is grandiose and unprecise, "The American Flag" may yet be yielded an advantage in point of style over Key's "Star-Spangled Banner," with which one naturally compares it.

Fitz-Greene Halleck.—The final quatrain of "The American Flag" was written by Drake's associate in the "Croaker Papers," Fitz-Greene Halleck (1790–1867). Halleck was a witty poet, who aimed at no lasting fame, but humorously chastised the passing follies of New York society, much as Lord Byron scourged society in London. He wrote clearly and gracefully, and was greatly overpraised in his time. His satiric poem "Fanny" (1819) was highly popular. "Marco Bozzaris," a lyric recital of the Byronic type, portrayed with a good deal of life, but with a suspicion of rant too, a dramatic incident in the struggle of modern Greece against the Turk. His tribute to Burns (1827) was warmly approved by the Scottish bard's sister: "nothing finer," she said in 1855, "has been written about Robert." "Red Jacket" and the monody on "Drake" also belong to

Halleck's early period. In fact, his main activity as a poet was confined to the ten or eleven years commencing with the death of Drake (1820). As Allston was the first of our poets to arouse much admiration abroad, so Halleck was the first to receive notable posthumous honours at home. In general, he owed a large measure of his inspiration to Washington Irving.

James Kirke Paulding.—So did James Kirke Paulding (1779–1860), though his "Lay of the Scotch Fiddle" (1813) was a parody of Walter Scott's "Lay of the Last Minstrel," and though his title to enduring fame, as he supposed, was an epic, "The Backwoodsman" (1818), representing life on the American frontier. Neither the clever ballad, nor the prosy epic, nor his second instalment of *Salmagundi* has outwitted the envy of time. In its own day Paulding's effort to repeat the first success of Irving was eclipsed by "The Croakers" of Halleck and Drake. His "Peter Piper" still lingers.

John Howard Payne.—A case similar to "Peter Piper" is that of a song in "Clari" (1823), one of the dramas by John Howard Payne (1791–1852). Payne, who tried his hand at various pursuits, was a friend of Irving, and acquainted with Coleridge and Lamb. At one time he was United States consul at Tunis. As an actor and a journalist he knew the temper of his American public; hence he was able to enjoy a considerable reputation as playwright. His "Brutus" (1818) was well received; yet he would be totally forgotten save for a single lyric in "Clari," "Home, Sweet Home," which successive generations of his countrymen have handed down as an heirloom of the people.

Woodworth, Morris, Hoffman, Willis, etc.—Two other writers of the same period, now known chiefly through brief and homely songs or rhetorical selections, were Samuel Woodworth (1785–1842), still remembered for "The Old Oaken Bucket" (1826), and George P. Morris (1802–64), whose "Woodman, Spare That Tree" and "The Main Truck" (otherwise called "A Leap for Life") have re-echoed from the platform of many a village schoolhouse, and given many a young rustic his principal conceptions of impassioned eloquence. The songs of Charles Fenno Hoffman (1806–84), while by no means so familiar as these, are not at all inferior. Hoffman was a student at Columbia College, bred up in the literary traditions of New York City. So also were James W. Eastburn (1797–1819) and Robert C. Sands (1799–1832). Under a rather indefensible nomenclature, all three would be included with Paulding and Halleck as members of the "Knickerbocker School," the bright luminary in which is Irving ("Diedrich Knickerbocker"). To these we may add McDonald Clarke (1798–1842), "the mad poet," irritatingly personal in his allusions to the belles of the metropolis; Park Benjamin (1809–64); and N. P. Willis (1806–67), whose reign of cleverness succeeded that of Halleck. Flippant, careless how or whom he hit, Willis made an extraordinary name at home, and was able to create a stir abroad. In America he published where and what he pleased, for the editors were glad to pay him well, so eager were people to read him. But he had the reward of a lightly won popularity: when the generation for whom he wrote had passed away he was deservedly neglected. His championship of American literature against the strictures of Lockhart and Marryat, and the redeeming candour of his opinions, make poor amends for his abuse of talents that might have improved, rather than satisfied, the taste of the garish day.

William Cullen Bryant.—However different in aim and permanence from the last mentioned adherent of the "Knickerbocker School," to the same general category may be assigned William Cullen Bryant (1794–1878), who from 1826 until his death was an active force in the literary life of New York. The author of "Thanatopsis" and one of the best verse translations of Homer was born in Cummington, Massachusetts, attended a local school, was taught Latin and Greek by private tutors, two clergymen of ability, and studied for part of a year at Williams College, where the standard of scholarship was then low. Leaving that institution in 1811, he made ready to enter the profession of law. During his preparation he had an interval of experience as adjutant in the State militia. After that, he practised as a lawyer in his native State, at Plainfield and Great Barrington, until 1825, when he yielded to the strong propensity of nature, and took up literature for the business of life.

As a mere child, Bryant showed an exceptional leaning toward poetry. He was unweariedly studious, and an omnivorous reader. He wrote verses before he was nine; in his youth, so he says, he varied his private devotions from the ordinary Calvinistic models, by supplicating that he "might receive the gift of poetic genius and write verses that might endure." The gift came to him through the instrumentality of Wordsworth's "Lyrical Ballads" (the American edition of 1802), whose mastery over him he afterwards acknowledged, and bore witness to in his practice. At first, however, he was imbued with the tendencies of his own predecessors in America. A Federalist in his political sympathies, he opposed the aims of Jefferson's administration—although later he grew to be a staunch supporter of "Jeffersonian Democracy." Encouraged by his father, a well-known physician, who himself indulged in verse, young Cullen, before he was fifteen, saw in print his political satire "The Embargo" (1808), a work in the manner of Freneau and Trumbull, in which Jefferson was invited to resign the presidency. In Wordsworth, fortunately, Byrant had a model choicer than the satirists. He became acquainted with "Lyrical Ballads" in 1810. Sometime in the autumn of 1811, his inward eye having been taught to see the operation of a benign and healing spirit in the world of nature, this thoughtful youth, now about to begin the study of law, and, as it were, to commence the effort of life, was moved to record his sentiments on the all-pervading fact of death: the universal debt is not an evil; to pay it is as natural as to be born; and to obey the voice of nature, to confide in her will, is the source of human satisfaction. That is the burden of "Thanatopsis."

When "Thanatopsis" was submitted by the poet's father to *The North American Review* (in 1817), people would hardly believe that such an exalted strain had been conceived outside of England. "Thanatopsis" and "To a Waterfowl" (written in 1815) are indeed in many ways Wordsworthian; the similarity is immediately noticeable. Yet the similarity is not complete. In the first place, they are founded, and very definitely founded, upon the natural scenery of Bryant's own New England environment; and they sprang out of a unified individual experience to which his personal observation contributed as much as his reading. But, as has been remarked before, the note of Bryant is a less joyous note than that of his great English exemplar, not only because of a difference in the selection of subjects, but through a difference in the treatment of detail as well. It is not to be expected that in perfection of technique a boy of seventeen could equal a poet who at the age of thirty-two (when Wordsworth first became at all generally known in America) was virtually master of his craft. Moreover, "Thanatopsis" as we now have it is actually an immense improvement upon the version that came out in *The North American*; yet in finality of expression it cannot vie with the "Lines" associated with Tintern Abbey, not to speak of certain portions of "The Prelude" or "The Excursion" written in the zenith of Wordsworth's power. Still, "Thanatopsis" was the first great American poem; in its ultimate form it bids fair to please most readers in all ages. The majesty of Thucydides is borrowed in the conception that the whole earth is the sepulchre of famous men; there is Homeric splendour of epithet in such expressions as the "all-beholding sun." The "healing sympathy" of nature, of course, is Wordsworthianism pure and simple; but the poem as a whole is tinged with a pantheism much more stoical than the pantheism of Wordsworth, and curiously out of keeping with the touch of New England moralising toward the end. This touch is even more pronounced in the verses "To a Waterfowl."

"To a Waterfowl" was published with several other poems, including "Thanatopsis," in 1821. According to that wayward genius Hartley Coleridge, it is the best short poem in the English language; a perilously sweeping judgment, like Shelley's on "France," the magnificent ode by Hartley's father. At all events, "To a Waterfowl" is hardly surpassed by any of Bryant's later work, and probably unsurpassed by anything of comparable subject and scope ever written in America.

In 1821, Bryant, then practising law at Great Barrington, was married to Miss Frances Fairchild. In 1825, he gave up the law and a secure livelihood, and, removing to New York, assumed the editorship of *The New York Review*. After a brief connection with *The United States Review*, he became assistant editor of *The Evening Post*; in 1829 he was made editor-in-chief. His lifelong guidance of this most influential paper is briefly touched upon elsewhere. It may be readily thought that Bryant's prolonged editorial labours interfered with his subsequent development as a poet. Yet his partial ownership of *The Post* finally gave him abundant means for travel and a widening of his experience in his own and foreign lands; and his habits of industry, supported by a temperate bodily régime, enabled him to achieve during his extended career a noble literary monument outside of journalism.

By 1832 he was ready to publish another edition of his "Poems," adding more than eighty pieces that were new—notably, the "Forest

Hymn," the "Song of Marion's Men," and "The Death of the Flowers." At intervals of a few years (1834, 1836, 1842, 1844, etc.) other editions or volumes followed; giving evidence that his imagination was not dormant, for they contained in each case material in part or wholly fresh. Thus the "Poems" of 1854 included "O Mother of a Mighty Race" and "Robert of Lincoln," the latter a favourite with many, though inferior to Bryant's general standard. Of the "Thirty Poems" issued ten years later (1864), twenty-seven were new; the presence of selections, in English, from Book V of the Odyssey is worthy of particular remark. They had already appeared, a few months before, in *The Atlantic Monthly*.

The achievement of Bryant's declining years was his translation of Homer. He had at various times amused himself with renderings of one or another passage that pleased him in foreign tongues. He was an ardent admirer of the Greek epics. He was dissatisfied with the versions of Cowper and Pope. It is possible that he was acquainted with the counsels of Matthew Arnold, called forth by the Homer of Francis Newman. The favour met by his attempts with the Odyssey encouraged him to try his hand at the Iliad. On the death of his wife, in 1866, he felt the need of some employment to distract his attention, and resolved to translate the Iliad entire. By 1869 he had finished the first twelve books, at the rate of from forty to seventy-five lines a day. These twelve books were published in February, 1870, the remainder of the Iliad in June. By the first of July he was engaged upon the Odyssey; on December 7, 1871, he sent his printers "the twenty-fourth and concluding book of [his] translation of Homer's Odyssey, together with the table of contents for the second volume." To misunderstand the repression of feeling in these simple words, with which the venerable Bryant takes leave of his final work, is to miss the hidden fire animating his whole existence. In a great poet there is little waste of energy in the outward expression. The moment feeling shows itself, it is transmuted into artistic form. The form is adequate, but it is something different from the sentiment that gives it life.

The excellence of Bryant's blank-verse translation of Homer is not a theme for long discussion here. He aimed at simplicity and faithfulness. He rejected several of the customary ornaments of modern verse, choosing for his medium that rhythm which is most nearly related to the cadence of everyday speech. Tested by its effect on the layman of the present day, his attempt is more successful than other well-known metrical versions, less than the cadenced prose of translators, like Myers and Lang, who have profited by the advice of Arnold with respect to diction, but in avoiding the trammels of metre have followed the example set by the scholars of King James in the Authorised Version of the Scriptures. However, Bryant's rendering is too noble a piece of imaginative scholarship to be passed over.

Bryant spent something like six years upon his Homer. He survived its completion by six years more, full of honours, rejoicing in a hale old age, still visited occasionally by poetical inspiration, still influential in the political thought of his nation, able at four score and four to make a public address in honour of the Italian patriot Mazzini. During this address, "his uncovered head was for a time exposed to the full glare of the sun. Shortly after, while entering a house, he fell backwards, striking his head upon the stone steps; concussion of the brain and paralysis followed." He died in New York, June 12, 1878, and was buried at Roslyn, on Long Island Sound, near the beautiful country home where for thirty-five years his literary toils had been "sweetened to his taste."

Owing to his artistic reserve, Bryant had the reputation of a temperamental coldness, a reputation that is belied both by the tenderness of his domestic ties and by his well chosen and enduring friendships. His patriotism also was unswerving. If he "let no empty gust of passion find an utterance in his lay," nevertheless he knew and valued

> ... feelings of calm power and mighty sweep,
> Like currents journeying through the boundless deep.

He was a devoted lover of humanity and life; he was a devoted lover of his art. For him, art and life were one. It is easy for the uninitiated to credit him with a lack of warmth. The fully emancipated are aware what union of fire and self-restraint, of vigour and delicacy, goes to the rearing of a fabric like the orderly and effective career of Bryant.

Like most, or all, great poets, Bryant wrote admirable prose. His essays in criticism have already been alluded to. As a stylist he was indefatigably painstaking even to the smallest detail: "He was not a fluent nor a very prolific writer.... His manuscripts, as well as his proofs, were commonly so disfigured by corrections as to be read with difficulty even by those familiar with his script." His capacity for intense application was a partial measure of his success both as poet and as critic. For oratory, his legal training stood him in good stead, and his later prominence in New York and in the country as a whole gave him many an occasion. If Bryant, as Matthew Arnold believed, was *"facile princeps"* among American poets, this eminence arose from no merely capricious outburst of genius; it was the natural efflux of a noble, well rounded, and representative human life.

Saxe, Melville, Alice and Phoebe Cary.—After Bryant it is convenient to speak of a few poets, very different from him, and for the most part from each other, whose contemporaneous presence in New York is almost the only thing that connects them. John G. Saxe (1816–87), a native of Vermont, in his time was counted a leader among satirists. He staggers now under the accusation of extreme superficiality; none the less is he lively and readable. He consciously imitated Hood; he could scarcely avoid imitating Wendell Holmes. Of himself he had a remarkable turn for epigram and for punning in rhyme. His burlesque adaptations of Ovid are smart and amusing. On the whole it may be said that Saxe was at his best in "The Proud Miss MacBride," where he girds at an upstart aristocracy:

> Of all the notable things on earth,
> The queerest one is pride of birth,
>   Among our "fierce Democracie."

Herman Melville (1819–91), who wrote a fascinating account ("Typee," 1846) of his stay among the aborigines of the Marquesas, also published "Battle-Pieces" (1866) and other poems. His verse is less objective and sincere than his prose. Alice Cary (1820–71) and her sister, Phoebe (1824–71), were born in Ohio, where they were locally appreciated. Removing first to Philadelphia, then to New York, they supported themselves by their pens. The talents of Alice Cary were manifestly superior; yet for a time, yielding to her admiration of Poe, she allowed the element of harmonious sound in her poetry to overbalance that of meaning. Her hymns, one of which is almost a classic, are noble in their purity of sentiment.

Dana, Sprague, Hillhouse, etc.—Although his life and activity were centred elsewhere, Bryant, as we have seen, was a product of western Massachusetts. From him and the city of his adoption we naturally turn to a number of writers whose careers are to be more closely identified with New England. Many of these, like Richard Henry Dana senior (1787–1879), of Boston, were poets only secondarily. Dana was a journalist and politician—an admirer of Wordsworth and a lecturer on Shakespeare. An edition of his prose and verse in 1833 contained a poem, "The Buccaneer," inspired by Coleridge's "Rime of the Ancient Mariner." His shorter poems are moral—

> Oh, listen, man!
> A voice within us speaks the startling word,
> "Man, thou shalt never die"—

and are mostly tame and artificial. Though inferior in native talent to his brother-in-law, Washington Allston, Dana was more widely known as a writer, partly because of his ability as literary critic. His verse was melancholy and his meditation not virile. As a poet he won a smaller audience than did Charles Sprague (1791–1875), also of Boston; yet it is not now easy to understand why Sprague's longest poem, "Curiosity" (1823), should have been "largely read and quoted in this country, and grossly plagiarised in England" (Onderdonk). James A. Hillhouse (1789–1841), who wrote a Biblical drama called "Hadad" (1824), published "Dramas, Discourses, and Other Pieces" in 1839. He is interesting as an early exponent of the dramatic art in America. His style shows a strange blending of elements from Lord Byron and the Scriptures. It would probably be fairer to judge him by "Demetria" than by "Hadad." A Byronic sentimentalism runs through the work of James Gates Percival (1795–1856), whose "Prometheus" (1820) luxuriates in the sorrows of men and the vanity of human wishes. His poetry often belies his everyday life, since for all his facile pessimism he was a man of genuine attainments and solid interest in science. He could not make his own experience the fundamental thing in his verse;—unlike his contemporary John Pierpont (1785–1866), a clergyman of Boston. In his hymns and patriotic odes, Pierpont was masculine and sane, a good representative of the New England abolitionist, as may be gathered from "The Fugitive Slave's Apostrophe to the North Star." "Warren's Address to the

American Soldiers" is even better known, and still withholds the name of Pierpont from oblivion. John G. C. Brainard (1796–1828) died before his poetical gift could find complete expression. He dealt with the scenery and legends of Connecticut, but is hardly remembered outside the histories of American literature.

Mrs. Brooks and Mrs. Sigourney.—The same generation produced several women of note, whose poetry demands some attention; in particular, Lydia Huntley Sigourney (1791–1865), a prolific maker of books, not to speak of "more than two thousand articles in prose and verse" which were issued during her long and quiet life in Hartford. Mrs. Sigourney was no genius, albeit she passed for "the American Hemans." She was a person of great moral worth and the most charitable disposition. It has been suggested that the beauty of her character was responsible for her extraordinary vogue. More probably the attention she gave to the legends of her own country, the not unwholesome cast of sentimentalism in her thought, and her readiness to contribute verses for any occasion, however slight, will in large part account for the unbounded admiration which she enjoyed. In 1822 appeared her poem, in five cantos, "Traits of the American Aborigines"; her "Lays of the Heart" were published in 1848. Besides her innumerable shorter articles, she is said to have been responsible for something like fifty volumes. "Maria del Occidente" (Mrs. Maria Gowen Brooks, 1795–1845) was of a different cast, less homely in her sentiments, a romantic soul, filled with the spirit of Southey and Moore, leaning toward the sensuous and exotic. When she bent her energies to verse, as in "Judith, Esther, and Other Poems" (1820), and "Zophiel, or The Bride of Seven" (1833)—a story based on the Apocryphal Book of Tobit—she showed herself far removed from Mrs. Sigourney and "The Power of Maternal Piety" or "The Sunday School." On the whole, the taste of "Maria del Occidente," as Southey called her, was worse than that of "the American Hemans"; and if Southey termed Mrs. Brooks "the most impassioned and most imaginative of all poetesses," he paid an astounding tribute to his own acumen as a critic. Emma H. Willard (1787–1870), like Mrs. Sigourney, was prominent as an educator, accomplishing more as the head of a female seminary in Troy, N. Y., than by her writings. She was the author of "Rocked in the Cradle of the Deep." In the next generation were Sarah H. Whitman (1803–78) and Frances S. Osgood (1811–50), who composed verse not lacking in merit, but who are recalled rather for their championship of Edgar Allan Poe. Mrs. Whitman was at one time betrothed to him.

Minor Poets of New England.—Among the minor New England poets who came slightly later, was Samuel Longfellow (1819–92)—younger brother of Henry W. Longfellow—a hymn-writer of singular purity. Sylvester Judd (1813–53), a Unitarian minister, wrote an epic entitled "Philo" (1850). William Wetmore Story (1819–95), who edited the life and letters of his distinguished father, Chief Justice Story, forsook the bar at an early age and went to Italy to engage in sculpture. He was a poet of refinement, touched with melancholy, intellectual rather than passionate—yet with a fondness for the intangible—influenced by Longfellow and Holmes, by Tennyson and Browning. In verse, his chief works were "Poems" (1847), "Graffiti d'Italia" (1868), "A Roman Lawyer in Jerusalem" (1870), "He and She" (1883), and "Poems" (1886). Among his individual pieces "Cleopatra" seems to be the best known. Theophilus W. Parsons (1819–92) shows a similar Continental influence, whose most valuable result was his free translation of Dante's "Inferno" (cantos I-X, 1843, completed in 1867); this was preceded by his fine lines "On a Bust of Dante" (1841), which are justly admired. Henry H. Brownell (1820–72) attracted notice by a poem on Farragut, and through Farragut's good offices entered the United States Navy. His "War Lyrics and Other Poems" (1866) contained a stirring piece, "The River Fight," on the exploits of Farragut, somewhat in the style of Tennyson's "Charge of the Light Brigade."

Poetry in the South.—The major poets of New England, Longfellow, Lowell, Whittier, Emerson, and perhaps one or two others, constitute the one group in America that may rightfully be dignified with the name of school. Before approaching them, however, let us give some consideration to the poets of the South.

Though the institution of slavery gave the dominant classes in the Southern States a leisure comparable to that enjoyed by classic Greece, plantation life was not favourable to a thorough and imaginative education; nor were there great civic centres to collect, for mutual inspiration, such individuals as showed artistic and literary bent. Furthermore, in modern times most of the poets have been furnished by a restless and aspiring middle class, which was virtually lacking in the South. Among

the owners of plantations, personal ambition rarely soared much higher than local, state, or sectional politics, and political and occasional
oratory, with some noteworthy exceptions, was flamboyant and insincere. Save for a few noteworthy exceptions, accordingly, the career of
poet languished, and literature of a high order failed of appreciation. The
leading poets of the South realised only too well the weight of inertia
against which they strove, in a civilisation where the odds were continually against their success.

The Forerunners.—Early and minor poets in the South need not long
detain us. William Crafts (1789–1826), of Charleston, South Carolina, a
graduate of Harvard, and an orator of repute, composed a "Raciad," or
epic on horse-racing, and "Sullivan's Island." His "Miscellaneous Writings" (1828) were published posthumously. William J. Grayson (1788–
1863), who was more voluminous, attempted in his poem "The Hireling
and the Slave" (1856) to represent slavery as a preferable state for the
negro. Richard H. Wilde (1789–1847), Edward C. Pinkney (1802–28),
George H. Calvert (1803–89), Philip P. Cooke (1816–50) and others, show
a range of imitation running all the way from Byron through Scott and
Moore to Tennyson. Cooke's "Florence Vane" was warmly admired by
Poe. Albert Pike (1809–91), should be remembered as the author of "Dixie," which, "set to a popular air which has been traced back to slavery
times in New York State, became, in a multitude of variations, a Southern Marseillaise" (Onderdonk).

Timrod, Hayne, and Simms.—Of a high order was the poetry of that
champion of the Southern cause Henry B. Timrod (1829–67). Denied by
fortune the sort of education that he craved, striving throughout much
of his life with poverty and sickness, and finally defeated, saddened by
personal bereavement as well as by the downfall of the South, Timrod
died before he could make adequate report of his endowments. His volume of "Poems" (1860), issued at the beginning of the Civil War, was
almost unnoticed; and even yet he has not obtained the recognition due
him. His devotion to the South was not greater than his reverence for his
art. Few of our poets have so clearly understood themselves and their
craft. Unusual courage breathes in all he wrote. In the year of his death,
a prey to disease and sorrow, he could say to the Confederate soldiers
buried "At Magnolia Cemetery":

> Sleep sweetly in your humble graves,
>   Sleep, martyrs of a fallen cause;
> Though yet no marble column craves
>   The pilgrim here to pause.
>
> In seeds of laurel in the earth
>   The blossom of your fame is blown,
> And somewhere, waiting for its birth,
>   The shaft is in the stone.

Timrod's works were brought to light again in 1873 by Paul Hamilton Hayne (1830–86), who, prior to the war, had united with Simms and Timrod to erect, if possible, the drooping spirit of poetry in the South. Hayne's "Poems" (1855) and "Sonnets and Other Poems" (1857) had a chance to make their way before the outbreak of hostilities; and he survived the conflict long enough to publish "Legends and Lyrics" (1872) and "The Mountain of the Lovers, and Other Poems" (1873). A complete edition of his poems appeared in 1882. "The Laureate of the South," as he was called, was an enthusiast in sub-tropical life and scenery, a word-painter and word-musician after the manner of Poe. His music is more obvious than Timrod's and not so likely to please a delicate ear; and he did not have Timrod's unity and clearness of conception.

Less careful still in his workmanship, and still more lacking in concentration, was the third of the trio, William Gilmore Simms (1806–70). Simms was a most abundant writer, known later for his novels and biographies rather than his poems. In his earlier poetry he was under the sway of Byron and Moore. His scanty advantages in the way of schooling were atoned for in part by voluminous indiscriminate reading; yet he never overcame certain defects in thinking to which self-taught men are prone. His first publication was "Lyrical and Other Poems" (1827). "Atalantis" (1832), a closet-drama in blank verse, in its general structure harks back to Shelley's "Prometheus Unbound." His selected works, in nineteen volumes, were published in 1859. Simms' commanding presence, the vigour of his personality, his determination to conquer all obstacles in his own path, and to vitalise the literary atmosphere of the South, make him an impressive, even heroic, figure.

Edgar Allan Poe.—The life of Edgar Allan Poe (1809–49) is duly re-counted in another place, where his prose fiction is handled at some length. When Poe ran away from the ledgers in his guardian's office, he carried with him in manuscript the first heir of his invention, "Tamerlane and Other Poems," for which he found a publisher at Boston (1827). "Al Aaraaf, Tamerlane, and Minor Poems" followed in 1829. In 1831, the year of his discharge from West Point, appeared the volume of "Poems" with which Poe thought to win the interest of the cadets. Thereafter, most of his poetry first saw the light in various periodicals; for example, "The Raven" (1845) in the New York *Evening Mirror*, "The Bells" (1849) in *Sartain's Magazine*, "Annabel Lee" (1849) in *The New York Tribune*.

In the opinion of the present writer, Poe's verse is generally rated above its value, even for those qualities in which it is supposed particularly to excel. Certain poetical gifts this author unquestionably had in abundance. He had the *copia verborum* which is indispensable to every literary artist. His sensations were vivid, if not numerous. He knew how to choose the symbols with which to attain his ends. If we are to trust the substance of his remarks in "The Philosophy of Composition," and of those which he made regarding "The Raven," his choice and manipulation of literary artifice were for the most part very conscious. He was able through the use of carefully selected diction and imagery to produce in his reader precisely the shade of feeling—the glimmer of the supernatural, the sense of grey and subdued, occasionally the sense of Weird and poignant, grief—which he desired. He never forgets the music of his words, and through habit, almost without trying, he can write continuously in a minor key. And yet, his music is not inevitable enough, nor does it undergo enough variation, or variation sufficiently delicate. It is too forced, too repetitious. His effects all lie within narrow limits, and he runs his gamut over and over again. This is altogether aside from his failure to make his music grow out of that strong underlying poetical good sense which is to be confidently expected of every great imagination. People too often forget how far Poe falls short of his master, Coleridge, in the mere element of harmonious sound; just as they too often forget how far Coleridge falls short of *his* master, Milton, in the union of ethereal as well as sonorous cadences with a finely modulated or robust thought and sentiment. Were Poe's appeals to the external senses more wonderful than they are, he would still lag behind those poets—and in the history of literature they are not after all so few—who can touch every chord, whether sad or joyous, known to the human ear, and still maintain that basis of firm reason without which human communication ceases to be broadly human. The intellect also has its music, lacking which no poetry has ever long survived.

Furthermore, all allowance being made for the tragic outcome of Poe's career, for the part of his fate which was not the outgrowth of his own character, or could not, humanly considered, be attributed at some point in his development to his own will, his poetry is not uplifting. True, in his handling of material he is, in the ordinary acceptation, entirely clean. That is, he is wholly free from obscenity, as he is free also from that more perilous seeming cleanness which so often cloaks real impurity. Nevertheless may he be dangerous food for those whom he most readily attracts. Poe is essentially pessimistic, hopeless, toward general human experience. His favourite topic is death; and his vision does not pierce beyond the worm and the grave. Nay, like his predecessors in England and on the Continent, he luxuriates in the tomb and the charnel. As in his stories, so in his verse, though less patently, he follows some of the most pernicious motives in art that the older civilisation afforded his age. And it is the lethal progeny—Baudelaire and the rest—of that movement in European literature typified by Ann Radcliffe and "Monk" Lewis that has been quickest to take up with Poe and exploit him abroad. We may seek to explain and exculpate him; we may sorrow for his blighted life; but the fact remains that what Poe wrote sprang out of his career, hence, on the whole, was morbid. The flowers of his poetry are the flowers of Lethe. The stimulants with which he catches the reader are violent and exciting. His ideal of intellectual beauty was detached and unnatural. It is little wonder, then, that he would not enter into sympathy with the English poet by whom the normal Bryant was inspired, and whose works, the most normalising and healthful influence that American literature thus far has felt, were purposely reactive against artificial and abnormal stimulation.

Sidney Lanier.—Among the representatives of the "New South," Sidney Lanier (1842–81), musician, poet, teacher of English, is easily foremost. He was born in Macon, Georgia, and received his education at Oglethorpe College, where, on graduating, he became a tutor; he volunteered in the Confederate Army (1860), toward the end of the war was captured, and perhaps owed his subsequent ill-health to his imprisonment of five months at Point Lookout. When the war was over, he taught again, in Alabama, read law, supported himself by his music—he was an adept on the flute—wrote for magazines, and by private study in Baltimore eventually fitted himself to take a lectureship in English literature at Johns Hopkins University. Courageous in his struggle with adverse circumstances, buoyant and energetic in spite of his long battle with disease, Lanier greatly resembles Timrod. Like Timrod, too, dying early, he left but a slender volume of poetry, uneven in excellence, an earnest of what he might have accomplished, hardly a standard by which to appraise him. Lanier's was a delicate and sensuous rather than a profound imagination; however, both in his observation of external nature and in the thoroughness and extent of his acquaintance with general literature, he was unusually well prepared for the office of poet. His interest in science fortified and disciplined his contemplation of the outer world; his poetical instinct was nurtured through industrious and select reading; and he brought to bear upon his own literary craftsmanship, and upon the literary work of others, the ear of a trained musician. His musical ear helped him greatly in his studies on metre, where his contributions to scholarship are distinctly more valuable than in his lectures on the English novel. Deeply sympathetic and generous and sane in all relations of life, Lanier had a subtle understanding for the realm that lies outside the haunts of men—for the domain of wild fauna and flora, for the seldom heeded and the escaping phenomena of the woods and the marsh and the sea. The poor reception given to his "Tiger Lilies" (1867), a novel based on experiences in the army, did not dishearten him. In 1875 he definitely announced himself by his poem entitled "Corn," published in *Lippincott's Magazine*, a vision of the South restored through agriculture. This brought him the opportunity of writing the "Centennial Cantata" for the Philadelphia Exposition, where he expressed the faith he now had in the future of the reunited nation. The Cantata finished, he immediately began a much longer centennial ode, his "Psalm of the West" (1876), which appeared in *Lippincott's Magazine*, and which, with "Corn" and "The Symphony," made part of a small volume published in the autumn of 1876. Lanier's important critical works were the product of the years between 1876 and his death. Some three years after he died, his poems were collected and edited by his wife. If we had to rely upon one poem to keep alive the fame of Lanier, thinks his biographer, Mr. Edwin Mims, we "could single out 'The Marshes of Glynn' with assurance that there is something so individual and original about it, and that, at the same time, there is such a roll and range of verse in it, that it will surely live not only in American poetry but in English." "He is the poet of the marshes as surely as Bryant is of the forests."

Maurice Thompson and Mrs. Preston.—Our notice of Southern writers may conclude with Maurice Thompson and Mrs. Margaret Preston. James Maurice Thompson (1844–1901) is commonly associated with the Middle West, since he was born and died in Indiana. His early life, however, was spent in Kentucky and Georgia, he saw service in the Confederate Army, and much of his verse and prose carries the stamp of his experiences in the South and his acquaintance with Southern literature. He was a lawyer by profession, but by instinct a natural scientist. In 1885 he was appointed State Geologist of Indiana. From 1890 on he was connected with the New York *Independent*. His style was crisp and neat, sometimes over-elaborate; but he kept an eye on the thing he was talking about, so that in general what he has said of nature is very acceptable. His devotion to the pastimes of fishing and archery gave him a good deal of literary material. His extensive and exact knowledge of the ways of birds enters into many of his poems, as for example "An Early Bluebird." The strain of regenerate patriotism in "Lincoln's Grave" is the same that we find in Lanier. Mrs. Preston (1820–97) was the daughter of the Rev. Dr. Junkin, founder of Lafayette College and afterward president of Washington and Lee University, in Virginia. Before her marriage, in 1857, she had done some writing. In 1866 she published "Beechenbrook, a Rhyme of the War"; in 1870, "Old Songs and New." Her "Cartoons" (1875) and "Colonial Ballads" (1887) show her at her best. She has been styled "the greatest Southern poetess"; there have been few claimants to dispute the title.

Major Poets of New England.—With this caption we return to the main stream of American verse, and reach the men whose lives and works may be said to justify a connected account of poetry in the United States. We shall take up Longfellow first. Whatever vicissitudes his literary standing has suffered, or is likely to suffer, he is bound for a long time to appear as the central figure among our poets.

Henry Wadsworth Longfellow.—The subject of this sketch was born in Portland, Maine, February 27, 1807. He came of a gifted stock. His father was a lawyer of ability, and his mother a woman of artistic temperament and varied attainments, so that the boy grew up in an atmosphere of study and refinement. Longfellow was a wise and gentle child, fond of books, not too sensitive, always normal and sane. Until 1821 he went to school in Portland; in 1822 he entered the sophomore class at Bowdoin College. Here he attained a good rank in scholarship, and became acquainted, not intimately, with the future novelist Hawthorne. Upon graduation in 1825, Longfellow went abroad, in order to fit himself for a professorship in modern languages which lay open to him at Bowdoin. He visited France, Germany, England, and the South of Europe; on his return in 1829 he gave himself up with ardour and success to the activity of teaching. In 1831 he was married to Miss Mary S. Potter. In 1835, having received an invitation to the chair of modern languages at Harvard, he went abroad again for further travel and study, this time mainly to Germany and the North. The death of his young wife, shortly after their arrival in Holland, filled his cup with bitterness, but did not swerve him from preparation for the duties of his chair at Cambridge. Nevertheless, as may be read beneath the surface of his romance "Hyperion," his determination that he must ultimately become a poet, and not end as a teacher in the classroom, can be traced to this critical epoch in his life.

Longfellow taught at Harvard from 1836 until 1854, with but one intermission, in 1842, when on account of his health he made his third trip to Europe. In 1843 he married Miss Frances E. Appleton, whom he had met in Switzerland sixteen years before, and whose presence and influence are likewise traceable in "Hyperion." Through the generosity of his father-in-law, he was able to establish a home in Craigie House, where he had been a lodger since 1837, a dwelling of Revolutionary fame. For a while, Longfellow's study was the room once occupied by Washington. Here, surrounded by his books and, as the years went on, by a growing family circle, he lived in comfort and felicity. His reputation spread, and the number of his acquaintances increased. Among his friends he reckoned Sparks and Prescott, the historians; Ticknor, his predecessor at Harvard, and Lowell, who afterward succeeded Longfellow; Fields, Emerson, Holmes, and Hawthorne; Felton, Sumner, Agassiz, and Norton. He read and wrote variously and extensively; he counted it a privilege to be interpreting Dante "to young hearts." In time, however, his duties as a teacher, above all the preparation of lectures, gradually wore upon him. He felt that he could not serve two masters, and he clave to poetry. At length, in 1854, he resigned his professorship, to devote himself exclusively to authorship. Seven years later, under the most distressing circumstances, he lost his second wife. From this catastrophe, Longfellow, though he eventually regained his outward cheerfulness, never inwardly recovered. "He bore his grief with courage and in silence. Only after months had passed could he speak of it; and then only in fewest words." In 1868 he made his last visit to Europe, where he was met with "a flood of hospitality." In London "he breakfasted with Mr. Gladstone, Sir Henry Holland, the Duke of Argyll; lunched with Lord John Russell at Richmond, ... received midnight calls from Bulwer and Aubrey de Vere.... The Queen received him cordially and without ceremony in one of the galleries of Windsor Castle." After a visit of two days with Tennyson, Longfellow and his party crossed to the Continent. They spent the summer in Switzerland, the autumn in France, the winter in Florence and Rome. When he returned to America, he "found Cambridge in all its beauty; not a leaf faded." "How glad," he wrote, "I am to be at home. The quiet and rest are welcome after the surly sea. But there is a tinge of sadness in it, also." The last ten years of Longfellow's life were quiet and serene, with a tinge of sadness in them, also. Yet they were filled with literary projects which, for a man of his age, he carried through with remarkable energy; and, until toward the end, his correspondence was enormous. In 1880 his health showed signs of failing. In 1882 he suffered a brief and sharp illness, and on Friday, March 24, "he sank quietly in death." "The long, busy, blameless life was ended."

At the age of thirteen, Longfellow printed four stanzas, "The Battle of Lovell's Pond," in a corner of *The Portland Gazette*. Within the next six years he wrote a considerable number of poems for *The United States Literary Gazette*. By 1833, in addition to text-books for his classes, he had, in various magazines, published original articles, stories, and several reviews; among them an important estimate of poetry, especially the poetry of America, in a notice of Sidney's "Defense of Poesy" contributed to *The North American Review*; as well as translations from the Spanish of Manrique and others, with an "Introductory Essay on the Moral and Devotional Poetry of Spain" (1833). "Outre-Mer," first published as a series of sketches, appeared in book form in 1835, "Hyperion" in 1839, and "Voices of the Night" in the same year as "Hyperion." "Voices of the Night" made Longfellow's reputation as a poet; the edition was immediately exhausted. "Hyperion," which eventually sold well, though at present it is not often enough read, was at first unfortunate, the publisher failing before this book had a fair start. Of Longfellow's better known works, published during the latter half of his lifetime, his "Ballads and Other Poems" appeared in 1841, "The Spanish Student" in 1843, "Evangeline" in 1847, "Kavanagh," another prose romance, in 1849, "Hiawatha" in 1855, "The Courtship of Miles Standish" in 1858, "The Golden Legend" in 1872, and "Aftermath" in 1873. The "Tales of a Wayside Inn" came out in 1863, 1872, and 1873, the First Day separately, the Second and the Third Day in company with other writings.

In consequence, it may be, of a latter-day tendency to disparage Longfellow's verse, there has been an effort of late to rehabilitate his prose; not so much, indeed, for its own sake, as for its importance in the history of our literature. "Hyperion," for example, is not merely what Longfellow called it, "a sincere book, showing the passage of a morbid mind into a purer and healthier state"; that is, it is not merely the veiled autobiography of our most popular poet. Its final reception and large sale are a proof that in the forties not a few Americans could be interested in German student life and in the discussion of Continental literatures. With this romance, one might say, began an American literature that, without ceasing to be native, could claim to be cosmopolitan. Possibly no single work produced in this country ever effected more in the dissemination of European culture. Its faults are on the surface. The style is not seldom forced and florid, having the colour of Jean Paul rather than Irving; and the sentiment here and there is gushing. Nevertheless, parts of "Hyperion" are good prose, the prose of a scholar who is aware of what he is saying and of a poet who knows how to avoid scraps of metre when he is not writing verse. The poet-scholar knows, too, on what sort of basis the best poetry is founded: "O thou poor authorling!... to cheer thy solitary labour, remember that the secret studies of an author are the sunken piers upon which is to rest the bridge of his fame, spanning the dark waters of Oblivion. They are out of sight; but without them no superstructure can stand secure."

The nature of Longfellow's secret studies is partly indicated by the extent of his published translations. Although one could hardly aver that the poet was anything like a linguistic investigator in the modern sense, he had a wide acquaintance with Germanic and Romance literatures; he spoke several modern tongues with fluency; and he had a sufficient command of idiom to translate with seeming ease from Swedish, German, Old English, French, Spanish, and Italian. His renderings from Tegnér's "Frithiof's Saga" seemed so true to the original that the Swedish poet urged Longfellow to complete the translation. The versions of Uhland and others which he made in Germany during the year 1836 were later on extraordinarily efficacious in popularising German literature for America. He may likewise be counted one of the pioneers among American students of Old English or, as he called it, "Anglo-Saxon." As a teacher of modern languages, he naturally gave heed to Greek and Latin secondarily, and there came a time when he deplored the fact that his familiarity with Greek had slipped away. Yet he loved the classics, his favourite among the Latin poets being Horace. In Horace, he said, one could find all that was worth while in the message of Goethe, expressed just as well, and uttered earlier. Of course the most considerable piece of scholarship undertaken by Longfellow was his translation of the "Divine Comedy," a task for which his enthusiastic teaching of Dante had helped to fit him, and one which he had commenced (1839) years before the death of his second wife; yet one which he resumed and mainly completed relatively late in life, and, like Bryant's Homer, something taken up as the resource of a soul bitterly bereaved, unable to accomplish spontaneous creative work. In compassing this task, Longfellow had the encouragement and the direct assistance of Norton and Lowell, to whose knowledge and taste the translation as it now stands is greatly indebted. Even so, it cannot rank high in artistic workmanship. First of all, the translator found that, in order to reproduce the sense with fidelity, he must sacrifice the rhyme, a dubious concession so long as metrical structure was to be retained at all. Still, Longfellow's translation is pure and lucid English; for the beginner in Dante the critical apparatus is valuable even now; and the three sonnets prefixed to the "Inferno," "Purgatorio," and "Paradiso" are in themselves an introduction to Dante of a sort hardly to be surpassed. The best spirit of America is blended in them with the best of the Middle Ages.

In considering Longfellow as an original poet, we shall not go astray if we remember his own conception of originality. To him the poetic gift meant, not the power of creating new material—as the vulgar suppose—but insight, the power of seeing things according to their eternal values. Doubtless he realised that one needs insight to discover how far the vulgar supposition is blind. At all events, we need not look for new ideas or new sentiments in the poetry of Longfellow, but for an attempt to make us see things as he sees them, after he has tried to see them as they are. In his dramas, and in his narratives—these latter being more important—he frankly took material furnished by his wide reading, or lying ready to his hand, and strove to clothe it in a new and more permanent form. "Evangeline" is an instance of his method. The story was given him by Hawthorne; in elaborating it, Longfellow consulted such works on Nova Scotia and the exile of the Acadians as were accessible to him; he was true to his sources. Had he known of better authorities, he would have read them, and his account of the exile would have been historically more precise. The metre of "Evangeline," suggested by that of Goethe's "Hermann und Dorothea," is one of the rare instances where dactylic hexameter has succeeded in English. One can truthfully say that whatever Longfellow took he really appropriated, that is, made his own. It was but seldom that his materials would not fuse, for he had a thorough command of technique. In "Hiawatha," which has been called "the nearest approach to an American epic," he employed a form of verse borrowed from the Finnish "Kalevala," in which to embody traditions of the Indians. As Freiligrath remarked, there is something odd in the notion of Hiawatha, child of the West Wind, meeting with historical Christian missionaries. However, Longfellow's daring synthesis of heterogeneous elements pleased that great authority on American antiquities Henry R. Schoolcraft; after many failures, a native poet had at length arisen to portray our aborigines, in a long poem, with fidelity and imagination. Ten thousand copies were sold in this country within four weeks, and the poem was translated into six modern languages.

The dramatic works of Longfellow have suffered in comparison with his narrative poems and lyrics. The causes of this are partly internal and partly external. In his "Christus," which he fancied would endure, he probably chose a subject of too great magnitude for his powers. Yet the second part at least, "The Golden Legend," at present operates less vitally than it should, largely because of its sympathy with the ideals of the Middle Ages—with ideals which we, still living in the Renaissance, are not ready to comprehend. "'The Golden Legend,'" said G. P. R. James, "is like an old ruin with the ivy and the rich blue mould upon it." Is it not more like a Gothic church before mould and ruin have crept in? It is a bit of wholesome, rejuvenated medievalism, an edifice whose threshold the intellectual pride of our age feels discomfort in crossing.

It is by his shorter poems that Longfellow now chiefly lives. Brief narratives such as "The Skeleton in Armour," and "The Wreck of the Schooner Hesperus," lyrics of sentiment and pathos—"Psalms of Life"— more rarely bits of humour like the German mechanic's song, "I know a maiden, fair to see," were soon established in the popular memory. It would be ungracious to say that the popular taste has been wrong in preferring what is sentimental and pathetic in Longfellow. A poet whose love of the hearth was so strong, and whose personal acquaintance with domestic happiness and domestic grief was so profound, did well to pour out his soul in verses which add sunshine to daylight for the happy, and in which the deeply afflicted may find pensive solace. Yet the popular taste has clung to "Tell me not in mournful numbers," where the sentiment is not above suspicion, and to "The Skeleton in Armour," where character, sentiment, and historical setting are for the most part incongruous; and it has almost let the sonnet on Milton fall asleep.

Longfellow was the most popular poet ever brought forth on this continent. His unparalleled vogue was destined to undergo a reaction. Among those who want better bread than is made of wheat, his poetry is not now counted a stimulating diet. However, when American scholarship shall succeed in reducing American literature to a true perspective, he will come to his own again. His patriotism will be rediscovered; his technical skill will be carefully appraised; the honours heaped upon him throughout the civilised world will be recognised as just; and the character from which flowed a well of undefiled poetry will stand out as one of the noblest products of occidental civilisation.

James Russell Lowell.—By general consent, Longfellow is our American poet, *par excellence*, Emerson our philosopher, James Russell Lowell our man of letters. Others, Lowell among them, have shared more richly than Longfellow in a distinctively lyrical temperament; others have thought more consecutively than Emerson. No one, however, when his initial talents are considered, has produced so much good poetry as Longfellow; no one in the realm of philosophic thought has been so patently influential as Emerson; and no one, not even Irving, has fared well in so many avenues of literature and popular scholarship as Lowell. He was poet, critic, professor, editor, diplomat, patriot, humanist; and withal he was a man and a friend.

He was born on Washington's birthday, February 22, 1819, at "Elmwood," Cambridge, a house still in the possession of his family. On his father's side he was of English blood, being descended from Percival Lowell, who came from Somersetshire to Massachusetts Colony in 1639; through his mother he drew his lineage from the folk of the Orkney Islands. His father was a well educated clergyman, faithful and affectionate; his mother, whether really gifted with second sight or not, was of a less usual type, imaginative, high-strung, with a tendency to mental derangement. During his infancy her youngest son heard ballads for lullabies. As a child he was read to sleep with Spenser's "Faerie Queene." When he grew older, he had the range of his father's generously stocked library. At the age of nine, he was devouring Walter Scott, and, like Scott at the same age, was astonishing his companions with improvised tales of fear and wonder. His imagination was not unduly stimulated; he lived a wholesome outdoor life, and he had a sound schooling in the classics. When he went to Harvard, in 1834, "he was a shy yet not very tractable youth, given, like so many boys who are shy from excess rather than from defect of ability, to occasional violence and oddity of expression or act." At Harvard, he gradually rebelled against the rigour of a fixed curriculum, but read omnivorously in English literature of the sixteenth and the nineteenth century, and, following the English romanticists of a generation previous, paid particular attention to Spenser and Milton. "Milton," he observes, "has excited my ambition to read all the Greek and Latin classics which he did." Lowell had gone through a precocious love affair at the age of ten; while in college he was again "hopelessly in love." His efforts in the way of serious writing were at this time facile and, naturally, not profound; his humour was naïve, and more engaging. His gradual neglect of the prescribed routine, in spite of his father's attempts to stir up in the young man a respect for academic honours, at length brought upon Lowell the open displeasure of the Harvard faculty; so that in his senior year he was temporarily suspended, and directed to regain his standing under the private instruction of the Rev. Barzillai Frost at Concord. Longfellow was one of his teachers in Cambridge; in his retirement, he met Emerson and Thoreau. When he left his tutor and returned to Harvard, Class Day was past; but he brought back his Class Poem finished, and allowed it to circulate among his friends. It is interesting as an evidence of Lowell's early freedom in using a variety of metres, of his feeling for nature, of his New England heritage of conservatism, of his inability as yet to enter into sympathy with the movement for the abolition of slavery, or with Emerson and Transcendentalism. It is interesting as a mixture of the old and the new; its touches of enthusiasm are in odd contrast with its general manner, which is strongly reminiscent of post-Revolutionary satire.

His course at Harvard over—for better or worse,—Lowell consigned himself, with misgivings and vacillation, to the study of law. An unfortunate love affair, the financial reverses of his father, uncertainty about his own livelihood, and his seemingly thwarted longing to become an author conspired to render him at times almost desperate. It appears that he even meditated suicide. His humour saved him. He continued his study of ancient and modern poets and certain aspects of their art; through this study, as well as through his mental sufferings, his knowledge of humanity was broadened and enriched. He began to understand the position of the Abolitionists. With his engagement to Miss Maria White, the horizon finally cleared. He had taken his degree in law. Though he could not immediately be married, the constant influence of Miss White, herself a poetess, and his contact with the circle of young people in which she moved—"the Band"—were from now on vital elements in his spiritual development. His head was full of literary plans. He would write a life of Keats; he would compose a "psycho-historical" tragedy. He became a contributor of verse to *Graham's Magazine*. In 1840 he brought out the volume of poetry entitled "A Year's Life," labelled by reviewers as "humanitarian and idealistic"; and in the next year or so he wrote for other periodicals an assortment of sonnets, prose sketches, and literary essays on the Elizabethan dramatists. By the close of 1842, he had resolved to abandon the law, and associated himself with Robert Carter in founding a magazine to be known as *The Pioneer*. The venture was short-lived, owing to Lowell's enforced removal to New York, where he was under the care of an eye-specialist. The failure of his periodical involved him in debt; however, he had gained valuable experience as an editor, and had widened his acquaintance among men of letters. Settling once more at Cambridge, he watched over the persons of his mother, whose mind was now astray, and his eldest sister, who already began to show signs of a similar malady. The fruit of two years of poetical activity appeared at the end of 1843 in his first series of "Poems." He married Miss White on December 26, 1844. Immediately afterward, he assumed for a brief space a position in Philadelphia on *The Pennsylvania Freeman*, he and his wife eking out a slender income by writing for The *Broadway Journal* of New York. An ardent Abolitionist now, Lowell, on his return to Cambridge, gave his attention during the next four years mainly to articles for *The National Anti-Slavery Standard*. From this point it is impossible in so short an account as the present to record many details of his productivity as a writer. In 1846 appeared the first of the "Biglow Papers," published in *The Boston Courier*; three more came out the next year. In 1848, besides a large sheaf of articles, Lowell issued the second series of his "Poems," his "Fable for Critics"—in which he handled contemporary American poets with levity but also with insight—and "The Vision of Sir Launfal," significant titles in any list of his works. His powers were near their height. His humour was almost as sure as it ever became; his criticism almost as pregnant, his imagination as vital, his attitude toward national issues as uncompromising. The defects in his style and treatment are such as we find even in his later work. Until 1853 Lowell's life was in the main happy, darkened indeed by the death of several children, and by anxiety over the fading health of his wife. From the grief and loneliness following her death, he sought relief in the preparation of a course of lectures on the English poets, to be delivered before the Lowell Institute in Boston. Their signal success brought him a call to the chair left vacant at Harvard by Longfellow. He gave a year or more to study abroad; returning in 1856, he spent the next sixteen years of his life in the duties of a college professor. He lectured on poetry and fine art, and offered courses in German, Spanish, and Italian literature. He was at his best in teaching Dante, where he could put in motion his belief "that the study of imaginative literature tends to sanity of mind"; that it is "a study of order, proportion, arrangement, of the highest and purest Reason," and shows "that chance has less to do with success than forethought, will, and work." Latterly he turned his attention to the literature of Old French. For a man who has been taxed with hereditary indolence, his industry was surprising. His connection with *The Atlantic Monthly* from its launching, in 1857, until 1861, and with *The North American Review* from 1864 until 1872, is mentioned elsewhere. His private reading was continuous and discursive. With the approach and outbreak of the Civil War, his heart and pen were enlisted in the service of the North. He wrote perhaps the most stirring political articles in American literature; and his verse ran all the way from a new series of "Biglow Papers" to the "Commemoration Ode" recited at the memorial exercises, July 21, 1865, in honour of the Harvard graduates who had given their lives for their country. After the war, *The North American Review* provided him with an outlet for many of his best known articles in literary criticism, for example, his essays on Chaucer, Pope, Spenser, and Dante. "The Cathedral," his most notable poem after the "Commemoration Ode," appeared in 1870. In 1869, and again in 1870, he delivered a number of lectures, on the poets, at Cornell University. In 1872, unable to secure a leave of absence from Harvard, he resigned his position there, in order to go abroad. After a stay of two years in Europe, where he was the recipient of distinguished honours, he resumed his post at Harvard, retaining it until 1877, when President Hayes appointed him Minister to Spain (1877–80). In 1880 Garfield made him Minister to England; here honours were showered upon him. "The Queen is recorded to have said that during her long reign no ambassador or minister had created so much interest and won so much regard as Mr. Lowell." Shortly after the death of his second wife, in 1885, he was supplanted in his diplomatic post. For a time he lived with his daughter at Southborough, Massachusetts. Among the later collections of his poetry was "Heartsease and Rue," published in 1887. The last two years of his life were passed at Cambridge, devoted in part to an edition of his works, in ten volumes. After a season of weakness and pain, borne with fortitude and humour, he died, where he first saw the light, at Elmwood, on August 12, 1891.

It is well-nigh impossible to characterise Lowell briefly. An attempt to sum up a personality that chose so many avenues of expression, and that at bottom was not thoroughly unified, can hardly do justice to the component parts. The most striking thing about the man was his fertility, if not in great constructive ideas, at all events in separate thoughts.

What he writes is full of meat. His redundancy is not in the way of useless verbiage; he wants to use all the materials that offer. A less obvious thing in Lowell is what we may term his lack of complete spiritual organisation. He lived in an age of dissolving beliefs and intellectual unrest. Though he was not tormented, as were some others, by fierce internal doubts, he yet failed ever to be quite clear with himself on fundamental questions of philosophy and religion. He was never quite at one with himself. As a writer, his serious and his humorous moods were continually interrupting each other. Partly on this account, he did not possess an assured style. Partly, of course, a kind of indifference, inherited or developed, was to blame; in his formative stage, he did not have the patience—as he himself told Longfellow—to write slowly enough. The result is, our enjoyment of his poetry comes from separate passages, not from organically constituted, harmonious wholes. In the occasional felicitous expression of an individual thought, few can surpass him:

> Coy Hebe flies from those that woo,
>   And shuns the hands would seize upon her;
> Follow thy life, and she will sue
>   To pour for thee the cup of honour.

As a colourist in words, when he happens not to overdo the impression, his art often seems masterly. Yet if we look closely, even in the much lauded "Commemoration Ode," his technique is seldom if ever inevitable. His prose is stylistically more continuous than his verse, owing to his experience as an editor. He healed others; himself he could heal at least partially. But even as a prose writer, in spite of his studies in the history of literature, he did not reach the point where science and the understanding are seen to be in harmony with poetry and the imagination. It appears that he did not succeed in distinguishing between what was temporary and what was permanent in science, so that he did not escape the danger of confusing the errors of scientists with their ideals; and as he was not in full sympathy, as Dante was, with minute literary research, so he was not willing to subject himself to the last, exacting, and detailed labours of the poet or essayist who determines to write verse or prose that shall endure. It follows that most of his writing, both poetry and prose, lacks finality. Thus in his article on Chaucer, though he met the approval of no less an authority than Professor Child, he could not ultimately have satisfied that great scholar and critic, since Lowell did not confine himself to generalisations based upon exhaustive induction. He does not clearly discriminate between "I think" and "I know."

The fact is that he wrote mainly for his own time, and was bound to have but a temporary reward. This is not saying that the reward was not worth while. His interpretations of Spenser, of Dante, of Milton, of the elder dramatists, sent to those poets many a reader who would not otherwise have gone; for America, he opened the road in the study of Chaucer; and his own "Vision of Sir Launfal" has unlocked many a hard heart to divine influences. When he wrote in dialect, as in the "Biglow Papers," he was manifestly writing for a time; but in their time the second series did more to justify the Northern cause than almost any other publication that could be mentioned, Whittier's poems not excepted. It may be thought that his wonderful command of dialect, contrasted with a less perfect and less instinctive success in any higher medium, marks him as above all else a satiric poet. When he was once sitting for his portrait, he so denominated himself, speaking generally—"a bored satiric poet." Yet were we to name Lowell the greatest of all American satirists, his urgent poems of patriotism—"The Washers of the Shroud," the "Commemoration Ode"—his "Vision of Sir Launfal," and "The Cathedral" would immediately proclaim him something greater than any satiric poet could be. Last of all, nobler than the sum of his writings was the work which he effected in bringing together his native land and the mother country, England, in a bond of sympathy unknown since their separation.

Ralph Waldo Emerson.—Emerson usually passes for a philosophical mystic and lay preacher. He deemed himself more of a poet than anything else, for he always hoped to attain perfect utterance in rhythmical language. Yet the fact that he wrote much more prose, however imaginative, than verse, has relegated the main treatment of him to another section of this volume. Such an arrangement, of course, is grounded in uncritical custom, not in reason.

Arbitrarily limiting ourselves here to his compositions in metre, we find that throughout his life (1803–82), or throughout the years in which he was productive, Emerson was responsible for much more poetry, in the narrower sense, than most of his readers are aware of, and that his poems are as well worth attention as his essays. In his verse, which was written for himself, he is, to be sure, less at home so far as concerns the form, but being less hampered by any regard for an audience, he is more spontaneous in his thought. At the same time, his stock of fundamental ideas and sentiments, however vivid and pure, was pretty much exhausted in his prose, so that, to a considerable extent, he repeated himself when he changed his medium of expression. Moreover, as the hierophant of intellectual independence, he did not come to a practical realisation of the way in which the opulence of the greatest poets and thinkers is related to the wealth and continuity of their reading. Emerson, indeed, read multifariously if not thoroughly; and it is true that his essays are liberal in the use of borrowed matter; the production of an essay on Montaigne might appear to mean little more than throwing together an anthology of excerpts, cemented with Emerson's own marginal notes. He rarely mastered any single author entire. His insight went by leaps and bounds, and he appropriated what he found congenial, not being pliant enough to enter steadily and long into the thought of another. His prose in general lacks plan. Some of his poems, on the contrary, are more unified, having an organic wholeness which is absent from his longer essays. In an essay, mere continuity of sentiment and preservation of individual style do not constitute an adequate link between the parts. In a lyric poem, such consistency may suffice. Virtually, all of Emerson's poetry is lyrical and meditative. The technique is seldom smooth, not for want of pains, since it was laboured and continually retouched, but for want of capacity in the artist. The style is apt to be brittle, the cadence is not maintained through passages of any length, and the separate sentences are easily detached from their context. Even so, they are not always clear, but may need commentary and parallel from the "Essays" to explain them. Emerson's poetry is largely autobiographical and, in no harsh sense, egoistic, a picture of the successive and recurrent states of his own soul. His vision of the universe in each of its parts, his belief in the immanence of God and the educational potency of solitude, and his confidence in the ability of Nature to prepare and suddenly to produce ideal or "representative" men, are ever near the surface. In his descriptions of the external world he is faithful to detail; but as he discovers in each individual thing an intrinsic value transcending the value of its dependence on the whole, he is likely to see the parts without being ready to seize the perspective. Among details his selection, if he makes any, seems altogether an affair of his mood, not of logic. His power of choice is nevertheless stronger than Whitman's. He has a more than Wordsworthian distaste for analytic science:

> But these young scholars, who invade our hills,
> Bold as the engineer who fells the wood,
> And travelling often in the cut he makes,
> Love not the flower they pluck, and know it not,
> And all their botany is Latin names.

None the less have science and scientific terms invaded his poetry; nor is it simply the larger and the elemental aspects of modern discovery that claim his regard. With his individualistic turn of mind, he can not choose but have an eye for the precise and specific:

> Ah! well I mind the calendar,
> Faithful through a thousand years,
> Of the painted race of flowers,
> Exact to days, exact to hours.

> *   *   *   *   *

> I know the trusty almanac
> Of the punctual coming-back,
> On their due days, of the birds.

He understands his own interest in such matters; not being very objective, he cannot understand the impulse of the young botanist. Lacking the dramatic and historical impulse, he wrote no long poems. "May-Day" is his longest and most sustained, although he never quite succeeded in ordering its parts. It "was probably written in snatches in the woods on his afternoon walks, through many years." The volume to which it gave its name (1867) marked a distinct advance in fluency over the collection of his poems that had appeared twenty years earlier. But even considering his own final selection (1876) or considering the now standard text of all his poetry (published in 1904), we can scarcely affirm that the longing he expressed in 1839 was ever fully satisfied: "I am naturally keenly susceptible to the pleasures of rhythm, and cannot believe but one day I shall attain to that splendid dialect, so ardent is my wish; and these wishes, I suppose, are ever only the buds of power; but up to this hour I have never had a true success in such attempts." It is probable that in spite of his New England good sense, his inherent esteem for propriety, his insight into the subtler workings of nature, he did not have the initial impulse of a Bryant and a Longfellow toward what he most needed in his education. Nature works also through the scientist and the pedagogue. Emerson doubts it:

> Can rules or tutors educate
> The semigod whom we await?
> He must be musical,
> Tremulous, impressional,
> Alive to gentle influence
> Of landscape and of sky,
> And tender to the spirit-touch
> Of man's or maiden's eye;
> > But, to his native centre fast,
> > Shall into Future fuse the Past,
> And the world's flowing fates in his own mould recast.

Henry David Thoreau.—Emerson had the originality that enables a seer to pierce beneath the surface, and to find a likeness in things where passive minds detect no brotherhood; he did not have the originality by virtue of which amply creative minds gather a multitude of elements, properly subordinated one to another, into new, harmonious, and embracing wholes. His is a crucial defect in American poetry, a defect in the constructive imagination. This defect is intimately associated with an unscholarly dread of minute research. Emerson's attitude of distrust toward science was shared by his friend and disciple Thoreau (1817–62), in whom the creed of individualism ran almost to the point of caricature. In his youth and prime, Thoreau wrote a great deal of verse, only a little of which has been preserved. The conception of Prometheus, suffering and isolated friend of humanity, tenacious in the assertion of his own will, was to Thoreau's taste; hence his rough but stirring translation from the tragedy by Æschylus. He had the Emersonian fondness for gnomic sentences and verses, such as he found scattered through the "Odes" of Pindar. His versions of Pindaric gnomes show that he was not afraid of difficult Greek; still, he hovered between belief and disbelief in scholarship. His ear was better than Emerson's. It is unfortunate that his unrivalled gift of observation did not more frequently leave a record of itself in lines like those "To a Stray Fowl." His mind was not without the New England love of the startling and paradoxical. Yet his search for hidden analogies borders oftener on true imagination than was the case with Holmes.

Oliver Wendell Holmes.—"The Autocrat of the Breakfast-Table" has already given evidence that it will outlast "Elsie Venner" and "The Guardian Angel"; yet if the miscellanies of Dr. Holmes (1809–94) possess more vitality than his novels, this is in some measure due to the "Autocrat's" occasional employment of verse. In the "Breakfast-Table" series appeared "The Chambered Nautilus" and "The Wonderful 'One-Hoss Shay,'" which, with his youthful "Old Ironsides," and "The Broomstick Train," have retained the firmest hold on the popular memory. Holmes was pleased to trace his ancestry back to Anne Bradstreet, the first American poetess. His own poetry commenced with a schoolboy rendering into heroic couplets from Virgil, and hardly ended with his tribute to the memory of Whittier in 1892. In the standard edition of his works his poems occupy three volumes. Many of them, corresponding to his turn for the novel, are narrative; for story-telling he had a knack amounting to a high degree of talent. His sense of order and proportion is stronger than that of other members of the New England school, and he has a command of at least formal structure. One may not unreasonably attribute this command in part to his studies in human anatomy. At the same time Holmes is beset with the temptation to value manner and brilliancy rather than substance, and he will go out of his way for a fanciful conceit or a striking expression. In the use of odds and ends of recondite lore his cleverness is amazing. He had a tenacious memory and a habit of rapid association, so that as a punster he is almost without a match. However, his glance is not deeply penetrating; he sees fantastic resemblances between things that are really far removed from one another, not so often the fundamental similarities in things whether near or apart. One may in vain search through Holmes for anything so truly poetic as Thoreau's comparison of sex in human beings and flowers. Accordingly, his mind may be classed as fanciful rather than imaginative. It ought not to be misunderstood, and will not be unduly detracting from his great excellence, if we say that the poetry of Holmes does not always evince the highest moral seriousness—a lack that is not fully supplied when he attempts moral subjects, as in "The Chambered Nautilus," where, though the comparison of the growing mollusk with the expanding human soul is beautiful, the preaching is a little trite.

As regards the form of his poetry, Holmes is a survival of the eighteenth century. In his boyhood, he was a devoted admirer of Pope, but instead of abandoning the style of the Augustans, as Bryant and Lowell abandoned or outgrew it, he chose rather to perfect himself in it; until, somewhat more plastic than it was in his models, somewhat modernised and provincial, that style became his normal accent. Having Holmes' purpose in view, one may add that no poet in America has acquired a surer control over his medium. Within this medium he was able to unite sparkle, humour, clearness, good sense, and oratorical emphasis. It is the opinion of several very able critics that no one in his century can vie with him in the art of writing verses for an occasion. Here is the source not only of his strength but also of his weakness. A large proportion of his verse is of mainly local or temporary interest. The poems which he offered year by year at the exercises of the Harvard Commencement will year by year engender less enthusiasm. A constructive criticism, however, will lay stress, not on his inheritance of New England provincialism or his slight tendency to be flippant, but on his kindliness, his inexhaustible good humour, his quick and darting intellectual curiosity, and on the appeal which his sprightly moralising makes to the young. It is not a little thing to say of a wit and a power of epigram like his that they were ever genial, and ever on the side of something better than a merely conventional morality.

John Greenleaf Whittier.—In so brief a section, it has seemed impossible to offer more than a few scattered remarks on the poetry that arose in both the North and the South in connection with slavery and the Civil War. Something has been said of Confederate writers, including Timrod and Lanier; more might be added on the patriotic verse of Lowell and Longfellow, Emerson and Holmes, and a throng of lesser men, who sang to the North of courage and consolation, or attacked those whom they considered the foes of the Republic at home or abroad. One poetess, yet living, Mrs. Julia Ward Howe (born in 1819), immortalised herself in 1862 by her "Battle-Hymn of the Republic," a piece breathing the very essence of righteousness and love of country, and having a value out of all proportion to the rest of her work. Something similar must be said of Thomas B. Read (1822–72) and his popular "Sheridan's Ride" (1865). The true bard of the battle-field and bivouac, of course, was Walt Whitman, who, as a nurse in the Union army, had actual experience of war. If, however, any one person is to be singled out from his century as the proclaimer of American freedom, this must be Whittier; and that too, it might almost be said, in spite of his heredity, his early hopes, and his natural bent. At least, his Quaker blood and his love for the peaceful ways of nature would not designate him for the office of poet militant. Furthermore, if Whittier's art and sentiment in the progress of years elicit more and more admiration from qualified arbiters, such admiration will be mainly bestowed, not on his war lyrics or his denunciations of slavery, but on his hymns, his legends of New England, and his rustic idyls—above all, on "Snow Bound."

He was born at Haverhill, Massachusetts, on December 17, 1807, springing from pious English stock, in a family that belonged to the Society of Friends. A minute and animated picture of his home and its inmates is given in "Snow Bound." Whittier's opportunities for regular schooling were slender. Though he did not inherit the rugged strength of his ancestors, his help was required on the farm; and his father, without absolutely discouraging the lad's effort to win an education, was reluctant to see him busied with a useless or dangerous plaything such as their sect generally regarded poetry. The boy attended district school, read the few books that were in his home, and even managed to obtain copies of Burns and Shakespeare, and a novel, perused in secret, of Scott. His mother was inwardly gratified by the lines which he wrote under the inspiration of Burns. When his sister clandestinely forwarded one of his poems to *The Free Press* of Newburyport, and thus paved the way for an acquaintance between Whittier and the editor, William Lloyd Garrison, the trend of the young man's life was determined. Thanks to the influence of Garrison, and by the strictest husbanding of his own means, Whittier was able to pass, in all, a year at the new Haverhill Academy. "Thus ended his school-days," says his biographer, Pickard; "but this was only the beginning of his student life. By wide and well-chosen reading, he was constantly adding to his stores of information. While revelling in the fields of English literature, he became familiar through translations with ancient and current literature of other nations, and kept abreast of all political and reformatory movements." In the development of his thought, he owed most to the Bible, to the tracts of the Friends, and to the poetry of Burns. The mainspring of his activity, whether as student, poet, politician, or anti-slavery agitator, was an intense desire to be useful to his kind, coupled with a burning belief in the sacredness of individual liberty. During his early manhood, he continued to write verse, sending it to various New England periodicals; and he became editor, successively of a Boston trade journal, of *The Haverhill Gazette*, and of *The New England Magazine*. Journalism helped him to enter politics, and in 1832 the Whigs of his native place seemed ready to elect him to Congress. After careful deliberation, he renounced his political aspirations, not without an inward struggle, and decided to lend his energies to the abolition of negro slavery, to assist the discredited and obscure band led by Garrison. "My lad," so in after years he counselled a youth of fifteen, "if thou wouldst win success, join thyself to some unpopular but noble cause." With all his idealism—let us rather say, on account of his thoroughgoing idealism—Whittier was thoroughly practical. He had keen insight into the characters of men, and knew how to turn their motives, both good and bad, to account; his political sagacity, which, with his untiring industry, made him one of the most capable workers on the side of Abolition, was largely responsible for the rise of Charles Sumner to a position of beneficent influence. Ever frail in health, yet labouring on, and subjected more than once to personal violence at the hands of opponents, Whittier had the satisfaction of seeing the movement which he championed emerge from persecution into triumph. Regarded superficially, his devotion delayed his own progress as an artist, and his best poetry came late. In a deeper sense, he could not have developed into the poet that he became without living the life that he did.

In a general way his work may be divided into two parts—that produced during his more active interest in journalism and politics, and that produced after his retirement. In 1831 he published his "Legends of New England in Prose and Verse," a pamphlet, and in 1832, another pamphlet, "Moll Pitcher," neither of them of much interest save in comparison with his better choice of subjects and better handling at a later date. A third pamphlet, "Justice and Expediency" (1833), published at his own expense and with a full consciousness of its probable effect, was the document that severed him from the dominant party and openly leagued him with the Abolitionists. "Mogg Megone" (1836), his first bound volume, which he afterward vainly tried to suppress, was published after he became a secretary of the American Anti-Slavery Society. The next year (1837), Isaac Knapp, without consulting Whittier, issued a collection of "Poems Written during the Progress of the Abolition Movement in America." It was followed in 1838 by an authorised collection. The poet represented Haverhill in the Massachusetts Legislature in 1835; ill-health prevented his finishing a second term. In 1837 he went to Philadelphia to aid "the venerable anti-slavery pioneer Benjamin Lundy, who was editing *The National Enquirer*," afterward called *The Pennsylvania Freeman*. In 1840 he retired to Amesbury, Massachusetts, taking up his abode with his mother and his sister Elizabeth. He never married. At Amesbury and at Danvers, in the same county, he spent the remainder of his life in quiet. The record is one of domestic peace and literary endeavour, whose first fruits were "Lays of my Home, and Other Poems" (1843). With this volume Whittier's writings began to be remunerative. Some of the more noteworthy subsequent dates in his life are as follows: Of his prose works, "The Stranger in Lowell" appeared in 1845, "Supernaturalism in New England" in 1847, "Literary Recollections" in 1854. From the founding of *The Atlantic Monthly*, in 1857, Whittier was a most welcome contributor. He also edited John Woolman's *Journal*, and in other ways displayed interest in the writings of the Friends. "Voices of Freedom" (1849) was the first comprehensive edition of his poems. He published "Songs of Labour" in 1850, "A Sabbath Scene" in 1853, "Home Ballads" in 1860, "National Lyrics" in 1865. After the war, his most important publications included "Snow Bound" (1866), "Maud Muller" (1867), "Ballads of New England" (1869), "Miriam and Other Poems" (1871), "Mabel Martin" (1874), "Hazel Blossoms" (1875), "Poems of Nature" (1885), "St. Gregory's Quest, and Recent Poems" (1886). His last collection, "At Sundown" (1890), was dedicated to E. C. Stedman, and closed with a valediction to Dr. Holmes. Many of Whittier's poems were first published in magazines; "Maud Muller" appeared in *The National Era*, in 1854.

Whittier's personality was one of indescribable attractiveness. He was gentle, yet full of repressed fire, an ardent nature that had steadily submitted to the Christian spirit of self-control. He had the inward beauty that springs from generous impulses under the habitual guidance of principle and forethought. Toward his opponents he showed no rancour; he strove against parties, not individuals; and he commanded the respect of his adversaries. If he had a foible, it was his delight in playful teasing. He never visited a theatre or a circus in his life. He is described in his early manhood as "tall, slight, and very erect," of a distinguished presence, yet bashful—but never awkward. His eye was brilliant and expressive. In maturity, his face in repose was almost stern, but a smile would light up his entire countenance. "His voice in reading was of a quality entirely different from that in conversation—much fuller and deeper." In later years, "while retaining a lively interest in all literary and political matters and keeping abreast of current events, he dwelt most intently ... upon the great spiritual and eternal realities of God. By the open fire in the evening he would talk for hours upon sacred themes, ever grateful for the rich blessings of his life and looking with reverent curiosity towards the future.... There was not the shadow of a doubt in his mind concerning the immortality of the soul." He died after a stroke of paralysis, on September 7, 1892, and was buried at Amesbury.

In a recent and praiseworthy volume of "The Chief American Poets," Dr. C. H. Page has included a longer list of selections from Whittier than from Longfellow, although the contributions representing Whittier occupy less space. This is significant. Whittier was mainly a writer of short poems. In the ballad he had a form suited to the general taste, and to his aim of stinging a sluggish populace into revolt against slavery. He painted that institution in its most repellent aspects, seeing nought of the glamour which Southern writers have shed over plantation life as it existed before the war. Living in the North, he saw something of escaping and recaptured negroes. His glance was very direct; he described matters simply; he accomplished the task that he set himself. Among his lyrics of the war, "Barbara Frietchie" is altogether the best known— not with complete justice to others, for example "The Watchers." To his treatment of tales and legends of colonial New England Whittier brought an inveterate hatred of persecution and oppression in every shape. Accordingly, many of his narratives, like "Cassandra Southwick," touch on wrongs attempted or inflicted upon the early Quakers. As an interpreter of colonial life Whittier comes second only to Hawthorne. As a herald of the beauty in flower and hill and stream, in "The Trailing Arbutus," "Among the Hills," "The Merrimac," he is second to none in America.

True, he does not always refrain from what Ruskin has called the pathetic fallacy, so that he descries in the face of nature moods that are really in the heart of man; but he does this more rarely than his contemporaries. In his revelation of humble and rustic types, "Maud Muller," "The Barefoot Boy," "The Huskers," he is almost the equal of Burns or Wordsworth. He is not their rival in perfection of style. More frequently than they he suffers from a bad line; and his rhymes are often defective. Yet one must not conclude that he was inattentive to technique. On the contrary, Whittier was a born artist. But the nice discipline of the ear which so many English poets have owed to the cultivation of Greek and Latin prosody was not vouchsafed to him; and for his manner he missed the advantage of rigorous criticism. The positive excellence of Whittier's verse is due to the harmonious blending and interworking in him of varied powers. His senses were alert and sure, his humour was fine, his intellect strong, his pathos firm. He was not afraid of a theme that was tragic. His realism might be compared to that of Crabbe, but it is more hopeful. In his religious poems there is a belief more satisfying than transcendental pantheism; and there is a quality of personal joy and optimism which, as we have previously observed, is not typical of American literature.

> Best loved and saintliest of our singing train,
>> Earth's noblest tributes to thy name belong.
> A lifelong record closed without a stain,
>> A blameless memory shrined in deathless song.

Such was Holmes' eulogy of Whittier. With it we may take leave of New England.

Bayard Taylor.—A Quaker poet of a different stamp was the meteoric Bayard Taylor (1825–78). His boyhood was distinguished by a passion for roving and for collecting objects of natural history. His devotion to books and his distaste for labour on a Pennsylvania farm did not always please his father, who laughed boisterously, however, when a phrenologist said of the son: "You will never make a farmer of him to any great extent: you will never keep him home; that boy will ramble around the world, and furthermore, he has all the marks of a poet." At the age of nineteen, having just published "Ximena: or The Battle of Sierra Morena, and Other Poems," and armed with some introductions from N. P.

Willis, Taylor engaged in a Byronic pilgrimage on the Continent. A half-year at Heidelberg rendered him fluent in German. By a circuitous route through northern Germany and Austria he proceeded on foot to Italy, and from Italy through France back to England, supporting himself by correspondence which he sent to *The New York Tribune*, *The Saturday Evening Post*, and *The United States Gazette*, and which on his return to America he collected in "Views Afoot" (1846). Our account of his life thus far gives a faint impression of his physical and mental activity. No adequate narrative may here be essayed of his wandering and eventful career throughout. "Views Afoot" made his reputation. By 1848 he had become head of the literary department of *The New York Tribune*. In 1849, as correspondent for *The Tribune*, he spent five months with the gold-diggers in California. In 1850 he married Miss Mary Agnew, who was dying of consumption, and who survived her wedding but two months. In 1851–53 he travelled in Egypt, Syria, Asia Minor, Ethiopia, Spain, India, and China. In 1856 he broke down from overwork in America—lecturing and writing—and he went to Europe again. In Germany (1857) he married the daughter of an eminent astronomer, P. A. Hansen. In 1857–58 he visited Greece. Two years later, at an expense of $17,000, he had built a home, near his birthplace, Kennett Square, Pennsylvania, calling his estate "Cedarcroft." To settle down in affluence had been his cherished ambition; but this dream, and his haste to realise it, embarrassed him financially, cost him much peace of mind, and eventually cost him his life. He never succeeded in resting. In 1862–63 he was Secretary of the Legation at St. Petersburg. During other intervals, he lectured in America. Among his lectures may be mentioned those delivered at Cornell University in 1870, 1871, 1875, and 1877. A large part of his correspondence is at present housed in the Cornell University Library. His translation of Goethe's "Faust," Part First, appeared in 1870; nearly all of the first edition was sold in one day. The Second Part came out in 1871. Excessive labour, an irregular and not abstemious way of life, and, more especially, financial worry told upon his constitution. He was destined never to finish his projected "Life of Goethe." He had barely entered upon his duties as Minister to Germany when the collapse came. His last words were, "I must be away."

"Taylor," says Albert H. Smyth, "wrote with such rapidity that he could complete a duodecimo volume in a fortnight.... In a night and a day, he read Victor Hugo's voluminous 'La Légende des Siècles,' and wrote for *The Tribune* a review of it which fills eighteen pages of his 'Essays and Literary Notes,' and contains five considerable poems that are translations in the metre of the original." His powers of memory are said to have been prodigious. He could repeat not only from his favourite authors but from the futile compositions of poetasters whose manuscripts he had read as an editor and rejected. He was in the habit of carrying his own poetry in his head until the process of correction was ended. Accordingly, the perfection of his "copy," which was written in the neatest hand imaginable, has led various critics into the error of thinking that he did not revise. His poetry was much more carefully worked out than his prose, upon which he had no thought of building a reputation. He would spend hours on the chiselling of a single couplet. His style resounds with echoes of word and phrase from Byron and Shelley, indeed from the whole circle of his reading in both English and German. Nor is it deficient in individuality. Taylor has a pronounced cadence of his own. Nevertheless his poetry wants some quality or other that would make it lasting. Although in 1896 there was a cult of younger men that studied and imitated him, his immense vogue as a prose writer had already waned; and his eclipse as a poet is now almost complete. In the history of American literature there is nothing stranger than this eclipse. Taylor's learning was wide and substantial. He shrank from no drudgery of preparation. At the age of fifty he was willing to begin the study of Greek. And it was not merely that he was in touch with his time on all sides, and able by brilliant arts to snare the popular fancy. When he wrote, he knew what he was talking about. His "Poems of the Orient" (1854), containing the Shelley-like "Bedouin Song," show deep sympathy with the customs and passions of the East. "Ross Browne's Syrian dragoman, when he listened to the reading of 'Hassan to his Mare,' 'sprang up with tears in his eyes, and protested that the Arabs talked just that way to their horses.'" Taylor had the suffrages of educated critics too. "The Picture of St. John" (1866) Longfellow reckoned "a great poem"; while Lowell said that, except "The Golden Legend," no American poem could match it in finish and sustained power. "The Masque of the Gods" (1872), an endeavour to combine the ideals of Christianity and Hellenism, also pleased Longfellow. "Lars, a Pastoral Poem" (1873), is a curious tale, with some historical basis; the unwonted background of Norwegian fiords makes part of the setting for a tragic romance among the Quakers. Of Taylor's dramatic poems we shall hazard no discussion; besides "The Masque of the Gods," he published "The Prophet" (1874), whose scene is laid among the Mormons, and "Prince Deukalion" (1877), a piece of symbolism in which the author tried to objectify his total conception of human life both here and hereafter. He felt as sure of the other world as of this. In such assurance he possessed the most vitalising belief that can inspire a poetic soul. Why, then, is his poetry now disregarded? Why is it that the production for which the present age is most ready to thank him is his version of Goethe's "Faust"? A tentative explanation is this. Taylor's life was full of disquiet. He never enjoyed the solitude necessary to the maturing of poetic sentiment. He was betrayed by temporal ambition into posting over land and ocean without rest. He was too determined to achieve fame. There are times for action, and there are times for a wise passiveness. They also serve who only stand and wait.

Walt Whitman.—His belief in immortality, in the absolute and eternal value of each individual person and thing, constitutes the main element of permanence in the writings of Walt (= Walter) Whitman. He too had in his veins a strain of blood from the Quakers; though he was born (May 31, 1819) in a family that took little cognisance of religion. His mother, Louisa Van Velsor, was of mingled Dutch and Welsh descent, illiterate, but in the eyes of her second child, the poet, always "perfect." When this child was four years old, his father and name-sake, a good carpenter and of honest Connecticut ancestry, but a slipshod householder, removed from West Hills, Huntington Township, Long Island, to the "village," as it then was, of Brooklyn; not before the impresses of rural life had entered unawares into the heart of the child; and not too late for the life of the future metropolis to become an imperishable part of his experience. The poet's formative years were passed in the midst of the growing population centred at New York. He attended the public schools of Brooklyn until he was thirteen, then, with a scanty knowledge of reading, writing, and arithmetic, entered a lawyer's office as errand-boy, his employers giving him access during free hours "to a big circulating library." "Up to that time," he says, "this was the signal event of my life." "For a time I now revel'd in romance-reading of all kinds; first the 'Arabian Nights,' all the volumes, an amazing treat. Then, with sorties in very many other directions, took in Walter Scott's novels, one after another, and his poetry." From errand-boy he became typesetter, varying his desultory labours for *The Patriot*, and *The Star*, by excursions on Long Island, by contributing "sentimental bits" to local newspapers, and by active participation in several debating societies. At eighteen he turned country schoolmaster; and shifting from that, he set up as editor of *The Long Islander*, hiring some help, but himself doing most of the work, including the distribution of his weekly sheet to its patrons. In 1841 he returned to New York, became editor of *The Daily Aurora*, wrote for *The Tattler*, and published stories in *The Democratic Review*. In later years it was his "serious wish to have all these crude and boyish pieces quietly dropp'd in oblivion." Meanwhile he attended the theatre, continued his observation of the crowds at the Brooklyn ferries and in the streets of New York, and his study of nature on the shores of Long Island, read newspapers, "went over thoroughly the Old and New Testaments, and absorbed ... Shakespeare, Ossian, the best translations [available] of Homer, Æschylus, Sophocles, the old German Nibelungen, the ancient Hindoo poems, and one or two other masterpieces, Dante's among them." A brief connection with *The Brooklyn Eagle* was terminated by Whitman's falling out with the radical faction of the Democrats; whereupon he seized "a good chance to go down to New Orleans on the staff of *The Crescent*, a daily to be started there." Accompanied by his younger brother, "Jeff," he crossed the Alleghanies, and took steamer down the Ohio and the Mississippi—"a leisurely journey and working expedition"; then "after a time plodded back northward, up the Mississippi, and around to and by way of the Great Lakes, ... to Niagara Falls and Lower Canada, finally returning through central New York and down the Hudson; travelling altogether probably 8000 miles this trip, to and fro." In the experiences of his life up to this point lay the materials for his "Leaves of Grass," which he published at his own expense in 1855, having done part of the typesetting himself. A copy sent to Emerson elicited from him a letter in which the book was characterised as "the most extraordinary piece of wit and wisdom that America has yet contributed." The next year Whitman brought out a second and amplified edition, printing Emerson's laudatory letter and his own answer in the Preface, and on the back the quotation, "I greet you at the beginning of a great career," with Emerson's name beneath. This act of questionable taste failed to augment the sale of the volume; nor was the edition of 1860 more successful. In 1862, Whitman's younger brother having been wounded during service in the Union Army, the poet was brought into contact with the army hospitals.

He continued his ministrations to the sick and suffering almost uninterruptedly until the hospitals in Washington were closed. "From cot to cot they called him, often in tremulous tones or in whispers; they embraced him, they touched his hand, they gazed at him. To one he gave a few words of cheer, for another he wrote a letter home, ... to another, some special friend, very low, he would give a manly farewell kiss. He did the things for them which no nurse or doctor could do, and he seemed to leave a benediction at every cot as he passed along." By sheer personal magnetism he saved many lives. The record of his connection with the war is to be found in his "Specimen Days," in the posthumous collection of letters entitled "The Wound-Dresser" (1898), in "Drum Taps," published in 1865, and in the "Sequel to Drum Taps," which contained his poems on Lincoln (among them the threnody, "O Captain! My Captain!"), published later in the same year. Shortly after the war was over, Whitman, who had found a place as clerk in the Department of the Interior, was discharged by Secretary Harlan, Harlan having discovered the authorship of "Leaves of Grass," in his opinion "an indecent book." The poet quickly received another position, in the office of the Attorney-General; and his enthusiastic friend and champion, W. D. O'Connor, brought out a defence of Whitman, written in terms of exaggerated praise, under the famous title of "The Good Grey Poet." A fourth edition of "Leaves of Grass," revised, and supplemented by "Drum Taps," was published in 1867; a fifth, including the "Passage to India," in 1871. The sixth and seventh editions appeared in 1876 and 1881–1882; the eighth (1888–1889) contained in addition "November Boughs," and the ninth (1891–1892) "Good-bye my Fancy." In 1873, Whitman, disabled by a stroke of paralysis, gave up his position in Washington and removed to Camden, New Jersey, where he lived with George Whitman until 1879. By this time he had so far recovered that he could make a journey to the West, followed by another, the next year, to Canada. In 1881, the sale of his works allowed him to settle, at Camden, in a home of his own. Here he lived in comparative comfort, the object of a good deal of curiosity, receiving visitors, some of them very distinguished, and, as his strength allowed, adding to his stock of verse. In 1888, he had a second stroke of paralysis, but he lived on, preserving his courage and mental alertness, until 1892. He died on March 26th of that year. If we can credit his statement made in 1890, he was probably survived by four out of six children that were not born in wedlock.

In many ways, Whitman corresponds to the ideal presented in the "natural man" of Rousseau; if space allowed, a profitable comparison might be made between "the good grey poet" and the French forerunner of American democracy. At the outset, the excessive sentimentalism of Rousseau would constitute a patent difference. But Whitman's assumption of equality among individuals, in so far as they are not spoiled by what he deems a false and artificial education, is nothing new to the reader of Rousseau; and his preference of the "powerful, uneducated," raw material of humanity has its counterpart in the sympathetic attitude of Rousseau toward the burgher and peasant classes which formed the part of society that he really understood. Moreover, both of these authors demand an individual standard—which is no standard—of judgment. Both desire to be appreciated, yet refuse to be appraised according to standards which the cumulative wisdom of mankind in the past, of the greatest democracy, has attained to and approved. Both try to regard organisation and the subordination of one person or thing to another as unnatural. In the case of Whitman at least, it is for want of philosophical standards, and for want of a consistent effort to determine what is meant by *nature* and *natural*, that the so-called literature of democracy has been so hard to measure.

In the first place, then, if we are to measure Whitman at all, we must make certain postulates. For example, we must postulate that restraint in literature, as in life, is a law of nature. This, Whitman is not disposed to admit. In private life, it is true, he was more temperate and continent than certain passages in "Leaves of Grass" led casual readers to surmise. But he saw fit to beget children, out of wedlock, without assuming the responsibility of their nurture and education. Are the duties which modern society lays upon parents less natural than the alleged practice of Rousseau, or are they more? Again, Whitman decides to address the public in the guise of a poet. Now in practice, be it observed, he is much truer to the demands of a poetic ear than are many of our conventional versifiers; and though he has a predilection for colloquial diction and syntax, he is in his own way not unscrupulous in the matter of technique. The changes that he made in successive editions of his main work, "Leaves of Grass," are of deep interest to the student of poetic art. At the same time, he repudiates literary convention, and recognizes no law as binding upon one who contracts to write for his fellow men, save the law of his individual being. There is, however, no law, or science, or art, of the individual as such. Poetry, according to the deepest thinkers on this subject, is the rhythmical utterance of the individual in harmony with universal law; and criticism has for its province the recognition of that universal law in the particular poet. In so far, then, as Whitman's irregularly trained personality succeeds in expressing what is true for all men, or for many, or for representative and typical men, uttering that truth in terms that are both choice and generally intelligible,—in so far as he actually conforms to the best conventions—he is a great poet, perhaps our greatest native poet. He succeeds often. It is to be noted that he is most successful when, as in his lament for Lincoln, he adopts a regular metrical form.

On Whitman's achievement as spokesman of modern democracy perhaps too much stress has already been laid. Following his own lead, his interpreters have been inclined to associate his idiosyncrasies, his departures from the normal, his lapses from good taste in referring to the physiology of sex, too closely with the nature of this achievement. In dealing with the "poetry of democracy," it seems to have escaped observation that an age of popular freedom and republican ideals may produce a literature of high refinement and perfect balance between literary tradition and the impulses of the individual author. It is well to remember that the masterpieces of art which ennobled Athens under Pericles were the expression of—for Greece—an age of democracy; and that the epics of Milton, however conventional in one sense, were the outpourings of a nobler champion of liberty than Whitman. Referring to the practice of studying his illustrious predecessors, Whitman has said: "Now, if eligible, O that the great masters might return and study me!" Something like this is sure to take place. In order to appreciate him rightly, we must confront him, full of the spirit of those authors, Sophocles, Dante, Milton, and their peers, by the standard of whom one is bound to estimate poetry. If thus confronted, Whitman's lustre, so bright in the eyes of his cult, begins to wane; still, the tributes paid him by W. M. Rossetti, Freiligrath, Dowden, Björnson, Symonds, may not lightly be set aside. Taken at its best, his poetry, as Emerson said, "has the best merits, namely, of fortifying and encouraging." His prose works ought not to be dismissed so summarily as must here be the case; being less subject to suspicious innovation than his verse, conforming naturally to expected canons, his prose, in particular his prose criticism, is well worth study. It is direct. Genius, said Whitman, is almost one hundred per cent directness.

Bret Harte, Joaquin Miller, Edward Rowland Sill.—We turn to the poetry of the Far West. Francis Bret Harte (1839–1902), born at Albany, New York, after a varied youth in California won a sudden renown through his "Heathen Chinee" and "Condensed Novels." His later success as a prolific writer of short stories tended to obscure his talent as a humourist in verse; and even in the present decade, when his death has called fresh attention to the value of his literary work as a whole, his poetry is hardly known as it should be. Probably in the course of years his "East and West Poems" (1871) and "Echoes of the Foothills" (1874) will entertain more readers than they now do in comparison with "The Luck of Roaring Camp." There is likely to come a time when pioneer life among the gold-mines will appeal less than it does to the present generation; whereas the permanent aspects of external nature, as Harte has caught them in "Crotalus," can never cease to interest. The details of his life are recounted in another part of this volume.

Cincinnatus Hiner Miller (born 1841), another celebrity of the West, was reared in a log-cabin in Indiana. After a few years of life on a farm in Oregon, he went to the gold-fields of California. When he had met almost every kind of experience imaginable, he studied law, and practised in Oregon. In 1870 he brought out a small volume of poems, one of them entitled "Joaquin," the name of a Mexican brigand, Joaquin Murietta, in whose defence he had already written, and henceforth his pen-name. His volume, "Songs of the Sierras," for which he at first vainly tried to find a publisher, produced, when finally accepted and issued, a sensation that recalled the days of Byron. His vogue has since declined, though he is still read, a collective edition of his poems having been published in 1897.

Much less famous than either Harte or Miller, not having the virility of the former, yet possessing a finer sensibility than the latter, was Edward Rowland Sill (1841–1887), a third poet of the Far West. Sprung from a family in Connecticut, a teacher in Cuyahoga Falls, Ohio, finally professor of English literature in the University of California, Sill, in "Hermione, and Other Poems," "The Hermitage, and Later Poems" (1867), "The Venus of Milo, and Other Poems," published (1888) after his death, sent forth a rill of poetry, slender but pure. In the opinion of his friends and many besides, Sill's death cut short a poetic career of unusual promise. His poems were collected in 1902, in a single volume, and again in 1906; in the latter edition they are arranged chronologically.

Miscellaneous and Later Poets.—Under this heading must be gathered a handful of writers whom the classification thus far adopted has not accounted for, some of whom would not easily admit of classification. However, it is not the purpose of this Manual to consider in detail the current writers of verse throughout America, among whom distinctions of value can rarely be established.

Hans Breitmann.—Charles Godfrey Leland (1824–1903) might be associated with Bayard Taylor. He is said to have neglected mathematics at Princeton for Carlyle and Spinoza; he studied abroad, returned to Philadelphia to engage in the practice of law, but gave this up for work as an editor. During the Civil War his pen was active in defence of the Union. Afterward he became popular through his "Hans Breitmann Ballads," in picturesque dialect displaying the humour of the shrewd jovial German immigrant before the war. Leland made himself an authority on gypsy lore, and was busy in several fields as a translator. During his long residence abroad, he enjoyed an acquaintance with many distinguished men of letters in Europe. Besides his ballads in dialect and translations from J. V. Scheffel, he wrote verse of serious intent; for example, "The Music Lesson of Confucius, and Other Poems," in which, like Taylor, he desired to unite the ideals of Christianity with those of Hellenism. The deaths of Leland, Stoddard, Aldrich, and Stedman within the last five years took almost the last survivors of an elder generation in American letters.

Richard Henry Stoddard.—In the year of his death, 1903, R. H. Stoddard was called by his friend, E. C. Stedman, "the most distinguished of living American poets." He was born in Hingham, Massachusetts, July 2, 1825. Educated in the schools of New York City, he supplemented by private reading his brief opportunities for regular study, and from worker in a foundry became connected with Bayard Taylor as a journalist. In 1853, Hawthorne aided him in securing a position in the New York Custom-House. From 1860 to 1870 he was literary editor of the New York *World*; in 1880 he took a similar post on *The Mail and Express*. His first volume of poetry, "Footprints" (1849), was afterwards suppressed; his second, "Poems" (1852), secured him an audience. "Songs of Summer" (1857) was a collection of poems that had been printed in various magazines. The latter part of his life was marked by great activity as an editor and biographer, somewhat after the fashion of Stedman. Most of his poetry subsequent to the collective edition of 1880 is included in "The Lion's Cub, with Other Verse" (1890). He preserved his lyrical quality to a great age. Like several of our leading poets, Stoddard reached his highest level in dealing with the theme of Abraham Lincoln.

Thomas Bailey Aldrich.—With his "Ballad of Babie Bell" (1855) in the New York *Journal of Commerce*, Aldrich (1836–1907) began a career whose high-water mark was the editorship of *The Atlantic Monthly* from 1881 to 1890. His initial volume of poetry, published in 1854, was "The Bells," which was succeeded in 1858 by "The Ballad of Babie Bell, and Other Poems." Of his numerous later poetical works, "Pampinea, and Other Poems" (1861), "Cloth of Gold, and Other Poems" (1874), "Flower and Thorn" (1876), etc., perhaps the tragedy of "Mercedes" ("Mercedes, and Later Lyrics," 1884) deserves particular notice, having been successfully staged, a test which few dramas by American poets have been able to endure. Aldrich was a master of his craft. Deep in his reverence for Tennyson, whom he ranks third in English poetry—after Shakespeare and Milton,—he sometimes exercises an almost Tennysonian harmony in the selection of detail; witness the Oriental luxury and splendour in "When the Sultan Goes to Ispahan."

Edmund Clarence Stedman.—Stedman's services to literature as a critic and anthologist are doubtless of much greater importance than his own poetry; but neither the one nor the other may be disparaged. He was born at Hartford, Connecticut, in 1833, his mother (by her second marriage Mrs. J. C. Kinney, the friend of the Brownings) being a woman of educated taste and herself a poet. Entering Yale at the age of fifteen, Stedman showed ability in Greek and in English composition, and shortly gained a prize by his poem on "Westminster Abbey." On account of a boyish prank he was compelled to leave college before the end of the course. Prior to the Civil War he was connected with *The Norwich Tribune* and *Winsted Herald*, and for a time with *The New York Tribune*; in this he printed his "Tribune Lyrics" (among them "Osawatomie Brown"). From 1861 to 1863 he was war correspondent of the New York *World*; later he was assistant to Edward Bates, Attorney-General under Lincoln. His interest in the first Pacific railroad brought him into relations with Wall Street, where, in 1869, he became an active member of the New York Stock Exchange. Here he remained until 1900, an influential man of affairs, respected by financiers as well as literary men, amassing and enjoying the means which he desired for the pursuits of literature. He was a thorough patriot, an earnest advocate of international copyright, above all a steady labourer for the education of public taste. His lectures on "The Nature and Elements of Poetry," delivered first at Johns Hopkins University, subsequently at the University of Pennsylvania, and again at Columbia, unfolded the dignity of a subject that is often regarded as a matter of indifference. By his "Victorian Anthology" (1895) he gave further evidence of the powers of selection displayed in "A Library of American Literature" (1888–1889), on which he collaborated with Ellen M. Hutchinson. His "American Anthology" (1901, etc.), several times reissued, contains selections from about six hundred American poets, with brief biographies, and is, to say the least, an indispensable volume to the general student of our literature. The present section of this Manual is much indebted to Stedman's "Anthology." One would hardly make too liberal an assertion in saying of Stedman that he was the most thoroughly read man of his time in the poetry of his own nation. It is possible that he was over generous in his recognition of the work of inferior authors; but let us not impute this to him as too serious a fault. Of the fifteen poems of his own to which he allowed admission in the "American Anthology" (sixteen, counting the "Prelude" to the volume), the best known are "The Discoverer," "Pan in Wall Street," and "The Hand of Lincoln." He died on January 18, 1908.

James Whitcomb Riley.—This artist in the "Hoosier" dialect of Indiana (born 1853), though still in middle life, seems to belong with the older rather than the younger generation of American poets. Unwilling to follow his father's profession of attorney, he early betook himself to a wandering life, gaining experience of the world as a vendor of patent medicines, sign-painter, actor, and the like. Settling at Indianapolis, he became known by his contributions to various newspapers, and when his reputation was established, won additional success by public readings from his poetry. His verse is bright and crisp, and he has pathos, humour, and good powers of description and narrative. He has an unusually keen understanding for the experiences of country life, particularly of youth and boyhood in rural villages and on the farm. "The Old Swimmin'-Hole, and 'Leven More Poems" (1883) was his first notable venture. "Afterwhiles" appeared in 1888. Within ten years or so he then published "Old-Fashioned Roses" (1888), "Pipes o' Pan at Zekesbury" (1889), "Rhymes of Childhood" (1890), "Neighbourly Poems" (1891), and, among other volumes, "A Child-World" (1896), and the "Rubaiyat of Doc Sifers" (1899). As a writer of dialect in verse, he falls not very far short of Lowell. His allusions to nature, to insect life for example, are simple and true. If but a bird or butterfly sit down beside him, he is as happy as if the same were a maiden-queen.

*   *   *   *   *

Space forbids any delay upon George Henry Boker (1823–1890), diplomat and dramatist, and his metrical drama, "Francesca da Rimini" (1856); or Francis Miles Finch (1827–1907), professor in Cornell University, and his celebrated poem "The Blue and the Gray" (in *The Atlantic Monthly*, 1867), a gift of healing from the North to the South; or John Hay (1838–1905), whose manifold services to his country were roofed and crowned with an abiding interest in literature ("Pike County Ballads," published in *The New York Tribune*); or Richard Watson Gilder (born 1844), editor of *The Century Magazine*, social reformer, and author of several volumes of finished verse; or Stephen Collins Foster (1836–1864), composer, whose songs, "The Old Folks at Home," "The Suwanee River," "My Old Kentucky Home," familiar the country over, are significant of the influence which the negroes have exerted on the language and art of the whites; or Will H. Thompson (born 1848), and "The High Tide at Gettysburg"; or John Townsend Trowbridge (born 1827), one of the original contributors to *The Atlantic Monthly*, author of "The Vagabonds" (1863), and steeped in the spirit of New England; or John Boyle O'Reilly (1844–1890), the Fenian, who escaped from imprisonment in Australia, and became a journalist in Boston ("Songs, Legends, and Ballads," "Songs of the Southern Seas," etc.); or Eugene Field (1850–1895), witty, eccentric, friend and student of children; or Richard Hovey (1864–1900), cut off in the flower of his promise ("Taliesin: a Masque," 1899); or Paul Laurence Dunbar (1872–1906), the negro poet, dead before his time, who wrote good and stirring English as well as pathetic dialect; or William Vaughn Moody, professor in the University of Chicago ("The Masque of Judgment," 1900); or Bliss Carman (born 1861) and Clinton Scollard (born 1860). All these and many more must pass with insufficient notice or none; otherwise the page would contain only a meaningless enumeration of names and dates. As was implied at the beginning, very few American writers who have won distinction in other ways have refrained from publishing a volume of lyrics "and other poems." Also, in spite of the slender encouragement from publishers to new authors of original verse, the occasional volume from the hitherto and hereafter unknown poetaster, who foots the bill for printing, continues to emerge and sink again at the present day.

The immediate outlook for poetry in the United States is not bright. It does not appear that with the material growth of the country we have developed a unified national spirit capable of expression at the hands of a great poet, were he to arise. It does not appear that we have among the younger men a first-class poet capable of expressing the national soul, were this more unified and precise. Furthermore, the type of humanistic education which fostered our elder poets of New England is generally discredited, and seems to be passing away without leaving any hope of a popular training in the near future worthy to succeed it. Simplicity, rigour, precision, and accuracy, all of them friendly to the poetic spirit, and among its necessary conditions, have fewer and fewer champions in the schools. Many subjects are studied, and almost nothing is mastered and retained. Memory, the mother of the Muses, is not in esteem. "Literature" is taught—though not learned; yet the children know no poetry. Worst of all, and a primary cause of much of the evil, the reading of standard works within the family is becoming less and less common. In particular, though there is much talk about the Bible, the Bible, like the classics, is becoming unfamiliar, to the great detriment of popular thought and style.

On the other hand, to offset the deficiency of our secondary schools and the decay of culture in the home, the last thirty years have witnessed an immense expansion in advanced scholarship, most notable, perhaps, in the investigation of the vernacular and related literatures. Graduate study of English, and of the literatures from which English literature has sprung, offers a refuge to such persons as have a serious and abiding interest in belles-lettres; it is undoubtedly developing the personalities of investigators to the highest point of efficiency possible under present conditions, and making ready for another generation, more fortunate, whose poetry shall find root in the fields that are to-day so thoroughly cultivated; working downward, it is already tending to bring about salutary changes here and there in the procedure of the schools, and hence eventually to have an influence in the home. A generation of scholars to clear the way, as in the beginning of the Renaissance—to produce the literary atmosphere which now is wanting—may be regarded as a hopeful sign of a generation of poets to come. Finally, if American poetry now seems moribund, we must yet remember the eternal power that the true poet is always in alliance with; the power that at any time can make the poet say of any literature: The maid is not dead, but sleepeth.[21]

IV. THE ESSAYISTS AND THE HUMOURISTS

English Influences on American Letters.—Springing from a common stock, the two branches of eighteenth-century English literature showed many similarities. The charge of imitation and even of plagiarism has been brought against the American writers of that period; but it seems in no way unsafe to point to the single origin as the probable cause of the same characteristics appearing in the literature produced here, and that produced in the mother-country. No one can deny, of course, that not a few of our authors went to school to Englishmen, but the assertion that America until recently has produced nothing but pinchbeck literature is as false as it is absurd. That like produces like may be a trite saying, but its frequent repetition does not impair its truth. The English mind, whether expressing itself at home or in the colonies, naturally put

---

21 In this sketch of American poetry, I have obviously had recourse not merely to the standard editions and biographies in the case of important authors, but in the case of these, to some extent, as well as of lesser authors, to a number of manuals and other compilations; among them the well-known works on American literature by Bronson, Hart, Richardson, and Onderdonk, and the anthologies, mentioned in the text, by Stedman and Page. I desire to express freely my sense of obligation to these sources.—L. C.

forth the same kind of shoots: that their development was not in all respects equally rapid, that in time they became so much unlike as to appear unrelated, can be traced, no doubt, to the unsheltered fortune of the American scion in early days, and to the complete removal of the slip from the parent stem in after-years.

With this thought in mind, the most thorough-going American may admit, without apologetic reserve, that the essayists of eighteenth-century England have counterparts in Irving and certain of his contemporaries, and that those of a slightly later date have much in common with Emerson and Thoreau. Should one feel, however, that excusable pride is to be taken only in those authors who exhibit qualities indigenous to America, one may triumphantly mention Warner, and Lowell, and Margaret Fuller; for, although these essayists show the racial instinct of English writers, they are none the less emphatically American in thought, tone, and expression. In passing, it is perhaps well to notice that a large number of American writers have tried their hands at more than one form of literature. For this reason Irving is discussed as an essayist, although he might be placed with the humourists, or perhaps better still, with fiction-writers, since he has the right to dispute with Poe the claim to be regarded as the progenitor of the American short story. Again, Emerson, like George Eliot, felt that his fame would eventually rest upon his poetry, but his readers almost always think and speak of him as an essayist. Lowell, Longfellow, and Whittier, on the other hand, are properly reviewed at large as poets, despite the fact that their prose work is not inconsiderable nor unimportant and must therefore receive some attention in even a rapid survey of the American essay.

Washington Irving.—Washington Irving (1783–1859), the first essayist of importance in the National Period of American Literature, was born in New York City. Unable on account of ill-health to continue his education, Irving went abroad in 1804. Returning two years later, he was admitted to the bar, but he never engaged in the actual practice of law. In 1815 Irving again went to Europe, this time upon matters connected with the cutlery business in which, as silent partner, he was engaged with his brothers. It was seventeen years before he again set foot upon his native soil, but when he did come back, he was widely known, both for his writings and for his diplomatic service as member of the American legations, first at Madrid (1826–1829) and later at London

(1829–1831). During the next decade, Irving was in this country, living quietly at Sunnyside, as he called his home at Tarrytown-on-the-Hudson. In 1842, accepting an appointment as Minister to Spain, he went to Europe for a third time and remained abroad four years. Upon his return home, he gave himself up entirely to writing, finishing his monumental work upon Washington but a short time before his death. He is buried in the Tarrytown Sleepy-Hollow Cemetery—within sight of the road down which one of his characters, Ichabod Crane, made his precipitous flight in mad endeavour to escape the headless horseman.

Irving's first book, "A History of New York," published as from the pen of "Diedrich Knickerbocker," appeared in 1809. It attracted immediate attention and established its author's reputation as a humourist; but unfortunately its fun at the expense of the ancestors of certain American families roused not a little rancour. Irving's next work, "The Sketch Book," was published, first in parts in 1819, and then in two volumes in the following year. This book and "Bracebridge Hall, or The Humourists" (1822), "Tales of a Traveller" (1824), "The Alhambra" (1832), and "Wolfert's Roost" (1855), are all miscellaneous collections of sketches, short stories, and character studies, of which one volume is not inferior to another. The first of them received cordial recognition from Scott, who arranged for its publication in London; and the last had a wide circulation both in America and in England.

During Irving's first visit to Spain, he became interested in certain biographical and historical material there easily accessible, and put it to use when he was writing "The Life and Voyages of Christopher Columbus" (1828), "The Chronicle of the Conquest of Granada" (1829), "The Voyages of the Companions of Columbus" (1831), "The Alhambra," already mentioned, and "The Life of Mahomet" (1849). Upon Irving's return to America his interest in the same kind of material continued, and led him to publish "The Life of Goldsmith" (1849), and "The Life of Washington" in six volumes (1855–1859). Irving's other works are "A Tour on the Prairies" (1835), "Astoria" (1836), and "The Adventures of Captain Bonneville" (1837).

Irving was the first American writer to gain literary reputation abroad; nor was the interest which he awakened there merely that of curiosity wondering what would come out of a wilderness. It may be that the great bulk of his work is not widely read at present, but such stories as "Rip Van Winkle," and "The Legend of Sleepy Hollow," such sketches as "The Stout Gentleman" and "Moonlight on the Alhambra" are perennial. Irving was hardly skilful in his use of pathos, degenerating not infrequently into the sentimental and even into the maudlin; yet the buoyancy of his fascinating and delicate humour has seldom been matched by any other American writer. His graceful, almost faultless style is akin to that of the writers of *The Spectator*, although it savours now and then of Goldsmith, and has, according to Scott, a dash of Swift. Perhaps Lowell best summed up the matter of Irving and his style in "A Fable for Critics":

> "To a true poet-heart add the fun of Dick Steele,
> Throw in all of Addison, *minus* the chill,
>
>   *   *   *   *   *
>
> Sweeten just to your own private liking, then strain,
> That only the finest and clearest remain,
>
>   *   *   *   *   *
>
> And you'll find a choice nature, not wholly deserving
> A name either English or Yankee,—just Irving."

Bryant and Others.—William Cullen Bryant (1794–1878) is generally thought of as a poet, but his prose was not inconsiderable either in amount or in value. During his long connection with the New York *Evening Post*, from 1826 until the end of his life, he wrote daily editorials of high literary quality, contributed to many other journals, and delivered frequent orations upon various subjects. A collection of Bryant's prose works in two volumes was published in 1894: one who reads them is convinced that their author was possessed of a clear, smooth style, an accurate, careful judgment, and good common sense. Whittier (1807–1892) and Longfellow (1807–1882) may not improperly be mentioned here, although, like Bryant, they also are best known as poets. Whittier was closely associated with William Lloyd Garrison in the Abolition movement and contributed much to its literature. Controversial writing, however, seldom lives, and Whittier's has not proved an exception to the rule. In addition to one or two attempts at novel-writing, Whittier published "Supernaturalism in New England" (1847), "Old Portraits and Modern Sketches" (1850), and "Literary Recreations" (1854); but these works are not important in style or in matter. The demands of metre and rhyme upon Whittier seem to have prevented the appearance, in his poetry, of certain crudities which sadly mar his prose. Longfellow's prose, on the other hand, is more important. It is marked by a delicacy and refinement which would go far towards keeping it well known, if the author's greater fame as a poet did not eclipse his renown as a prose writer. In addition to two romances, he published "Outre Mer" (1825), a volume in aim and content somewhat like Irving's "Sketch Book"; and under the title of "Drift Wood" he included in the first edition of his "Complete Prose Works" (1857) a collection of stray essays and book reviews originally contributed to various periodicals.

Edgar Allan Poe.—Edgar Allan Poe (1809–1869), like the three authors just mentioned, was a poet, yet to his own time he was perhaps even better known as a short story writer and essayist. Opinions about the value of his literary work have been as various as those respecting his character; but it is safe to claim for him no mean place among writers of criticism. In this department of literature he undertook to bring about a reform among American authors who had passed from timid deference to English opinion into the stage of noisy and indiscriminate praise of every piece of writing produced in this country. From a study of Coleridge, Poe had come to the conclusion that poetry was a matter of "intellectual happiness"; its soul was the imagination. A person of metaphysical acumen, therefore, by noting how poetic moods are excited, could produce a finer poem than one who, lacking the analytical faculty, could only feel the emotions he desired to arouse in his readers. Poe laid great stress, too, on perfection of form as of the utmost importance in producing an effect; truth was a secondary matter, except in detail, and as a means of securing assent to a conclusion which might be essentially untruthful. The object of poetry, he thought, is to arouse a subtle, indefinite pleasure; this was imparted by music; hence the necessity of melody, of the refrain.

As a critic, Poe was often savage in the extreme; but it must be remembered, as we look back upon him, that the urbanity of the modern book reviewer was then a thing unknown. Poe's literary judgments have in the main been justified, although some of his unsparing attacks in "The Literati of New York" arouse resentment even at this late day, while his equally unrestrained laudation of certain of his now wholly forgotten contemporaries leads one near to contemptuous amusement. Poe's most important contribution to the theory of writing are two essays usually reprinted with his poems; of these "The Philosophy of Composition" first appeared in *Graham's Magazine* for April, 1846, and "The Poetic Principle," originally a lecture, was printed in *Sartain's Magazine* for October, 1850. Perhaps an essay "On Critics and Criticism" ought also to be mentioned; it was first published in *Graham's Magazine* for January, 1850.

Ralph Waldo Emerson.—Ralph Waldo Emerson (1803–1882), serious, high-minded, and well balanced, affords a striking contrast in almost every way to Poe. Born in Boston, he was graduated from Harvard College at the age of nineteen. After teaching school for a time, he became minister of the Old North Church in his native city, but in 1835 withdrew from his charge because of his aversion to the rite of the Lord's Supper. Taking up his residence at Concord, Massachusetts, he spent the rest of his years in writing and lecturing. While engaged in the latter work he went as far west as California and made two visits abroad. During the first, Emerson met Wordsworth, Coleridge, Landor, and De Quincey, who received him graciously, George Eliot, who referred to him as "the first man she had ever seen," and Carlyle, who found in the visitor a hero well worthy of sincere admiration. Dignified and simple in manner, deep and kindly in thought, he found contentment in an uneventful career; sympathising strongly with those who would live the life of the spirit, he supported in theory the Brook Farm experiment; advocating anti-slavery ideas, he opened his church to Abolition agitators; but objecting on principle to war, he proposed to buy the slaves and educate them morally. He went down to his grave loved by his neighbours and honoured by many who knew him only through his works.

Emerson made his earliest appearance as a writer in a book entitled "Nature" (1836), but he first attracted real attention by his Phi Beta Kappa oration before Harvard College in 1837. This address, now published in his collected works as "The American Scholar," made so strong an appeal to his listeners to break away from the influence of England in matters of authorship that Holmes with his usual felicity termed it "our literary Declaration of Independence." For three or four years, beginning in 1840, Emerson was editor of *The Dial*. In 1841 he published his first collection of "Essays"; and three years later his second. From then on at irregular intervals other volumes of like content appeared; of these the most important, in all probability, are "Representative Men" (1850), "The Conduct of Life" (1860), and "Society and Solitude" (1870). There is no need of an enumeration of Emerson's books, since they are all similar in form, content, and purpose. While Emerson is in no true sense a philosopher, he did project a theory of life. Sincerity he regarded as fundamental, and his belief in the formative influence of great men was almost identical with that held by Carlyle. By the possession of "transcendental reason," man, according to Emerson, becomes intuitively aware of the truth. This truth or doctrine has been reduced by some critic to three propositions: (1) God is in all things and all things are in God. (2) Each created existence is essential to every other created existence. (3) Nothing which has once existed ever ceases to exist. To the average reader these ideas are bewildering and have been collectively designated as "a new philosophy maintaining that nothing is everything in general, and everything is nothing in particular." It is related as a fact, that after an address by Emerson before a college society, the minister in charge of the meeting devoutly prayed that the hearers might be preserved from ever again being compelled to listen to such transcendental nonsense. At the close of the meeting Emerson imperturbably remarked that the gentleman seemed a very conscientious, plain-spoken man.

The distance between Emerson's thought and that of most men laid him open to the charge of obscurity, an accusation which is still widely repeated by those who do not trouble themselves to read or to think. It cannot be denied that Emerson is often mystical, and that he must find spiritual insight and almost poetic imagination in those who would penetrate to the heart of his teachings; but it is unfair to give the impression that, save to the initiated, he is nearly always incomprehensible. Page after page of his writings offers no difficulty whatever to the most cursory reader, and his work as a whole is within the ken of any serious and unprejudiced reader. In style Emerson is sometimes forbidding through a strong tendency to condensation of expression; but the beauty of his thought frequently draws to itself a diction and order which transform his prose into veritable poetry. His strong, earnest spirituality is never fanatical, his perfect trust in what he called the Over-Soul is never sentimental, his full confidence that the world is making for ultimate good is never unpractical. Looking upon the universe as "one vast symbol of God," he escaped pantheism on one hand and materialism on the other. As a teacher uttering his uplifting thought through literature, Emerson, it may be confidently said, stands without a rival among American writers.

Henry David Thoreau.—Henry David Thoreau (1817–1862) is by many readers coupled with Emerson. Born in Concord, Massachusetts, he spent the greater part of his life in his native town and its vicinity. He was graduated at Harvard College in 1837, although he refused his diploma on the ground that it was not worth five dollars. He gave occasional lectures and wrote many books: of these he himself published but two, "A Week on the Concord and Merrimac Rivers" (1849) and "Walden, or Life in the Woods" (1854). To these have been added from time to time since Thoreau's death several volumes entitled "Excursions in Field and Forest" (1863), "The Maine Woods" (1864), "Cape Cod" (1865), and "A Yankee in Canada" (1866). The greater part of his voluminous journal was published in 1906 and 1907, though extensive selections had been previously printed in four volumes bearing respectively the names of the four seasons of the year. More than any other well-known American author, Thoreau strove to get at Nature's inmost heart. Withdrawing to Walden Pond, he spent the larger part of his time for two years in reading and meditation; feeling then that his object had been accomplished, he returned to town life. For a brief period, Thoreau lived as an inmate of Emerson's household and became an unconscious disciple of the man who entertained him. A transcendentalist imbued with a strong spirit of otherworldliness, he may perhaps be best summed up in Emerson's words. "He was bred to no profession; he never married; he lived alone; he never went to church; he never voted; he refused to pay a tax to the state; he ate no flesh; he drank no wine; he never knew the use of tobacco; and though a naturalist he used neither rod nor gun." Thomas Wentworth Higginson has pointed out that Thoreau's fame has survived two of the greatest dangers that can beset reputation—a brilliant satirist for critic (Lowell), and an injudicious friend for biographer (Channing).

Minor Transcendentalists.—Minor transcendentalists, and connected therefore with Emerson and Thoreau, were Amos Bronson Alcott (1799–1888), and Sarah Margaret Fuller (1810–1850). Both, like Emerson, were contributors to *The Dial* but unlike him did not hold aloof from the Brook Farm experiment. Alcott's chief works were "Tablets" (1868), "Concord Days" (1872), and "Table Talk" (1877); Margaret Fuller's, "A Summer on the Lakes" (1843), "Woman in the Nineteenth Century" (1844), and "Papers on Literature and Art" (1846). Other essayists who may be mentioned as identifying themselves with the Brook Farm movement or with the Transcendental Club out of which it grew, were three noted clergymen, William Ellery Channing (1780–1842), the founder of the club; Theodore Parker (1810–1860), the pulpit representative of its theories, and James Freeman Clarke (1810–1888), a frequent contributor to its organ, *The Dial*. In later years each of these men published works which are still occasionally read. Channing's numerous writings were brought together in five volumes in 1841, and, under the title "The Perfect Life," a selection from them was made in 1872. He must not be confused with a younger William Ellery Channing (1818–1901), his brother's son, the author of a monograph on "Thoreau, the Poet Naturalist" (1873) and of "Conversations from Rome" (1902). Parker's chief works aside from his sermons were "Miscellaneous Writings" (1843) and "Historic Americans" (1870); Clarke's, "Orthodoxy, its Truths and Errors" (1866) and "Ten Great Religions" (1871).

The Transcendental Movement appealed to all sorts and conditions of men: philosophers exchanged ideas with journalists, and ministers with writers of fiction. Of the members who later became known as editors the most important were George Ripley (1802–1880), Charles Anderson Dana (1819–1897), and George William Curtis (1824–1892), all of whom at some time or other were upon the staff of *The New York Tribune*. Ripley and Dana were joint editors of "The American Encyclopedia" (1857–1863); but they also worked independently, the former putting together fourteen volumes entitled "Specimens of Foreign Standard Literature" (1838–1842), the latter making that still famous collection "The Household Book of Poetry and Song" (1857). Curtis' interests were so many and so various that he has been classified as journalist, orator, publicist, and author. His most important works were "Lotus Eating" (1852), "Potiphar Papers" (1853), and "Essays from the Easy Chair" (1891), the last a collection of brief papers originally contributed to *Harper's Magazine*.

Oliver Wendell Holmes.—Oliver Wendell Holmes (1809–1894) stands in some contrast to the chief writers of the Transcendental School. On the whole they were marked by deliberate seriousness, but he possessed a clear, crisp spontaneity which often broke forth into sparkling fun. Born in Cambridge, Massachusetts, a member of what he facetiously styled "The Brahmin Caste" of New England, he counted among his ancestors more than one English governor of the Colonial period and that famous woman of her time, Anne Bradstreet, "the Tenth Muse." After being graduated from Harvard College in 1829, he studied law for a year and then turned to medicine. Completing his education in Paris, Holmes returned to America in 1835 to enter upon the practice of his profession, but in 1839 accepted a professorship of anatomy at Dartmouth College, in New Hampshire. The following year he entered upon a similar position in the Harvard Medical School, and remained there until 1882. In 1886, Holmes visited Europe and received honorary degrees from Edinburgh, Oxford, and Cambridge. The eight remaining years of his life he spent quietly at his home in Boston, graciously receiving even strangers, who felt that they had not really seen that city unless they had shaken Dr. Holmes by the hand.

Of Holmes' prose work his "Breakfast Table" series best defends his right to claim a permanent place of fame. "The Autocrat of the Breakfast Table," after appearing serially in the first and second volumes of *The Atlantic Monthly* (1857–1858), was immediately republished in book form, and was succeeded by "The Professor at the Breakfast Table" (1859), "The Poet at the Breakfast Table" (1872), and "Over the Tea-Cups" (1891). These works, which have been rather aptly characterised as "a cross between an essay and a drama," contain comments on almost everything in the heavens above, the earth beneath, and the waters under the earth. The books are at times delightfully whimsical and scintillatingly witty, at others deeply serious and minutely analytic, and at still others tenderly generous and movingly pathetic. Holmes' other important works in prose are two volumes of biography, a "Memoir of John Lothrop Motley" (1879) and a "Life of Ralph Waldo Emerson" (1884); one book of essays, "Pages from an Odd Volume of Life" (1883); and one diary of travel, "Our Hundred Days in Europe" (1887).

Willis, Mitchell, and Warner.—Nathaniel Parker Willis (1806–1867), Donald Grant Mitchell (born in 1822), and Charles Dudley Warner (1829–1900) are suggested by the mention of Holmes, for they, like him, were writers of the "genial" essay. Willis was born in Portland, Maine, and was graduated from Yale at the age of twenty-one. Entering upon a journalistic career in 1828, he spent a considerable number of years abroad, whence he sent home for the periodicals of his day frequent accounts of his foreign travel and experiences. His complete works have been collected into thirteen volumes, but the best of his writing may be found in two books published during his lifetime, "Pencillings by the Way" (1835) and "Letters from Under a Bridge" (1840). Willis wrote with most painstaking care. It has been left upon record by James Parton that Willis "bestowed upon everything he did the most careful labour, making endless erasures and emendations. On an average he blotted one line out of every three that he wrote, and on one page of his editorial writing there were but three lines left unaltered." It may be added, in passing, that Willis' father in 1827 founded the well known and widely read *Youth's Companion*. Mitchell, for many years better known as "Ik Marvel," was, like Willis, a New Englander by birth and a graduate of Yale College. He, also, spent a few years abroad, acting, in fact, as United States Consul at Venice in 1853–1855. His works were many, but he is best known as the author of "Reveries of a Bachelor" (1850) and "Dream Life" (1851). Warner was in many respects the strongest writer of this group. A New Englander by birth, he was graduated at Hamilton College, Clinton, New York, then studied law at the University of Pennsylvania, and finally began the practice of his profession in Chicago. In 1860 he was called to Hartford, Connecticut, as editor of a daily paper, and from then on gave himself up to journalism and other literary interests. His works were many and varied; the most important are "My Summer in a Garden" (1870), "Backlog Studies" (1872), "My Winter on the Nile" (1876), and a "Life of Washington Irving" (1881).

Some Travellers.—Bayard Taylor's experiences abroad found their expression in a number of books; but, readable as they all are, the first, "Views Afoot" (1846), is the best. It is a work to be compared with Irving's "Sketch Book" and Longfellow's "Outre Mer"; it may not be far wrong to assign it to a place between the two, inferior to the first, superior to the second. From Taylor's numerous works in other departments of pure literature, "Studies in German Literature" (1879) and "Essays and Notes" (1880) may be chosen for mention.

At the risk of departing somewhat from chronological order, one may mention at this point a few authors who, like Taylor, left records of their travels and adventures. The earliest of these, an older man in fact than Taylor, was Elisha Kent Kane (1820–1857), the Arctic explorer, who related in "The Grinnell Expeditions" (1854–1856), the story of the two unsuccessful attempts to find Sir John Franklin. Much nearer to our time were Henry M. Stanley (1841–1890) and George Kennan (born in 1845). Stanley was born in Wales, it is true, and was knighted by Queen Victoria in 1890; but his explorations in Africa were made while he was a citizen of the United States. His best-known work is his first, "How I Found Livingston" (1872). Kennan experienced adventures in still another part of the world. Sent to Siberia by the American Telegraph Association to superintend the construction of lines, he published, in 1870, "Tent Life in Siberia." Several years later he returned to the same country as correspondent of *The Century Magazine* to investigate social and political conditions there. He published the results of his observations in "Siberia and the Exile System" (1891).

Holland, Lowell, and Others.—The essay of travel, it will have to be admitted, has carried us pretty well out of the realm of pure literature and brought us down to very recent times. If we have seemed to ignore certain writers, some less and some greater, it was but to return to them for fuller mention. Josiah Gilbert Holland (1819–1881) was born in Belchertown, Massachusetts, and while still a young man became associate editor of *The Springfield Republican*. In 1870 he assisted in the foundation of *Scribner's Monthly* and became its editor-in-chief. He tried his hand at various forms of literature and at one time was not far from being the most popular writer in the United States. To this day there is hardly an American household unprovided with a copy of one of the early editions of "Timothy Titcomb's Letters" (1858), "Gold Foil" (1859), or "Plain Talks on Familiar Subjects" (1865). James Russell Lowell (1819–1891) contributed many articles to *The Atlantic* and *The North American*

Review; some of this work has not yet been collected, but the best of it may be found scattered through the seven volumes of his complete prose works (1890–1891). During his lifetime Lowell published several collections of essays; the most valuable are "Fireside Travels" (1864), "Among my Books" (1870), and "My Study Windows" (1871). As one looks over their contents, one is surprised at the versatility of their writer. The essay of reminiscence, "A Moosehead Journal" or "Cambridge Thirty Years Ago," balances the essay of travel, "At Sea" or "A Few Bits of Roman Mosaic"; the historical essay, "New England Two Centuries Ago," is matched by the nature study, "My Garden Acquaintance"; the purely literary sketch, "Shakespeare Once More," stands beside the book review "Witchcraft" or "A Great Public Character"; and the political speech, "Democracy" or "Tariff Reform," adds a certain virility to the notes of a response to the toast "Our Literature" or to the address on "Books and Reading" delivered at the opening of a free public library. Lowell is ironical in "On a Certain Condescension in Foreigners," witty in "A Good Word for Winter," genial in "A Library of Old Authors," sympathetic in "Emerson the Lecturer," just in "Thoreau," firm in "Reconstruction" and "Abraham Lincoln," thoughtful in "The Rebellion: Its Causes and Consequences," and scholarly in "Chaucer" and "Dante." Aristocratic in the best sense of that much abused term, cultured in manner, robust and vigorous in thought, clean and fresh in mind, Lowell still stands forth as America's finest representative man of letters.

The greatness of Lowell has by no means dimmed the renown of certain of his lesser contemporaries. Edward Everett Hale (born in 1822), Thomas Wentworth Higginson (born in 1823), and Charles Eliot Norton (1827–1908) deserve at least passing mention, although the first two are better known for contributions to magazines than for books, and the last has gained attention mainly through his biographical work and his translation of Dante. Owing to the popularity of a story, "The Man Without a Country," Dr. Hale has unfortunately become known as an author of one book, but his "Puritan Politics in England and New England" (1869) is valuable, and his "Franklin in France" (1887), written with the assistance of his son, is interesting and trustworthy. Mr. Higginson has tried his hand at biography, historical memoranda, criticism, and fiction: probably his best work is found in "Outdoor Papers" (1863), "Atlantic Essays" (1871), and "The New World and the New Book" (1891). Of the three authors here mentioned, Dr. Norton is the most important; he is more than a writer; he is in addition a scholar. Knowing intimately all of the foremost writers of this country, he was hardly less well acquainted with the most important English authors of the middle and later Victorian period. In addition to his monumental prose translation of Dante's "New Life" (1858) and "Divine Comedy" (1892), he has edited such books as "The Early Letters of Thomas Carlyle" (1886), "The Letters of James Russell Lowell" (1893), and "The Letters of John Ruskin" (1904). His chief original works are "Notes of Travel and Study in Italy" (1859) and "Historical Studies of Church-Building in the Middle Ages" (1880). The scholarship of Dr. Norton immediately suggests that of other men. George Ticknor (1791–1887) by the date of his birth seems to belong to a period slightly earlier than that of Norton; in fact he immediately preceded Longfellow as professor of belles-lettres at Harvard. His chief work was "A History of Spanish Literature" (1849). As a valuable piece of criticism, it has not been superseded, and even in Spain is accepted as authoritative. Somewhat later than Ticknor in point of time was Francis James Child (1825–1896). Educated at Harvard College, he was a professor there for nearly half a century. Devoting himself to the study of the ballad as a literary form, he published the results of his work in eight volumes under the title "English and Scottish Popular Ballads" (1857–1859). Closely connected with these several authors was James Thomas Fields (1817–1881). Founder of *The Atlantic Monthly* and member of a famous publishing house, he was acquainted more or less intimately with every important American writer of the last half of the nineteenth century. He was not without literary skill himself, publishing among other works "Yesterdays with Authors" (1872) and "Underbrush" (1881). His wife, Annie Adams Fields (born in 1834), has written a number of books in a similar vein: the most valuable, perhaps, are "A Shelf of Old Books" and "Authors and Friends," both published in 1896.

Shakespearean Scholars.—Harking back to Norton and Ticknor as representative American students of foreign literatures, one naturally takes pleasure in seeing that the field of Shakespearean scholarship has been by no means neglected in this country. Henry Norman Hudson (1814–1886) may be said to have been the first American to turn a furrow; for, after publishing "Lectures on Shakespeare" (1848), he devoted himself to a critical study of the plays and finally produced a work still mentioned with respect, "Shakespeare: His Life, Art, and Characters" (1872). Meanwhile Richard Grant White (1822–1885) had published "The Authorship of the Three Parts of Henry VI." (1859) and "Memoirs of the Life of Shakespeare" (1865). Interested in other subjects for a time, he wrote "Words and Their Uses" (1870) and "England Without and Within" (1881); then, returning to his early interests, he produced "Studies in Shakespeare" (1885). Perhaps Edwin Percy Whipple (1819–1886) deserves mention at this place, for after writing "Essays and Reviews" (1849), and "Character and Characteristic Men" (1866), he published "The Literature of the Age of Elizabeth" (1869). Nor is it possible to overlook Thomas Raynesford Lounsbury (born in 1838), who added to his extensive "Studies in Chaucer" (1892) a trilogy of studies entitled "Shakespeare as a Dramatic Artist" (1901), "Shakespeare and Voltaire" (1902), and "The Text of Shakespeare" (1906). But easily the foremost Shakespearean scholar in America is Horace Howard Furness (born in 1833), whose "Variorum Shakespeare" as a painstaking and authoritative work stands unsurpassed in any language. Recently Mr. Furness has associated his son with him in his investigations, and we may therefore expect with some confidence that a study of Shakespeare on the largest scale up to this time attempted may be completed according to the traditions with which it was begun.

Literary Historians.—Widely interested as the scholars of this country have been in the greater writers and the more important literature of other lands, there has been no dearth of attention to our own. Moses Coit Tyler (1835–1900), sometime professor of American history at Cornell University, was the author of two valuable works, "History of American Literature during the Colonial Times" (1878) and "Literary History of the American Revolution" (1897). Charles Francis Richardson (born in 1851), professor of English in Dartmouth College, has covered the whole range of our literary history down to 1885 in his "American Literature" (1887); and Barrett Wendell (born in 1855) of Harvard University, in his "Literary History of America" (1901), has brought his treatment of the same topic down to the beginning of the present century. Professor Wendell has written upon other American topics in "Stelligeri" (1893), and "A Life of Cotton Mather" (1891). More recently he has published two works, both the result of his residence abroad as a lecturing professor: the substance of the first, "The Temper of the Seventeenth Century in English Literature" (1904), was delivered before Trinity College, Cambridge; that of the second, "The France of To-Day" (1907) was gathered while he was giving a course of lectures in Paris.

Members of other American college faculties have given evidence of minute research and strong inspiration in books not a few. James Brander Matthews (born in 1852) of Columbia University, and George Edward Woodberry (born in 1855), for many years connected with the same university, have both written books that have gained popular approval; of the former, "French Dramatists of the Nineteenth Century" (1881) and "The Historical Novel" (1901) certainly deserve mention; of the latter, "The Life of Poe" (1885) and "The Appreciation of Literature" (1907). No less significant than these men are Felix Emmanuel Schelling (born in 1858) of the University of Pennsylvania, whose latest work is "The Elizabethan Drama" (1908), and Vida Dutton Scudder (born in 1861) of Wellesley College, who cannot be left unnoticed, so thorough and satisfactory are her "Life of the Spirit in the Modern English Poets" (1895) and "Social Ideals in English Letters" (1898). Woodrow Wilson, president of Princeton University, has spared time from his political and historical studies to write an interesting volume of essays called "Mere Literature" (1896); President Wilson's former colleague, Bliss Perry (born in 1860), now editor of *The Atlantic Monthly* and professor of belles-lettres at Harvard, has published a valuable "Study of Prose Fiction" (1902), and another Princeton professor, Henry Jackson Van Dyke (born in 1852), has written an especially useful study called "The Poetry of Tennyson" (1889), and has also shown himself a master of the leisurely essay in "Little Rivers" (1895) and "Fisherman's Luck" (1899).

The Nature Writers.—Professor Van Dyke's "outdoor essays," as they are sometimes called, carry us back to the earlier nature writers, for between him and Thoreau there is no wide hiatus. John Burroughs (born in 1837) has written a considerable number of books dealing with his observations out of doors, although he has by no means neglected the purely literary topic. The mention of his earlier works gives an adequate index of all his subject-matter. "Wake-Robin" appeared in 1870, "Birds and Poets" in 1875, and "Whitman, a Study" in 1896. To be closely associated with Mr. Burroughs is Bradford Torrey (born in 1843); his chief works are "Birds in the Bush" (1885), "The Footpath Way" (1892), and "A World of Green Hills" (1898). Nor can Olive Thorne Miller (born in 1831) be overlooked: she began to write studies of birds about 1880, and among other works, all of considerable interest, she has published "In Nesting Time" (1888), "A Bird-Lover in the West" (1894), and "Under the Tree-Tops" (1897). The writers just mentioned are not to be regarded, of course, as scientists or even as scientific writers in the commonly accepted sense of those terms. They look upon nature with the loving rather than the analytic eye, and register their appreciative feelings rather than their minute observations. They have much in common, therefore, with the purely literary essayists whose names are not far from legion. Although unable to mention all who have recently attracted attention, we must not forget William Winter (born in 1836), whose best prose works date back but a quarter of a century: he published "Shakespeare's England" in 1888, "Gray Days and Gold" in 1891, and "The Life and Art of Edwin Booth" in 1894. Neither can we ignore Hamilton Wright Mabie (born in 1845), literary editor of *The Outlook*. His books are many and widely popular: probably the series of three volumes called "My Study Fire" (1890, 1894, and 1899) and "Shakespeare: Poet, Dramatist, and Man" (1900) are best known. Not less significant is Paul Elmer More (born in 1864) of the editorial staff of *The Nation*. In addition to translations from Sanskrit and from Greek, he has published five books all bearing the title "Shelburne Essays" (1904–1908).

Other Essayists.—Finally, so far as essayists are concerned, some rapid review must be made of the novelists and the later poets who have not restricted themselves to the fields of their chief labour. This takes us back as far as Nathaniel Hawthorne (1804–1864), whose "Our Old Home" (1863) is a collection of valuable essays on various English topics. The saying "Like father, like son" was exemplified when Julian Hawthorne (born in 1846) brought out "Saxon Studies" (1876), a book of like purport with his father's. The mention of more than one writer in a family suggests the elder Henry James (1811–1882) and his two sons, William and Henry. The father is best remembered as a theological and philosophical writer through his "Moralism and Christianity" (1852) and "Lectures and Miscellanies" (1852). The elder son, William James (born in 1842), for many years professor of psychology in Harvard University, besides being the author of several technical works in the science to which he is devoted, has written "The Will to Believe, and Other Essays" (1897),

"Is Life Worth Living?" (1898), and "Pragmatism" (1906). The younger Henry James (born in 1843), in addition to being a novelist, is also the author of "A Little Tour in France" (1884), "Partial Portraits" (1888), and "Essays in London and Elsewhere" (1893). For some reason not strongly apparent, William Dean Howells (born in 1837) is almost always associated in the minds of readers with Henry James the novelist. Editor for a time of *The Atlantic Monthly*, and later connected first with the staff of *Harper's Magazine*, and afterwards with that of *The Cosmopolitan*, he has made many books of essays. The best are "Venetian Life" (1866), "Italian Journeys" (1867), and "Criticism and Fiction" (1895). Belonging by birth to a later decade, Francis Marion Crawford (born in 1854) is near to being America's most prolific writer. His most important work, outside the domain of the novel, is a small volume connected in content with the art which he chiefly affects, "The Novel, What It Is" (1903). It attracted much attention upon its appearance, and is still often quoted. Mr. Crawford is also the author of "The Rulers of the South" (1900) and "Gleanings from Venetian History" (1905). The woman novelists cannot be ignored as writers of essays, for not only do they possess powers of penetration and insight, but two of them, at least, have swayed public opinion to no inappreciable extent. Harriet Beecher Stowe (1811–1896) in addition to her many books of fiction wrote a very much discussed study entitled "Lady Byron Vindicated" (1870) and "The American Woman's Home" (1869), at one time thought to be the final word upon domestic questions. A writer of hardly less importance was Helen Hunt Jackson (1831–1885), still popularly known by her pseudonym of "H. H." Her most valuable study was "A Century of Dishonour" (1881), in which she laid bare the ill-treatment accorded the American Indians; she succeeded through its pages in doing much to ameliorate their unfortunate condition. Mrs. Jackson's "Bits of Travel" (1873) and "Between Whiles" (1887) are interesting and readable.

The more important later poets who have contributed to essay literature are led by that erratic but remarkable genius, Walt Whitman (1819–1892). His collected "Prose Works," published in the year of his death, contain much more true common sense than his writings are popularly assumed to show. The main titles included in the contents are those of small volumes printed at various intervals: "Specimen Days" (1882), "November Boughs" (1888), and "Good-Bye, My Fancy" (1891). Edmund

Clarence Stedman (1833–1908) and Thomas Bailey Aldrich (1836–1907), who in their poetry followed the traditions established by Longfellow and Lowell, were the authors of not unimportant prose works. The former wrote three valuable books: "Victorian Poets" (1875), "Poets of America" (1885), and "The Nature and Elements of Poetry" (1892); the latter author produced two volumes of travel and reminiscence: "From Ponkapog to Pesth" (1883) and "An Old Town by the Sea" (1893). Possibly allied rather with Whitman than with the other poets just mentioned, Sidney Lanier (1842–1881) may justly stand at the close of our list of American critical writers. He subjected the methods of metrical composition to minute scrutiny, and published the results of his investigations as "The Science of English Verse" (1881). Turning then to a study of fiction, he wrote an important work entitled "The English Novel and Its Development" (1885). Since Lanier's death, his executors have brought together many of his lectures and papers under the titles of "Music and Poetry" (1898), and "Shakspere and his Forerunners" (1902).

The Humourists.—It is a far cry from the serious thought of Sidney Lanier to the ludicrous perversities of Mark Twain; yet between these two lies an extensive territory freely admitted by foreign critics to be distinctly and perhaps typically American. The humour of this country is different from that found anywhere else in the world. At times, it is true, it exhibits the sparkling characteristics of the Irishman's wit, at others the keen shrewdness of the Frenchman's *bon-mot*; certainly it is never less sprightly than the work of the English joker, nor less spontaneous than that of the German jester. In fact it may savour of any one, or of all the qualities just mentioned, and even of many others. The truth of the matter is, composite as a nation, we preserve in our humour the best traits of the elements out of which we are formed, and pretty generally add to the mixture a flavour indigenous to the soil upon which we flourish.

Humour of the Colonial Period.—In the early periods of our history, conscious humour did not exist. The colonists were too intent upon subduing the wilderness and safeguarding their religion to spend time in making fun. Their steeple-crowned hats, their staid garb, and the severe simplicity of their speech and conduct may seem ridiculous to us now; but, depend upon it, these were very serious matters to the Puritans themselves. A sudden outbreak of frivolity, whether it showed in a departure from the accepted dress or in an unusual use of language, would have been looked upon as sufficient cause for an immediate ecclesiastical investigation and solemn condemnation. Surely a community that in all seriousness could pass a law making it a finable offence in a man to kiss his wife on Sunday, would have been horror-stricken at the irreverent flippancy of Eli Perkins and of George Ade, and would no doubt have called down anathema upon Bill Nye and possibly even upon Carolyn Wells.

Humour of the Revolutionary Period.—Nor did circumstances permit the rise of humour in the Revolutionary period. The great joke of that time was the struggle between the pigmy and the giant, ending in the discomfiture of the latter to the tune of

"Yankee Doodle came to town."

A few grim remarks have come down to us, it must be admitted, remarks which amuse us now, but which could have been little provocative of laughter when they were uttered. Certainly we have no record of hilarious mirth filling the chamber when at the signing of the Declaration of Independence, Franklin sharply replied to the remark, "Well, in this matter I suppose we must all hang together," with the words, "Yes, or we shall all hang separately!" Life indeed was far too serious in both the earlier periods of American history and literature to be made a source of amusement. True, we have not a little work, satiric in tone, from such writers as the patriot, John Trumbull (1750–1831), and the Tory, Jonathan Odell (1737–1881), of whom the first in his "M'Fingal" (1775–1782) imitated Butler's "Hudibras," and the second in his "Word of Congress" (1779) and "The American Times" (1780) followed models set up by Dryden, Pope, and Churchill. Joel Barlow (1754–1812), too, deserves passing mention here for his mock-heroic poem, "The Hasty Pudding" (1793); and Philip Freneau (1752–1832) must be named on account of several briefer pieces of verse intended, no doubt, to be funny, but succeeding only in being abusive and vituperative of British leaders and British methods. On the whole, the efforts of all these writers, so far as humour is concerned, were little better than clumsy; and nowadays, if we bother with their works at all, we laugh at the authors rather than with them.

The Imitative School.—Conscious or deliberate American humour, then, can hardly be said to have shown itself before the early years of the nineteenth century. When it did appear, moreover, it was strongly imitative of English models and exhibited itself not as the most striking trait, but as only one of many qualities characterising an author's style. Indeed, barring the work of a mere handful of writers, we find such American humour as is likely to live woven into books which endure for other reasons than because they awaken laughter. For the earliest instance of any importance, we may mention Washington Irving, a writer already discussed as an essayist. He exhibits in various parts of his work a sparkling effervescence which, if a little more spontaneous than that found in *The Spectator*, is none the less strongly suggestive, like his more serious work, of Addison and Steele, and perhaps also of Goldsmith and Swift.

The Restrained School.—Less noticeably imitative of foreign work, the whimsicalities of Oliver Wendell Holmes, of James Russell Lowell, and of Charles Dudley Warner have been deemed sufficiently important to make each the subject of a chapter in more than one English work vainly endeavouring to analyse and classify that subtle something which makes American humour funny. With apparent gravity Holmes could ask the startling question, "Why is an onion like a piano?" and in answer convulse his readers with the atrocious pun, "Because it smell odious!" His characterisation of an afternoon reception as "Giggle, gabble, gobble, git," is worthy of frequent quotation; and one passage in his "Music Grinders" is of perennial value. Wearied by the discordant tunes issuing from a hurdy-gurdy, the distracted poet at last exclaims:

> "But hark! the air again is still
>   The music all is ground,
> And silence, like a poultice, comes
>   To heal the blows of sound."

The man who has had the experience here set down, appreciates both the pathos and the humour of a passage like that. Lowell's humour is akin to that of Holmes. It breaks out in nearly every essay that he wrote, and almost runs riot in some of his poems. Speaking of the destruction of a certain hill that a city street might be improved, he remarked in "Cambridge Thirty Years Ago" (1854): "The landscape was carried away cart-load by cart-load, and, dumped down on the roads, forms a part of that unfathomable pudding which has, I fear, drawn many a teamster and pedestrian to the use of phrases not commonly found in English dictionaries." There is much humour in Lowell, more stirring than this, but the quotation exhibits the readiness with which he would give an unexpected turn to a sentence, or throw in an unlooked-for reference or expression, too delicate to be shocking, too subtle to arouse loud laughter, but capable none the less of sending a ripple of amusement over the calmest gravity. For work professedly humorous throughout, we must turn to "A Fable for Critics" (1848) or to "The Biglow Papers" (1848). Both contain much good hard common sense, but the humour instead of being a mere accident of expression is the real reason for the existence of the greater part of each work. More closely allied to Lowell, perhaps, than to either Irving or Holmes, Warner produced no work exclusively funny. Still there is hardly a page of "My Summer in a Garden" (1870) or of "In the Wilderness" (1878) which does not have at least one laughable sentence. For this reason Warner defies quotation: his chapters must be read in their entirety rather than in chance snatches.

The Professional Humourists.—Turning now from those writers of humour who have been looked upon by some critics as forming an "imitative school" and by others as constituting what they have more happily termed a "restrained school," we come upon a widely extended group of writers who profess to have no higher calling than the awakening of mere laughter. If we call them collectively the "professional school of American humourists," we need not feel ourselves debarred from regarding them as falling naturally into several classes, to each of which we may give some special name, such as "the milder school," "the women humourists," "the boisterous group," and the like. We must not forget, however, that no hard and fast dividing lines can be drawn between the different classes, since the fact that a writer is a woman does not necessarily prevent her writing boisterous humour, or that a man who is generally almost clown-like may not sometimes produce a rare and refined piece of fun. Furthermore, it happens that the very naturalness with which the humourists fall into groups and classes prevents their being discussed in chronological order. The milder fun-makers have existed side by side with their hilarious brethren from the beginning, so that one must ignore, except in the slightest way, the order determined mainly by accidents of birth, or dates of publication.

The Women Humourists.—Politeness demands that we speak of the women humourists first: in the fore-front of these we must place Mrs. Frances Miriam Whitcher (1811–1852). She made her first appearance as a writer in *Neal's Saturday Gazette* about 1845, and to that paper contributed a long series of articles purporting to come from the pen of "the Widow Bedott." From the first she attracted attention, and interest in her work has never wholly ceased. Such was the demand for her writings that after her death two collections of articles from her pen were made and published as "The Widow Bedott Papers" (1855), and "Widow Sprigg, Mary Elmer, and Other Sketches" (1867).

Closely related in form and content to "The Widow Bedott Papers" was a book published in 1873 with the title "My Opinions and Betsy Bobbet's." Although immediately popular, it was for many years supposed to be the work of its professed author, Samanthy Allen; but by the time "P. A. and P. I. or Samanthy at the Centennial" appeared, in 1876, the secret had leaked out that "Josiah Allen's Wife" was the pseudonym of Marietta Holley (born in 1844), a native of Adams, New York. A contributor to *Peterson's Magazine*, *The Christian Union*, *The Independent*, and other periodicals, and the author of numerous books, she has gained considerable renown. Her earlier works are her best; for as time went on she diluted her skill in fun-making by permitting her interest in the temperance question, the woman-suffrage movement, and negro education to interfere with the power of her wit. Miss Holley's work has attracted some attention abroad, and has been translated into several foreign languages. Merely pausing to mention Mary Abigail Dodge (1830–1896), a native of Hamilton, Massachusetts, who, forming her pseudonym from a part of her own name and from that of her birthplace, made herself famous as "Gail Hamilton" in work both grave and gay; and stopping only to call attention to the fact that Harriet Beecher Stowe in "Old Town Folks" (1869) gave us an unusually funny book, we may choose from the host of women who are moving us to laughter the most industrious of them all, Carolyn Wells. As a writer of the verse form called the *limerick* she has more than once equalled Edward Lear, and as a parodist she shocks a reader to silence by her audacity.

The Milder Humourists.—In what may be called the milder school of American humourists Seba Smith (1792–1868) was the leader in point of time. Graduated from Bowdoin College in 1818, Smith began almost immediately to contribute editorially to the papers of Portland, Maine. In addition to more serious works, he wrote, under the pen-name of "Major Jack Downing," a series of political articles in New England dialect, thus anticipating Lowell's "Biglow Papers" by several years. Smith was the author of a number of books, the best known of which are probably "Way Down East" (1853) and "My Thirty Years Out of the Senate" (1859), the latter a homely and vigorous parody of Senator T. H. Benton's "Thirty Years' View of the American Government." Writing not long after Seba Smith, John Godfrey Saxe (1816–1887) early sprang into fame. The author of a considerable amount of prose, he attracted far wider attention by his verse. In the latter he showed the working of a strong English influence; indeed, it is not too much to say that had there been no Thomas Hood, there would have been no Saxe. Born at Highgate, Vermont, and graduated from Middlebury College in 1843, he soon became interested in both journalism and politics; but he is now best remembered by his work in verse. His "Humorous and Satirical Poems" (1850) fairly bristle with puns from beginning to end, and the surprising fact about them is that they are so good and so well set in their places that rarely does a reader feel inclined to accuse Saxe of overstraining his powers.

Leland, Field, Riley, and Harris.—Merely mentioning in passing the name of Saxe's contemporary, Frederick Swartwout Cozzens (1818–1869), author of "The Sparrowgrass Papers" (1856), we call attention to Robert Henry Newell (1836–1901), whose "Orpheus C. Kerr Papers" in three volumes (1861–1869) contained presumably funny comments on the Civil War, and to David Ross Locke (1833–1888), who, writing under the pseudonym of "Petroleum Vesuvius Naseby," wittily supported the administration of Lincoln, and attacked that of Johnson, in newspaper articles afterward collected into a book entitled "Divers Views, Opinions, and Prophecies of Yours Truly" (1865). These three men, although deserving mention on account of the position they once held, are now little read, but their contemporary Charles Godfrey Leland (1824–1903) seems to have established something like permanent renown for himself. Graduated from Princeton in 1846, he became prominent in various fields of journalism and authorship. His best-known work is "Hans Breitmann's Ballads," of which a collected edition appeared in 1895. These poems are written in the dialect known as Pennsylvania Dutch, and relate the exploits of their clownish hero in various exigencies and circumstances. In this same school of mild humourists we may class also a number of writers most of whom are still in the prime of life. From the host we select three as typical. Eugene Field (1850–1895), whose untimely death cut short a career of promise already blossoming into fulfilment, may be mentioned first. In addition to much serious work, he published "The Tribune Primer" (1882), a mock imitation of a child's first reading-book, and "Culture's Garden" (1887), a series of clever skits directed against those who make a pretence of ultra-refinement. With Field for some reason James Whitcomb Riley (born in 1853) has always been popularly associated, possibly because both wrote poems having childhood as subject-matter. Mr. Riley's humorous work is scattered through his several books, of which "Rhymes of Childhood" (1890) and "Home Folks" (1900) are typical, if not the best. An author of a series of books which appeal at once to students of popular tradition and to general readers whether young or old is found in Joel Chandler Harris (1848–1908). Publishing a book in 1880 on Afro-American folk-lore under the title "Uncle Remus, His Songs and His Sayings," Mr. Harris found to his surprise that he had an audience who listened to him with mirth instead of gravity. It is improbable that more than a mere handful of his readers suspect for even a moment that the several stories put into the mouth of Uncle Remus are a real contribution to anthropological data. In his later years, Mr. Harris wisely threw all his reports into literary form, with the result that there was a steady rise in his popularity as he gave us successively "Nights with Uncle Remus" (1883), "Mingo, and Other Sketches" (1884), and "Daddy Jake, the Runaway" (1889).

The Boisterous Humourists.—Turning now to the "boisterous school" of American humour, we may dwell for a time upon the chief characteristics exhibited by members of the group. In the first place, most of them have forgotten how to spell. There is something ludicrous in the appearance of the word "through" masquerading in the garb "thru," whatever may be the plea of the society of spelling reformers to the contrary; and certainly no one, except a school-teacher, can be other than amused to see such common words as "laugh," "feel," "funny," and the like making their bows as "laff," "feal," and "phuny." Laughable as this may be, however, it is not too much to insist that, if the appeal is only to the eye, if the wit evaporates when the words are not seen but merely heard, then the humour is not of very high order. In the second place, most of the members of the boisterous school, along with their loss of power as spellers, have also forgotten how to tell the truth. "This inclination towards outrageous exaggeration," said Lowell, "is a prime characteristic of American humour." "There is," he says elsewhere, "something irresistibly comic in the conception of a negro so black that charcoal made a white mark on him, or in the idea of a soil so fertile that a nail planted in it becomes a railroad spike before morning." This example of untruthfulness might also be taken as an illustration of the third trait of the group now under discussion—that of producing the most absurd paradoxes and of bringing into juxtaposition the most diverse uses of the same word. This is more than mere word-play; it is rather what might be termed the apotheosis of the pun. It underlies the majority of jokes that are found in the American newspaper, and is at once the admiration and the despair of those who try to analyse or to imitate the subtlety of our humour.

Josh Billings.—With these three characteristics in mind we may now give some brief attention to the humourists themselves. Of the "boisterous school" the earliest were Henry Wheeler Shaw, Benjamin Penhallow Shillaber, and Charles Farrar Browne. If by chance these names seem quite unfamiliar, the strangeness will disappear when attention is called to the fact that the three men respectively wrote under the *noms de plume* of "Josh Billings," "Mrs. Partington," and "Artemus Ward." Shaw (1818–1885) was born in Lanesborough, Massachusetts, and died in Monterey, California. To complete his formal education he entered Hamilton College in Clinton, New York; but tiring of the life there, he went on to the West and spent a number of years undergoing the many experiences offered by frontier life. Returning East in 1858, he became an auctioneer in Poughkeepsie, New York, where he also began to contribute to various magazines and newspapers. He attracted little attention until he invented an amusing system of phonetic spelling supposed to represent his homely method of pronunciation. His chief works were his "Farmer's Allminax" published annually between 1870 and 1880, "Every Boddy's Friend" (1876), and "Josh Billings' Spice Box" (1881). A quotation or two will exhibit both the thought and the form which characterise the contents of his several volumes of writing:

"Fallin' in luv is like fallin' in molases—sweet but drefful dobby."

"Yu can't tell what makes a kis taste so good eny more than you kin a peech. Eny man who kin set down wher it is cool and tell what a kis tastes like hain't got eny more taste in his mouth than a knot-hol hez."

Mrs. Partington.—Benjamin P. Shillaber (1814–1890) was influenced by Sheridan even more strongly than was Saxe by the elder Hood. Mrs. Partington is America's Mrs. Malaprop. Her misuse of the English language Shillaber recorded in three books bearing the several titles, "Life and Sayings of Mrs. Partington" (1854), "Partingtonian Patchwork" (1873), and "Ike and his Friend" (1879). Mrs. Partington's likeness to her English predecessor, or, as she would undoubtedly have said, her "predecessoress," may be seen in her chance remark: "I am not so young as I was once, and I don't believe I shall ever be, if I live to the age of Samson, which, heaven knows as well as I do, I don't want to, for I wouldn't be a centurion or an octagon and survive my factories and become idiomatic by any means. But then there is no knowing how a thing will turn out till it takes place, and we shall come to an end some day, though we may never live to see it."

Artemus Ward.—Charles F. Brown (1834–1867), the third of the humourists writing about the middle of the last century, was born in Waterford, Maine, and lived in various parts of the United States as his newspaper work called him first to one town and then to another. He made extensive lecture trips, and finally went in 1866 to England, where he died in March of the following year. He had the distinction of being the first American contributor to *Punch*. He published during his lifetime a number of books, among which were "Artemus Ward: His Book" (1865), "Artemus Ward: His Book of Goaks" (1865), and "Artemus Ward in London" (1867). Undoubtedly his best single work was a lecture giving an account of his visit to the Mormons. Learning from Brigham Young that he was married to eighty wives and sealed to as many more, Artemus remarked that the prophet was "the most marriedest man" he ever saw. Ward then went on to say: "In a privit conversashun with Brigham I learnt the follerin' fax: It takes him six weeks to kiss his wives. He don't do it only onct a year and sez it's wuss nor cleanin' house. He don't pretend to know his children, there is so many of 'em, tho they all know him. He sez about every child he meats call him Par and he takes it for granted it is so."

Later Writers of Boisterous Humour.—Taking up now the writers who were born in the decade immediately preceding the turning point of the nineteenth century, we may regard as worthy of special mention Charles Heber Clark, Charles Bertrand Lewis, Robert Jones Burdette, and Edgar Wilson Nye. Of these, all save one are still living and still writing. Mr. Clark was born in Berlin, Maryland, in 1841. For many years he has been the editor of *The Textile Record*, published in Philadelphia, to which he has contributed a number of articles on economic themes. He is best known, however, by two books of humour: "Out of the Hurly Burly" and "Elbow Room," both written under the *nom de plume* of "Max Adeler." Mr. Lewis (born in 1842) is best known by his pseudonym, "M. Quad," a title drawn from the parlance of printers. Mr. Lewis' earlier work was much more spontaneous than that which he is producing now. Connected with *The Detroit Free Press*, he contributed to it a steady stream of character sketches of great variety. Collecting them later, he published them under various titles. Of these volumes the best are "Brother Gardener's Lime-Kiln Club," "Quad's Odds," and "Mr. and Mrs. Bowser."

Edgar W. Nye (1850–1896), best known as "Bill Nye," was born in Shirley, Maine, and died near Asheville, North Carolina. Educated in Wisconsin, he first turned his attention to the study of law. Abandoning that pursuit after having been admitted to the bar, he dabbled in several different occupations, and finally became a newspaper correspondent. For a short time he travelled with James Whitcomb Riley, the two giving a series of entertainments which proved widely popular. Nye's published works were many, but they have little chance of permanent life. As good as any are "Bill Nye and the Boomerang" (1881), "A Comic History of the United States" (1894), and "The Railroad Guide" (1888), the last written in partnership with Mr. Riley. Mr. Burdette, the last of the quartette here mentioned together, was born in Greensboro, Pennsylvania, in 1844, and received his schooling in Peoria, Illinois. During the Civil War he was a soldier in the Union Army. At the close of the struggle, Mr. Burdette returned to Peoria, where he was connected with first one and then another of the newspapers published there. Finally, failing in a paper issued under his own proprietorship, he went to Burlington, Iowa, and became a member of the staff of *The Hawkeye*. While engaged in newspaper work, Mr. Burdette began to write funny things to amuse his invalid wife; and these, published later in the columns of the paper, have made him known throughout the United States. He was licensed as a Baptist preacher in 1887, since when he has signed himself Robert Burdette, D., on the ground that the abbreviation *D.* is the next thing to that of *D.D.* Mr. Burdette's best humorous work may be read in "The Rise and Fall of the Moustache and other Hawkeyetems" (1877) and "Chimes from a Jester's Bells" (1897).

Mark Twain.—Of American humourists "Mark Twain," known in private life as Samuel Langhorne Clemens, is readily placed foremost by critics and admirers both at home and abroad. He has the right to be considered the Nestor of our writers, for, born in 1835, he began to produce his earliest work when Irving was in his prime, and has therefore seen at least one phase of every school in our literature. His younger years were those of the decline of the Knickerbocker writers; he saw the rise and fall of the Concord group, the Cambridge poets, and the New York writers; and now he is present at the general upward movement all over the country, including the South and the West. His relation to our literature is not unlike that of Fanny Burney to the novel; she was born before Richardson published "The History of Sir Charles Grandison," and did not die until twelve years after the birth of George Meredith, thus being contemporaneous with the greatest English novelists from the first to the last. Mr. Clemens was born in Florida, Missouri, and when scarcely thirteen years old was apprenticed to a printer. Barring a few years spent as pilot upon the Mississippi, he has devoted his life to literary work. His writings include "The Innocents Abroad" (1869), the humorous record of a trip in the countries of the Eastern Hemisphere; "The Gilded Age" (1873), a novel written conjointly with Charles Dudley Warner; "The Adventures of Tom Sawyer" (1876), and "The Adventures of Huckleberry Finn" (1884), both books about boys whose exploits are interesting to young and old alike; "A Connecticut Yankee at the Court of King Arthur" (1889), a cruel parody of Malory's "Morte d'Arthur"; and "Christian Science," an attempt, despite all the fun it makes, to report sincerely upon a careful investigation of the claims of Mrs. Mary Baker Eddy and her disciples. It is unfortunate for Mr. Clemens that he is a humourist, for he has had to suffer the lot long ago mentioned by Holmes as the fate of the fun-producer: no one can ever take such a man seriously; no one can believe that he ever has any other purpose than to tickle our fancy or awaken our laughter. Yet it is not impossible that future critics may come to regard "The Prince and the Pauper" (1882) and "The Personal Recollections of Joan of Arc" (1896), two serious and dignified pieces of writing, as Mr. Clemens's best work.

Within recent years Oxford University has conferred the degree of D.C.L. upon Mr. Clemens in recognition of his contributions to literature. This action by a great institution of learning has filled many minds with surprise, nor have all of them quite recovered their mental equilibrium yet. Some, indeed, are still asking the old question, "Is Saul also among the prophets?" and can hardly believe their ears when they receive the answer, "Yea, verily!" Humour at last seems to be coming to its own. Said Mr. Meredith a few years ago: "Comedy, we have to admit, was never one of the most honoured of the Muses. She was in her origin, short of laughter, the loudest expression of the little civilisation of men." While it must be admitted that when he wrote this the greatest English writer now living had in mind something much more delicate, much more refined, much more subtle, than anything yet produced in America, it is not beyond thought that even he would let us classify the fun-makers of this country as true humourists. They deal little in satire, little in irony, but they have much in common with those to whom Mr. Meredith said: "If you laugh all round a person, tumble him, roll him about, deal him a smack, and drop a tear on him, own his likeness to you, and yours to your neighbour, spare him as little as you shun, pity him as much as you expose, it is a spirit of Humour that is moving you."

V. THE ORATORS AND THE DIVINES

The Historical Background.—In America, oratory has been the most fortunate of all the arts. Whether in the era prior to the Revolution, or in the formative years of the Republic before 1800, or in the first half and more of the nineteenth century—in the pulpit as well as at the bar and in the forum, American orators have drawn their inspiration directly from the political or religious life of the nation. From the nature of things, no other art, neither poetry, nor painting, nor music, could bear so intimate a relation to the course of our national existence as the utterance of the public speaker. Every crisis in our history, the Revolution itself, the War of 1812, the struggle between North and South, was hastened by the spoken word. Trained poets have been wanting among us; trained speakers, in so far as their powers could develop without a correspondingly high development of poetry and music, we have always possessed; men skilled in rousing enthusiasm and reverence throughout congregations of the pious, men alert to kindle the intelligence of a legislature or to sway the minds of judge and jury. From the first, this training was continuous and effective. In the bare colonial churches thought, word, and action of the pastor were criticised by an audience that had braved the sea and the savage for the privilege of listening. From the colonial courts of justice spread the education which warranted Burke in saying of a litigious populace: "In no country perhaps in the world is the law so general a study. The profession itself is numerous and powerful.... But all who read, and most do read, endeavour to obtain some smattering in that science." With this knowledge of law, every other colonist was a keen debater for his private rights and, when the time came, for the rights of his community or nation. From a population thus educated sprang the forensic leaders of the Revolution; and to its sources in eighteenth-century popular education we follow back the steady stream of American eloquence which in the nineteenth century runs strong and full in the noblest efforts of American literature—say Webster's tribute to Massachusetts in the reply to Hayne, and Lincoln's undying speech at Gettysburg.

So close indeed is the bond between juridic and political history on the one hand, and the achievement of the great American orators on the other, that they can be sundered, as in the following pages, only for purposes of general reference. Since a political history of the United States from the year 1783 is not here expected, we must limit ourselves to brief notice of a few representative men, taken in something like chronological order, and mainly between the years 1800 and 1865. With the Civil War, or perhaps with the second inaugural address of President Lincoln, ended the golden age of national eloquence.

Precursors of the Nineteenth Century.—The careers of James Otis (1725–83), Samuel Adams (1722–1803), Josiah Quincy, Junior (1744–75), and Patrick Henry (1736–99), fall largely in the period covered by the pages from Tyler; and the orations and political writings of the Revolutionary Period itself do not come within the scope of the present sketch. Of course it is impossible to make a line of sharp division in the case of public men whom we instinctively couple with the earliest days of the Republic, but whose voices were heard to the verge of the next century, or even beyond. The "Farewell Address" of Washington to his countrymen in 1796, so long regarded with veneration, was, in spite of its conservative form, its Johnsonian balance, a document with matter for the coming age. However, it is clear that statesmen who were in their prime at the time of Washington's death in 1799 more particularly require our attention.

Fisher Ames.—Among these is Fisher Ames (1758–1808). Admitted to Harvard at the age of twelve, after graduation he first engaged in teaching, then studied law, and entering politics, became a force among the Federalists. Long the victim of ill health, he nevertheless made his superior mental endowment felt in the counsels of the nation. His "Tomahawk Speech" (1796), on Jay's treaty with Great Britain, contained passages of splendour on the fear of Indian massacres. For the eloquence of this speech he has been compared to Wilberforce, Brougham, Burke, Pitt, and Fox. He could not have resembled them all. Ames had a fastidious taste, was cautious and dignified in his utterances, and was not desirous of a cheap popularity. "To be the favourite of an ignorant multitude," he observed, "a man must descend to their level." Four years before he died, his health constrained him to decline the presidency of Harvard.

The Early Nineteenth Century.—The activity of Rufus King (1755–1827) and others continued somewhat later. This friend of Alexander Hamilton, and collaborator with him in the political essays signed "Camillus," was in 1796 accorded the delicate function of Minister to England. In 1813 the Legislature of New York elected him to the United States Senate; here he won laurels for his speech on the destruction of Washington by the British. He returned to the Senate in 1820, and he was Minister to England again under President Adams.

John Marshall.—The name of John Marshall (1755–1835) we naturally associate with his momentous work of interpreting the Constitution. The dry light of his intellect and his lack of passion were more suited to purely legal exposition than to the eloquence of debate. When he went to Congress in 1798, the cogency of his argument was already known. It is sufficiently demonstrated by his speech in Robbins' case (1800), a case that involved the international law governing murder committed upon the high seas by a citizen of one country sailing on the ship of another. Marshall's uninspiring "Life of Washington" is valuable as a repository of plain fact.

Morris and De Witt.—Gouverneur Morris (1752–1816) was early famous for his eloquence. His thought was orderly, his style finished. Successful in the practice of law, and distinguished for his services during the Revolution, he became a zealous Federalist, entering the United States Senate in 1800. Here his most notable effort was his "Speech on the Judiciary" (1802). Clinton De Witt (1769–1828), who was Mayor of New York City most of the time between 1803 and 1815, was also in the Senate for two years, and opposed the redoubtable Morris on the question of navigation on the Mississippi. De Witt was a man of wide interests, being something of a scientist and historian; his practical sense recognised the value of inland waterways. He merits more attention than can here be given him.

Gore, Dexter, and Others.—The same is true of the following: Christopher Gore (1758–1829), who in 1814 reached the Senate, to remain three years, and who spoke on "The Prohibition of Certain Imports" (1814) and on "Direct Taxation" (1815); Samuel Dexter (1761–1816), Secretary of War and Secretary of the Treasury; James A. Bayard (1767–1815), lawyer, Senator, Commissioner at Ghent in 1814; William Branch Giles (1762–1840); Edward Livingston (1764–1836), jurist, diplomat, Secretary of State; John Sergeant (1779–1852), candidate for Vice-President on the Clay ticket of 1832; John J. Crittenden (1787–1863), lawyer and statesman; James Hillhouse (1789–1846), orator as well as poet.

William Pinkney.—Among the noteworthy orators during the first twenty years of the last century was William Pinkney (1764–1822). The son of a sympathiser with England, he was himself devoted to the cause of American freedom. His prominence in the affairs of Maryland ushered him into national concerns. He took part in the War of 1812, and was wounded. He was Attorney-General under Madison, but resigned for the sake of his private practice. He was made Minister to Russia in 1816; in 1820 he entered the United States Senate. A specimen of his eloquence may be seen in his argument before the Supreme Court (1815) in the case of the prize ship *Nereide*. Pinkney was fond of classical learning, and well versed in current literature. He prided himself on his accuracy in the use of English. This made him over-conscious in his style, so that his thought seems artificial. His death is said to have been partly caused by his labours in the preparation and delivery of an argument.

Quincy, Gallatin, and Emmet.—Josiah Quincy (1772–1864), son of Josiah Quincy of Revolutionary fame, was president of Harvard from 1829 to 1845. Besides his "History of Harvard University," he was the author of many pamphlets and public addresses. "His career in Congress was distinguished chiefly for his opposition to the Embargo, to the War of 1812, and to the admission of Louisiana." Albert Gallatin (1761–1849), leaving his birthplace, at Geneva, Switzerland, came to Boston in 1781, taught French in Harvard, went to Virginia, and there became the friend of Patrick Henry. He was sent to Congress in 1795, and thereafter entrusted with special missions to Holland and England. He was also Minister to France (1816), and Minister to England (1826). Gallatin's intuitions were as quick and sure as his character was upright and urbane. His information, as in his speech (1796) on the earlier British treaty, was ample and exact. Among his innumerable services to the country of his adoption, not the least were his efforts on behalf of internal commerce and the improvement in methods of banking. Thomas Addis Emmet (1764–1827) was also a foreigner—a native of Cork. He studied medicine in Edinburgh, but turning to law, was admitted to practice in 1791 and settled at Dublin. For his share in the Irish insurrectionary movement he was imprisoned; after his release he emigrated to New York, where he became an eminent pleader. He had a "dignified but earnest attitude, forcible and unstudied gestures," and a "powerful and expressive voice." "No orator knew better how to enlist his hearers on the side of his client."

Red Jacket and Tecumseh.—Foreign, likewise, although bred within our borders, was the eloquence of the Indians, Red Jacket and Tecumseh. Red Jacket was the nickname of Sa-go-ye-wat-ha ("He keeps them awake"), otherwise known as "the last of the Senecas." He was a lover of peace, resisting entanglements, counselling the Indians neither to fight, nor yet to mingle, with the whites, dissuading them against the adoption of Christianity, settled in his ancestral reverence for "the Great Spirit." His simple and direct language was full of sudden poetic energy. He died at a great age in 1830. Tecumseh (1770?-1812), in many things his opposite, was killed at the Battle of the Thames, where he fought with the English against the United States. A born leader was Tecumseh, magnificent in his proportions, noble in his bearing, fiery and magnetic. Prior to the War of 1812 he tried to enlist the Indians of the South and West in a general insurrection against the government. He went from tribe to tribe, reproaching them with their debasement through white civilisation, and abusing the Federal authority.

William Wirt.—Of Swiss descent, one of the ablest men this country developed in his time was William Wirt (1772–1834). His arraignment of Aaron Burr at the latter's trial in 1807 was masterly, and made Wirt's name familiar to the public ear. From 1817 to 1828 he was Attorney-General. In private as in national life his character was without stain; his correspondence discloses an honesty and consistency of statement and purpose almost unequalled. His imaginative "Letters of the British Spy" (1803) described Virginian society and American eloquence as they might appear to an unbiassed traveller. "The Life and Character of Patrick Henry" (1817) was roundly praised by Jefferson. Of Wirt's occasional addresses none was more admired than that delivered in 1830 before the students of Rutgers College.

Judge Story.—The voluminous works of Joseph Story (1779–1845), including text-books on law, are in part made up of his discourses. He began life as a poet, but attained his first eminence as a lawyer. Before his appointment to the United States Supreme Court, he was heard on the floor of the House of Representatives. As professor in the Harvard Law School he proved an acceptable lecturer.

John Quincy Adams.—The younger Adams (1767–1848), sixth President of the United States, received from his father, the second President, specific training for the career of statesman; even his boyhood was passed in the midst of political and diplomatic life. He studied at Leyden, then at Harvard, where, during an interim in his public activities, he afterward held the chair of rhetoric and belles-lettres. He saw diplomatic service in Holland, Russia, England, was in the Senate, and was in the House of Representatives. He was a foe of slavery, but not a Garrisonian Abolitionist. In 1836 he urged upon Congress its right under the Constitution, as he believed, to abolish slavery by legal enactment. His influence was strong for freedom of debate. This "old man eloquent" continued speaking when he was over eighty, and died on the floor of the House of Representatives. He was a diarist, a poet, a translator. He was a clear, fluent, not very terse speaker, having the agglomerative and developing style of the parliamentary orator. When he desired, he could be ironical.

The High Tide of American Oratory.—The burning questions of the rights of an individual state as against its duties to the central government, of the extension of negro slavery, or its territorial limitation, or its entire abolition, brought on the crisis of the Civil War, which is the central fact in American history. Correspondingly, during the interval between the War of 1812 and the War of the Rebellion, their eloquence fired by these and related questions, lie the careers of our greatest orators.

"Old Bullion."—Thomas Hart Benton (1782–1858) cannot be reckoned one of these. Indifferent to the spread of slavery, he was in favour of developing the great Western territories at any cost. He urged a reduction of the prices charged by the government in the sale of public lands, and promoted the interests of a railroad to the Pacific. As an advocate of specie currency he acquired the sobriquet of "Old Bullion." Retiring from the Senate after extended usefulness there, he published his "Thirty Years' View," a history of the workings of the American Government from 1820 to 1850, highly commended by Bryant for its taste and simplicity of style.

Henry Clay.—Slightly the senior of Benton, Henry Clay (1777–1852) was in public life for an even longer time. By birth he was a Virginian. In the face of early hardship he rose to be Senator from Kentucky (1806–1807); from 1811 until 1852, for forty-one years, he was almost steadily in the eye of the nation. A leader of the Whig party, he sided with his great opponent, Calhoun, against the more timid Madison, in precipitating the second war with England; and he was prominent in the negotiations for peace that followed. Clay was four times Speaker of the House of Representatives, and four times unsuccessful candidate for President of the United States. The influence which he had shown over juries in Kentucky he likewise exercised in the national legislature. In the management of conflicting interests, and in furthering the measures of his party, he had a genius for detecting what was possible or expedient. The Missouri Compromise of 1820, the Tariff Compromise of 1833, and the Slavery Compromise of 1850 were largely owing to him. He was a master in effecting legislation. According to Blaine, "Mr. Webster argued the principle, Mr. Clay embodied it in a statute." Among his celebrated speeches were those on the New Army Bill (1813), on the Seminole War (1819), and on the Tariff (1824). At his death, a colleague, Joseph R. Underwood, said in the Senate:

> The character of Henry Clay was formed and developed by the influence of our free institutions. His physical and mental organisation eminently qualified him to become a great and impressive orator. His person was tall, slender, and commanding; his temperament ardent, fearless, and full of hope; his countenance clear, expressive, and variable—indicating the emotion which predominated at the moment with exact similitude; his voice cultivated and modulated in harmony with the sentiment he desired to express ...; his eye beaming with intelligence, and flashing with coruscations of genius; his gestures and attitudes graceful and natural. These personal advantages won the prepossessions of an audience, even before his intellectual powers began to move his hearers; and when his strong common sense, his profound reasoning, his clear conceptions of his subject in all its bearings, and his striking and beautiful illustrations, united with such personal qualities, were brought to the discussion of any question, his audience was enraptured, convinced, and led by the orator as if enchanted by the lyre of Orpheus.

John Caldwell Calhoun.—The character and intellect of John Caldwell Calhoun (1782–1850) were admired even by those who least cared for his opinions. A South Carolinian of Scotch-Irish extraction, he graduated from Yale, in 1804, with the highest honours. He towered in political life from 1808 until he died: as leader of the war party under Madison; in upholding the doctrine of nullification—that is, the right of each state to resist a Congressional enactment which the state might deem injurious; in the annexation of Texas; and in the defence of slavery. Calhoun was fearless and precise in the discharge of his duties as Secretary of War under Monroe, reducing expenses, and rendering petty defalcation impossible. He was Vice-President in 1825. His ruling ideas are contained in his "Disquisition on Government" and "Discourse on the Government of the United States" (in the first volume of his works), and in speeches before the Senate—for example, on Nullification and the Force Bill (1833) and on the Slavery Question (1850). He was thus characterised by Webster:

> The eloquence of Mr. Calhoun ... was plain, strong, terse, condensed, concise; sometimes impassioned—still always severe. Rejecting ornament, not seeking far for illustration, his power consisted in the plainness of his propositions, in the clearness of his logic, and in the earnestness and energy of his manner.... His demeanour as a Senator is known to us all—is appreciated, venerated by us all.

Hayne and Randolph.—When Calhoun was Vice-President, his spokesman in the Senate was a fellow Carolinian, Robert Young Hayne (1791–1840), who was a soldier in the War of 1812, but who, in his vindication of state rights, refused the Attorney-Generalship of the country to be Attorney-General of South Carolina. He also retired from the Senate to be Governor of his State. In his unlucky debate with Webster in 1830 he carried sectional jealousy—of the South against New England—into the question concerning the sale of public lands in the West. Graceful in person, of a fine countenance, industrious, commonly amiable, Hayne "had a copious and ready elocution, flowing at will in a strong and steady current, and rich in the material that constitutes argument." His prejudices, however, could distract him from the subject in hand. The bellicose Virginian, John Randolph of Roanoke (1773–1833), was in Congress at the age of twenty-six. His bitterness toward England seems excessive. Eccentric, singular also in appearance, biting and unexpected in retort, he was a figure of interest when he came to the Senate in 1825. His duel with Henry Clay is a matter of unpleasant history. Enthusiastic contemporary estimates of him by Paulding and others have not worn well.

Daniel Webster.—The prince of American orators, and one of the great orators of modern times, was born in Salisbury, New Hampshire, on January 18, 1782. His ancestry was Scotch. He had the stinted education of a village school whose doors were open for a short term in winter. Yet he could never recollect the time when he could not read the Bible; and this and the few other books that he could obtain he perused so often that he virtually had them by heart. He was fond of committing passages to memory. But at Exeter, where he prepared for college, there was one thing which he could not do: "I could not speak before the school." The efforts of his father made it possible for him to attend Dartmouth College. He read by himself with the avidity of a Lowell—but he also pursued with good intent the regular course of studies. Finishing this course in 1801, he studied law, earned a little money by teaching in Maine, and at length entered the office of Christopher Gore in Boston—"a tall, gaunt young man, with rather a thin face, but all the peculiarities of feature and complexion by which he was distinguished in later life." There followed some years of practice with meagre remuneration, but of unceasing study. In 1813 he was sent to Congress from New Hampshire. His speech in that year on the repeal of the Berlin and Milan Decrees elicited praise from Chief Justice Marshall, and throughout the country. Webster immediately advanced to the front rank of debaters. It is baffling even to suggest the range and importance of his subsequent labours. When the famous Dartmouth College case, apparently a forlorn hope, was carried before the United States Supreme Court in 1818, Webster's opening argument as junior counsel brought an unlooked for settlement in favour of the College; since then the case has furnished a ruling precedent in interpreting the Constitutional clause which prohibits state interference with the terms of a past contract. In 1820 he was engaged on the revision of the Massachusetts State Constitution. From 1823 to 1827 he was in the House of Representatives; from 1827 to 1841, and again from 1845 to 1850, in the Senate. He was Secretary of State under Harrison and Tyler, and under Fillmore. Through supposed concessions to slavery in his speech of March 7, 1850, on the Constitution and the Union, he estranged his best friends in the North, and had to endure the taunt of faithlessness in Whittier's "Ichabod." Historians, however, have justified the loftiness of his statesmanship even here. He died as Secretary of State under Fillmore, October 24, 1852.

During his reply to Hayne in 1830, when Webster uttered his encomium on the State of Massachusetts, strong men were moved to tears. One cannot read it at this distance without strange emotion. Passages in the second address at Bunker Hill, or the argument in Knapp's trial—the passage on the conscience of the murderer, or more especially that at the end on the universal sense of duty—rise to the point where the ethical and æsthetic values of eloquence are one and eternal. One might go on to mention his eulogy on "Adams and Jefferson," his "First Settlement of New England"—but we should hardly finish a mere enumeration of the speeches he delivered during his forty years of public life.

> Consider [said Choate] the work he did in that life of forty years—the range of subjects investigated and discussed; composing the whole theory and practice of our organic and administrative politics, foreign and domestic; the vast body of instructive thought he produced and put in possession of the country; how much he achieved in Congress as well as at the bar; to fix the true interpretation, as well as to impress the transcendent value of the Constitution itself ...; how much to establish in the general mind the great doctrine that the government of the United States is a government proper, established by the people of the States, not a compact between sovereign communities ...; to place the executive department of the government on its true basis ...; to secure to that department its just powers on the one hand, and on the other hand to vindicate to the legislative department, and especially to the Senate, all that belonged to them ...; to develop the vast material resources of the country, and push forward the planting of the West ...; to protect the vast mechanical and manufacturing interests ...; how much for the right performance of the most delicate and difficult of all tasks, the ordering of the foreign affairs of a nation, free, sensitive, self-conscious ...; how much to compose with honour a concurrence of difficulties with the first power of the world.

His style is simple, clear, free from tricks, unstudied in its details, the easy outflow of a mind nourished on choice and repeated reading, with the English Bible as its main source; not avoiding allusion to himself, but quickly mounting with the subject to universal application; not deficient in grace, yet on the whole massive, orderly, and neglectful of lighter emotions. In private life Webster was genial. He was fond of the open country, delighting in the rod and gun. "Black Dan" he was familiarly called, on account of his deep-set, lustrous eyes, over-shadowing brows, and commanding, swarthy countenance. The proportions and majesty of his head were in keeping with the dignity of his figure.

William Lloyd Garrison.—With the main agitator of the Abolitionist movement there was no thought of compromise. Orator as well as writer, William Lloyd Garrison (1805–1879), though the herald of self-restraint, and preaching the doctrine of non-resistance, carried his principles to their extreme length. He condemned the churches for their tolerance of slavery, and disliked the Constitution for permitting it. He favoured ending the Union, if the national disease could be removed by amputation. He could not tolerate gradual treatment or the doubtful promise of an incomplete cure.

Charles Sumner.—Garrison's brave, handsome, and gifted friend, and the friend of Longfellow, Charles Sumner (1811–1878), was trained in the law under Judge Story. It was partly through Whittier's influence that he entered politics, but when he succeeded Webster in the Senate his place as a leader was assured. The infamous assault upon him by Brooks in 1856, during the debate over the affairs of Kansas, left Sumner incapacitated until 1859. When "the eloquent vacant chair" was filled again, crowds gathered whenever announcement was made that Sumner would speak. His intellect was not equal to that of his illustrious predecessor; yet his sound judgment and winning personality, aided by a captivating delivery, put him, in the Senate, at the head of the new Republican party. His "Orations" have been published in eight volumes.

Thaddeus Stevens.—While Sumner was in the Senate, Thaddeus Stevens (1792–1868), a less admirable character, led the Republicans in the House. He also was a bitter foe of slavery, and was urgent with Lincoln to emancipate the negroes. "A clear, logical, and powerful debater," he was feared for his mordant invective. Influential with the rank and file of politicians, he rejoiced in the borrowed title of the "Great Commoner."

Wendell Phillips.—Of course the trumpet of the Abolitionists was the impassioned Wendell Phillips (1811–1884), ever supporting the hands of Garrison, and similarly uncompromising. On graduating from Harvard in 1831, he studied law; but he refused to engage in its practice, since this would entail his swearing to uphold a national Constitution which tolerated slavery. He was a master of sarcasm, irony, and epigram, of choice and varied wit; serene in the presence of his enemies, capturing and holding their attention. When the Civil War was over, and the cause of Abolition won, he turned to the remedy of other evils, speaking in favour of woman's rights, and championing labour reform. In the guise of a general redresser of wrongs he lost prestige as well as something of his own sense of dignity.

Rufus Choate.—The most famous of a famous family, Rufus Choate (1799–1859) was distinguished for his pleading at the bar, his literary attainments, and, during the time that he was there (1841–1845), the exercise of his talents in the Senate. A pupil of no less a lawyer than William Wirt, Choate, in his unrivalled success with juries, and his stirring if florid occasional addresses, was indebted not alone to his natural ardour and personal magnetism, but also to thorough analysis and unremitting preparation. His eulogy on Webster at Dartmouth College, July 27, 1853, was the tribute of an eminent graduate of that institution to the noblest.

Stephen A. Douglas.—Stephen Arnold Douglas (1813–1861) was born in Brandon, Vermont, studied law in Canandaigua, New York, continued this study in Ohio, and proceeded thence to Illinois to teach, and to practise his calling of lawyer. He was in the United States Senate from 1847 to 1861, doing his best to avert the Civil War. In 1858 and 1860 the "Little Giant" boldly appeared before audiences in the South and denied the right of any state to secede from the Union. His speech on the Kansas-Nebraska Bill (1854) shows his attitude of *laissez-faire* in the matter of slavery. When he matched his wits with Lincoln in their joint debate, he unintentionally hastened his antagonist's advance toward the Presidency.

William H. Seward.—Cautious, clear, incisive, firm in his grasp of the laws of political history, William Henry Seward (1811–1872) foresaw what Douglas could not, that the struggle with slavery was an irrepressible conflict. In New York State, of which he became Governor, he was the untiring enemy of political opportunism in every shape. An unsuccessful aspirant in 1860 for the Presidency, he eventually overcame his lack of confidence in Lincoln, and as Lincoln's Secretary of State was of inestimable service in maintaining our relations with England during the course of the Rebellion. His "Diplomatic History of the Civil War in America" was published posthumously.

Salmon P. Chase.—Lincoln's Secretary of the Treasury, Salmon Portland Chase (1808–1873), was not a facile speaker, but, tall and commanding, one of the handsomest men in the Senate, he was both dignified and impressive. Like Choate, he graduated from Dartmouth and studied with William Wirt. As a practising lawyer he engaged (1837) in the defence of persons on trial for alleged violation of the Fugitive Slave Act; in the debate upon the Kansas-Nebraska Bill (1854) he advocated "free soil," and insisted upon "the absolute divorce of the General Government" from all connection with slavery. He was a Senator both before and after holding the governorship of Ohio, and again just before Lincoln summoned him into the Cabinet. In 1864 he was made Chief Justice of the Supreme Court, a position which he honoured till his death.

Edward Everett.—In the delivery of Edward Everett (1794–1865) "there was nothing in manner, person, dress, gesture, tone, accent, or emphasis too minute for his attention." From boyhood he had the gift of eloquence, which he developed by assiduous practice. Taking high honours at Harvard when but seventeen, he went into the Unitarian ministry, and began preaching at the Brattle Street Church in Boston, with immediate success. Invited to assume a chair at Harvard, he studied abroad in preparation, and then from 1819 to 1825 taught Greek. He left his professorship to become a member of the House of Representatives. Ten years later he was elected Governor of Massachusetts. In 1841 General Harrison appointed him Minister to England; on his return he accepted the presidency of Harvard. He succeeded Webster as Secretary of State under Fillmore; and in the national election of 1860, representing the forces that desired a compromise between North and South, he was candidate for Vice-President of the United States. During his stay in the Senate Everett also was heard on the Kansas-Nebraska Bill. His orations were published in four volumes. His "Lecture on the Character of Washington" (1856), frequently repeated, and his "Eulogy on Webster" (1859) were among his most splendid efforts. He made a remarkable address at Gettysburg, though it now seems academic beside that of Lincoln on the same occasion.

Abraham Lincoln.—For a manual of literature the essential thing in the life of President Lincoln (1809–1865) is the ennoblement that went on in his eloquence, as his character developed under the increasing gravity and tension of his public career, and as his individual spirit became more and more identified with the agonising soul of a nation. The simplicity and directness of his mental operations are apparent in any of his earlier letters and speeches; they were sufficiently evident to those who heard his debate with Douglas. But his utterance gained in dignity and closeness of texture when his native impulses for good became free from idiosyncrasy, and when his innate moral rightness grew into a deep and conscious religion. In all literature there are few things more significant than the chastening of style that accompanied the chastening of Lincoln's personality. There is a noticeable difference even between the manner of his first and that of his second inaugural address. In the meantime he had pronounced his speech at the dedication of the National Cemetery on the battlefield of Gettysburg, November 19, 1863. There, devoid of all pretence to rhetorical artifice, yet in the perfection of English style, Lincoln gave to the world a masterpiece of literature, issuing as it were from the life-blood of the people; a masterpiece in which art and life are married, and imaginative and literal truth are become one flesh. Says Mr. Bryce:

> That famous Gettysburg speech is the best example one could desire of the characteristic quality of Lincoln's eloquence. It is a short speech. It is wonderfully terse in expression. It is quiet, so quiet that at the moment it did not make upon the audience, an audience wrought up by a long and highly-decorated harangue from one of the prominent orators of the day, an impression at all commensurate to that which it began to make as soon as it was

read over America and Europe. There is in it not a touch of what we call rhetoric, or of any striving after effect. Alike in thought and in language it is simple, plain, direct. But it states certain truths and principles in phrases so aptly chosen and so forcible, that one feels as if those truths could have been conveyed in no other words, and as if this deliverance of them were made for all time. Words so simple and so strong could have come only from one who had meditated so long on the primal facts of American history and popular government that the truths those facts taught him had become like the truths of mathematics in their clearness, their breadth, and their precision.

Miscellaneous and Later Orators.—It is obvious that the lives of many ante-bellum orators overlapped upon the era of Reconstruction; and the fifty years of political activity since the Civil War have brought forth an ever growing number of men concerned in affairs of state. However, there are few in this last to compare in eloquence with those of the preceding half-century. Among recognised orators a quieter tone on the whole has prevailed; not altogether that of Lincoln, nor yet that characteristic of the best speakers in the time of Madison and the younger Adams; nevertheless marking an improvement upon the flowery and pedantic effusions of an intermediate age represented by Choate, Winthrop, and, to a certain extent, Everett. The passage of laws and the expediting of other public business have come to depend more upon influence and effort exerted off the floor of the House and the Senate, and less upon forensic argument and persuasion. With the enormous growth of the population and the corresponding increase in the size of our legislative bodies, public orators have in most cases been satisfied, perforce, with a local reputation. The following are chosen miscellaneously.

John B. Gough (1817–1886) was an English editor, who fell a victim to alcoholism, and being rescued from his habit by a friend of temperance, dedicated himself to the cause of rescuing others. He lectured widely in America, enthralling large audiences by his descriptions of the ruin worked by alcoholic beverages, and by his graphic narratives of lapsing and reformed drunkards.

George William Curtis (1824–1892) was in youth (1842) attached to the community at Brook Farm. On returning from studies in Berlin and Italy, he became connected with the publishers of Putnam's Magazine. The management of this periodical failing, Curtis assumed a financial liability for which he was not legally responsible, and spent twenty years in lecturing, to pay off the indebtedness. He was noted as editor of *Harper's Monthly*, and as a writer for *Harper's Weekly* and *Harper's Bazar*. He was a virile speaker on civil-service reform and other subjects involving the national welfare. Wherever he went he inculcated high political ideals. His "Orations and Addresses" were edited by Professor Charles Eliot Norton.

James G. Blaine (1830–1893), a Pennsylvanian, commenced life as an editor in Maine, became a member of the State Legislature there, and thence proceeded to Congress. He made a brilliant record as Speaker of the House of Representatives (1869–1875). In 1876 he was appointed United States Senator from Maine. Several times a Presidential possibility, he was the Republican nominee in 1884, when he was unexpectedly defeated by Cleveland. Blaine's speech on the remonetisation of silver (1878) has been often cited. He was clear and forcible, save for a slight lisp, but his character was not such as to force conviction home.

It is impossible in the space allotted to proceed further with recent or contemporary orators in political or secular life. One ought not to neglect such men as Carl Schurz (1829–1906) or Bourke Cockran (born in 1854), or among the last few presidents, Benjamin Harrison (1833–1901). Mr. Harrison, an astute lawyer, could, on short notice, and seemingly without effort, deliver the choicest of addresses, well turned, fluent, and of a convenient length. An account of American political eloquence properly ends with a reference to the distinguished statesman, now President, and after Washington and Lincoln the third among our sons of light, to whom this volume is dedicated. From the most conspicuous of public orators at the present day, we return to the early divines and theologians.

American Divines.—In his "Annals of the American Pulpit"—"from the Early Settlement of this Country to the Close of the Year 1855"—the Reverend William B. Sprague (1795–1875) collected the biographies of thirteen hundred or more divines who had earned as he thought a lasting memorial.[22] "From the commencement of this work," he observes, "I have been quite aware that nothing pertaining to it involves more delicacy than the selection of its subjects, and that no degree of care and impartiality can be a full security against mistakes." Far more difficult is the matter of selection, when in a sketch of barely a dozen pages we try to include the names of those who, during the nineteenth century, have most deeply wrought upon the private life of our citizens. The separation of church and state in America renders all the wider the ordinary cleft between public and private life, and the multiplicity of religious sects still further tends to keep the eloquence and motive force of great spiritual leaders from becoming generally known. Even among those whose power and fame have overleaped the confines of their own parish or denomination, our choice is necessarily limited to a scanty few.

Clergymen as Educators.—The influence of notable preachers—not to speak of the clergy as a whole—in American life is incalculable. Outside of the church and the home, it has been most evident in higher education; until a short time since, educational leadership was vested, as it should be, in the ministers of religion. As significant as the important colleges more or less directly founded for the training of pastors is the long line of college presidents taken from the ranks of that profession. At Princeton, Jonathan Edwards, head of that institution (1758) during the last month of his life, was succeeded ten years later by John Witherspoon (1722–1794), a lineal descendant of John Knox, and a signer of the American Declaration of Independence. The philosopher, James McCosh (1811–1894), was eleventh president in the same illustrious succession. At Yale we have such men as the poet, Timothy Dwight (1752–1817), and his grandson of the same name (born in 1828); Jeremiah Day (1773–1867), mathematician and commentator on Edwards; Theodore Dwight Woolsey (1801–1889), classical scholar and authority on international law, under whose presidency was trained a generation

---

22 In nine volumes, New York, 1857–1869. For the section entitled "The Orators and the Divines," the following works, among others, have also been consulted: "American Eloquence, a Collection of Speeches and Addresses by the Most Eminent Orators of America," etc., by Frank Moore, two volumes, New York, 1895 (published 1857); "American Orations," etc., edited by Alexander Johnston, re-edited by J. A. Woodburn, four volumes, 1896–1897; "The Clergy in American Life and Letters," by D. D. Addison, 1900; "A Manual of American Literature," by John S. Hart, 1878.

of organisers to guide the affairs of newer universities; and Noah Porter (1811–1892), whose treatise on "The Human Intellect" became a general text-book. At Union College was Eliphalet Nott (1773–1866), who, during an administration of sixty-two years, manifested consummate wisdom in the management of students. On the death of Hamilton at the hands of Aaron Burr, Nott eloquently attacked the barbarous practice of duelling. In his "Lectures on Temperance" (1823), he assisted the vigorous movement of Lyman Beecher and others against "even the common use of ardent spirits." At Harvard was the versatile Edward Everett (1794–1865), to mention none of his predecessors. At Brown was Francis Wayland (1796–1865), the metaphysician; at Williams, Mark Hopkins, in his teaching a veritable Gamaliel. Aside from presidents, the peaceful army of college instructors chosen from the ministry is beyond reckoning—men like Frederick Henry Hedge (1805–1890), a Unitarian, professor of the German language and literature at Harvard, author of "Ways of the Spirit, and Other Essays," "Prose Writers of Germany," "Atheism in Philosophy," etc.; or Edwards Amasa Park (1808–1900), descended, as his first name suggests, from a celebrated stock. Park was professor of philosophy at Amherst College, and afterward professor at Andover Theological Seminary. He was a hymnologist as well as a theologian, a biographer, as in his "Life of Nathanael Emmons," and a contributor to the *Bibliotheca Sacra*. He had an individual, curiously periphrastic, way of putting things.

Divines as Special Students.—Although the large denominations of the Methodists and Baptists have not insisted on the possession of learning by their ministers, in their own province of scholarship American clergymen, while rarely independent of foreign, especially German investigators, have undertaken many researches of much value. Edward Robinson (1794–1863), a professor at Andover and then at Union Seminary, made a harmony of the Gospels in Greek, and another in English, compiled a lexicon to the New Testament, and wrote on the topography of the Holy Land. In this he assisted the sagacious missionary, Eli Smith (1801–1857), whose long residence in the Orient gave him peculiar advantages as a Biblical geographer. Similar advantages were enjoyed by William McClune Thomson (1806–1894), and bore good fruit in "The Land and the Book" (illustrations of the Bible from customs and scenery in the East) and "The Land of Promise, or Travels in Modern Palestine." Nor should the translation of the Scriptures into Burmese by that great apostle, Adoniram Judson (1788–1850), go unmentioned. At home, George Rapall Noyes (1798–1868), professor of Hebrew at Harvard Divinity School, translated the New Testament into English. Leonard Bacon (1802–1881), pastor of the Centre Church in New Haven, takes rank with the ecclesiastical historians for his "Genesis of the New England Churches." Thomas Jefferson Conant (1802–1891), of the same generation, a Baptist, was a Hebrew scholar of repute, in the main devoting himself to studies on the Old Testament, and editing critical texts of the Book of Job, of Proverbs, of Genesis, and of the Psalms. Thomas F. Curtis (1815–1872), President of Lewisburg University, Pennsylvania, compiled a history of the Baptist Church, publishing it in the year, 1857, when Sprague began to issue his monumental "Annals of the American Pulpit," already referred to. Still another Baptist, Horatio Balch Hackett (1808–1875), for thirty-one years professor at Newton Seminary, and for five at Rochester, made himself an authority on Christian antiquities. Henry Boynton Smith (1815–1877) from 1854 to 1874 taught the subject of systematic theology at Union Seminary; he is important among the church historians—not so important, of course, as the indefatigable Philip Schaff (1819–1893). Born in Switzerland, educated in Germany, and recommended by the most distinguished German theologians, Schaff in 1844 accepted a call from this country to the Seminary at Mercersburg, Pennsylvania; here he quickly established his reputation as an encyclopedist of religious knowledge. His greatest work was an edition, thoroughly revised, of Lange's "Commentary on the Bible." Professor William Greenough Thayer Shedd (1820–1894), who taught English literature in the University of Vermont, from there migrated to the chair of Biblical literature in Union Seminary (1863–1890). Besides a "History of Christian Doctrine," and other theological works, he published an edition, which has not yet been improved upon, of the works of Coleridge. William Henry Green (1825–1900), of the Theological Seminary at Princeton, an Orientalist, was a frequent writer for *The Princeton Review*. Crawford Howell Toy (born in 1836), since 1890 professor of Hebrew and related languages in the Harvard Divinity School, is the author of meritorious published researches, including a work on "The Religion of Israel" (1892) and a commentary on the Book of Proverbs. If Charles Augustus Briggs (born in 1841) had preserved all the objectivity of a scientific historian, and not turned controversialist, he probably would not have been subjected to trial by the Presbyterians on the charge of heresy. To his studies in Biblical history and the growth of dogma has often been attached the badly chosen term, "Higher Criticism," that misnomer for the historical interpretation of the Scriptures. A severe loss to American scholarship has recently come through the death of Alexander Viets Griswold Allen (1841–1908), biographer of Jonathan Edwards and Phillips Brooks, and author of "The Continuity of Christian Thought" (1884) and "Christian Institutions" (1897). In him the scholar became the constructive artist.

Writers of Hymns.—Between the publication of "The Bay Psalm Book" (1640) and the revision of Watts' version of the Psalms by Joel Barlow and by the elder Dwight at the end of the eighteenth century, sacred poetry in America underwent much refinement. From Dwight and his generation down, the writers of hymns have been many and able. Henry Ustick Onderdonk (1789–1858), William Augustus Muhlenberg (1796–1877), George Washington Doane (1799–1859), Protestant Episcopal Bishop of New Jersey at the age of thirty-three, Leonard Bacon (1802–1881), George W. Bethune (1805–1862), Samuel Francis Smith (1808–1895), George Duffield (1818–1888), Samuel Longfellow (1819–1892), above all, Ray Palmer (1808–1887), are a few of the most eminent.

Miscellaneous Preachers.—*Samuel Hopkins.*—A disciple of Jonathan Edwards, the institutor of the Hopkinsian form of divinity (1721–1803) sought, according to Hildreth, "to add to the five points of Calvinism the rather heterogeneous ingredient that holiness consists in pure, disinterested benevolence, and that all regard for self is necessarily sinful." He inculcated the doctrine of the free agency of sinners. A forerunner of the Garrisons, Whittiers, and Sumners, he was an early and persistent foe of negro slavery.

Nathanael Emmons.—A typical predecessor of the nineteenth century, whose great age brought him far into it, was Nathanael Emmons (1745–1840), of Connecticut, and of Wrentham, Massachusetts. He wished to be "a consistent Calvinist," yet to harmonise a difficult creed with the truths of common experience. He was an excellent reasoner on the evidences of moral government, establishing unexpected chains of inference, and from gladly accepted premises leading his hearers to less pleasant but unavoidable conclusions. "He was skilled," says Park, "in disentangling a theory from its adscititious matter, and scanning it alone." "He made but few gestures; his voice was not powerful; but men listened to him with intense curiosity, and often with awe." Emmons had his own conception of eloquence: "I read deep, well-written tragedies for the sake of real improvement in the art of preaching. They appeared to me the very best books to teach true eloquence." Again: "Style is only the frame to hold our thoughts. It is like the sash of a window: a heavy sash will obscure the light." And once more: "First, have something to say; second, say it." His writings—essays, sermons at ordinations, sermons at installations, funeral sermons, thanksgiving sermons, "A Sermon on Sacred Music" (1806)—are numberless.

Henry Ernst Muhlenberg.—Of a different but well-known type was the son (1753–1815) of the German-American Henry Melchior Muhlenberg (1742–1787). Henry Ernst was sent abroad while a boy, studied at Halle, returned, became a pastor among the Germans of Pennsylvania, and finally died at Lancaster in that State. He was endowed with an exceptional physique, walking with ease from Lancaster to Philadelphia, a distance of sixty miles. Discursive in his studies—he was an Oriental scholar and a botanist—he was tolerant in his belief, clinging to the fundamental truths of Christianity. In his discourses, he took the familiar attitude of a parent addressing his children.

Alexander Campbell.—The founder (1788–1866) of the sect known to the rest of the world as the Campbellites, a man of prodigious energy, was without question one of the remarkable spirits of his time. His writings, over fifty volumes, represent but a moiety of his labours: he built printing-presses in the interests of his movement for religious reform; he debated in public with all comers—for example, in 1829 with the infidel, Robert Owen. Self-possessed on the platform, he indulged in little action, and he spared his voice. But his distinct and beautiful enunciation expected and received attention, his audience listening, as to a master, in perfect silence.

William Ellery Channing.—Although "he lacks critical acumen," "lacks also the sentiment of great originality," "lacks that which America has so far lacked—high intellectual culture, critical knowledge," "does not know the general result of what is known to his age," still Channing

(1780–1842), in the words of Renan, "has been unquestionably the most complete representative of that exclusively American experiment—of religion without mystery, of rationalism without criticism, of intellectual culture without elevated poetry—which seems to be the ideal to which the religion of the United States aspires." An exemplary student at school and college (Harvard), Channing went to the South as a private tutor. His path being deflected into the ministry, he returned to New England, and was installed (1803) in the Federal Street Church at Boston. In this church he was active for twenty years, and he was at least the nominal head of it for forty. His health was delicate, and his capacity for continued exertion limited. Channing's religion might be described as a form of ethics, allied to the political doctrines of Rousseau, too simple and theoretical for common life, and in the main salutary so far as it was a generous reaction against the harsher tenets of Calvin. The severity of Calvinism, that "vulgar and frightful theology," in his eyes inevitably led to gloomy superstition. "God is good," he kept repeating, and human nature in its origin also good. "He ... fell in with those who consider the human race to be actually degenerated by the abuse of free will. In Jesus Christ he recognised a sublime being, who had wrought a crisis in the condition of humanity, had renewed the moral sense, and touched with saving power the fountains of good that were hidden in the depths of the human heart." Channing wrote no books; his literary remains consist of essays, sermons, and addresses. His "Discourse on the Fall of Bonaparte" (1814), his lecture on "Self-Culture," and his "Address on West India Emancipation" (1842) display various aspects of a beautiful and courageous personality.

Horace Bushnell.—"I have never been a great agitator, never pulled a wire to get the will of men, never did a politic thing," said Bushnell (1802–1876). He graduated at Yale in 1827; from 1833 until 1859, when he retired on account of ill-health, he had charge of the North Church in Hartford, Connecticut. Thereafter he devoted his time to the preparation of special sermons and addresses and to researches in American history and the history of his own State. He took a vital interest in political questions. Bushnell was a clear and independent thinker, without bias, not given to controversy, none the less eloquent and persuasive. His sermons were collected and widely circulated. The problems of religious experience, of suffering and evil, and of education he attempted to solve in "Nature and the Supernatural," "The Vicarious Sacrifice," and "Christian Nurture." In the last-named work he objected to the doctrine of natural depravity, contending for a gradual development in the child of the religious sentiment and the higher imagination, as against a sudden and crucial "conversion." Among Congregationalists the supposed latitude of his theological opinions involved him in the charge of a leaning toward Unitarianism.

Theodore Parker.—In his day, Theodore Parker (1810–1860) was considered the most daring of rationalists, and so "advanced," as we now call it, in his beliefs or disbeliefs as to be outside the pale of Christianity. Present-day rationalists find him a congenial spirit. He was a man of undoubted genius, caustic, flashing, vehement, incessant in labour, dying early from sheer exhaustion. His collected works in fourteen volumes (edited by Cobbe) reveal the nature of his industry. He was unweariedly accurate in detail, being determined to leave no pebble unturned in his search for truth. His sermon on "The Transient and the Permanent in Christianity" (1841) and "A Discourse of Matters Pertaining to Religion" (1842) gave evidence of his departure from the accepted form of Unitarianism. In 1845 he openly broke away, regarding the Church as an unnecessary organisation. In general, his criticism was destructive, and his attention to detail not balanced by powers of synthesis. His own convictions like iron and brooking no denial, he disregarded the tenderest feelings of other men, and in a mistaken sense of duty would trample underfoot those things which his neighbour might hold most sacred. His intellect flourished at the expense of his imagination, and his want of perspective resolves itself into a defect of taste, all the more injurious through the violence of his affections. This man, most cordially hated and feared by those whom he opposed, most ardently loved by his friends, would shed tears like a child when he met with a trivial act of kindness.

The Beechers.—Lyman Beecher (1775–1863) represents the other extreme, of traditional orthodoxy, and the reaction against the trend of Unitarianism. He was a stern and virile personality, rigorous in habit, and in his expectation of righteousness in others, withal friendly and benign. His son, Henry Ward Beecher (1813–1887), according to the testimony of the daughter and sister, Harriet Beecher Stowe, as a child was deficient in verbal memory—a thing which he never outgrew,—diffident, sensitive, thick and indistinct in his speech. In the midst of a talented family that was much given to theological argument, his powers were gradually developed. At Laurenceburg, Ohio, his first charge, he was sexton as well as preacher. He came before the public through his defence of the negro in *The Cincinnati Journal.* At Indianapolis his reputation grew, for his independent spirit and direct, informal style proved very attractive; and when he had been called to Plymouth Church in Brooklyn, the people crowded over from New York to hear him. Beecher studied every-day life in the streets and shops of the metropolis; his discourses on popular topics, good government and the like, unconventionally treated, gave his audiences what they liked. His sympathies were non-sectarian, he had his finger on the pulse of every gathering, his well of common sense was overflowing, and he was fearless to the point of audacity, carrying the art of the mimic into the very pulpit. His preaching, in fact, sometimes bordered upon dangerous self-assertion. He rose to eminence, as Bacon might say, by a combination of good with questionable arts. But the mixture was mainly good. In Beecher's discussion of slavery, Calhoun, who was not easily deceived, saw that the preacher knew how to get to the bottom of his subject. His good-humour, and pluck, and immense patriotism before hostile crowds in England (1863) greatly helped to deter that nation from recognising the Southern Confederacy.

Theorists on Pulpit Eloquence.—Beecher's "Yale Lectures on Preaching" disclose how large an element there was in his oratory of conscious adaptation of means to ends. They belong to an extensive and interesting branch of American literature, to which Phillips Brooks, J. A. Broadus, E. G. Robinson, R. S. Storrs, J. W. Alexander, and many others have made contributions. James Waddell Alexander (1804–1859), son of Archibald Alexander of Princeton Seminary, left his "Thoughts on Preaching" to be published in 1864. "The Preparation and Delivery of Sermons," by John Albert Broadus (1827–1895), President of the Southern Baptist Theological Seminary, represents the theory of a trainer of preachers, himself a winning orator with a consciously developed instinct: "Everybody who can speak effectively knows that the power of speaking depends very largely upon the way it is heard, upon the sympathy one succeeds in gaining from those he addresses." To insure sympathy—his watchword,—Broadus preached without manuscript. In general, as here, his syntax is not finely moulded. With these might be mentioned another clergyman, Chauncey Allen Goodrich (1790–1860), for forty-three years professor at Yale, whose "Select British Eloquence" set a standard of illuminating scholarship.

Richard Salter Storrs.—Dr. Storrs (1821–1900), descended from a line of clergymen, was from 1846 on in high repute as a preacher in the Church of the Pilgrims, Brooklyn. He was also in demand as a lecturer, and contributed freely to the *Bibliotheca Sacra* and other periodicals. His "Conditions of Success in Preaching without Notes" partly tells the secret of his own eminence; his rich voice, distinct utterance, and stately bearing further explain it. In youth a student of the law, he caught something of his eloquence from Rufus Choate. But the moral elevation of character in Storrs was the ultimate support of all his art.

T. De Witt Talmage.—In Brooklyn, where he preached from 1869 to 1894, Thomas De Witt Talmage (1832–1902) had a "Tabernacle," as it was called, to which everyone was welcome, and which commonly was filled by an audience of four thousand. In 1894 he removed to New York. For twenty-nine years the sermons of Talmage were published every week, latterly in countless journals; they have had an immense circulation, not alone in his own country, being translated into many foreign, even Asiatic languages. It is possible that no other preacher in the world has during life enjoyed so extensive and regular a following. His physical activity was unbounded; his utterance clear, though his voice was not pleasing, and his message simple, violent, and undiscriminatingly conservative. In espousing what he took to be orthodox, he was hasty and inaccurate; he was utterly careless, too, what means he used to work upon his hearers. To the cultured his writings have little worth. His value to the state and the great world is not so easily decided.

Phillips Brooks.—Phillips Brooks (1835–1893), after Henry Ward Beecher the greatest pulpit orator in America since the Civil War, was a native of Boston, nurtured in the best traditions of New England. A brilliant and popular undergraduate at Harvard, he strangely enough failed in his subsequent brief experience in teaching. He then studied for the ministry, at the Episcopal Seminary in Alexandria, Virginia. As a young rector in Philadelphia, he showed his power and fearlessness in his patriotic sermons during the Rebellion. "In their relation to the politics of the land," he contended, "the great vice of our people ... is cowardice." He himself dared openly to lay the crime of Lincoln's martyrdom, not alone upon the assassin, but upon the supporters of slavery in the South. From Philadelphia, he went to Trinity Church, Boston, in 1869. Two years prior to his death he was made Bishop of Massachusetts. "The Yale Lectures on Preaching," delivered in 1877, "constitute," says Allen, his best interpreter, "the autobiography of Phillips Brooks.... It is a book which owes nothing to predecessors in the same field.... He confines himself to preaching as he had experienced its workings, or studied its method, or observed its power.... The book captivates the reader, simply for this reason alone,—the transparency of the soul of its writer, between whom and the reader there intervenes no barrier." This was the quality also of his sermons.

> He stands in the pulpit [reported an observer] smooth-faced, full-voiced, as self-reliant a man as ever occupied such a station. He indulges in few gestures; he has no mannerisms. If, under any circumstances, he might realise the popular conception of an orator, he does not betray the possibilities here. He provokes no attention to predominant spirituality by inferior vitality. There is a splendid harmony of strength, bodily and mental, which prevents the measurement of either. It is only when he is out of his desk and level with his audience that you realise his stature. In the lecture-room or crowded street, he stands like Saul among the people. The well-balanced head and strong shoulders draw your eyes at once. He dresses well, lives well, and holds his own decidedly in social circles.... His power is not limited to his church ministrations, nor is he making himself known by some brilliant special development. It is the whole man—mentally, morally, and spiritually, leader, helper, friend—which is attaining such pre-eminence. But when he preaches, you are carried away to the need of men and of your own shortcomings, and have no present consciousness of the personality of the speaker. A transparent medium is the purest. You do not think of Phillips Brooks till Phillips Brooks gets through with his subject.

Brooks was a wide reader and a careful and original student of church history and theological discussion; he was not the profound and searching scholar that Renan vainly sought in America. He had a roomy mind, a teeming imagination, and a heart full of generosity, energy, and optimism. He lived by admiration, hope, and love. His ideas, which were large and luminous, although they did not have the final tempering that comes from passage through the slow fire of a rigorous critical method, became vital from sharing in his warmth and purity of sentiment.

> In regard to his intellectual habits and methods [remarks Allen] one thing is clear, that Phillips Brooks worked through the poetic imagination rather than by the process of dialectics, although he could show great dialectic subtlety when occasion demanded. When we conjoin this power of the poetic imagination and his other gifts, the "unparalleled combination of intensity of feeling with comprehensiveness of view and balance of judgment," we can understand how he could quickly penetrate to the heart of intellectual systems, how a hint to his mind was like a volume to others, and he preferred to work out the hint in his own way.

VI. THE SCIENTISTS

General Remarks.—The beginnings of science in America date from colonial days and have been touched upon by Professor Tyler. The interest of Americans in science has never abated. Readers of standard scientific literature are numerous. *The Scientific American*, founded in 1845, *The Popular Science Monthly*, founded in 1872, *Science*, dating from 1883, and several other journals of science are read by many non-professional persons. The various sciences have, in the last quarter-century at least, won a place of prominence in our college curricula. The number of disinterested scientific observers and investigators has always been large. The largest scientific organisation in the United States, the American Association for the Advancement of Science, which developed from the old Association of American Geologists and Naturalists in 1847, now has a membership of over five thousand; and in addition to this and other general scientific bodies there is for workers in nearly every individual science a national organisation, meeting regularly and publishing the results of investigations. In almost every science America has produced scholars of note; in some she has furnished leaders of the world.

This is not, of course, the place, even if the writer were competent to furnish it, for a narrative of American scientific achievement. We can only touch upon a few of the greater names in mental and moral, political and legal, ethnological and linguistic, and natural and physical science.

Mental and Moral Science.—It cannot be said that America has taken a place of pre-eminence in the philosophical thought of the nineteenth century. English, French, and German savants still lead in this realm of thought. Yet American philosophy has made enormous strides in the last half-century and many of its exponents have won universal recognition. Porter and McCosh have expounded the views of the Scottish School; German thought has been elucidated and criticised by Harris, Bowne, and Royce; the writings of Draper, Fiske, and Schurman on the evolutionary theories of Darwin and Spencer are well known. The psychologists Ladd, Stanley Hall, Baldwin, Titchener, and James have international reputations. In the number and equipment of her psychological laboratories America leads the world. The number of periodicals devoted to psychology, ethics, and cognate sciences is considerable. Philosophical studies enjoy great favour at our universities, both as electives and as required subjects. Some of the men briefly considered below are perhaps more famous as teachers than as writers; yet all have left their mark on the philosophical thought of their day.

Francis Wayland.—Francis Wayland (1796–1865), a Baptist clergyman and for twenty-eight years (1827–1855) president of Brown University, wrote several well-known works on moral and political science. After graduating from Union College in 1813, he studied medicine and began practice at Troy, New York; but from 1816 on devoted himself to the ministry. His "Elements of Moral Science" (1835), his greatest work, was long a standard text-book. "The Elements of Political Economy" appeared in 1837; "Limitations of Human Reason," in 1840; "Thoughts on the Present Collegiate System of the United States," in 1842; and "Elements of Intellectual Philosophy," in 1854. Wayland is most important as a teacher of morals. For him education and religion went hand in hand.

Although he was not a thinker of the highest order, his treatises were lucid, exact, and attractive. He was one of the great educational and religious leaders of his day.

Mark Hopkins.—Another great educator was Mark Hopkins (1802–1887), whose birthplace was Stockbridge, Massachusetts, and who graduated from Williams College in 1824. Like Wayland, he first practised medicine, then became a minister and teacher of moral philosophy. He was professor of moral philosophy at Williams for fifty-seven years, and president from 1836 till 1872. He wrote "The Influence of the Gospel in Liberalising the Mind" (1831), "The Connexion between Taste and Morals" (1841), "The Evidences of Christianity" (Lowell Institute lectures, 1844), "Miscellaneous Essays and Reviews" (1847), "Moral Science" (also Lowell lectures, 1862), "The Law of Love and Love as a Law" (1869), "An Outline Study of Man" (1873), "Strength and Beauty" (1874), and "The Scriptural Idea of Man" (1883). Few men in America have been more potent as intellectual and moral forces than was Mark Hopkins. President Garfield used to say that a student on one end of a log and Mark Hopkins on the other would make a university anywhere. Great as an original thinker and expounder, he was greater as a teacher; "he built himself into the mental fabric of two generations of men."

Laurens P. Hickok.—Laurens P. Hickok (1798–1888), a Congregational clergyman, and professor successively in Western Reserve College, Auburn Theological Seminary, and Union College (of which he was virtually president 1860–1868), wrote a number of philosophical and theological works, among which are "Rational Psychology" (1848), "Moral Science" (1853), "Mental Science" (1854), "Rational Cosmology" (1858), "Humanity Immortal" (1872), "Creator and Creation" (1872), and "The Logic of Reason" (1875). He also contributed to theological and philosophical reviews.

Francis Bowen.—A conservative resolutely opposed to the teachings of Fichte, Kant, and Mill on the one hand and of Darwin on the other, Francis Bowen (1811–1890) is remembered as a strong and clear writer and an enthusiastic teacher. Nine years after his graduation from Harvard (in 1833), we find him editing Virgil and publishing "Critical Essays on Speculative Philosophy." He edited *The North American Review* from

1843 till 1854, then became Alford professor of natural religion, moral philosophy, and civil polity in Harvard College. Of his voluminous writings we can mention only a few: "Lectures on the Application of Metaphysical and Ethical Science to the Evidences of Religion" (1849), "Lectures on Political Economy" (1850), "The Principles of Political Economy" (1856), an edition of "The Metaphysics of Sir William Hamilton" (1862), "Modern Philosophy from Descartes to Schopenhauer and Hartmann" (1877), and "A Layman's Study of the English Bible" (1885).

Noah Porter.—Professor of moral philosophy and metaphysics at Yale College for forty-six years, and president of Yale University for fifteen years, Noah Porter (1811–1892) made a strong impression in both the philosophical, and the educational world. He was the son of the Rev. Noah Porter, for fifty years minister of the Congregational Church in Farmington, Connecticut, and graduated at Yale in 1831. He was a minister at New Milford, Connecticut, and Springfield, Massachusetts, for ten years; then he assumed his chair at Yale. His chief work, "The Human Intellect" (1868), ably champions the theistic view of the universe, and has had wide use as a text-book, as has also his "Elements of Intellectual Science" (1871). He wrote also "The Elements of Moral Science" (1885) and "A Critical Exposition of Kant's Ethics" (1886); besides several books on education, of which we may mention "American Colleges and the American Public" (1870) and "Books and Reading" (1870). He also edited the revised editions (1864, 1890) of Webster's Dictionary.

James McCosh.—The Scottish philosophy was vigorously championed in America by President James McCosh (1811–1894). Born in Ayrshire, Scotland, of a sturdy middle-class family, he was educated at Glasgow and Edinburgh. His graduation essay on the Stoic philosophy won him the honorary degree of A.M. Becoming a minister of the Established Kirk, he seceded with Chalmers and rendered valuable service to the Free Church. His "Method of the Divine Government, Physical and Moral" (1850) laid the foundation of his fame as a philosophical writer, and doubtless led to his appointment in 1852 to the professorship of logic and metaphysics in Queen's College, Belfast. From Belfast, after an active literary and educational career, he was called to the presidency of Princeton College, and thenceforward was a distinguished figure in the American intellectual world. His numerous writings after 1868 include

"The Scottish Philosophy, Biographical, Expository, Critical" (1874), "The Emotions" (1880), "Philosophical Series" (1882–1885, eight volumes), "Psychology of the Cognitive Powers" (1886), "Realistic Philosophy Defended" (1887), "The Religious Aspect of Evolution" (1887), and "First and Fundamental Truths" (1894). Dr. McCosh was one of the first to point out the theological bearing of Darwinism and to announce his acceptance of it when properly understood. "Touching the thought of his time," says Professor Sloane, "at its salient points and with tremendous vitality, he constantly insisted on the few central truths of his system in their application to each new question as it arose. Incisive, intense, and real, or rather concrete in his thinking, he felt a loyalty to truth which he sought to instil with all his might into the minds of others."

William Torrey Harris.—William T. Harris (born in 1835) left Yale in 1857 to become a teacher in St. Louis, where he was superintendent of schools from 1867 till 1888. From 1889 till 1906 he was United States Commissioner of Education. Although leading a busy life as a teacher, he found time for philosophical work. He founded (1867) and has since edited *The Journal of Speculative Philosophy*, the first philosophical periodical in English. His "Hegel's Logic" (1890), while highly technical, is one of the clearest and most scholarly expositions of Hegelian thought. He has written also "An Introduction to the Study of Philosophy" (1889), "Psychologic Foundations of Education" (1898), and many smaller educational and philosophical studies.

John Fiske.—One of the greatest of modern expositors of science was John Fiske (1842–1901). He was born at Middletown, Connecticut, and entered Harvard as a sophomore in 1860, graduating in 1863. The works of Spencer and Darwin opened a new world to his vigorous imagination and he devoted many years to elucidating and applying their doctrines, in "Myths and Myth Makers" (1872), "Outlines of Cosmic Philosophy" (1874), "The Unseen World" (1876), "Darwinism, and Other Essays" (1879), "Excursions of an Evolutionist" (1883), "The Destiny of Man Viewed in the Light of His Origin" (1884), and "The Idea of God as Affected by Modern Knowledge" (1885). His later years were devoted to studies in American history, the events of which he interpreted as the result of evolutionary processes. His work reveals a uniform optimism.

Some Living Writers.—Among living writers on philosophical themes space will permit the mention of only two or three. The son of Henry James, the theologian, and the brother of Henry James, Jr., the novelist, William James (born in 1842) was educated privately and at Harvard, from which he received the degree of M.D. in 1870. Two years later he became an instructor and in 1881 a full professor, the subjects of his later interest being psychology and philosophy. He has written, among a large number of books and articles, "Principles of Psychology" (1890), "The Will to Believe, and Other Essays in Popular Philosophy" (1897), "Human Immortality" (the Ingersoll Lecture, 1898), "The Varieties of Religious Experience" (Gifford Lectures at Edinburgh University, 1902), and "Pragmatism" (1907). Especially noteworthy is his work in analytical psychology. Always clear and fresh in style, his writings have exerted a marked influence on thought both in Europe and in America.

Borden Parker Bowne (born in 1847), who, after graduating at New York University in 1871, studied at Halle, Göttingen, and Paris, in 1876 became professor of philosophy at Boston University. He has written "The Philosophy of Herbert Spencer" (1874), "Studies in Theism" (1879), "Metaphysics" (1882), "Introduction to Psychological Theory" (1886), and "Principles of Ethics" (1892).

Jacob Gould Schurman (born in 1854) has made some worthy contributions to the literature of ethics; it is a matter of regret that administrative work has of late kept him from writing more for the general public. He was born at Freetown, Prince Edward Island, and studied at Acadia College. In 1875 he won the Gilchrist Dominion Scholarship in the University of London, from which he graduated in 1877. He later studied at Edinburgh, Heidelberg, Berlin, and Göttingen, and in Italy. From 1886 till 1892 he was professor of philosophy in Cornell University, of which he became president in 1892. He has written lucid studies of "Kantian Ethics and the Ethics of Evolution" (1881), "The Ethical Import of Darwinism" (1888), "Belief in God" (1890), and "Agnosticism and Religion" (1896).

Josiah Royce (born in 1855), a Californian who studied at the University of California, Leipsic, Göttingen, and Johns Hopkins, has done much to interpret and popularise the thought of Hegel, and has made valuable original contributions to contemporary idealistic thought. His philosophical works include "The Religious Aspect of Philosophy" (1885), "The Spirit of Modern Philosophy" (1892), "The Conception of God" (1895), "Studies of Good and Evil" (1898), "The Conception of Immortality" (1900, an Ingersoll Lecture), and "The World and the Individual" (1900–1901). A close thinker, he writes in a remarkably fresh, vigorous, and informal style.

Political and Legal Science.—In the fields of political, economic, social, and legal science the most that can be claimed for American writers is that a fair number of them have achieved genuine distinction and enjoy international reputations. America is still too young to be expected to have produced independent schools of thought in these lines. What Dr. Sherwood says of the economists may have a larger application here:

> The chief reason for our failure to make large contributions to economic science [he remarks in his "Tendencies in American Economic Thought"] is the same reason which explains the meagreness of our contribution to general science, viz., the all-absorbing problem of making use of the advantages within our grasp. Within a century we have been compelled to work out several most difficult problems: how to unite in a solid empire many vigorous, large, and discordant nationalities; how to stretch this empire over the adjacent territories, so as to remove dangerous enemies; how to get rid of slavery without disrupting the Union; how to make our general education keep pace with our growth in numbers and with the advance of science; how, with the rapidly shifting forms of industrial organisation, to maintain purity of government and social order; how to govern an empire without an emperor; how to push forward material civilisation without going backwards in intellectual and moral civilisation; how to stimulate invention so as to win wealth for all, with inadequate labour and capital.

These practical problems have kept us from producing men with wealth and leisure for working out solutions of the large abstract questions raised in these sciences. Nor have our writers yet succeeded in handling large masses of facts with the skill of some foreign writers. The best comprehensive work on American institutions remains Bryce's "American Commonwealth," the work of an Englishman. Yet in Marshall, Kent, and Story we have produced some great jurists; in Wheaton, Lawrence, and Woolsey some great writers on legal science; in Carey, Wells, Walker, and George writers of commanding importance in the sphere of political economy.

John Marshall.—Pre-eminent among the jurists of America is John Marshall (1755–1835), for thirty-four years Chief-Justice of the United States Supreme Court. Marshall served as an officer in the Revolution; in 1780, being without a command, he attended Chancellor Wyeth's lectures on law at William and Mary College. Entering upon the practice of law, he quickly became known for his acumen. His accession to the Supreme Court bench (1801) marks an epoch in our legal and constitutional history. He had, as it were, to blaze a trail. The Constitution had been adopted; it had yet to be construed. A thousand questions arose as to what it meant, what it included, what it was meant not to include. Marshall's decisions, recorded in thirty-two volumes of reports, reveal the impartial workings of a master legal mind. Such men do not often appear; it was fortunate that the American Government in its early years was guided by Marshall's constitutional constructions. They virtually form a system of law, a system which has not since been seriously modified. "The judge who rears such a monument to his memory," says Mr. Magruder, his biographer, "will never be forgotten; in the united domain of English and American jurisprudence there are not half a dozen such memorials; but not the least distinguished is that of Marshall."

James Kent.—It has been said of Kent's "Commentaries upon American Law" (1826–1830) that they had a deeper and more lasting influence upon the American character than any other secular book of the nineteenth century. James Kent (1763–1847) graduated from Yale in 1781 and then practised law, first at Poughkeepsie, and after 1793 in New York City. In the same year he became professor of law in Columbia College. The Federalist leaders rapidly advanced him; he was made Chief-Justice of the New York Supreme Court in 1804 and Chancellor in 1814. Retiring in 1823, he resumed his teaching at Columbia, and later published many of his lectures in the "Commentaries." His Chancery decisions, to be found in Caines' and Johnson's reports, were of fundamental importance and form the basis of American equity jurisprudence.

Joseph Story.—With Chancellor Kent, Joseph Story (1779–1845) shares the glory of having laid the foundations of American equity jurisprudence. Story graduated from Harvard in 1798 and was admitted to the bar in 1801. Becoming a leader of what was later the Democratic party, in 1808 he entered Congress and in 1811 was appointed an Associate Justice of the United States Supreme Court. From 1829 on he was also a professor of law at Harvard. For some time after Marshall's death he was acting Chief-Justice. Many of his opinions in patent and admiralty law are still authoritative. Some of his writings are "Commentaries on the Constitution of the United States" (1833), "The Conflict of Laws" (1834), "Commentaries on Equity Jurisprudence" (1835–1836), and treatises on agency, partnership, bills, and notes.

Henry Wheaton.—Less known than Story, yet in his day a prominent figure in the legal world, was Henry Wheaton (1785–1848), of Providence, Rhode Island, a graduate of Brown University in the class of 1802. He was a lawyer, an editor, and a diplomatist (from 1837 till 1846 Minister Plenipotentiary to Prussia). His "Elements of International Law" (1836, republished in several editions, and translated into French, Chinese, and Japanese) remains one of the leading authorities. Another important work was his "Histoire du progrès des gens en Europe depuis le paix de Westphalie jusqu'au Congrès de Vienne" (1841, English translation 1846). He was widely respected for sound learning and diplomatic ability.

Francis Lieber.—Francis Lieber (1800–1872), a native of Berlin and a Ph.D. of the University of Jena (1820), came to America virtually a political exile, and, though an ardent worshipper of freedom, was at first, as Dr. Harley remarks, obliged to make his home in the very heart of the slave power. For twenty-one years he was professor of history and political economy in South Carolina College, being "the first great teacher in this country of history and politics as co-ordinated subjects." From 1856 till 1860 he held the chair of political economy in Columbia College; and from 1860 till his death he was professor of political science in the Columbia Law School. The great works on which his fame rests are his

"Political Ethics" (1838), "Legal and Political Hermeneutics" (1839), and "Civil Liberty and Self-Government" (1853). In writing these books he was a pioneer, and pointed out some important principles of American liberty. In his later years he gave much attention to international and military law. From his proposals originated the Institut de Droit International, started at Ghent in 1873, "the organ for the legal consciousness of the civilised world."

William Beach Lawrence.—Another writer whose name is linked with Columbia College is William B. Lawrence (1800–1881). Born in New York City, he graduated from Columbia in 1818, was admitted to the bar in 1823, and gave attention chiefly to international law. For a time he lectured at Columbia on political economy, defending free trade. Removing to Rhode Island, he served as acting Governor in 1852. In 1872–1873 he lectured on international law in the Columbian University at Washington. His works are marked by breadth of view and soundness of judgment. They include "The Bank of the United States" (1831), "Institutions of the United States" (1832), "Discourses on Political Economy" (1834), "The Law of Charitable Uses" (1845), "Commentaire sur les éléments du droit international" (1868–1880), and "The Treaty of Washington" (1871).

Theodore Dwight Woolsey.—Theodore D. Woolsey (1801–1889) had a varied preparation for his notable career. Graduating at Yale in 1820, he studied law in Philadelphia, theology at Princeton, and Greek at Leipsic, Bonn, and Berlin. From 1831 till 1846 he was professor of Greek at Yale. Becoming president of Yale in 1846, he thenceforward confined his teaching to history, political science, and international law, and became eminent as a writer on subjects in these fields. Among his works are "An Introduction to the Study of International Law" (1860), "Essays on Divorce and Divorce Legislation" (1869), "Political Science" (two volumes, 1877), and "Communism and Socialism, in Their History and Theory" (1880).

Henry Wager Halleck.—Chiefly known as a soldier, and as general of the armies of the United States from July, 1862, till March, 1864, Henry W. Halleck (1815–1872) was after all more skilled in the science of war than in its practice in the field. He studied at Union College and West Point, from which he graduated in 1839. Before the Lowell Institute in

1845 he lectured on the science of war; his lectures, published as "Elements of Military Art and Science," were much used later as a training manual. The chief of his other works, "International Law, or Rules Regulating the Intercourse of States in Peace and War" (1861), abridged in 1866 for college use, still ranks among the highest authorities.

Henry Charles Carey.—In his day the foremost champion of governmental protection to private industry was Henry C. Carey (1793–1879). The eldest son of Matthew Carey, the Philadelphia publisher, he devoted his early years to carrying on the bookselling and publishing business, retiring in 1835. His essay on "The Rate of Wages" (1835) was soon expanded into "The Principles of Political Economy" (1837–1840), which found favour abroad and was translated into Swedish and Italian. His other leading works were "The Credit System of France, Great Britain, and the United States" (1838), "The Past, the Present, and the Future" (1848), "Letters on the International Copyright" (1853), "The Principles of Social Science" (1858), and "The Unity of Law" (1873). Carey was originally a free-trader, but early became a supporter of protection on the ground of temporary expediency. Some of his views have been attacked as unwarranted and dogmatically expressed; it must be conceded, however, that he had a strong grasp of facts and that his works are an invaluable contribution to economic and social science.

David Ames Wells.—For many years, it is safe to say, the leading economist in America was David A. Wells (1828–1898). He was descended from Thomas Welles, Governor of Connecticut in 1655–1658, was born at Springfield, Massachusetts, and was graduated from Williams College in 1847 and from the Lawrence Scientific School of Harvard in 1852. For some years he taught physics and chemistry, and was engaged also in writing school text-books on these subjects. An essay ("Our Burden and Strength") on the resources and financial ability of the United States (1864) brought Wells into prominence, while it did much to restore confidence in the Federal Government. President Lincoln summoned Mr. Wells to Washington, and appointed him chairman of the Revenue Commission of 1865–1866. As special commissioner of the revenue (1866–1870) he completed vast reforms in the complex system of revenue which had grown up during the war. Thereafter he was largely engaged in writing and speaking on economic topics. Among his books are "Robinson Crusoe's Money," illustrated by Nast (1876), "Our Merchant Marine: How It Rose, Increased, Became Great, Declined, and Decayed" (1882), "Practical Economics" (1885), "A Study of Mexico" (1887), "The Relation of the Tariff to Wages" (1888), and "Recent Economic Changes" (1898).

Francis Amasa Walker.—Born in Boston, Francis A. Walker (1840–1897) graduated from Amherst at twenty, then served in the Union Army, becoming a brigadier-general. In 1869 he was put at the head of the Bureau of Statistics; he was superintendent of the Ninth and the Tenth Census, and held other prominent positions, including (1873–1881) the professorship of political economy and history at the Sheffield Scientific School of Yale and (1881–1897) the presidency of the Massachusetts Institute of Technology. He was a prolific writer; of his economic works we can mention only "The Indian Question" (1874), "The Wages Question" (1876), "Money" (1878), "Money in its Relations to Trade and Industry" (Lowell Institute lectures, 1879), "Political Economy" (1883), "Land and its Rent" (1883), and "International Bimetallism" (1896). Walker's influence as an economist was felt especially in connection with the theory of wages. "The central idea of his theory," says Dr. Sherwood, "that the amount of wages under free competition tends to equal the product due to the labour, has been generally accepted, although not altogether as the direct result of his writing."

Henry George.—The theories of Henry George (1839–1896) have been widely discussed. They were first put forth in "Our Land and Land Policy" (1871), in which he held that the burden of taxation should be borne by the land and not by industry, and that thus opportunities for progress would be equalised. His most important book was "Progress and Poverty" (1879), which in a few years made George virtually the apostle of a new economic and social creed. Conservative economists have been slow to accept his single-tax theory; it has, however, called attention to the enormous waste and wrong that result from granting public franchises to private corporations without due compensation. His theory of wages, that they arise from a value created by the efficiency of the labourer, has been generally accepted and may be regarded as a real contribution to economic science.

Some Other Writers.—More than a generation of Williams College men sat under the teaching of Arthur Latham Perry (1830–1905), for thirty-eight years professor of history and political economy. Perry published his "Elements of Political Economy" in 1865; some twenty editions have since appeared. His advocacy of free trade in the sixties cost him many friends. He published also a work on "International Commerce" (1866) and smaller treatises on political economy. Elisha Mulford (1833–1885), a graduate of Yale College and an Episcopal clergyman, was the author of two highly powerful and stimulating books: "The Nation" (1870), dealing with the philosophy of the state, and "The Republic of God" (1880), a religious work of similar character. William Graham Sumner (born in 1840) became prominent for his advocacy of free trade and of the gold standard. Graduating at Yale in 1863, he studied at Göttingen and Oxford, then took orders in the Episcopal Church. Since 1872 he has been professor of political and social science at Yale. He has written "A History of American Currency" (1874), "Lectures on the History of Protection in the United States" (1875), "What Social Classes Owe Each Other" (1882), "Collected Essays in Political and Social Science" (1885), "The Financier and Finances of the American Revolution" (1892), and "A History of Banking in the United States" (1896). Another well known political economist is Richard Theodore Ely (born in 1854), a graduate of Columbia College (1876) and of Heidelberg (Ph.D. *summa cum laude*, 1879), who, as director of the School of Economics, Political Science, and History in the University of Wisconsin, has trained more teachers of economic science than any other American living and has exerted marked influence on the thought of his time. He has to his credit a long list of valuable publications; some of them are "French and German Socialism in Modern Times" (1883), "The Labour Movement in America" (1886), "Taxation in American States and Cities" (1888), "Socialism, an Examination of Its Nature, Its Strength, and Its Weakness, with Suggestions for Social Reform" (1894), "The Social Law of Service" (1896), and "Monopolies and Trusts" (1900). The tendency of the Government to regulate economic movements is in harmony with a doctrine of which he has been a bold champion. Another equally high authority on trusts and currency problems is Jeremiah Whipple Jenks (born in 1856), since 1891 professor of political economy at Cornell University. His "The Trust Problem" (1900) and "Trusts and Industrial Combinations" (1900) have circulated widely. President Woodrow Wilson (born in 1856) of Princeton, discussed elsewhere as a historian, must also be mentioned here for his standard work on "The State: Elements of Historical and Practical Politics" (1889), "An Old Master, and Other Political Essays" (1893), and "Mere Literature, and Other Essays," in which large and sound views of government and its functions are set forth in a clear and attractive style.

Ethnological and Linguistic Science.—In the broad field of ethnological research the work of American scholars has been chiefly devoted to the native and primitive races of America. This offers, as has been pointed out by Mr. McGee,[23]"the finest field the world affords," exhibiting nearly every stage of development and nearly every type of mankind; and American contributions to ethnology and anthropology have been correspondingly important. The names of Gallatin, Schoolcraft, Morgan, Powell, Brinton, will be at once recalled; probably the last named is our best known ethnologist. In the science of language our showing is, in point of numbers, somewhat more creditable. The lexicographical work of Webster, Worcester, Whitney, and March, and the grammatical work of Child and Gildersleeve have been recognised and appreciated the world over. In these sciences America's debt to Germany is a heavy one. Most of our greater teachers of language received their professional training in Germany; and while fewer of our students now go to Germany for the doctor's degree, the influence of German scholarship is still strongly felt among us.

Pierre Étienne Duponceau.—Duponceau (1760–1844) was one of the pioneers of American philology. Born in France, he came to America in 1777 as secretary to Baron Steuben, served in the American army as captain till 1781, and afterward practised law in Philadelphia, becoming well known. He wrote treatises on law: "Exposition sommaire de la constitution des États-Unis d'Amérique" (1837); and in linguistics: "English Phonology" (1818), "Mémoire sur le système grammatical des languages de quelques nations indiennes de l'Amérique du Nord" (1838), which was awarded a medal by the French Institute, and "A Dissertation on the Nature and Character of the Chinese System of Writing" (1838).

Albert Gallatin.—The long and illustrious political career of Albert Gallatin (1761–1849) must not detain us here. Most of his literary and ethnological work was done in his later years. In 1836 he published

---

23   *The Atlantic Monthly*, September, 1898, lxxxii. 319.

his "Synopsis of the Indian Tribes within the United States, East of the Rocky Mountains, and in the British and Russian Possessions in North America." In 1845 appeared his "Notes on the Semi-Civilised Nations of Mexico, Yucatan, and Central America." He founded the American Ethnological Society in 1842; and he is rightly known and will be remembered as the father of American ethnology.

Henry Rowe Schoolcraft.—Among the most prominent of early American ethnologists was Henry R. Schoolcraft (1793–1864). His grandfather, James Calcraft, formerly a British soldier under Marlborough, had kept a large school in Albany County, New York, and because of this his name was changed to Schoolcraft. At an early age Henry Schoolcraft became a student of mineralogy, chemistry, natural philosophy, and medicine. In connection with his father's glass-making enterprises in New Hampshire, Vermont, and western New York, he was engaged for some time in building glass-works, and in 1817 began to publish a work on "Vitreology." Conceiving a desire to travel in the Far West, he started in 1818 on a journey down the Ohio and up the Mississippi. A book resulting from this, on the mineralogy of the West, made him well known. Another expedition was described in "Travels in the Central Portions of the Mississippi Valley" (1825). In 1828 he was the leader in founding the Michigan Historical Society and in 1832 he helped found the Algic Society, for the reclamation and study of the Indians. A narrative of his work and experiences was embodied in "Personal Memoirs of a Residence of Thirty Years with the Indian Tribes on the American Frontiers, 1812 to 1842," a work full of the flavour of the primitive West. Other works were "Algic Researches" (1839), a collection of Indian allegories and legends; "Oneota, or The Characteristics of the Red Race in America" (1844–1845); "The Red Race of America" (1847); and "American Indians, their History, Condition, and Prospects" (1850), an immense work covering a wide range of subjects. His books did much to promote knowledge of Indian life and thought.

Charles Pickering.—Another well-known ethnologist, Charles Pickering (1805–1878), born in Susquehanna County, Pennsylvania, graduated at Harvard College in 1823 and took his degree in medicine in 1826. He accompanied Commodore Wilkes in the *Vincennes* on its exploring voyage around the world in 1838–1842 and later visited India and Eastern

Africa. His great work was "The Races of Man and their Geographical Distribution" (1848); later works of importance were "The Geographical Distribution of Animals and Man" (1854) and "The Geographical Distribution of Plants" (1861).

Lewis Henry Morgan.—Lewis H. Morgan (1818–1881), born at Aurora on Cayuga Lake, New York, and graduated from Union College in 1840, became interested in studying the Indians through having organised a society called "The Grand Order of the Iroquois," which he wished to model after the ancient Iroquois Confederacy. The first literary fruits of his studies were his "Letters on the Iroquois" (in *The American Review* in 1847). Finding that he must neglect his law practice or abandon his Indian studies, he determined to publish all his materials and then cleave to law. In 1851, then, appeared "The League of the Iroquois," in which were fully explained the organisation and government of the celebrated Iroquois Confederacy, and which formed the first scientific account of an Indian tribe. A few years later, urged by Henry, Agassiz, and others, he took up his studies again, and began an investigation which was extended to embrace the whole world, and which resulted in his scholarly "Systems of Consanguinity and Affinity of the Human Family," published in 1871, as No. 17 of the Smithsonian "Contributions to Knowledge." In 1881 he gathered his materials on tribal organisation into an epoch-making philosophical treatise on "Ancient Society," which materially helped to lay the foundations of our modern science of governmental institutions.

John Wesley Powell.—Major John W. Powell (1834–1902) became conspicuous both as a geologist and an anthropologist. He studied at two or three small Western colleges, served in the Civil War, and then taught geology in two Illinois universities. In 1867 he travelled in the Colorado Rockies and thenceforward for many years was busied with surveys and explorations of the Far West. From 1881 till 1894 he was director of the United States Geological Survey, resigning to become director of the Bureau of Anthropology. He made many important contributions to the sciences which interested him, publishing "Exploration of the Colorado River of the West and Its Tributaries" (1875), "Report on the Geology of the Uinta Mountains" (1876), "Report on the Arid Region of the United States" (1879), "Introduction to the Study of the Indian

Languages" (1880), "Studies in Sociology" (1887), "Canyons of the Colorado" (1895), and "Physiographic Processes, Physiographic Features, and Physiographic Regions of the United States" (1895).

Daniel Garrison Brinton.—Daniel G. Brinton (1837–1899) of Philadelphia was one of the leading archæologists of the New World. Graduating at Yale in 1858 and at the Jefferson Medical College, Philadelphia, in 1860, he served as a surgeon in the war and from 1867 to 1887 was editor of *The Medical and Surgical Reporter*. From 1886 until his death he was professor of American linguistics and archæology at the University of Pennsylvania. He has to his credit a long list of important books and papers, only a few of which can be mentioned here. He began to publish in 1859 ("The Floridian Peninsula, Its Literary History, Indian Tribes, and Antiquities"). From boyhood he took a deep interest in the study of the American Indians; and in 1868 he published "The Myths of the New World." He also wrote, on Indian subjects, "American Hero Myths" (1882), "The American Race" (1892), and numerous ethnological and linguistic papers. He also both edited (for the most part) and published "The Library of Aboriginal American Literature" in eight volumes (1882–1885). In the controversies between science and theological dogma he was a pronounced radical. Along with his scientific labours Dr. Brinton found time for some studies in poetry, especially of Browning and Whitman.

Noah Webster.—Among students of linguistic science the first to be mentioned in point of time, and one of the first in importance, is Noah Webster (1758–1843), a native of Hartford, Connecticut, and a graduate of Yale College, whose "Grammatical Institute of the English Language" (spelling-book, grammar, and reader) appeared in 1783–1785. These books had an immense sale. The grammar showed originality, but was partly superseded by Murray's. Webster published also "Dissertations on the English Language" (1789), a more advanced "Philosophical and Practical Grammar of the English Language" (1807), and "Origin, History, and Connection of the Languages of Western Asia and of Europe" (1807); the last being one of the first fruits of Sir William Jones' identification of Sanskrit in 1786. The great work of Webster's life, however, was his "American Dictionary of the English Language," first published in 1828. Revised in 1847, 1864, and 1890, this is now the "International" and enjoys a large sale. The edition of 1901 contains 2528 pages.

Lindley Murray.—Lindley Murray (1745–1826), a native of Pennsylvania, made a fortune in trade at the time of the Revolution, and then settled at Holdgate, near York, England. Here he wrote his "Grammar of the English Language" (1795), which by 1816 had swollen to two volumes. In 1818 he published an "Abridgement," which went through some six-score editions. It laid great stress on syntax, and was a terror to generations of students.

Joseph Emerson Worcester.—For many years the only rival of Webster's Dictionary was Worcester's. Like Webster, Joseph Emerson Worcester (1784–1865) was a graduate of Yale College. After teaching for a time at Salem, Massachusetts, he settled at Cambridge. After various lexicographical labours, he issued "A Universal and Critical Dictionary" (1846), containing "in addition to the words found in Todd's edition of Johnson's Dictionary, nearly 27,000 words for which authorities are given." In 1860 this was expanded into the quarto "Dictionary of the English Language," which included about 104,000 words. In a memoir of Dr. Worcester, Ezra Abbot said:

> The tendency of his mind was practical rather than speculative. As a lexicographer, he did not undertake to reform long-established anomalies in the English language: his aim was rather to preserve it from corruption; and his works have certainly contributed much to that end. In respect both to orthography and pronunciation, he took great pains to ascertain the best usage; and perhaps there is no lexicographer whose judgment respecting these matters in doubtful cases deserves higher consideration.

Goold Brown.—Most of our grandfathers got their knowledge of English grammar from the text-books of Goold Brown (1791–1857). His education was obtained at the Friends' School in Providence, Rhode Island, his birthplace. He became a successful teacher and for twenty years conducted an academy in New York City. His "Institutes of English Grammar" appeared in 1823 and with an elementary work had an enormous circulation. His "Grammar of English Grammars" (1851), which brought him wide reputation, has been called "the most exhaustive, most accurate, and most original treatise on the English language

ever written." This is absurdly high praise; yet the book is undoubtedly
a monument of industry, and has been for many earnest souls "a court of
last resort on matters grammatical."

George Perkins Marsh.—In his day a distinguished diplomatist and
man of letters, George P. Marsh (1801–1882) made substantial contributions to philology. He graduated at Dartmouth College in 1820 and
studied law. He soon turned to studies in language and in 1838 printed
privately a translation of Rask's "Icelandic Grammar." His "Lectures on
the English Language" (1861) were delivered originally at Columbia; his
"Origin and History of the English Language" (1862) was a course of
Lowell Institute lectures.

Samuel Stehman Haldeman.—Samuel S. Haldeman (1812–1880) attained a respectable place as a philologist, but was also known as a
naturalist and an archæologist. He went to Dickinson College two years,
but not liking the course of study, left to study by himself. Shortly after
his marriage in 1835, he settled at Chickies, Pennsylvania, became a
silent partner with two brothers in the iron business, and spent most of
his time in his library, where, for many years, he worked sixteen hours
a day. His nature-studies resulted in "Fresh-Water Univalve Mollusca of
the United States" (nine parts, 1840–1845); "Zoölogical Contributions"
(1842–1843); "Zoölogy of the Invertebrate Animals" (1850); and more
than seventy papers. He began early to take interest in the Indian languages, and published papers on them, as well as on the languages
of Europe and China, and on spelling reform. These writings are now
valuable chiefly as landmarks in the history of linguistic science; but this
does not impair Haldeman's contemporary reputation as a learned and
accurate linguist. His last works were a monograph on "Pennsylvania
Dutch" (1872) and "Outlines of Etymology" (1878).

James Hammond Trumbull.—Well known as a thorough student of
Indian languages was James H. Trumbull (1821–1897) of Hartford, Connecticut. He studied at Yale in the class of 1842, but was prevented by
ill health from graduating. On linguistics he wrote "The Composition
of Indian Geographical Names" (1870), "The Best Methods of Studying
the Indian Languages" (1871), "Notes on Forty Algonkin Versions of the
Lord's Prayer" (1873), and "Indian Names of Places in and on the Bor-

ders of Connecticut, with Interpretations" (1881). He also edited Roger Williams' "Key into the Language of America" (1866).

Francis James Child.—Francis J. Child (1825–1896), created a tradition of zeal for broad and sound learning, the influence of which is still strong. A Boston youth, he stood at the head of his class at Harvard, that of 1846. For forty-five years he was a professor in Harvard. In addition to some excellent editions of texts, he published an epoch-making monograph, "Observations on the Language of Chaucer" (1862), "Observations on the Language of Gower's Confessio Amantis" (1866), and a monumental edition of "English and Scottish Popular Ballads" (1857–1858, revised and enlarged edition in ten volumes, 1882–1898), which is a model of accurate, comprehensive work, and which it is safe to say will not soon be superseded. It is due largely to Child that Harvard has become one of the leading centres of English study in America.

Francis Andrew March.—The Nestor of living American philologists is Professor Francis A. March (born in 1825), since 1855 a teacher in Lafayette College. He graduated at Amherst College in 1845. At first he pursued philosophical studies, but was later drawn to the study of language. His "Method of Philological Study of the English Language" appeared in 1865. His "Comparative Grammar of the Anglo-Saxon Language" (1870) was a pioneer, and with the "Anglo-Saxon Reader" (1870) did good service in introducing the subject into American colleges. For many years Dr. March has been an ardent apostle of spelling reform.

William Dwight Whitney.—Probably William Dwight Whitney (1827–1894) is best known as a writer of textbooks and popular expositor of linguistic problems. Among scholars, however, his chief monument is his work in Sanskrit. Born at Northampton, Massachusetts, he was graduated at eighteen from Williams College. In the winter of 1848–1849 he began the study of Sanskrit; this study he continued under Salisbury at Yale, Weber at Berlin, and Roth at Tübingen. In 1854 he was appointed professor of Sanskrit and comparative philology at Yale, and held this chair until his death; being for many years accounted the leading philologist in America. He was a most industrious and systematic worker. His bibliography includes 360 titles. He wrote simple and lucid grammars of English (1877), French (1886), German (1869), and Sanskrit

(1879); "Language and the Study of Language" (1867); "Oriental and Linguistic Studies" (1873–1874); "The Life and Growth of Language" (1875); several translations, with commentaries, of Sanskrit texts; and numerous papers and reviews. He was also editor-in-chief of "The Century Dictionary" (1889–1891) and read every proof of its 21,138 columns. But his greatest service to the cause of science was in holding up to his pupils a lofty ideal and a rigorous scientific method.

> Hellenists, Latinists, and linguists of every sort [said Professor Perrin in a memorial address], and even historical students in the more restricted sense, all over this country and Europe, are now labouring, each in his chosen field, with a more equable spirit, a broader method, and a loftier ideal, because they have caught them all, directly or indirectly, from the master whose memory we honour.

Basil Lanneau Gildersleeve.—Valuable work in classical philology has been done by Basil L. Gildersleeve (born in 1831). After graduating at Princeton in 1849, he studied at Berlin, Bonn, and Göttingen, receiving the degree of Ph.D. from Göttingen in 1853. For twenty years (1856–1876) he was professor of Greek (for five years, of Latin also) at the University of Virginia. In 1876 he was called to a similar chair at Johns Hopkins University, which he has since held. He founded (1880) and has since edited *The American Journal of Philology*, and has published, among other books, "A Latin Grammar" (1876, twice revised), "Essays and Studies, Educational and Literary" (1890), "The Syntax of Classical Greek" (part i., 1900, with Charles W. E. Miller), and editions of Justin Martyr, Persius, and Pindar.

Natural and Physical Science.—It is in the natural and physical sciences that our attempt to cover the ground will at once appear most hopeless. In some of these sciences, for example astronomy, physics, and geology, American scholars stand concededly among the foremost in the world; to practically all of them Americans have contributed noteworthy studies and discoveries. Lack of space prevents even the mention, with one or two exceptions, of living writers.

John James Audubon.—Among the naturalists of America no name is more illustrious than that of the chief of our ornithologists, John James

Audubon (1780–1851). His father was a French naval officer who had settled upon a plantation near New Orleans and married a lady of Spanish descent. When but a child Audubon used to draw pictures of birds; of those which were not satisfactory he made a bonfire at each birthday. When he was about eighteen, his father settled him on a farm near Philadelphia; here he gratified the naturalist's passion to such an extent that he was good for nothing else. "For a period of twenty years," he wrote later, "my life was a series of vicissitudes. I tried various branches of commerce, but they all proved unprofitable, doubtless because my whole mind was ever filled with my passion for rambling and admiring those objects of Nature from which alone I received the purest gratification." He lived with his family successively in Kentucky, Ohio, Mississippi, and Louisiana; drawing and studying birds incessantly. Visiting England in 1826, he arranged for the publication of "The Birds of America" (1830–1839). It was to be published in numbers of five folio plates each, the whole to be in four volumes and to be sold for $1000 a copy. The work was to cost over $100,000; yet he had not money enough to pay for the first number. He supported himself by painting. He was elected (1830) a Fellow of the Royal Society. Audubon accompanied his "Birds" with "Ornithological Biographies" (five volumes, 1831–1839), the literary value of which is important; "it presents," says one writer, "in language warm from his having been a part of the scenes, a virgin past of our country, and its forests and prairies, which can never be restored or so well described again." "The Viviparous Quadrupeds of North America," with 150 plates, appeared in three volumes in 1845–1848; in this undertaking he was assisted by his two sons and the Rev. John Bachman of Charleston, South Carolina. The last three years of his life were spent in mental darkness. His claim to honorable rank in American letters cannot be denied.

Spencer Fullerton Baird.—No American naturalist exerted a wider and deeper influence than Spencer F. Baird (1823–1887). A native of Pennsylvania and a graduate of Dickinson College (1840), he was the friend and in some work the collaborator of Audubon, Agassiz, and other zoölogists. Appointed assistant secretary of the Smithsonian Institution in 1850, he directed much of the scientific exploration of the West; organised the National Museum (1857); succeeded Henry in 1878 as secretary of the Smithsonian and largely developed its work; and in 1874 became head of the Commission of Fish and Fisheries, and organised the science and practice of fish culture in America. He was besides a voluminous writer. His books and papers down to 1882 include 1063 titles. Of them we may mention "Catalogue of North American Reptiles" (1853), "The Birds of America" (with John Cassin, 1860), "The Mammals of North America" (1859), and "History of American Birds" (with Thomas M. Brewer and Robert Ridgway, 1874–1884).

Alpheus Hyatt.—In zoölogy and palæontology one of the celebrated scholars of his day was Alpheus Hyatt (1838–1902). Born in Washington, D. C., he received his education at the Maryland Military Academy, Yale College, and under Agassiz at the Lawrence Scientific School of Harvard, from which he was graduated in 1862. After the Civil War, in which he rose to be a captain, he continued his studies in natural history and became active in fostering these studies in general. He helped to found *The American Naturalist* in 1868, and was the principal founder of the American Society of Naturalists, organised in 1883. In 1881 he became professor of zoölogy and palæontology in the Massachusetts Institute of Technology and in Boston University. He was equally active in teaching, in popularising science, and in research. Some of his books are "Observations on Freshwater Polyzoa" (1866), "Revision of North American Poriferæ" (1875–1877), long the only work on North American commercial sponges, "The Genesis of the Tertiary Species of Planorbis at Steinheim," a long and important monograph on the influence of gravity on certain shells, published by the Boston Society of Natural History in its "Memoirs" (1880), "Genera of Fossil Cephalopods" (1883), "The Larval Theory of the Origin of Cellular Tissue" (1884), giving his theory of the origin of sex, and "The Genesis of the Arietidæ" (1889). He also edited a series of "Guides for Science-Teaching," of several of which he himself was also the author. Few Americans indeed have done so much to make natural science popular as did Hyatt. His work in research was immensely fruitful. He has been called the founder of the new school of invertebrate palæontology, while in systematic zoölogy he made several discoveries which led to important revisions in biological classification.

Alpheus Spring Packard.—The son of a Bowdoin College professor of the same name, Alpheus S. Packard (1839–1905) naturally entered Bowdoin and there came under the influence of Dr. Paul Chadbourne, who encouraged his inclination toward zoölogical study. After graduating from Bowdoin in 1861 and from the Maine Medical School in 1864, he worked under Agassiz at Harvard, devoting himself largely to the study of insects. In 1867 he became curator of invertebrates and in 1876 director, of the Peabody Academy of Science in Salem, Massachusetts. In 1878 he was appointed professor of zoölogy and geology in Brown University, retaining this post till his death. He was one of the founders and for twenty years editor of *The American Naturalist*. Besides hundreds of papers, he wrote a "Guide to the Study of Insects" (1869); "The Mammoth Cave and Its Inhabitants," jointly with F. W. Putnam (1872); "Life Histories of Animals" (1876), the first attempt since the Lowell Institute lectures of Agassiz to attempt a summary of embryological discoveries; "Insects Injurious to Forest and Shade Trees" (1890), "A Naturalist on the Labrador Coast" (1891), "A Text-Book of Entomology" (1898), and "Lamarck, the Founder of Evolution: His Life and Work" (1901). Apropos of the last book it will be remembered that Packard, Cope, and Hyatt were the founders and chief exponents of the Neo-Lamarckian school of evolution. Packard was an indefatigable investigator and his contributions to entomology and zoölogy immensely advanced those sciences.

Edward Drinker Cope.—Another celebrated naturalist was Edward D. Cope (1840–1897) of Philadelphia, whose studies in fossil vertebrates were of epoch-making significance. He studied at the University of Pennsylvania. From 1864 till 1867 he was professor of natural sciences in Haverford College. For twenty-two years thereafter he was engaged in exploration, research, and editorial work. In 1889 he became professor of geology and palæontology in the University of Pennsylvania. Before he was thirty he had laid his foundations in five chief lines of research, ichthyology, amphibians, reptiles, mammals, and evolutionary philosophy. On all of these subjects he wrote much and wisely. He was the author of over four hundred volumes, papers, and memoirs, to say nothing of hundreds of editorial articles in *The American Naturalist*, which he edited from 1878 until his death. On the subject of evolution alone his most important works are "The Origin of Genera" (1868), "The Origin of the Fittest" (1886), and "The Primary Factors of Organic Evolution" (1896). His activity in research may be judged from the fact that he himself named and described 1115 out of some 3200 known species of North American fossil vertebrates. Naturally, in attempting so much, he fell short of perfection in some things.

His life-work, [says Professor Osborn,[24]] bears the marks of great genius, of solid and accurate observation, and at times of inaccuracy due to bad logic or haste and over-pressure of work. The greater number of his Natural Orders and Natural Laws will remain as permanent landmarks in our science. As a comparative anatomist he ranks, both in the range and effectiveness of his knowledge and his ideas, with Cuvier and Owen.... As a natural philosopher, while far less logical than Huxley, he was more creative and constructive, his metaphysics ending in theism rather than agnosticism.

Elliott Coues.—Distinguished as an ornithologist, Elliott Coues (1842–1899) became favourably known also for researches in biology and comparative anatomy. After taking degrees at the Columbian University in 1861–1863, he entered the Union Army as assistant surgeon, studying flora and fauna wherever he went. In 1873–1876 he was surgeon and naturalist to the United States Northern Boundary Commission and in 1876–1880 was connected with the United States Geological and Geographical Survey of the Territories. He helped found the American Ornithologists' Union and edited its organ, The Auk. His "Key to North American Birds" (1872, rewritten 1884 and 1901) is of great significance. He wrote also on "Birds of the Northwest" (1874), "Birds of the Colorado Valley" (1878), and with Winfrid A. Stearns, "New England Bird Life" (1881).

David Starr Jordan.—David Starr Jordan (born in 1851) has in recent years been regarded chiefly as an educator; he became known through his studies on fishes. Entering Cornell University in 1868, he was appointed instructor in botany in 1870 and graduated M.S. in 1872. After teaching and studying science for some years, he was made (1879) professor of zoölogy at Indiana University, of which he became president in 1885. Since 1891 he has been president of Stanford University. Some of his books are "A Manual of the Vertebrate Animals of the Northern United States" (1876), "Science Sketches" (1887), "Fishes of North and Middle America" (1896–1899), "Footnotes to Evolution" (1898), and "The Food and Game Fishes of North America" (1902). He is a leader both in his chosen scientific field and in educational thought.

---

24 *Science,* May 7, 1897, n. s. v. 717.

Asa Gray.—The best-known botanist of his epoch was Asa Gray (1810–1888) a native of Paris, Oneida County, New York. He graduated in medicine at Fairfield College in 1831, but soon gave up medicine for botany and in 1842 was elected to the Fisher professorship of natural history in Harvard University. Any adequate narrative of Gray's tremendous activity as a writer and teacher is out of the question here; we can only say that his widely known and long standard text-books on botany (beginning with the "Elements of Botany," 1836, which grew into the "Structural and Systematic Botany" of 1879, and including his "How Plants Grow," 1858, and "How Plants Behave," 1872) represent but a small part of his literary activity. With Dr. Torrey he began (1838) the "Flora of North America"; he wrote also valuable botanical memoirs and many valuable articles for *The North American Review* and *The American Journal of Science*.

Edward Hitchcock.—Edward Hitchcock (1793–1864), a Congregational clergyman, and for thirty-nine years a professor of science in Amherst College, was especially devoted to geological study. A large number of his books and papers relate to geological subjects, which he helped to make popular; among these books are "Economical Geology" (1832), "Geology of Massachusetts" (1841), "The Religion of Geology and Its Connected Sciences" (1851), and "Ichnology of New England" (1858). He was the first president of the Association of American Geologists, and was president of Amherst College from 1845 till 1854.

Louis Agassiz.—The celebrated naturalist Jean Louis Rodolphe Agassiz (1807–1873) was of Swiss birth and did not come to America to live until he was forty-one years of age, and had already become famous for those studies of glacial phenomena set forth in "Études sur les glaciers" (1840) and "Système glaciaire" (with Guyot and Desor, 1847). For twenty-five years (1848–1873) he was professor of natural history at Harvard, and in that time, besides training some of the most eminent of living American scientists, he did much to arouse popular interest in science and scientific progress. Of the "Contributions to the Natural History of the United States" which he planned to publish in ten volumes, he lived to issue only four (1857–1862). For Agassiz Nature was "the expression of the thought of the Creator." In opposing the Darwinians as to the origin of species, Agassiz unfortunately took the wrong side of the question of how the Creator expressed His thought; but he remains nevertheless distinguished both as a scientist and as an educator; a singularly great and gentle nature, strong and true.

Arnold Henry Guyot.—Less distinguished than his compatriot Agassiz, but of enduring fame, was the geographer Arnold Guyot (1807–1884). Born near Neuchâtel, Switzerland, he studied there and in Germany, receiving the degree of Ph.D. from Berlin in 1835. Like Agassiz he became known for his glacial discoveries; and like Agassiz he came to America in the troubled year 1848. From 1854 until his death he was professor of geology and physical geography at Princeton. His text-books and maps revolutionised the teaching and study of geography. He wrote also many scientific papers and memoirs, among which may be noted especially those describing his studies in the Appalachian Mountains. American science owes much to his unselfish devotion.

James Dwight Dana.—James D. Dana (1813–1895), born in Utica, New York, was attracted by the fame of the elder Silliman to Yale College, where he graduated in 1833. To the Sillimans he became allied by his marriage with Henrietta F. Silliman in 1844; and like them he had a long and notable career closely connected with Yale College, where he became (1835) Silliman professor of natural history and geology. He wrote many reports on geological, zoölogical, and mineralogical subjects, besides "A Manual of Mineralogy" (1851), "A Manual of Geology" (1862), "On Coral Reefs and Islands" (1853), "Science and the Bible" (*Bibliotheca Sacra*, 1856–1857), and "Corals and Coral Islands" (1872).

Alexander Winchell.—Another noted geologist was Alexander Winchell (1824–1891). Graduating from Wesleyan University in 1847, he became a teacher of science in various schools, and in 1853 professor of physics and civil engineering in the University of Michigan; being soon transferred to the chair of geology, zoölogy, and botany. He afterward taught at Syracuse and Vanderbilt Universities. From the latter institution in 1878 he was dismissed because his views on evolution were "contrary to the plan of redemption." The next year he was recalled to Michigan. Besides being a leading spirit in forming the Geological Society of America, and in establishing *The American Geologist*, he was a voluminous writer, especially of scientific works for popular use, and endeavoured in these works to show the essential harmony between science and Christian dogma. Thus he did the work of a peacemaker in what has long been a heated conflict.

Nathaniel Bowditch (1773–1838) was a pioneer in the study of astronomy and mathematics in America. At first a cooper and then a ship-chandler, he was studious, and learned Latin in order to read Newton's "Principia." As supercargo on a merchant vessel during several voyages, he became expert in the theory of navigation and published in 1802 "The New American Practical Navigator," which in a revised form is published by the United States Hydrographic Office and is the standard compendium for navigators. In 1829 he translated Laplace's "Méchanique céleste," adding valuable notes.

Benjamin Peirce.—In the annals of mathematics and astronomy the name of Benjamin Peirce (1809–1880) has a place of distinction. Born at Salem, Massachusetts, he became a pupil of Bowditch, and graduated at Harvard in 1829, in the class with Holmes. He became a tutor at Harvard in 1831, professor of mathematics and physics in 1833, and nine years later Perkins professor of mathematics and astronomy, holding this chair till his death. From 1867 till 1874, succeeding Dallas Bache, he was superintendent of the Coast Survey. He wrote an important series of mathematical text-books; "System of Analytical Mechanics" (1857); "Linear Associative Algebra" (communications to the National Academy of Sciences, collected in 1870); and Lowell Institute lectures on "Ideality in the Physical Sciences" (1881). He obtained eminence, it has been said, equally in mathematics, physics, astronomy, mechanics, and navigation.

The Sillimans.—In the annals of American science no other name is so long and favourably known as that of the Sillimans. Benjamin Silliman (1779–1864) was for fifty years, beginning in 1802, professor of chemistry in Yale College and founded (1818) *The American Journal of Science and Arts*, which he edited for twenty-eight years. His son, Benjamin, Jr. (1816–1885), taught and studied chemistry, mineralogy, and geology in Yale, and was associate editor (1838–1846) of his father's *Journal*. For the rest of his life he was a professor of chemistry, first in what is now the Sheffield Scientific School of Yale, then at Louisville University, and later in the Academic and Medical Departments at Yale. In 1858 he published "First Principles of Natural Philosophy or Physics"; and he was the author of many scientific memoirs, addresses, and reports. He was one of the pioneers in science-teaching in America, and his influence on scientific education was deep and abiding.

Joseph Henry.—Joseph Henry (1797–1878) was one of the most illustrious physicists of his day. Born and educated at Albany, New York, he began (1827) researches which resulted in important discoveries in the field of electro-magnetism, one of which made the telegraph possible. From 1832 till 1846 he was professor of natural philosophy in the College of New Jersey (Princeton), and from 1846 till his death was secretary of the Smithsonian Institution, which he had helped to organise. He published "Contributions to Electricity and Magnetism" (1839) and many papers, especially in the Smithsonian reports. A brilliant and profound investigator, he did signally important service in organising great scientific enterprises. "To Henry," says Dr. Woodward, "more than to any other man, must be attributed the rise and the growth in America of the present public appreciation of the scientific work carried on by governmental aid."

Alexander Dallas Bache.—Alexander Dallas Bache (1806–1867), a great-grandson of Benjamin Franklin, after graduating in 1825 at West Point, at the head of his class, at twenty-two resigned a lieutenant's commission to become professor of natural philosophy and chemistry at the University of Pennsylvania. Having made a name for his researches on steam, magnetism, etc., he was called in 1843 to be superintendent of the United States Coast Survey, and performed his duties with marked efficiency. Gifted with quick apprehension and broad intelligence, he possessed great powers of leadership. He published nearly two hundred scientific papers, memoirs, and reports. "To him," declared his eulogist Benjamin Gould, "the scientific progress of the nation was indebted more than to any other man who had trod her soil."

Matthew Fontaine Maury.—Matthew F. Maury (1806–1873) is well known to students of meteorological science and also to the educational world. He was a Virginian of Huguenot extraction, who went to sea at nineteen and became not only a good sailor but also an authority on navigation. His "Treatise on Navigation" (1835) was favourably received abroad and was used as a text-book in the United States Navy. As "Harry Bluff" he published in *The Southern Literary Messenger*, about 1840, under the title of "Scraps from the Lucky-Bag," a series of papers on nautical matters, which brought him fame and resulted in placing him in charge of the Depot of Charts and Instruments at Washington, an office which later became the Naval Observatory and Hydrographical Department. One of his first tasks was to compile some charts of winds and currents. These charts proved immensely valuable by shortening voyages and lowering the expense of commerce. His "Physical Geography of the Sea and its Meteorology" (1855) at once took the highest rank in its field, and the geographical text-books which he wrote in his later years have done great service to education and in a revised form still satisfy the needs of many schools. He was the author also of many pamphlets and official papers.

Josiah Parsons Cooke.—Josiah Parsons Cooke (1827–1894), a pioneer in chemical education, was born in Boston and graduated at Harvard in 1844. In 1851 he became professor of chemistry and mineralogy at Harvard. He did much to further the study of chemistry in colleges and was one of the first to urge the laboratory method of instruction. He published, among other things, "Chemical Problems and Reactions" (1853), "Religion and Chemistry" (1864), "The New Chemistry" (1871), and "The Credentials of Science the Warrant of Faith" (1888).

John William Draper.—John W. Draper (1811–1882) is known in the annals of science as a chemist and physiologist; he won eminence also as a historian. Born at St. Helens, near Liverpool, the son of a Wesleyan Methodist minister, he studied chemistry under Turner in London, and coming to America in 1833, graduated in medicine from the University of Pennsylvania in 1836. He now began investigating the chemical action of light, and published in 1844 a "Treatise on the Forces which Produce the Organisation of Plants." His memoir "On the Production of Light by Heat" (1847), a valuable contribution to the subject of spectrum analysis, appeared thirteen years before Kirchoff's celebrated memoir, which used to be thought of as marking the beginning of spectrum analysis. He was also the first to succeed (1839) in taking portraits of the human face by photography. In 1839 he became professor of chemistry, and in 1850 of physiology also, in the University of New York. His "Treatise on Human Physiology, Statical and Dynamical" (1856) at once took its place as a standard text-book. He wrote also a "Text-Book on Chemistry" (1846); a "Text-Book on Natural Philosophy" (1847); "History of the Conflict between Religion and Science" (1874), an able and comprehensive treatment of a vast subject; and "Scientific Memoirs" (1878), a collection of papers on radiant energy. Two of his sons, Henry and John Christopher, also became well known physiologists and chemists.

Charles Augustus Young.—Of the more recent astronomers of America, Charles A. Young (1834–1908) was one of the foremost. Born in Hanover, New Hampshire, the son of Professor Ira Young of Dartmouth College, he graduated from Dartmouth in 1853. From 1856 till 1866 he was professor of mathematics, astronomy, and natural philosophy in Western Reserve University. In the latter year he returned to Dartmouth as professor of natural philosophy and astronomy, remaining there till 1877, when he became professor of astronomy at Princeton. He was prominently connected with several important astronomical expeditions and produced some notable inventions, among them an automatic spectroscope which has been widely used by astronomers. He made some significant observations on the sun, including a verification by experiment of Doppler's principle as applied to light, by which he was able to measure the velocity of the sun's rotation. He also discovered the thin solar shell of gaseous matter called "the reversing layer." He wrote "The Sun" in "The International Scientific Series" (1882), "A General Astronomy" (1889), "Elements of Astronomy" (1890), and "A Manual of Astronomy" (1902).

Robert Henry Thurston.—Distinguished as an educator, an inventor, and a writer on engineering subjects was Robert H. Thurston (1839–1903). He was born in Providence, Rhode Island, and graduated from Brown University in 1859. During the Civil War he served as an engineer in the Federal Navy; in 1865 he was appointed assistant professor of natural and experimental philosophy at the United States Naval Academy. In 1871 he became professor of engineering at the Stevens Institute of Technology, remaining here until 1885, when he was made director of Sibley College in Cornell University. His writings, always clear, exact, and authoritative, have circulated widely among engineers. They include "A History of the Growth of the Steam Engine" (1878, revised in 1901, and translated into French and German), "Materials of Engineering" (three volumes, 1882–1886), "Manual of the Steam Engine" (1890–1891), "Manual of Steam Boilers" (1890), with other valuable works, and about 250 scientific papers. Thurston served on several important government engineering commissions. Of him it has justly been said that "he made engineers better scientists, promoted engineering education, helped to put engineering upon a higher professional plane, and constantly was on the watch to dispel the fogs of prejudice by help of the truths of science."

The Youmans Brothers.—The life of Edward Livingston Youmans (1821–1887) was spent chiefly in popularising science. Born in Albany County, New York, he inherited a strong bent toward scientific study. For many years he wrestled with threatening blindness, and was never well. His "Class-Book of Chemistry" (1851) was remarkably successful. "There was," Mr. Fiske says of it, "a firm grasp of the philosophical principles underlying chemical phenomena, and the meaning and functions of the science were set forth in such a way as to charm the student and make him wish for more." He spent many years in delivering lyceum lectures, for which he was well fitted. His "Handbook of Household Science" (1857) was a carefully written treatise on the applications of science to the problems of food, light, heat, and sanitation. Its popularity led him to plan a comprehensive "Household Cyclopædia" which he did not live to finish. Besides editing "The Correlation and Conservation of Forces" (1864), a series of expositions by Grove, Helmholtz, Mayer, Faraday, Liebig, and Carpenter, and "The Culture Demanded by Modern Life" (1867), a collection of addresses and arguments in favour of scientific education, Youmans published several addresses and papers, and did much to give the views of Darwin and Spencer a favourable reception in America. He was the originator and general editor of "The International Scientific Series," of which fifty-seven volumes appeared in his lifetime. It was a difficult but eminently useful task to secure popular scientific books by masters; and the series of seventy-nine volumes has done much for education. Youmans was also the founder of *The Popular Science Monthly* (begun in 1872) and edited the first twenty-eight volumes.

> While it was his main intent [to quote Mr. Fiske again] to
> give in popular form an account of the progress of the sev-
> eral departments of science, he never lost sight of the aim
> to show wherein the scientific method was applicable to
> the larger questions of life—of education, social relations,
> morals, government, and religion.

William Jay Youmans (1838–1901) first studied chemistry at Columbia and Yale and privately with his brother Edward, then took a medical
course at New York University. After practising medicine for some three
years, he became connected with *The Popular Science Monthly*, which
he edited from 1887 till 1900. He wrote "Pioneers of Science in America"
(1895).

Henry Carrington Bolton.—Henry Carrington Bolton (1843–1903)
did much for the bibliography of chemistry; his "Select Bibliography of
Chemistry, 1492–1892" (1893–1905) comprises over 12,000 titles in twen-
ty-four languages. He also wrote many papers on the history of chemistry. His "Counting-out Rhymes of Children" (1888) gave him prominence
as a folklorist, and he published also some important papers on various
other subjects in folklore.

VII. THE PERIODICALS

Their Importance.—No apology need be offered for including in this
volume a section on the history of American periodicals. As Professor
Smyth has well said, in speaking of the early magazines of Philadelphia,
such a division "helps to exhibit the process of American literature as an
evolution." Much of our best literature made its first appearance in periodicals; and the remuneration received by authors from this source has
great significance in the economics of literature. Likewise much of our
best and most searching criticism, whether reprinted or not, appeared
originally in newspapers and magazines, which have thus had a prominent part in the making of American literature. In 1810 there were only
about thirty periodicals altogether; in 1900 there were 239 classed as
general and literary, some of them having a considerable circulation on
the other side of the Atlantic. In the brief space allotted to this section
it will be impossible to do more than to mention a few of the most im-

portant literary periodicals; the full extent of the journalistic activity of the United States may be inferred from the fact that in 1900 over eight billion copies of periodicals were circulated, having a market value of nearly $225,000,000.

The Eighteenth Century.—The eighteenth century will not long detain us. Only ten years after Edward Cave had founded *The Gentleman's Magazine* in London (1731), Andrew Bradford and Benjamin Franklin founded in Philadelphia the first monthly magazines in America. Of Bradford's venture, *The American Magazine*, edited by John Webbe, only three numbers appeared; while Franklin published only six numbers of *The General Magazine*. In the course of the century several others appeared, among them *The American Magazine and Historical Chronicle* (Boston, 1743–1746); *The Independent Reflector* (New York, 1752–1753), among whose contributors were Governor William Livingston, John Morin Scott, and Aaron Burr; *The American Magazine* (Philadelphia, 1757–1758, revived in 1769), which Professor Tyler calls "by far the most admirable example of our literary periodicals in the colonial time," edited by Rev. William Smith, first provost of the College of Philadelphia; *The New American Magazine* (Woodbridge, New Jersey, 1758–1760), edited by S. Nevil; *The Royal American Magazine* (Boston, 1774–1775); *The Pennsylvania Magazine* (Philadelphia, 1775–1776), edited by Thomas Paine, to which articles were sent by Francis Hopkinson, John Witherspoon, and William Smith; *The Columbian Magazine* (Philadelphia, 1786–1790), edited at first by Matthew Carey and later by Alexander J. Dallas, and changed in 1790 to *The Universal Asylum* (1790–1792; to this Benjamin Rush was a faithful contributor); *The American Museum* (Philadelphia, 1787–1792, 1798), for which Carey abandoned *The Columbian* and which was "the first really successful literary undertaking of the kind in America"; *The Massachusetts Magazine* (Boston, 1789–1796); *The New York Magazine* (1790–1797); *The Farmers' Museum* (Walpole, New Hampshire, 1793–1799), of which Joseph Dennie, the editor from 1796 to 1799, boasted that "it is read by more than two thousand individuals, and has its patrons in Europe and on the banks of the Ohio"; and *The Monthly Magazine and American Review* (New York, 1799–1800), founded by Charles Brockden Brown, and carried on in 1801–1802 as *The American Review and Literary Journal*. But the reading public of those days was small, and other conditions were unfavourable to publishers; in consequence, almost none of these publications lived into the next century.

The Nineteenth Century.—Of the literary magazines established before 1850, only one or two have survived. Yet we now begin to see the periodicals exhibiting greater vitality; and gradually they come to deal more and more with native literature and to exhibit a greater self-reliance on the part of American writers. The first half of the century was the period in which the national spirit took deep root and made rapid growth; and this national spirit is fully reflected in the literature of the time.

In 1801 Joseph Dennie and John Dickins began to publish, in Philadelphia, *The Port Folio*, which was destined to live for twenty-six years. Among its contributors were John Blair Linn, author of "The Powers of Genius," "The Death of Washington," etc.; Robert H. Rose, author of "Sketches in Verse"; John Sanderson, who wrote a book of Parisian sketches entitled "The American in Paris"; Alexander Graydon; Gouverneur Morris; Joseph Hopkinson, author of "Hail, Columbia," and of articles on Shakespeare; and Alexander Wilson, poet and ornithologist, whose works were edited by Alexander B. Grosart (Paisley, Scotland, 1876).

From 1803 to 1811, the Anthology Club maintained in Boston a sprightly magazine called *The Anthology and Boston Review*. The best minds of Boston contributed to it; among them George Ticknor, William Tudor, Joseph Buckminster, John Quincy Adams, Dr. John Sylvester, Edward Everett, and John Gardiner. The magazine never paid expenses; but the contributors cheerfully paid for their pleasure. The club did much to give Boston its literary prestige, and was the forerunner of the famous Boston Athenæum.

The Literary Magazine and American Register (Philadelphia, 1803–1808) was likewise founded by the novelist Brown, who published therein, among other things, his "Memoirs of Carwin, the Biloquist."

Washington Irving began his literary career with the publication of *Salmagundi*, which he founded in New York in 1807, in conjunction with his brother William and James Kirke Paulding. The little sheet, in yellow covers, was issued by an eccentric publisher, David Longworth, the front of whose house was entirely hidden by a colossal painting of the crowning of Shakespeare. The magazine was modelled after Addison's *Spectator*. Paulding was Launcelot Langstaff and Irving was Pindar Cockloft, the poet. "Our intention," wrote the editors, "is simply to instruct the young, reform the old, correct the town, and castigate the age; this is an arduous task, and therefore we undertake it with confidence." The work soon became popular throughout the United States for its clever reproductions of society foibles. After twenty numbers, however, it was discontinued, because, as Paulding said, "the publisher, with that liberality so characteristic of these modern Mæcenases, declined to concede to us a share of the profits, which had become considerable." Twelve years later, Irving being then in Europe, Paulding attempted a second series (Philadelphia, May to August, 1820), which, though inferior to the first series, still contained some interesting pages.

The Select Reviews and Spirit of the Foreign Magazines, begun by Samuel Ewing in Philadelphia (1809), later became *The Analectic Magazine* (1812–1821). In 1813–1814 Irving was its editor and contributed to it some biographies of heroes of the War of 1812 and some of the essays afterwards collected in "The Sketch Book." Other contributors were Gulian C. Verplanck, James K. Paulding, Alexander Wilson, and William Darlington. *The Analectic* published in July, 1819, the first lithograph made in America.

The Portico (Baltimore, 1815–1819) numbered among its contributors John Neal, whose lengthy review of Byron appeared as a serial. Neal continued to write for *The Portico* "until he knocked it on the head, it is thought, by an article on Free Agency."

The Idle Man (New York, 1821–1822) was edited by Richard H. Dana the elder; in it were printed his novels "Tom Thornton" and "Paul Felton" and some contributions from Bryant and from Washington Allston.

The New York Mirror, a weekly, was begun in 1823 by General George P. Morris and Samuel Woodworth, the author of "The Old Oaken Bucket." Woodworth soon gave way to Theodore S. Fay and he in turn (1831) to Nathaniel P. Willis. Morris and Willis conducted it with great success until 1842. Fay contributed "The Little Genius," satirical letters on New York society, and "The Minute Book," letters from Europe. Willis spent some years abroad as foreign correspondent of the paper (1832–1836), his letters being eagerly read and widely copied. Morris and Willis subsequently conducted *The New Mirror* (New York, 1843–1844), which in October, 1844, became a daily, and *The Home Journal*(New York, from 1846 on), which as *Town and Country* still continues.

The Atlantic Magazine (New York, 1824–1825), edited by Robert C. Sands, was continued till 1826 as *The New York Review and Athenæum Magazine*. In its later form it was edited by Henry J. Anderson and William Cullen Bryant. In it appeared many of Bryant's poems and some of his prose, as well as contributions by Longfellow, Dana, Willis, Bancroft, and Caleb Cushing. In March, 1826, the *Review* was merged with *The New York Literary Gazette*. In July this was in turn combined with *The United States Literary Gazette*, which had been founded in Boston in 1825 and edited by Theophilus Parsons, the new title being *The United States Review and Literary Gazette*. James G. Carter, and later Charles Folsom, were the Boston editors, and Bryant was the New York editor. The periodical did not long survive.

The American Monthly Magazine (New York, 1829–1831) was established and edited by Nathaniel P. Willis, who enlisted a number of younger writers, such as Richard Hildreth, Park Benjamin, Isaac McLellan, Albert Pike ("Hymns to the Gods"), Rufus Dawes, and Mrs. Sigourney. In 1831 the *Magazine* was absorbed by *The New York Mirror*, of which Willis now became an associate editor.

The Illinois Monthly Magazine (Vandalia, Illinois, 1830–1832), edited and mainly written by James Hall, was the earliest literary publication in the West; it was superseded by *The Western Monthly Magazine* (Cincinnati, 1833–1836), edited by Timothy Flint.

One of the most popular of the Philadelphia magazines was *Godey's Lady's Book* (1830–1877), which as early as 1859 circulated 98,500 copies, and which published compositions by Paulding, Park Benjamin, Holmes, Irving, Poe, Bayard Taylor, Longfellow, Harriet Beecher Stowe, Simms, Willis, Buchanan Read, Thomas Dunn English, and Lydia H.

Sigourney. Poe's contribution on "The Literati of New York," published in its columns in 1846, created a great sensation at the time. For more than thirty years *Godey's* was edited by Mrs. Sarah J. Hale, who is also famous as the author of "Mary had a little lamb," and through whose exertions our national Thanksgiving Day was secured.

The New England Magazine, established in Boston in 1831 by Joseph T. and Edwin Buckingham, published contributions from Hildreth, Park Benjamin, Whittier, Holmes (who published here the first two papers, never by authority reprinted, of his "Autocrat" series), Longfellow, William and Andrew Peabody, George S. Hillard ("Literary Portraits" and "Selections from the Papers of an Idler"), and other eminent writers. In 1835 Park Benjamin took it to New York and continued it till 1838 as *The American Monthly Magazine*.

The North American Quarterly Magazine (Philadelphia, 1833–1838) was conducted by Sumner Lincoln Fairfield, author of "The Cities of the Plain," and of an unpublished poem, "The Last Night of Pompeii" (finished in 1830), from which he alleged that Bulwer, to whom he sent the manuscript, stole the plot of his "Last Days of Pompeii."

Much more successful was *The Knickerbacker or New-York Monthly Magazine*, founded in the same year and quietly changed with the seventh number to *The Knickerbocker*. The founder was Charles Fenno Hoffman, who edited three numbers. Some contributors were Harry Franco, Bryant, Irving ("Crayon Papers"), Longfellow, Lewis Gaylord Clark (for a time the editor), William L. Stone, the brothers Duyckinck, Frederick S. Cozzens, Simms, Park Benjamin, John L. Stephens (letters from Egypt), and Parkman ("The Oregon Trail"). With some exceptions it must be said that the contents of *The Knickerbocker* were not of very great merit; and in its later years there were too many stories on the order of "Carl Almendinger's Office, or, The Mysteries of Chicago," which ran as a serial in 1862. In 1864 the title was *The American Monthly Knickerbocker*, and from July till October, 1865, when publication was suspended, the title was *The Fœderal American*.

The Southern Literary Messenger, published monthly at Richmond, Virginia, between 1834 and 1864, exerted a marked influence upon the literary taste of the whole South. In it were first published many of Poe's stories and criticisms, and he was the editor of the second volume. Other contributors were Paulding, Park Benjamin, John W. Draper, Willis, Henry C. Lea, R. H. Stoddard, Simms, John B. Dabney, Matthew F. Maury, Philip Pendleton, and John Esten Cooke, Henry Timrod, Paul H. Hayne, Aldrich, Moncure D. Conway, Thomas Dunn English, John P. Kennedy, James Barron Hope ("Henry Ellen"), and W. Gordon McCabe.

In 1837 William E. Burton, the comedian, established in Philadelphia *The Gentleman's Magazine* to do for his sex what *Godey's* was doing for the ladies. Beginning with July, 1839, Poe became joint editor. The next year Burton sold out to George R. Graham, who combined the magazine with *The Casket* (begun by Samuel Coate Atkinson in 1827) to form *Graham's Lady's and Gentleman's Magazine*. For years *Graham's* was the most famous and truly national periodical in America. Graham understood the reading public as did few other men. He paid contributors liberally for those days, and collected a brilliant list of writers, including every name well known in letters at the time except Irving, who confined himself to *The Knickerbocker*. To *Graham's* Longfellow contributed his "Spanish Student," "Childhood," "The Builders," "The Belfry of Bruges," "The Arsenal at Springfield," "Nuremberg," etc. Poe contributed "The Mask of the Red Death," "The Murders in the Rue Morgue," "The Conqueror Worm," "Life in Death," and some minor pieces. Here were first published also many of Hawthorne's "Twice-Told Tales." Simms, Paulding, Geo. H. Boker, Henry W. Herbert, Robert T. Conrad, E. P. Whipple, and John G. Saxe were "principal contributors." Lowell and Bayard Taylor were editorial writers. Cooper received $1800, then a very high price, for "The Islets of the Gulf, or Rose Budd," later republished as "Jack Tier, or The Florida Reefs," and $1000 for a series of biographies of distinguished naval commanders. Nathaniel P. Willis wrote much between 1843 and 1851. In 1852, Graham boasted that in the decade previous he had paid American contributors between eighty and ninety thousand dollars. The circulation of the magazine for a long time was 40,000 copies. About 1854 Graham sold out. In competition with *Harper's* and *Putnam's*, *Graham's* soon declined. In 1859 its name was changed to *The American Monthly*, and it quickly disappeared.

In 1839 Willis began, in connection with Dr. T. O. Porter, to issue a weekly, *The Corsair*, from the basement of the Astor House, New York. Willis was the chief writer, contributing romantic stories, dramatic criticism, letters from Europe entitled "Jottings Down in London," and gossip. While in England he met Thackeray, whom he induced to contribute eight letters. In all, fifty-two numbers were printed, the last dated March 7, 1840.

The Transcendental Movement, which will be discussed elsewhere, found expression in 1840 in a Boston quarterly called *The Dial*, which flourished till 1844, and which was edited successively by George Ripley, Margaret Fuller, and Emerson. The last contributed more than thirty prose articles and poems, among them "The Conservative," "Chardon Street and Bible Convention," "The Transcendentalist," and in verse "The Problem," "The Sphinx," and "Woodnotes." Bronson Alcott sent his "Orphic Sayings," the mystery of some of which has never been fathomed. Other writers were Theodore Parker, George Ripley, Thoreau, James Freeman Clarke, William H. and William Ellery Channing, Eliot Cabot, John S. Dwight, Christopher P. Cranch, Mrs. Ellen Hooper, and Charles A. Dana. "Conceived and carried on in a spirit of boundless hope and enthusiasm," the magazine encountered much ridicule among the Philistines. *The Knickerbocker* said of the first number:

> It is to be devoted to that refinement upon common-sense literature, just now so much in vogue at the East; which, like the memorable science of Sir Piercie Shafton, shall indoctrinate the dull in intellectuality, the vulgar in nobility, and give that "unutterable perfection of human utterance"; that eloquence which no other eloquence is sufficient to praise; that art which, in fine, when we call it *literary Euphuism*, we bestow upon it its richest panegyric.

Yet in spite of such strictures, the contents of *The Dial* are now immensely significant of the social agitation then going on in New England; and much of its matter has become a part of our permanent literature.

The New World, a large weekly established in New York by Park Benjamin (1840–1845), reprinted much from the English magazines, but included also contributions from Epes and John Osborne Sargent, James Aldrich, Herbert, Charles Lanman, Edward S. Gould, Charles Eames (editor for a time), and John Jay. George P. Putnam, the publisher, was for some years its London correspondent.

It was in *Peterson's Ladies' National Magazine* (a fashion journal begun in Philadelphia in 1841) that Frances Hodgson Burnett published her first story, "Ethel's Sir Lancelot" (November, 1868). The magazine, long popular among readers of light literature, was a few years since merged with *The Argosy*.

The Union Magazine (New York, 1847–1848), edited by Mrs. Caroline M. Kirkland, was bought by John Sartain, the engraver, and William Sloanaker, who had withdrawn from the managership of *Graham's*, and reappeared in Philadelphia (1849–1852) as *Sartain's Union Magazine of Literature and Art*, attaining great popularity. It published works by Longfellow ("The Blind Girl of Castel Cuillé," "Resignation"), Boker, Mrs. Sigourney, Lucy Larcom, Henry T. Tuckerman, Poe ("The Bells"), Park Benjamin, R. H. Stoddard, and Charles G. Leland.

Harper's New Monthly Magazine (New York), established by the Messrs. Harper in June, 1850, has long enjoyed a deservedly large circulation. For a considerable time it contained chiefly articles, especially fiction, reprinted from English periodicals. In later years it has included much more from American writers, and its contents have in general been of a high order of merit. Its records of travel and of scientific progress have been valuable. For many years the "Easy Chair," conducted by George William Curtis, and later by William D. Howells, has been an interesting feature. In *Harper's* first appeared Howells' "Annie Kilburn" and "Their Silver Wedding Journey," Warner's "Studies of the Great West" and "A Little Journey in the World," Constance F. Woolson's "Jupiter Lights," "East Angels," and "Anne," Poulteney Bigelow's "White Man's Africa," Stockton's "Bicycle of Cathay" and "The Great Stone of Sardis," John Fox, Jr.'s "Kentuckians," Stephen Crane's "Whilomville Stories," Mark Twain's "Personal Recollections of Joan of Arc," Woodrow Wilson's "Colonies and Nation," Mary E. Wilkins' "Portion of Labor," Mary Johnston's "Sir Mortimer," and Margaret Deland's "Awakening of Helena Richie." *The International Magazine*, founded by Rufus W. Griswold in New York in 1850, was two years later merged with *Harper's*.

Putnam's Monthly Magazine began publication in New York in 1853. Its earlier editors were Charles F. Briggs (whose pen name was "Harry Franco"), Parke Godwin, George W. Curtis, and George P. Putnam. Among the more important of the early contributions may be mentioned "Shakespeare's Scholar" by Richard Grant White, "Early Years in Europe" by George H. Calvert, "The Potiphar Papers" and "Prue and I" by George W. Curtis, a series of political essays by Parke Godwin, "Fireside Travels" and "A Moosehead Journal" by James Russell Lowell, the "Sparrowgrass Papers" by Frederick S. Cozzens, "Cape Cod" by Henry W. Thoreau, "Wensley" by Edmund Quincy, and "Israel Potter" by Herman Melville. *Putnam's* was one of the first of American magazines which restricted its pages to original contributions, and which gave special attention to the encouragement of the work of American writers. Published till 1857 and from 1868 till 1870, it was revived in 1906 as *Putnam's Monthly*, under the editorial direction of Joseph B. Gilder and George H. Putnam. *Putnam's* is still to be described as a literary magazine, although space is given also to illustrated articles on popular topics. *Putnam's* arranges with certain of the English magazines, such as *The Cornhill Magazine* and *The Fortnightly Review*, to share contributors, English as well as American. The essays of Mrs. Richmond Ritchie (Thackeray's daughter) and of Mr. Arthur C. Benson, for instance, have, under such an arrangement, been published simultaneously in *The Cornhill* and in *Putnam's*.

The year 1857 is memorable for the founding of *The Atlantic Monthly* by the publishing firm of Phillips & Sampson of Boston. James Russell Lowell became the first editor, accepting the post on condition that Dr. Holmes, who suggested the name, should be engaged as the first contributor. Among those who wrote for the first number were Longfellow, Lowell, Emerson, Motley, Holmes (who began "The Autocrat"), Whittier, Charles Eliot Norton, J. T. Trowbridge, Harriet Beecher Stowe, and Parke Godwin. Most of these were already well known authors. The list of contributors to *The Atlantic* during the half-century of its life includes all of the most illustrious of American writers—not only of New England, but of all parts of the country. In religious thought its attitude has been reverent but liberal. The achievements of science have been set forth by men like Agassiz, Percival Lowell, Simon Newcomb, John Trowbridge, George F. Wright, and George H. Darwin. The new political and economic questions have been discussed by such men as President Roosevelt, former President Cleveland, Richard Olney, Woodrow Wilson, Carl Schurz, John W. Foster, Henry Loomis Nelson, Edward M. Shepard, Benjamin

Kidd, John Jay Chapman, and Thomas Nelson Page. The fiction of *The Atlantic* has been produced mainly by American writers—Hawthorne ("Septimius Felton"), Henry James, Jr. ("Roderick Hudson," "The Portrait of a Lady"), Aldrich ("The Stillwater Tragedy," "Prudence Palfrey"), Bret Harte, Howells ("Their Wedding Journey," "A Chance Acquaintance," "The Lady of the Aroostook"), Mark Twain, Marion Crawford ("A Roman Singer," "Paul Patoff," "Don Orsino"), Stockton ("The House of Martha"), S. Weir Mitchell ("In War Time"), Hopkinson Smith ("Caleb West"), Cable ("Bylow Hill"), Paul Leicester Ford ("The Story of an Untold Love"), Mary Johnston ("To Have and to Hold," "Audrey"), Sarah Orne Jewett ("The Tory Lover"), Margaret Deland ("Sidney," "Philip and His Wife"), Kate Douglas Wiggin ("Penelope's Progress"), and many others. An equally brilliant list might be made of the essayists whose best work has made its initial appearance in the form of *Atlantic* articles. The editors have been Lowell (1857–1861), James T. Fields, of the firm of Ticknor & Fields, then the publishers (1861–1871), William Dean Howells (1871–1880), Thomas Bailey Aldrich (1880–1890), Horace E. Scudder (1890–1897), Walter H. Page (1897–1899), and Bliss Perry—an illustrious roll. *The Atlantic* has never changed its original purpose.

> It is still [to quote a recent writer] an American magazine for American readers.... It holds that the most important service which an American magazine can perform is the interpretation of this country to itself, by the promotion of sympathy between the different sections of our varied population, the frank examination of our national characteristics, the study of our perplexing problems, the encouragement of our art and literature, and the reinforcement of those moral and religious beliefs upon which depends the success of our experiment in self-government.

These ideals largely explain the success and permanence of *The Atlantic*. *The Galaxy*, founded in New York in 1866, after furnishing for several years an entertaining literary and scientific miscellany, was in 1878 incorporated with *The Atlantic*.

Lippincott's Magazine, established in Philadelphia in 1868, continues to devote its chief energies to fiction, though it has also published some notable poetry. Here appeared Lanier's "Corn," Edward Kearsley's

"CampFire Lyrics," and some of the verse of Emma Lazarus, Maurice Thompson, Paul H. Hayne, Celia Thaxter, and Philip Bourke Marston.

The Overland Monthly (San Francisco, 1868–1875, 1883 to the present time) has faithfully mirrored the picturesque and stirring life of the Far West. It absorbed *The Californian* (1880–1882). The first five volumes were edited by Bret Harte, and a large number of his stories, probably forming his best literary work, first appeared in its columns.

Old and New (Boston, 1870–1875) was conducted by Edward Everett Hale with the intention of "squeezing from the Old its lessons for the New" and of combining amusing with instructive literature after the manner of the *Revue des Deux Mondes*.

In 1870, Dr. Josiah G. Holland and Roswell B. Smith projected *Scribner's Monthly* (New York), and for eleven years Dr. Holland was its editor. In 1881 it was changed to *The Century Magazine* and under the editorship of Richard Watson Gilder has taken high rank as a distinctively popular magazine. It has given special attention to popular history, and its literary, historical, and scientific articles, generally substantial and meritorious, have appealed to a wide range of readers. Like *Harper's*, it has drawn upon all of the leading writers, for example Harte ("Gabriel Conroy"), Cable ("The Grandissimes," "Dr. Sevier"), Howells ("A Modern Instance," "A Woman's Reason," "Silas Lapham"), Stockton ("Rudder Grange," "The Merry Chanter," "The Hundredth Man"), Boyesen ("Falconberg"), John Hay ("The Bread-Winners"), Henry James, Jr. ("Confidence," "The Bostonians"), Eugene Schuyler ("Peter the Great"), Joel Chandler Harris ("Uncle Remus"), Hamlin Garland ("Her Mountain Lover"), Mary Hallock Foote ("The Led-Horse Claim," "Cœur d'Alene"), Marion Crawford ("Via Crucis"), Mark Twain ("Pudd'nhead Wilson"), S. Weir Mitchell ("Characteristics," "Hugh Wynne"). Many poems of merit have also been printed in *The Century*.

In 1887, *Scribner's Magazine* was established by Charles Scribner's Sons, and has since taken rank as among the first of American monthlies. It devotes proportionately more space to literature than is given by its competitor, *The Century Magazine*, and pays less attention to so-called popular subjects. Like *The Century*, it contains illustrations, which are characterised by a high artistic standard. *Scribner's* is under the editorial management of Mr. Edward L. Burlingame. Like *The Century*, it is published in London as well as in New York.

Among the other literary periodicals established within the last quarter-century are *The Bay State Monthly* (Boston, 1884–1885), which became in 1886 *The New England Magazine*, and which confines itself chiefly to the history and literature of New England; *The Forum* (New York, since 1886), devoted to the discussion of present-day questions; *The Cosmopolitan* (New York, since 1886), a typical popular monthly miscellany; *The Arena* (New York, since 1889), which has been a fearless exponent of advanced liberal thought; *Munsey's Magazine* (New York, since 1891), well illustrated, and claiming a circulation of over 600,000 copies; *McClure's Magazine*, established by S. S. McClure in New York in 1893, which by the end of its first year circulated 150,000 copies; *The Bookman* (New York), edited since 1895 by Harry Thurston Peck; and *The Reader*(Indianapolis, Indiana, 1902), now merged in *Putnam's Monthly*.

The Annuals.—In the twenties and thirties of the last century, too, the annuals were popular in America as in England. Almost all of the leading authors contributed to them. Among the best were *The Talisman* (New York, 1828–1830), written by Bryant, Verplanck, and Sands, and illustrated by Inman, Samuel F. B. Morse, and others; and *The Token*(Boston, 1828–1842), edited by S. G. Goodrich ("Peter Parley") and (in 1829) N. P. Willis, in which appeared contributions by Longfellow, Hawthorne (some "Twice-Told Tales"), Mrs. Child, Mrs. Sigourney, and Mrs. Hale. In general, however, the American, like the British annuals, included a large amount of mediocre writing.

The Reviews.—The American reviews begin with *The American Review of History and Politics*, founded by Robert Walsh (Philadelphia, 1811–1813). In 1815 *The North American Review and Miscellaneous Journal* was founded in Boston and has consequently had the longest life of all the periodicals now in existence. Its founder, William Tudor, was, we have seen, a member of the Anthology Club, and a writer of fine taste, who later did good service in a diplomatic career in South America. The *Review* was at first published every two months in numbers of 150 pages each; after the seventh volume it appeared quarterly in numbers of 250 pages each and at the same time ceased to publish poetry and general news, thus conforming more closely to the leading type of contemporary British reviews. The most voluminous contributors to the first sixty volumes were Judge Willard Phillips (editor in 1817), Tudor, Edward and Alexander Everett (editors in 1819–1822 and 1830–1836 respectively), Jared Sparks (editor in 1822–1830), Bancroft, Francis Bowen (editor in 1843–1853), Nathan Hale, George S. Hillard, John G. Palfrey (editor in 1836–1843), Oliver, William, and Andrew Peabody, Caleb Cushing, Cornelius C. Felton, William H. Prescott, and Charles Francis Adams. Much of Whipple's criticism originally appeared here. Among recent editors have been Lowell, Charles Eliot Norton, Henry Adams, and Henry Cabot Lodge. Bryant's "Thanatopsis" first appeared here in September, 1817. The book reviews, especially between 1850 and 1870, were probably better than those usually found in any other American periodical. In recent years the character of *The North American* has largely changed. It now offers monthly a collection of signed articles chiefly on current political and social problems.

Other early reviews were *The Christian Examiner and Theological Review* (Boston, 1824–1869, in 1870 merged with *Old and New*), in which appeared some of the most virile criticism of the time; *The American Quarterly Review* (Philadelphia, 1827–1837), another of Walsh's ventures and a quarterly of merit; *The Southern Review* (Charleston, 1828–1832, revived 1842–1855), started by William Elliott and Hugh S. Legare; *The Western Review* (Cincinnati, 1828–1830), founded by Timothy Flint; *The New York Review*(1837–1842), established by Francis L. Hawks and later edited by Joseph G. Cogswell and Caleb S. Henry; *The Boston Quarterly Review* (1838–1842), edited by Orestes A. Brownson, and merged with *The United States Magazine and Democratic Review* (Washington and New York, 1837–1852), which became *The United States Review* (1853–1859); *The New Englander* (New Haven, Conn., 1843–1892), for religious, historical, and literary articles; *The American Whig Review* (New York, 1845–1852), started by George H. Colton and later edited by Dr. James D. Whelpley; *The Literary World* (New York, 1847–1853), ably edited by Evart A. Duyckinck; *The Massachusetts Quarterly Review*(Boston, 1847–1850), edited by Theodore Parker; *The New York Quarterly Review* (1852–1853); and *The National Quarterly Review* (New York, 1860–1880).

The Nation was founded as a weekly in New York in 1865 by Edwin Lawrence Godkin, who remained its editor for a third of a century. Since 1881, when Mr. Godkin assumed the editorial control of the New York *Evening Post, The Nation* has been issued as the weekly edition of *The Evening Post.* During the forty-three years of its existence, *The Nation* has held a leading position in American criticism and also as an exponent of American politics considered from an independent point of view. From 1881 to 1905, *The Nation* was under the editorial management of the late Wendell Phillips Garrison. It is now under the direction of Mr. Hammond Lamont. The literary department is conducted by Mr. Paul E. More, who had, before assuming this editorial post, made a name for himself in literary criticism.

The International Review (New York, 1874–1883) printed many articles of solid worth. *The Dial*, semi-monthly, was established in Chicago in 1880 by Francis F. Browne. It has made a noteworthy reputation for a high standard of American criticism, and has retained the services of some of the ablest of American reviewers. *The Critic* was founded, as a weekly literary journal, in New York, in 1881, by Jeannette L. Gilder and Joseph B. Gilder. It did good work in literary criticism and in the presentation of literary news for twenty-five years, when it was absorbed by *Putnam's Monthly. The Sewanee Review*, a quarterly founded at the University of the South, Sewanee, Tennessee, in 1892, and *The South Atlantic Quarterly*, founded at Durham, North Carolina, in 1902, are publishing the best literary criticism in the South to-day.

Newspapers.—The plan of this Manual permits but a brief reference to the more important of the newspapers which have given attention to the interests of literature. The New York *Evening Post* was founded in 1801, and was for fifty-two years (1828–1880) edited by Bryant. In 1819, it printed the well-known "Croaker Papers" by Drake and Halleck. James K. Paulding was an occasional contributor, and Whitman was one of its Washington writers during the first year of the Civil War, 1861. Bret Harte was for a time on the editorial staff, and the list of the literary critics includes the names of John R. Thompson and John Bigelow. During the years 1881–1902, *The Evening Post* was under the editorial control of Edwin L. Godkin, who was an Irishman by birth, an Englishman by education, and an American by what may be called natural selection.

His editorials in *The Evening Post* constitute a most important contribution to the literature of journalism, or it may be more precise to say to the journalism of literature. They were forcible, witty, and incisive, and always represented the earnest convictions of the writer. *The Evening Post*, which still gives a full measure of dignified and effective consideration to literature, is now under the editorial direction of Messrs. Rollo Ogden and Oswald G. Villard. Its literary department is managed by Paul E. More.

The New York Tribune was founded in 1841 by Horace Greeley, who must also take rank as one of the noteworthy American editors. For thirty-one years, George Ripley had the chief responsibility for its literary department, and among his associates were Bayard Taylor and Margaret Fuller. A number of the more important reviews, particularly those having to do with English criticism and with poetry, were the work of Edmund C. Stedman. Miss Ellen Hutchinson, later associated with Mr. Stedman in editing the "Library of American Literature," was for many years on the literary staff of *The Tribune*.

The Sun was founded in 1833, and was for many years managed by a third great American editor, Charles A. Dana. The incisive force and stirring wit of Dana's editorials have probably never been equalled in American journalism, unless it were in the columns of Godkin's Post. *The Sun* has always given much attention to literature, and the weekly contributions of Mr. Mayo W. Hazeltine have for many years taken first rank among the critical literary essays of the day.

The Times was founded in 1851 by Henry J. Raymond, an early associate of Horace Greeley. During the past twelve years, *The Times* has given a larger measure of attention to literature than any other paper in the country. Its literary department finally became sufficiently important to call for a separate printing, and it is now issued as a weekly literary supplement. The present editor of the supplement, which presents a convenient and comprehensive summary of the publications of each week, is Mr. William Bayard Hale. The literary supplement has secured for its regular contributors a number of the more capable critics of the day, among whom may be mentioned Mr. Edward Cary, Miss Elizabeth Luther Cary, Miss Hildegarde Hawthorne, and Mr. Montgomery Schuyler.

Of the other New York papers, *The World* was founded in 1860, and during the years 1862–1876 was associated with the name of Manton Marble, one of the scholarly editors of his day. It is now controlled by Mr. Joseph Pulitzer. *The Express*, founded in 1836, and for a series of years the organ of the remarkable brothers James and Erastus Brooks, was, about 1880, merged with *The Mail*, also founded in 1836. *The Commercial Advertiser*, founded early in the nineteenth century, became about 1890 *The Commercial Advertiser and the Globe*, and later *The Globe*. *The Herald*, founded in 1831 by the elder James Gordon Bennett, is still under the control of the Bennett family. It is most valuable to the community in its presentation of news, but has not been distinctive on its literary side. *The Eagle*, published in what is now the Borough of Brooklyn, was founded about 1850. It has always taken high rank for independence of political conviction and also for the excellent literary quality of its editorials and reviews. It has for many years been under the editorial direction of St. Clair McKelway.

In New England, *The Boston Transcript*, founded in 1830, devotes much space to reviews and discussions of literature and stands high for its catholicity of judgment and discriminating taste. Among the papers in the smaller New England cities should be specified *The Republican*, of Springfield, Massachusetts, founded in 1824, the ownership of which has for three generations been in the Bowles family. It has included among its contributors some of the ablest writers of New England. *The Courant*, of Hartford, Connecticut, had the advantage for many years of the editorship of Charles Dudley Warner.

In the Middle West, the Chicago *Tribune*, founded in 1847, is to be recalled for its association with the life-work of one of America's ablest journalists, Joseph Medill. In Cincinnati, *The Commercial* had the advantage for many years of the editorial direction of Murat Halsted. In the Southwest, the Louisville (Kentucky) *Journal*, founded in 1830, will always be associated with the name of George D. Prentice. *The Journal* was in 1868 merged with *The Courier* and, as *The Courier-Journal*, has since been under the direction of Mr. Henry Watterson, a survivor of the type of "strenuous" Southern journalism.

The Washington *National Era*, published between the years 1847 and 1860, is to be noted as having presented to the world "Uncle Tom's Cabin." In the contest for abolition which this book did so much to bring to a triumphant end, *The Liberator* (1831–1866), carried on by William Lloyd Garrison, and *The National Anti-Slavery Standard* (1840–1872), conducted by Wendell Phillips, should also be mentioned. These two men differed sharply from each other from time to time as to the methods to be pursued, but were at one in their fierce antagonism to slavery and in their readiness to devote their lives, if need be, to its extinction.

AMERICAN AUTHORS REPRESENTED IN
THE TAUCHNITZ EDITION

Adams, Henry	1838–
Alcott, Louisa M.	1832–1888
Aldrich, Thomas Bailey	1836–1907
Atherton, Gertrude Franklin	1859–
Bellamy, Edward	1850–1898
Benedict, Frank Lee	1834–
Bierce, Ambrose	1842–
Burnett, Frances Hodgson	1849–
Carnegie, Andrew	1837–
Chance, Julia Grinnell Cruger (Julien Gordon)	1859–
Churchill, Winston	1871–
Clemens, Samuel L. (Mark Twain)	1835–
Cooper, James Fenimore	1789–1851
Craigie, Pearl Mary Teresa (John Oliver Hobbes)	1867–1906
Crawford, F. Marion	1854–
Cummins, Maria Susanna	1827–1866
Davis, Richard Harding	1864–
Deland, Margaret	1857–
Dixon, Thomas, Jr.	1864–
Eggleston, Edward	1837–1902
Emerson, Ralph Waldo	1803–1882
Fletcher, Julia Constance (George Fleming)	1853–
Frederic, Harold	1856–1898
Freeman, Mary E. Wilkins	1862–

Gunter, Archibald Clavering	1847–1907
Habberton, John	1842–
Halsted, Leonora B.	1855–
Harland, Henry	1861–1905
Harte, Francis Bret	1839–1902
Hawthorne, Nathaniel	1804–1864
Hay, John	1838–1905
Holmes, Oliver Wendell	1809–1894
Howells, William Dean	1837–
Irving, Washington	1783–1859
Jackson, Helen Hunt (H. H.)	1831–1885
James, Henry	1843–
Kimball, Richard B.	1816–1892
Longfellow, Henry Wadsworth	1807–1882
Lorimer, George Horace	1868–
McKnight, Charles	1826–1881
Norris, Frank	1870–1902
Osbourne, Lloyd	1868–
Parkes, Elizabeth Robins (C. E. Raimond)	1862–
Pike, Mary Hayden Green (Mary Langdon)	1825–
Poe, Edgar Allan	1809–1849
Prentiss, Elizabeth Payson	1818–1878
Riggs, Kate Douglas Wiggin	1857–
Roosevelt, Theodore	1858–
Savage, Richard Henry	1846–1903
Sheppard, Nathan	1834–1888
Stanton, Theodore	1851–
Stockton, Frank R.	1834–1902
Stowe, Harriet Beecher	1811–1896
von Teuffel, Blanche Wilder Howard	1847–1898
Wallace, Lewis	1827–1905

Warner, Anna B. (Amy Lothrop)	1820–
Warner, Susan (Elizabeth Wetherell)	1819–1885
Wetmore, Elizabeth Bisland	1861–
Wharton, Edith	1862–
Williamson, Alice Muriel	1870–

Made in the USA
Monee, IL
07 July 2026

56552362R00217